CITY OF THE GOOD

City of the Good

NATURE, RELIGION, AND THE ANCIENT
SEARCH FOR WHAT IS RIGHT

MICHAEL MAYERFELD BELL

PRINCETON UNIVERSITY PRESS
PRINCETON & OXFORD

Copyright © 2018 by Princeton University Press

Published by Princeton University Press,
41 William Street, Princeton, New Jersey 08540

In the United Kingdom: Princeton University Press,
6 Oxford Street, Woodstock, Oxfordshire OX20 1TR

press.princeton.edu

Cover photograph: Avignon, France, courtesy of the author

First paperback printing, 2020
Paperback ISBN 978-0-691-20291-4
Cloth ISBN 978-0-691-16509-7

Library of Congress Control Number: 2017945408

British Library Cataloging-in-Publication Data is available

This book has been composed in Arno Pro

For my mother
Island dweller, "four" yeller
Skiff rower, flower grower
Tongue trainer, word explainer
Wisdom giver, full life liver
Old Lady of the River

CONTENTS

Preface

"WHERE DID THE KIDS GO?" my wife asked—a classic question one parent asks another.

"I don't know. I thought they were with you," I replied—the classic response to that classic question.

Not that we were really worried. The Vatican Museum channels the thousands in one direction through its long galleries, with little opportunity for deviation. Even pausing for a moment to linger on an object or painting sets up eddies in the flow, building a pressure of impatience that soon gets the feet moving again on toward the Sistine Chapel, where we had just arrived. Besides, our son was then twenty-six and our daughter eighteen. Besides, it was the Vatican.

"I'll go back and see if I can find them," Diane said, continuing with the whispered tones we had been using.

A brave offer. The river into the Sistine Chapel pours through one narrow door, flooding into a lake of all manner of humanity that eventually trickles out the other end via another small door. She would have to squirm hard to go upstream.

"Okay. Best leave me your backpack, though," I said with a hush. "So you can wiggle through a bit easier."

"Thanks. You stay right here. Don't move."

Off she went. I turned my eyes upward and all around, joining the collective quiet wonder at Michelangelo's vision of the divine in *The Last Judgment*, forty-five feet high up the Sistine Chapel front wall and continuing onto the ceiling, humbling believer and nonbeliever alike.

But I soon found my mind drifting toward reflection on what was not in that vision. Maybe it was the oppressive stuffiness of the packed room. Maybe it was the over-loud announcement in Italian and then English that periodically curdled the air with "This is a holy place of reflection. Please maintain silence. No photographs." Or words to that effect—a disembodied voice of rules coming down from on high. I don't know. For whatever reason, the mood the chapel conjured in me was analytic, not beatific. I started mentally ticking off the absences from the presences. No animals. No forests. No gardens, aside from Adam and Eve being evicted from Eden in one of Michelangelo's ceiling panels. No farming. No eating. No laughing. No sex. No politicians. No people of color. Almost no women. Such a heaven seemed a starkly limited place. But what troubled me most was the space's grand declaration that this was all for the good.

My neck was tired by the time Diane came back, still without Sam and Eleanor. She motioned a shush at me, as I started to inquire. I stood by as Diane took her own look at the fabulously painted walls and ceilings. She was getting it more than me. But Diane, too, soon had her fill of wonder, perhaps limited by mild parental separation anxiety. We headed for the door, fresher air, and freedom to talk aloud.

Eventually we washed up in the coffee shop and took turns standing outside it at a corner between two corridors—one leading to the outdoors and one to the shop, a corner past which every visitor must eventually course—until Sam and Eleanor appeared with excited looks. They had found some side passages we had missed, leading to whole other lands of art. Literally. The Vatican's Egyptian Museum. Its Ethnological Museum. Its Cartography Museum. And its fabulous gallery of Greek and Roman busts.

The children must, in time, lead the parents. Diane and I followed delightedly, taking another look through the long Vatican galleries until they showed us the entrances to the side passages we had missed. Here there were animals, often combined with images of a highly diverse divine. Here there were representations of forests and farms and gardens, of streams and rivers and oceans, and of human labor in them. Here there was overt sexuality (albeit with many a fig-leaf later added to the genitals of statues). Here there were lots and lots of political figures—kings, queens, emperors, pharaohs, chiefs, and more. Here there were gods and goddesses in conflict, pursuing projects and ambitions, often involving the conflicts, projects, and ambitions of humans. And here there were many representations of women and people of color. Here we found life more nearly as it is really lived, an entanglement of world, being, and passion—of nature, faith, and the human community—where the good and the bad are not easily separated and where politics cannot be escaped.

The ecologically and egalitarian minded have to wonder why the world's dominant religions have long relegated these basic experiences of the human condition mainly to their side passages. The same question could, and should, be asked of our dominant philosophies of nature and environment. In this book, I try to answer that question—a question that, at last, traditions of nature and religion increasingly find themselves asking as well. They ask it because many among the newer generations, and some among the older ones, no longer rush past those other corridors, and find much meaning and even delight there. So I wish might we all.

ACKNOWLEDGMENTS

NOT JUST A CITY but a whole landscape of good people contributed to the writing of this book. Indeed, a whole lifescape: people from across the sweep of my sixty years show up in various ways in its pages, many explicitly, many more implicitly.

My greatest thanks go to my editor at Princeton, Meagan Levinson. She gave the manuscript a very close read—something I fear many editors no longer seem to find time for. Meagan's reading was immensely helpful, at every level: sentence, paragraph, chapter, and the argument of the whole book. Thank you, Meagan.

Also at Princeton, I want to give sincere thanks to my copy editor, Joseph Dahm. It's a bit of a phantom experience, working with a copy editor these days. We've never met. But his careful eye, his sensitivity to my narrative style, and his gentle way of prodding me along were models of the copy editor's craft. I hope we do meet one day. Thank you, Joseph.

The rest of Princeton's staff were also great to work with. Thanks especially to Jenny Wolkowicki, my production editor, and to Eric Schwartz, the former sociology editor at Princeton who initially recruited me and talked me through a lot of issues at the early stages of my writing. He's at lucky Columbia University Press now.

I was lucky too with the two excellent anonymous reviewers that Princeton arranged for the book. One of them subsequently identified himself: the environmental author Jules Pretty, who is also professor of environment and society at the University of Essex in the United Kingdom. Jules and the other reviewer helped me immensely in figuring out where the book was heading and how to get there.

I also had the benefit of many readers whom I arranged from among my own friends and colleagues. I especially want to thank Samer Alatout, James Knight, Katherine Scahill, and Kalyanakrishnan Sivaramakrishnan for their help with my understanding of, respectively, Islam, Christianity, Buddhism, and Hinduism. As well, Brad Brewster pointed me to St. Augustine's parallels with Thoreau. Barbara Decre helped me research the ecological dimensions of the Qur'an. And Abby Letak gave the references a thorough, much-needed polishing. Thanks to you three, too.

I had a lot of reading to do myself, exploring some five thousand years of writing on nature, religion, and the good. Many highlights of that writing appear in the text of this book. I thank Liverpool University Press for permission to quote liberally from their translation of Aristophanes's play *Wealth* (Sommerstein, 2001 trans.) and Oxford University Press to quote liberally from their translation of *The Qur'an* (Hallem, 2008, trans.).

I wrote the book in part by teaching a lecture course on it at the University of Wisconsin–Madison for five years: Community and Environmental Sociology 541—"Environmental Stewardship and Social Justice (Special Topic: Nature, Faith, and Community)." My students over those many years tested and contested these ideas, sharpening my thinking immensely and helping me find better ways to express my points. I owe an equal debt to the five wonderful graduate students who in turn served as the teaching assistant for the course: Alex McCullough, Amanda McMillan-Lequieu, Valerie Stull, Loka Ashwood, and Kerem Morgul. I learned a great deal working with them on how to present the material—which often entailed collectively rethinking it a good bit too! Thank you Alex, Amanda, Valerie, Loka, and Kerem.

And thanks to the people of Wisconsin who have had the grace to employ me at the University of Wisconsin–Madison since 2002, both to teach courses like that and to do the research and writing that continue the growth of the society and ecology we share. Long live the "Wisconsin Idea" that makes the borders of the university the borders of the state and the world—indeed, the universe, the universe being what a university is about.

One of my greatest teachers about the universe of nature and religion is my friend and colleague Mpumelelo Ncwadi. Through our work together on the LAND (Livelihood, Agroecology, Nutrition, and Development) Project in South Africa, he has guided my learning in so many ways relevant to this book, but especially about the continuing vitality of ancestor veneration to the amaXhosa people. He graciously agreed to allow me to share some of his explanations and stories in this book. But let me add one more here: Mpumi's motto "you don't know if you don't go," which is his translation of a traditional isiXhosa saying. I did go, and I certainly can't say that I now fully know, but I do think that I understand a lot better. I hope I've been able to communicate in this book some of what I've learned from Mpumi and the villagers of KuManzimdaka. Thank you, Mpumi, and thank you to the villagers, especially MamBhele Ncapayi.

Frederico, even though it was decades and decades ago, and I fear you may have long since passed on to the company of your Cabécar ancestors, let me offer my sincere thanks to you as well. The week I spent in your company in the Talamanca Mountains rainforest in Costa Rica was one of the most transformative of my life. I'm sorry I lost track of you soon afterward, and I regret that you will likely never read or learn of these words. You too were one of my great teachers. Gracias sinceras, or, in your own tongue, wi'ktebala.

But for sure my greatest teachers have been my own family. My wife Diane Mayerfeld and our children Sam Bell and Eleanor Mayerfeld were especially vigorous testers and contesters of my ideas and interpretations. We do not eat in silence. Dinner together is always a feast of the mind. Our many family adventures often make an appearance in this book. Plus Diane gave the entire manuscript a complete reading, catching many annoyances and mistakes large and small. My mother, to whom I dedicate the book, also long ago cultivated in me a fascination and enchantment with both nature and religion, addicting me, like her, to gardening, rowing skiffs, walking in the woods, gathering wild blackberries, reading *Biblical Archaeology Review*, and lighting candles once a week. Hugs to you all.

These, then, are among the many logics in this book, the many hands who helped cut something that I hope is at least decently reflective from the rough stone of my experience and what I have gathered from theirs. May the cutting, and the recutting, never cease.

CITY OF THE GOOD

1

The Conundrum of the Absolute

EARLY ONE MORNING in the New England autumn, a lonely man took a walk in the woods. He headed west as he walked, drawn by, as he later put it, a "subtile [*sic*] magnetism."[1] He walked alone, at least alone of other humans. He found company with the trees and the scurry of wildlife shuffling through the foliage, occasionally pausing to note the passing bearded figure. Such companions do not contradict your mood, your ideas, your plans. Their lives move to other concerns. So it was peaceful.[2] But the east rumbled with tumult, conflict, and confusion. For to the east lay the bellowing city: Boston.

It was a contentious time, even more than ours is today. The Abolition Movement was growing in strength and controversy. By the time the lonely man's essay about his walk appeared in print in 1862, the American Civil War had begun. How should we live? What is just? What is sacred? What is true? How can we best steward the world and care for all its inhabitants, human and nonhuman alike? People found themselves so divided that they were willing to kill each other to settle these questions. The "more perfect union" promised in the US Constitution had never seemed so elusive and unlikely. Eleven states had seceded from the Union. The battles were bloody, some of the bloodiest ever seen—especially the September 17, 1862, Battle of Antietam, where twenty-three thousand soldiers died on a single day, each killed by someone who a few years prior had considered himself a fellow citizen. Bloody as they were, the battles remained inconclusive, and more awful fighting seemed certain to follow.

In the face of such contention, of social life turned to horror, there was much to be said for the lonely life apart from society. As this hardy walker put it, "I wish to speak a word for Nature, for absolute Freedom and Wildness, as contrasted with a Freedom and Culture merely civil,—to regard man as an inhabitant, or a part and parcel of Nature, rather than a member of society."[3] Here we might learn that "we have a wild savage in us" and that "a savage name is perchance somewhere recorded as ours."[4] Here one might escape "Man and his affairs, church and state—and school, trade and commerce, and manufactures and agriculture,—even politics, the most alarming of them all."[5] Here one might find a "portion of the earth's surface where a man does not stand from one year's end to another and there consequently politics are not, for they are but as the cigar smoke of a man."[6]

The 1850s and early 1860s were also a time of bounding scientific and technological discovery. Henry Bessemer patented a means to mass produce steel in 1855. The world's first oil refinery came on line in 1856. In 1859, Darwin published *On the Origin of Species*, and digging began for the Suez Canal. Henry Gatling patented the Gatling gun, generally regarded as the first workable machine gun, in 1861. The first section of the London Underground opened in 1863. Factories grew in size and output, changing the clothes people wore, the food they ate, the homes they lived in, and the techniques of daily living they used to accomplish their myriad mundane needs. Humans dominated the natural world as never before, bending it to their wishes, and sometimes bending it out of recognition.

These advances were not unmixed blessings, at least in the mind of the lonely walker, ever turning west. "Now a days, almost all man's improvements, so called, as the building of homes, and the cutting down of the forest, and of all large trees, simply deform the landscape, and make it more and more tame and cheap."[7] Yes, the science and industry of the east enabled welcome comforts. But we were losing as much as we gained. As he put it, "We have heard of a Society for the Diffusion of Useful Knowledge. It is said that Knowledge is power; and the like. Methinks there is equal need of a Society for the Diffusion of Useful Ignorance, what we will call Beautiful Knowledge, a knowledge useful in a higher sense."[8] For "a man's ignorance sometimes is not only useful, but beautiful, while his knowledge, so called, is oftentimes worse than useless beside being ugly."[9] Which is why the lonely man found that "Eastward I go only by force; but westward I go free."[10] As he put it in his most famous of many famous lines: "The West of which I speak is but another name for the Wild; and what I have been preparing to say is, that in Wildness is the preservation of the world."[11]

We are not all like Henry David Thoreau, lonely walkers through the woods of the world, turning ever outward to find the ever inward.[12] But ideas that resonate with Thoreau's sensibilities continue to resound through the thoughts and social debates that most of us moderns today find ourselves caught up in.

("Moderns" is not a perfect word to describe the "us" I have in mind, and our origins, but it will do for the present.) Like Thoreau, most of us are deeply concerned about human domination of ecology. Like Thoreau, most of us are deeply concerned about human domination of each other. We often seek in nature a basis for living more lightly and more justly, a basis for the good.

And whether we search for the good in the lonely woods or not, we moderns all find ourselves doing some walking, looking for paths that take us beyond the conflicts of human communities—for absolutes that give us a sense of respite from the smoky vapors of our ceaseless politics.

———

It's an old problem. In 387 CE, one man sought his respite in a quiet garden in Mediolanum—the city we today call Milan—the western capital of a splintering Roman Empire. He was a confused man in a confused time. "Thither my inner turmoil carried me," he later described, "where no one could interfere with my deep conflagration."[13] The confused man was accompanied only by a close friend, "loyal at my side." And he carried a copy of the letters of the Apostle Paul, bound together into a book, a new means of assembling writing that was fast replacing the scroll.[14]

He had much on his mind—not least his ambitious mother, who had followed him to Mediolanum from their hometown in Numidia, a Roman province in North Africa. Her goal was to straighten him out. She strongly disapproved of his fifteen-year-long relationship with a concubine he had met as a young man in Carthage, and of his lack of a proper wife. Plus his mother was a devout Christian. She had long been disturbed by the confused man's commitment to Manichaeism, a religion started a hundred years earlier by a Persian sage named Mani. Manichaeism revered the teachings of Jesus, but also those of Zoroaster and the Buddha, seeing them all as divine windows into the same goodness that Mani called simply "light" in the face of the evil forces of the "dark." The confused man had come to question Manichaeism. The more he considered it, the more simplistic he found it. He had been having many deep conversations with Ambrose, the Christian bishop of Mediolanum. But he had not committed to Christianity. Not yet.

His mother could not deny that he was doing well, though. Although only thirty-two, the confused man held the position of professor of rhetoric in Mediolanum. He could count hundreds of adoring students, and dozens of influential friends, such as Ambrose. He had written a book on aesthetics. But his mother hoped for more, maybe even the governorship of a province like Numidia.[15]

The confused man was certainly plenty ambitious. But did he really want a governorship—especially if it was his mother's idea? In any case, for a governorship he would need a real wife, one from a wealthy family with the money and status to promote his career. His mother convinced him to send the concubine packing, back to Africa. She arranged for a marriage with a girl with the necessary pedigree. But the girl was only eleven. The confused man would have to wait two more years until she came of age. Plus he didn't love her, and he very much loved the concubine. "My heart, to which she had been grafted, was lacerated, wounded, shedding blood," he wrote concerning his mistress's departure.[16]

Many found the times confusing, not just this man in the garden with his friend and a book. As Thoreau's day would later also experience, a civil war raged, one with a long and complex history. A century before, the Roman Empire had split into two, then into four, with four capitals, one of which was Mediolanum—all in addition to Rome, which still held much traditional power, although none of the four emperors lived there. (In a way, there were five capitals.) Eventually, the powerful figure of Constantine pulled the empire back together into one brute being. That didn't last long, though. On his death, Constantine's three sons split the empire into three dominions, one for each. They then promptly set about attacking each other until a solitary brother remained to rule the whole empire again. After a few more wars and murders, the Roman Empire split back into two, and then into three again.

In other words, there was ambition aplenty, and thus politics aplenty, in the Roman Empire.

And much more to come. From 376 to 382, the empire struggled to deal with a major invasion by a large group of desperate Goths, who had been displaced from Germania by Huns advancing from the east. No sooner had the Gothic War concluded than a man with the singularly immodest name of Magnus Maximus, general of the British divisions of the Roman army, sailed his forces across to Gaul to start a civil war. After winning Gaul, he invaded Italy and headed for Mediolanum—and was met by an equally large army drawn from other parts of the empire. The situation was tense. After negotiations led by Ambrose, the bishop who later befriended the confused man, Magnus Maximus settled for being declared emperor of the Western Roman Empire, and agreed to go back to Gaul.

A few months later, the confused man arrived in Mediolanum. His mother followed shortly afterward.

So the confused man indeed had a lot on his mind that day in the garden. His meddlesome mother. His own ambitiousness. His breakup with his partner of fifteen years. An impending marriage that horrified him. Civil war compounded by invasion, in both Roman politics and the politics of his personal life, all of which seemed far from over. A deep doubt over the very basis of truth, justice, and legitimate motivation had taken root in his moral thought.

"I was at war within," he wrote. "So sick was I, so tortured, as I reviled myself more bitterly than ever."[17]

He needed to be completely alone, and moved off deeper into the garden, leaving his friend behind. He lay down beneath a fig tree, "loosing the reins on my sobbing, as tears tore themselves from my eyes."[18] Then he heard "the voice of a boy—or perhaps a girl, I could not tell—chanting in repeated singsong: Lift! Look!"

He could think of no children's game that used such a chant, and concluded it must actually be divine prompting. So he lifted himself up, as the chant instructed. The commandment to look could mean only the book of Paul's letters, which he had left with his friend. He raced back, grabbed it, and the book fell open, by chance, at these lines:

> Let us then lay aside the works of darkness and put on the armor of light; let us live honorably as in the day, not in reveling and drunkenness, not in debauchery and licentiousness, not in quarreling and jealousy. Instead, put on the Lord Jesus Christ, and make no provision for the flesh, to gratify its desires.[19]

That was it, the origins of his tortures, and those of everyone else: *desire*— and not just desire for sex and other bodily pleasures but for material gain and other forms of power. Confused no more, at that moment the man who would be known as St. Augustine of Hippo decided to become a Christian and a priest.

Becoming a priest was probably a good career move—although not exactly the career his mother had advocated, despite her promotion of Christianity. It could not have escaped Augustine's attention that Christianity had become the state religion in 380, when the three emperors who then jointly ruled the Roman Empire issued the Edict of Thessalonica. Instead of persecution, Christian leaders like Ambrose were now entrusted with the most delicate tasks of state. Being a priest did require celibacy, though, for Pope Siricius of Rome had issued the *Directa Decretal* in 386, which stipulated that all priests follow "the splendor of chastity." But stop, lift, and look: celibacy also presented a way out of his engagement to the eleven-year-old.

Still, we cannot doubt that St. Augustine's conversion was deeply felt in the innermost tissues of his morality, as is plain on every page of his *Confessions*, from where we get the story of his garden encounter with the divine. It is equally plain on every page of his *De Civitate Dei*, or *The City of God*, the book he spent fourteen years writing between 412 and 426. By then, Augustine was serving as Bishop of Hippo—a major Roman city in the north African province of Numidia, likely making him as powerful as he would have been as governor. But power, he wrote, was not what he sought. What he sought was to understand power and the origin of our urge for it. Like Thoreau, Augustine saw the source of that urge as lying deep in our urban humanness, in the politics of "the city of this world, a city which aims at dominion, which holds nations in enslavement, but is itself dominated by that very lust of domination."[20] He exhorted us to seek the *Summum Bonum*, the Supreme Good, which is free of politics and cigar smoke and that most basic of desires: pride, or what he also termed "self-love." For, he asked, "what is the origin of our evil will but pride?"[21]

Thoreau found this supreme, absolute good in nature. Augustine found it in supernature, in his faith in the divine. And both shared a deep distrust of the political ways they associated with the city. Nonetheless, Augustine conceived absolute goodness through the image of a city—albeit a very different kind of city, what he called the "Heavenly City." Give up the enticements of "the earthly city, which lives by man's standards," he counseled. Instead, seek "the Heavenly City, which lives according to God's will."[22] For "the two cities were created by two kinds of love: the earthly city was created by self-love reaching the point of contempt for God, the Heavenly City by the love of God carried as far as contempt of self."[23]

Billions today look to this second form of love, hoping such goodness will direct us truly, guiding us through and beyond the ceaseless vortex of human desires. Whether conceived as the nature Thoreau sought by walking west or the divine guidance Augustine sought by looking up, we hope to live not just in a city of God but in a city of the good, sheltered by edifices of the absolute.

———

Nevertheless, despite our searches for goodness, we've been arguing a lot lately, as a people and as a planet. And the absolutes we've regularly been using to make our various cases don't seem to be helping us resolve matters. What we thought would settle our debates—what nature and science say, what God and his scriptures say, and so what I say too—have only unsettled them the more, for we are not all using the same absolutes. The arguments go on and on unproductively, one absolute clashing with another, until we turn away in frustration and go a-walking in the woods like Thoreau, or in an urban garden like

Augustine, seeking to escape the stench of the cigar smoke and the cacophony of the smokers.

A great rush of books of late has taken a look at the religious origins of this frustration. Robert Wright has told us about *The Evolution of God*. Richard Dawkins has told us about *The God Delusion*. Karen Armstrong has told us about *The History of God*, *The Great Transformation*, and *The Case for God*. Elaine Pagels has told us about *The Gnostic Gospels*, *The Origin of Satan*, and *Revelations*. Reza Aslan has told us about the life of the historical Jesus in *Zealot*. These are all valuable books, however they may differ in their predilections and prescriptions.

A great rush of writers have also looked at the ecological troubles that cause us to point fingers at each other, and go away snarling. Charles Wohlforth has described *The Fate of Nature*. Michael Pollan has pointed out *The Omnivore's Dilemma*. Jared Diamond has warned us about *Collapse: How Societies Choose to Fail or Succeed*. Al Gore has tried to get us to pay attention to *An Inconvenient Truth*. Bill McKibben has worried about *The End of Nature*, offered a vision of *Hope: Human and Wild* and a *Deep Economy*, and asked us to prepare for *Eaarth: Making a Life on a Tough New Planet*.

I have a feeling these concerns and frustrations are connected. In this book, I trace the social history of both these basic forms of the absolute—the natural and the supernatural—and their interrelationship with ideas and boundaries of human community. Nature, faith, and community together form what I find helpful to envision as an *ancient triangle* of beliefs, with nature and faith forming the two sides of the base, sometimes supporting and sometimes conflicting in how they uphold community life, and sometimes supporting and sometimes conflicting with that life.

Today it seems we find more conflict than mutual support emanating from the sides of the base. Yes, some now work to green religion and to sanctify ecology.[24] Some have tried to bring concern for climate change to the pulpit and to bring respect for spirit to our battles over pipelines and the latest housing development proposal. They find this mutual support both possible and necessary. But they take on this good work because it needs to be done. It isn't done already.

This good work isn't done in part because we don't agree on what constitutes the good. We don't agree because we can't agree. The very way we usually conceive of our most cherished beliefs makes talking through our differences nearly impossible. If what makes the good is that it is not human, what good is it to debate the good with a human?

This is unproductive. On the thought that we might be better equipped to resolve our troubles if we knew their origins, in this book I offer an explanation for how this triangle of beliefs came about, and how it has been used in the layout, the moral design, of the city of the good. For there was not always a trigonometry of separations, nature from the divine from the human, just as there isn't one everywhere today to the same degree and sharpness. Perhaps it need not be anywhere so.

Here's the gist of my explanation. Why do we so often embrace absolutist notions, even when they seem an unhelpful basis for discussing how we should live together with each other and the planet? Because of an old cultural habit that emerged out of a mighty transformation in human affairs: the expansion of cities in growing states and empires. Inequality grew along with accumulating urban wealth. Desire seemed the new coin of social life. People were troubled by this challenge to justice, either to defend inequality or to confront and critique it. And they found a powerful manner of moral thought to justify their passions: what I will term a *natural conscience*, based on faith in forms of absolute goodness we regard as free of the human and thus free of politics—but that often divide us nonetheless. They sought absolution in the absolute, absolving the human by removing the human.

We still often seek this absolution because it comforts yet today—until you encounter someone who uses a different basis for the absolute. Nature versus the divine, say. Or a different religion. Or a different interpretation of what is natural. Such fundamental differences—truly differences in our fundamentals—can be deeply disturbing, not just emotionally but socially.

So we shut, even shout, conversation down. For to debate the implications of one's moral differences is to risk implicating oneself and all one's close associates. Our ideas are never just ideas. They create and manifest social ties. To trust an idea is to trust the well and watershed from which it springs. To threaten an idea is to threaten our trust in the well and watershed, the idea's source and source's source: community itself. To a social being, there can be hardly any threat greater. And so, largely without deliberate intention, we often use absolutes to close ourselves down to the logics others present to us about social and ecological life. Alas, rather than comfort, much pain and difficulty result, for in so doing we cut ourselves off not only to potentially worthy ideas but to one another. We need what I will term a *multilogical* approach to truth and moral thought to better articulate, learn from, and identify with our varying passions and commitments to each corner of the ancient triangle.

That's an overview of my explanation for the divide that emerged, and that has largely remained, between the top and the bottom of the triangle— between the human apex and nature and the divine along the base.[25] Here it is in a clause: because of the moral attraction to urbanizing societies of a foundation for justice apart from human desires. But what about the sides of the base? Why did nature and the divine also separate from each other?

Again for reasons associated with the rise of cities, states, and empires. Culturally, the concept of nature offered to an absolute conception of the divine an account of the origin of desire: in the nature of the body and its ecology. To overcome our nature was to overcome desire, and thus politics. As well, this negative view of nature culturally resonated with a second economic inequality. Not only did the expansion of cities manifest an intensified vertical social conflict over class. It also manifested an intensified horizontal conflict between urban and rural, between what I will term the *bourgeois* and the *pagan*. The wealth accumulation that was the basis for the rise of social class in the city had its own basis in milking wealth from the countryside, harvesting the harvest through taxes and tithes. Associating the people of the countryside with nature's moral backwardness helped justify this horizontal inequality. And it also led to neglect and even disdain for ecological questions, due to the comforting distance that wealth and trade provided from the vagaries of climate, crop disease, soil health, and other matters of sustenance.

Nature was not always seen in a negative way, however. Nearly from the very origin of the concept during periods of urban expansion and social class development in ancient Greece, India, and China, nature could be an absolute goodness in its own right, separate from the politics of human desire. Indeed, advocates of nature as an absolute have often seen religion as a human institution, and thus an institution of human politics, not a preserve apart from politics. Religion, in this view, obscures the absolute and its essential nature. Consequently, either nature or the divine—sometimes together, sometimes in conflict with each other—can serve to ground a natural conscience. But significantly, whether conceived as nature or supernature, the idea of absolute good is historically an urban idea, a bourgeois idea, even if today it is also often strongly held by rural people. (You no longer need to live in the city to be largely bourgeois.)[26] The city of the good began as the good of the city.

All of which indicates that we have not always separated nature from the divine and from the human. Nor do we everywhere, or anywhere fully, today. The pagan view was and is that nature and the divine are *entangled* with the human—and not necessarily good.[27] There is no triangle in the pagan view, except through triangulation from the bourgeois. The ancient triangle is not so ancient as that, nor as universal today as that. (You no longer need to live in the countryside to be largely pagan either.) Perhaps we have more potential than we commonly recognize for a multilogical relationship to each other and our ecologies, from pagan to bourgeois.

———

I head far back into human history, and range far across the globe, to explain and substantiate these claims. The book travels among the ancient Sumerians, Greeks, Romans, Chinese, Hebrews, Christians, Buddhists, Hindus, Muslims, Mayans, and more. It follows developments in moral thought about the good up to the present day, from religion to science to environmentalism, often conversing along the way with contemporary indigenous and other fine folk that I have had the fortune to encounter in my own travels. Throughout, I relate these developments to their urban and rural circumstances—not to give analytic priority to material and economic conditions, but rather to give analytic balance with the cultural and symbolic.[28]

I do not intend to be comprehensive about any of this. With so much to cover, to be comprehensive would risk being incomprehensible. My approach is to visit intimately with places and peoples in the fullness of moments, much like I have done already with Thoreau and St. Augustine. By going small, the book aims to connect to the big through an understanding of contexts and their interconnections.

———

Back in the late 1940s, following the horrors of National Socialism, social philosopher Karl Jaspers found himself searching for something encouraging to say about modernity and its contexts. He hit upon a powerful empirical observation, closely related to the argument I make in this book. Beginning around 800 BCE, he observed, thinkers in several major civilizations came up with a similar new take on faith. The divine was one, good, and transcendentally universal, promoting a new "consciousness" of the "unity of mankind," as Jaspers put it. Zoroaster, Mahavira, Siddhartha Gautama, Plato, Laozi, Vyasa, Hillel, Jesus, and Muhammad all made this case in various ways that remain extremely influential.[29] Jaspers called this pivotal period the "Axial Age," arguing it was as transformative as the Enlightenment.[30]

Jaspers also noted that these ideas emerged within societies developing from the local social relations of agrarianism into cities and city-states. Expanded trade was leading to new connections, he suggested, and thus a new sense of connectedness. A universal, unified, and transcendent sense of the divine, and the sense that this transcendent universality was good, resonated with the new connectedness. We are all one, and it is part of that recognition that we also envision the divine as a universal unity of the good, he contended.

We cannot doubt Jaspers's main empirical point: the rise of universalistic, unified, and transcendent notions of divine goodness was closely associated with a dramatic expansion of cities, states, and empires. Karen Armstrong's many books document this main point in far greater detail (and far more compellingly) than Jaspers himself did.[31] And like Jaspers, Armstrong seeks something encouraging to say about modernity, especially in the face of our constant wars, many of them religiously inspired.[32] The social critic Robert Wright makes a related case about the "evolution of god" toward overcoming "zero-sum thinking" that divides ethnicities, nations, and other social groups.[33] We increasingly love a god of the good as we ourselves become good, and vice versa, the Axial theorists contend.

But Axial theory does not consider the ecological implications of these new urban ideas. Nor does it reckon with the social inequalities that accompanied the rise of the new religions. The Axial theorists suffer from what we might call a civilizationist bias—emphasizing the ways in which our growing urbanism, technological development, and globalization reflect an increasing commitment to good things like democracy and justice. I do not wish to turn the tables here and argue the reverse. My point is not that the city of the good is really the city of the bad. Yet the motives and consequences of the growth of cities, states, and empires seem to me considerably more complex and contradictory. A new commitment to the good there may have been, but at the same time the new urban societies, states, and empires saw a new disregard for ecological questions and a dramatic rise in social inequality, both vertical and horizontal.

The Axial theorists also imply, and sometimes overtly state, another bias closely related to civilizationism: an evolutionary bias toward seeing social change as directional. Here they are joined by an old academic line of argument, especially pronounced in the writings of Émile Durkheim and Ferdinand Tönnies, two of the founding figures of my own profession, sociology.[34] Durkheim and Tönnies suggested that it is helpful to distinguish between two broad ways of organizing community life. Durkheim called the differentiation of roles most characteristic of the city "organic solidarity" and the ties of similarity he found most characteristic of the countryside "mechanical solidarity." By organic solidarity, he had in mind ties between professions like doctors and lawyers, carpenters and plumbers, all of whom rely on each other's difference. By mechanical solidarity, he had in mind the kinship of family and tribe, the members of which rely on each other's similarity. Tönnies made a related distinction between the instrumental social relations of the city, what he termed "gesellschaft," and the affective ties of the countryside, what he called "gemeinschaft." Although they framed the matter somewhat differently, both Durkheim and Tönnies suggested that human social life is steadily evolving away from the past of mechanical solidarity, gemeinschaft, and the rural toward the organic solidarity, gesellschaft, and urbanism of the future. Durkheim and Tönnies were a bit ambivalent about whether this change was a wholly good thing, though. The Axial theorists are not: the Axial ideas that emerged in cities are morally better, they contend.

Again, I do not intend to argue the reverse. But I think we need to take care not to mistake history for evolution. Yes, the idea of the good—envisioned, as I will argue, via a triangle of separations, nature from the divine from the human, and thus emancipated from politics—first arose in cities. Yes, people of the countryside had different concerns and ways of community. But those concerns and ways did not go away. They did not go away in the countryside, nor did they fully diminish in the city. In their better moments, Tönnies recognized that "the essence of both gemeinschaft and gesellschaft is found interwoven in all kinds of associations," and Durkheim noted that mechanical solidarity and organic solidarity "are two aspects of one and the same reality."[35] These are matters of social context, not the unstoppable flight of time's arrow.

I offer the terms "bourgeois" and "pagan" as more contextually sensitive terms. Different contexts raise different concerns. By "bourgeois"—a word derived from the Latin for a fortified town—I mean the concerns over the justice of desire and the vicissitudes of wealth that originally arose in the city, but are no longer so confined. By "pagan"—a word derived from the Latin for a country dweller—I mean the concerns over the troubles of disloyalty and the vicissitudes of agriculture and ecology that originally arose in the countryside, but are also not so confined. They are not so confined because our contexts are not so pure. (And I should stress that by "pagan" I do not mean New Age. I mean the ancient and living traditions that descend from the concerns of rural context the world over.)

However, we should not switch from determinism by time to determinism by context. Our ideas are not so compliant. Ideas have an independence of their own that we carry with us into a context, as anyone who has ever found that they misunderstood a situation (which must be everyone) will know, or as anyone who has ever surprised themselves with how well they coped with a situation (which I hope is everyone) will also know. Our ideas often serve us well. And they often do not.

I have tried to write the book in a way that manifests a sensitivity to both time and context, without slipping into a determinism of either. Although the book follows a loosely historical narrative, I often bounce from instance to instance and situation to situation. One moment I am talking about the ancient Maya, the next I am talking with a Cabécar Indian from Costa Rica, and the next with my old friend Mpumelelo Ncwadi, who hails from present day South Africa. I do so to make connections and comparisons between pasts, between presents, and between pasts and presents. And our potential futures.

––––––––

For better or for worse, most of us now live in dominantly bourgeois societies, whether we live in town or in the countryside. Bourgeois concerns increasingly worry all of us, in both developed countries and developing, and our moral orientations need to speak to those anxieties. We also remain more pagan than we generally recognize, and I believe we need ways to attend to those passions as well. But I do not write to advocate a rejection of bourgeois concerns.

Nonetheless I am troubled by how dominantly bourgeois people like me typically seek the good. Orienting our moral thought around ideas of absolute goodness helps resolve many issues for us, but many other issues come with that form of consideration. We have come to love the absolute, in its many manifestations, as a way to resolve the moral troubles raised by bourgeois life. Placed back in social context, however, such comfort soon leads to discomfort. We've got a lot of talking to do. Yet absolute answers that are beyond discussion make it very difficult to have a discussion. Starting with positions that we believe are good because they are beyond the political makes it very hard to have good politics. Rather than dialogue, we fall into monologues, shouted by bullhorn from the heads of our advancing armies of supporters and conscripts. For if our views are absolute, we feel no compulsion to listen to what others have to say. Our minds, and our motives, are made up already.

A heartbreaking consequence is what might be called the *conundrum of the absolute*. Some of the most wonderful, selfless, and beautiful things that people have ever done have been in the name of absolutes, variously understood. But as well, some of the most horrific, selfish, and ugly things we have ever done have been in the name of absolutes.

Magnificently, in the name of community with nature, we have saved the tiger, the elephant, the American bison, and the California condor. We have established vast wilderness preserves, feeling, like Thoreau, that in wildness is indeed the preservation of the world. We have begun to clean up the water, air, and land upon which all life depends, generally in the face of political forces who have strongly and slyly opposed these efforts. We have found common cause with others because we recognized in them the same natures we find in ourselves.

Through faith in supernature, we have fed the starving and given shelter to the homeless and the ill-housed. We have strengthened commitments at home and abroad, reaching in to reach out, reaching out to reach in. We have limited ambitions that, on reflection, served only to advance our dominance in our own little realms and no broader purpose. In service of both nature and supernature, we have sacrificed much of our selves for collective ends that we came to understand we should hold dearer.

Yet in the name of nature, we have also expropriated land from the poor to make way for parks and tourism. We have competed with the disadvantaged on unequal terms for homes and lives that are comparatively free of the pollution and danger of industrialism. We have tortured, enslaved, and slaughtered those we deemed to have natures apart from and beneath our own. In the name of our faith in supernatural absolutes, we have waged divisive moral campaigns. We have suppressed the rights of others and crushed their self-regard. And we have tortured, enslaved, and slaughtered those who committed to supernatures we deemed apart from and beneath our own. Our transcendent beliefs are supposed to motivate our compassion and faith in the golden rules of human and ecological relationships. Sadly, they have often motivated and justified cruelty and leaden rules of relationships.[36]

For these moral ideas are also ideas of community and its boundaries. Our conceptions of both nature and the divine have led us to open our ears and our eyes to others, but also, when envisioned as absolutes, to shut them. We come to fear difference rather than relish the creativity of the multilogical that comes from dialogue and debate, through which we are always learning and becoming, even when we do not fully agree (which may always be the case).[37] We come to fear difference especially in moments of political conflict. Such moments are precisely when we find the monological character of the absolute the most seductive, for monologue suppresses difference. Such moments are equally when those seeking means to manipulate the many find the absolute most useful to their goals. As we look out across the world, we seem to be in such a moment of heightened political conflict today, and thus heightened attraction for answers from beyond—even as they lead us, or are used to lead us, astray. Absolutes are always deeply political, at the same time that they appear to provide a basis for action that is beyond politics.

These are the perils of innocence. Yet, the Russian social philosopher Mikhail Bakhtin noted, monologue is never completely absolute. As Bakhtin put it, "there is neither a first nor a last word."[38] Monologue always contains strains of dialogue and the multilogical, for it must take its audience at least a bit into account to make its case. And often more than a bit. In other words, the absolute is never absolute. Across the long history of natures, faiths, and communities, we have oscillated from more monologic to more multilogical moments and modes of interaction and debate. Sometimes even in the midst of heightened conflict we have found ways to open conversation, to learn from each other, to jointly construct new alternatives with broad and diverse benefit.

I find much cause for hope in this potential non-absoluteness of our absolutes—hope that we may come to accept the certainty of uncertainty in a world that is ever unfinished, always open, full of difference and conflict, and therefore ceaselessly intriguing, alive, and creative.

The Pagan

2

Nature Before Nature

CAVES CONJURE A SENSE of the profound. The echoing darkness obscures our usual means for estimating distance, summoning awe of the vast. The stillness and constant climate give us little sense of motion, encouraging a feeling of timelessness. The twisting contours of the walls suggest some alien logic of construction, raising suspense and mystery. As well, caves go deep into where we cannot ordinarily go, constituted as we are. Caves confront us with our limits just as they give us access to the unseen foundations of the normal.

Caves are cool.

Or so I found myself thinking the summer of 2011 as I stood in the middle of the hundred-foot high main room of the Ideon Cave, more than five thousand feet above the Mediterranean Sea, set into the face of Mount Ida, or Psiloritis, as the locals call it, the tallest mountain on Crete. A daily stream of visitors makes the dry, rocky hike up Psiloritis, eager like me to exercise their legs and their imaginations. The Ideon Cave has been a religious pilgrimage site for over four thousand years, at least since Minoan times, if not earlier. The path to the Ideon Cave is very deeply worn.

The Minoans lit the first fires of ancient Greek religion. Long before mainland Greeks did, the Minoans divined the existence of Zeus. The Minoans themselves seem to have gotten the idea of Zeus from Proto-Indo-Europeans—peoples known to scholars by the happy acronym PIE—through various cultural pathways now lost to us. The PIE peoples had called their chief god by almost the same name: Dyeus.[1] Like Zeus, Dyeus was a male god of sky and thunder.[2] The Romans picked up on Dyeus too. The name "Jupiter" came from *dyeu-pater*, PIE for god-father. Later on, the Romans equated Jupiter with Zeus, a kind of double derivation from Dyeus. The Romans also generalized *dyeus* into *deus*, meaning "deity." The English word "deity" itself derives from *dyeus*. And so do the English words "theology" and "divinity."

These are all very old words. People have been thinking about this stuff for a long time.

It was in the Ideon Cave that Dyeus became Zeus. For legend has it that here his mother Rhea hid the baby Zeus from the violent eye of his father, Cronus, who wanted to eat him.[3] Rhea was the goddess of motherhood, and Cronus—the Greek equivalent of the Roman god Saturn—was then ruler of the gods. Cronus had earlier overthrown his own father, Uranus, to take the throne. But an oracle said that a son of Rhea would one day overthrow Cronus in turn. So Cronus caught and ate every baby his wife bore. Then Rhea hit on the idea of showing Cronus a stone wrapped in swaddling clothes when she next gave birth. Cronus, in his fear and haste, promptly ate the stone. Meanwhile, Rhea hid her new child in the Ideon Cave to protect him until he was strong enough to take on his father.

Everyone worried that Cronus would eventually figure out what had happened. So local men guarded the cave entrance to protect Zeus. The ancient myths call them the *curetes*, the original inhabitants of Crete, for whom Crete is named. Every time the baby Zeus cried the *curetes* would dance and bang their shields with their swords, so Cronus wouldn't hear him. (Cretan men still do this dance at local village festivals.) The nymphs Melissa and Amalthea helped Rhea raise Zeus, feeding him on goat's milk and honey. And sure enough, when he had grown up, Zeus fulfilled the prophecy. He forced Cronus to disgorge his five brothers and sisters. Together, led by Zeus, the siblings imprisoned Cronus and the other Titans in Tartarus, a dungeon deep below the surface of the Earth. Some say the Titans are there to this day.

It's quite a tale. So, like me, the curious and faithful have long made the trek up to the very spot where so much of the story takes place, eager to feel the unfelt.[4] Archaeologists have recovered thousands of artifacts from the Ideon Cave. Ivory sculptures. Hundreds of clay lamps. Bronze shields such as those Zeus's guards were supposed to have used in their dances. Outside the cave you can still see a stone altar, carved out of the living rock, where millennia of Zeus's followers have offered him gifts and implored him for better fortunes for themselves and their loved ones. Plato, Pythagoras, and Epimenides received their initiation into the sacred mysteries of Zeus here.[5]

It's not hard to imagine why the Minoans and later Greeks connected this story to this particular place. One's imagination of the sky god, and chief of the gods, readily accepts an association of him with Psiloritis, the highest mountain in the region—what, for the people who originated this story, was likely the highest mountain that they knew.[6] (Psiloritis means "high mountain" in Greek.) It is easy to envision other associations. The howling of the wind around the mountain peaks with the squalling of the baby Zeus. The sounds of thunder with the rattling clatter of the *curetes'* shields on high. The goat milk and honey with the delicious foodstuffs that even these arid heights can produce with abundance. The region's many earthquakes with the bellowing and pounding of Cronus and his fellow Titans, struggling to escape Tartarus, deep in the Earth.

In other words, the story of Zeus in the Ideon Cave is in large part a story about nature—except that nature did not yet exist.

———

I say "did not exist" because the idea of a nature that we may identify and talk about as a category of thought, as something we can separate out from other matters we might consider, did not exist for the Minoans and other early peoples. Nor does it, as we will see, for some contemporary peoples as well. To be sure, matters that a scientist might refer to with the word "nature" existed as concerns: the sky and the wind, storms and lightening, pastures that yield milk and honey, earthquakes that shatter our lives. But the evidence of stories like Zeus's upbringing in the mountain caves of Crete suggests that early peoples, like some others today, combined these concerns with the ways of the supernatural and even with the ways of people, such as the *curetes*. It was not the goddess Rhea and the nymphs Melissa and Amalthea alone who protected the baby Zeus from Cronus. People, goats, and cave worked together with the divine. The story of Zeus's upbringing presents an *entangled* vision of nature, supernature, and the human all matted together, rather than seeing nature as a separate matter, worthy of a word that distinguishes it. There was a tangle, not a triangle.

In addition to a vision of entanglement, we should immediately note two other key points about what I will call *nature before nature*. First is that the characters in these stories are not necessarily good. Cronus is certainly presented as a rather bloodthirsty fellow, and Zeus's response was not exactly gentle and affectionate. Second is that, although Zeus clearly has far-ranging powers, the story of the Ideon Cave allows one to experience his presence in a very specific spot. Ancient Greek religion emphasized *immanence* in places, like the Ideon Cave or like Mount Olympus, the home of the gods, over the *transcendence* so familiar to us in the modern world religions. Many spirits, like nymphs, in fact inhabited only one place—a specific rock, tree, river, or mountain.

———

And not only in ancient Greece. Thanks to the care of an eighteenth-century Christian friar, Francisco Ximénez, we have a rare record of another entangled vision of nature before nature: the *Popol Vuh*, one of the few surviving scriptures of ancient Mayan religion.

Christian clergy have not always been respectful and protective of the faith traditions of others, especially Spanish clergy in the centuries following Cortez's defeat of the Aztecs in 1521. One horrific moment that stands out is the scene at the Franciscan monastery at the town of Maní in the Yucatan on July 12, 1562.[7] There, a monk by the name of Diego de Landa ordered the burning of all the scriptures and idols of the Maya. He was able to round up forty Mayan books, as well as reportedly some twenty thousand Mayan religious objects. He forced hundreds of Maya to watch as he commanded the books and objects to be burned, calling them "the deceit of the devil."[8] Other monks followed suit whenever they encountered Mayan books through to 1697 when the last Mayan city was conquered—a place called Tayasal, which held out so long because of its location on an island in a lake in the middle of the Guatemalan jungle.

But it turned out the monks didn't quite burn them all. Over the next couple of hundred years, three ancient Mayan books turned up in Europe, and part of a fourth in Mexico. Intrigued by the artistry and exoticness of the hieroglyphics, travelers brought three home to Europe as souvenirs. The fragment of a fourth showed up in the 1960s on the black market, apparently looted from a cave in Chiapas.[9]

Plus the text of one more ancient Mayan book of scriptures has also turned up, albeit not the original and without any hieroglyphics. But it is perhaps the most important ancient Mayan book of all: the *Popol Vuh*, a striking work of nature before nature. The name *Popol Vuh* translates as the "Book of the People" or the "Book of the Community." Some now call it the "Mayan Bible." It recounts Mayan history—or, more specifically, the history of the Quiché branch of the Maya—from creation up to the time of the Spanish conquest. What has come down to us is a transliteration of the original Mayan into Roman letters, and a translation of the transliteration into Spanish, made by an obscure friar named Francisco Ximénez, who made the transliteration and translation sometime between 1700 and 1715.[10] It lay moldering in his papers for a century and a half before it finally came to light.

We know very little about Friar Ximénez and how he learned the *Popol Vuh*, aside from a few brief references in his writings. Some scholars think that a Mayan priest—or perhaps several Mayan priests—must have trusted him enough to give him a private recitation of the *Popol Vuh*, likely over the course of several days, and slowly enough that Ximénez could transcribe it as a transliteration and later translate it. Probably the hieroglyphic version was already lost, and the recitation was from memory. Another theory is that a native Quiché speaker who knew Latin characters made the transliteration, which Ximénez later translated.[11] However it happened, the intent of local people seems to have been to preserve the *Popol Vuh* before it was lost entirely. The Preamble states that "we shall bring it to light because now the *Popol Vuh*, as it is called, cannot be seen any more. . . . The original book, written long ago, existed, but its sight is hidden to the searcher and to the thinker."[12]

What follows is a wild, oftentimes perplexing story, full of politics and violent conflict—a description that could also apply to many sections of the Bible (for reasons I'll come to a couple of chapters hence). Also like the Bible, the *Popol Vuh* begins by recounting the creation of the world through to the development of human society, including the founding of cities and the genealogy of kings.[13] Along the way, it tells the story of the heroic twins, Xbalanqué and Hunahpú, sons of the corn god, and how they revenge their father's death.[14] The lords of Xibalba, the Mayan name for the underworld, kill the twins' father. But the twins defeat the lords of Xibalba and resurrect their father. In a series of adventures, they also kill many divine trouble makers—a bird monster, a volcano monster, a monster who produces earthquakes, as well as the lords of Xibalba—before rising into the sky to become the sun and the moon.[15]

A number of the stories resonate closely with biblical accounts, particularly in the early part of the *Popol Vuh*. The world is created from nothing by "the word."[16] The gods send a massive flood to wipe out an early version of humans because "they no longer remembered the Heart of Heaven."[17] And the mother of the heroic twins becomes pregnant with them through a form of immaculate conception (albeit from spittle that dripped from the skull of their father, the corn god, who was then still dead).[18] These stories may be original to the Quiché Maya. Yet by the time Ximénez recorded the *Popol Vuh*, the Maya were already strongly influenced by Christianity. Many had converted, or had at least professed conversion. (After all, Ximénez had come there to encourage them to become Christians.) So there is reason to suspect some blending of traditions. But there is also much that is strikingly Mayan.

For one thing, the story of the *Popol Vuh* is in large measure the story of corn. The famed Mayan archaeologist Michael Coe interprets the *Popol Vuh* as "fundamentally agricultural, relating to the annual planting and harvest cycle of maize [corn], the Maya staff of life."[19] The resurrection of the corn god from the underworld is the resurrection of the plant from the kernel out of the dark and mysterious depths of the soil.

For another, nature does not exist in the *Popol Vuh*—at least not nature in the sense of a category, realm, or power separate from humans and the divine.[20] There is a great deal of ecology in its stories, however. One passage explains the origin of what Western ecologists today would call "food chains" and "trophic levels." The grandmother of the heroic twins tries to send them a secret message, hidden in the stomach of a louse. But before the message gets to the twins, the louse is swallowed by a toad. The toad is swallowed by a snake, which is in turn swallowed by a hawk. The twins don't know any of this, and for amusement they shoot the hawk in the eye with a blowgun. Annoyed, the hawk refuses to give them the message unless they fix its eye, which the twins do. Then the hawk vomits out the snake, which vomits out the toad—which tries but fails to vomit out the louse. It fails because the louse tricked the toad when it was first swallowed and stayed stuck to the toad's teeth, to prevent being fully eaten. The twins get the louse out of the toad's mouth anyway, and receive their grandmother's message. "From then on this was the food of snakes," the *Popol Vuh* recounts, "who still today swallow toads." And "from that time, this has been the food of hawks, who devour snakes in the fields." But because "the toad was tricked . . . the kind of food to give it is not known," evidently reporting on the state of ecological knowledge at the time and place of the *Popol Vuh*'s composition.[21]

These are not the kinds of stories Western parents would likely read in the evening to gentle a child to sleep—even though the swallowing, vomiting, and shooting of the hawk in the eye are fairly mild violence compared with many other stories in the *Popol Vuh*. The gods are fierce, the animals are fierce, and the human heroes are fierce. There is much pain and gore. This is not a world of goodness, mildness, and mercy.

But another feature of the state of ecological knowledge in the *Popol Vuh* is that the divine is inseparably entangled with ecology—the gods with corn and with creating the foods of animals—as are, heroically, people themselves.

————

Many indigenous peoples still profess an entangled view. In the mid-1970s, I had the chance to experience such an understanding among the Cabécar of Costa Rica. At the time, I was working as a field geologist for a US mineral exploration company, interested in mining copper in Costa Rica's Talamanca Mountains. It would have been a terrible thing to do to the region's inhabitants, human and nonhuman alike. The kind of copper we were looking for is called "porphyry copper," a massive but low-grade type of deposit. You basically need a whole mountain of the stuff to make it worth mining. Plus, once the ore has been dug out and crushed and the copper removed, you wind up with about twice the volume in waste rock. So you also need a couple of adjacent valleys to fill in. And you need a rail line and a port facility to get the copper to the coast and into boats to ship around the world. It would have been a mess of imperialist proportions. But I was only nineteen, ignorant of the implications and the politics, and eager for a semester of adventure to escape from college and a strong case of sophomore slump.

These mountains are high—the highest in Central America—and quite remote. The area where we were working was a two-day walk from the nearest road. The forestry companies hadn't been there yet, and may never, because it is now a United Nations Biosphere Reserve, as well as a reserve for native peoples. They say that the biodiversity is as great as anywhere in the world. I remember being told it was possible to encounter over two hundred different species of trees on a single hectare.

In order to explore for copper in high mountains covered by dense rain-forest, where the rocks usually aren't visible because of all the vegetation, you must walk up and down streams, collect little sample bags of sand, send them off to a laboratory, and watch for spikes in metal content in the lab reports.[22] Since the sand must have come from upstream of the sample location, you can pin down the source well enough for the exploratory phase of copper mining. So that's what I did, along with a couple of Costa Rican coworkers. I walked up and down mountain streams in rubber boots and filled bags with sand. A helicopter would drop us off in a natural clearing, generally on the stony banks of a river that was not flowing at full volume, this being the dry season (really, the less rainy season). We would set up camp in the rain forest, slinging hammocks and mosquito netting between trees, with tarps above, and moving every few days as we finished sampling an area. Sample bags of sand weigh your pack down pretty quickly, though. We sometimes found ourselves hauling fifty or sixty pounds of sand each, in addition to our camping gear. So the helicopter would come back once a week or so to take our filled sample bags and give us more food.

It was tough going. One time I lost my footing fording a swift river, and was swept toward a waterfall that poured into the entrance of a steep canyon. It was an Indiana Jones moment, but it was fully real. Fortunately (or I wouldn't be writing this sentence right now), I was able to direct myself enough to land— yes!—feet first on a boulder at the top of the waterfall that split the current more or less in two. One of my colleagues tied a rope around his middle, while the other tied the other end around his own waist. Then he waded out as far as he could stand in the river, and tossed me the end of a second rope. It was pretty risky. The far end of the first rope should have been tied around a tree, not to a person, in case one of my colleagues stumbled and they both wound up being swept down the river too. But we didn't have a choice. The ropes weren't long enough to do it any other way. And after a few tosses, it worked.

After this incident, we decided it would be a good idea, where possible, to hire one of the local native folk to guide us. In this way, I got to know a Cabécar man we knew only as Frederico, and his wife Ismarelda. (Their given names were in Cabécar, but they assumed Spanish names when dealing with outsiders.) As is characteristic of the Cabécar, Frederico and Ismarelda lived alone in a grass-roofed homestead with a small farm carved out of the rainforest, miles from anyone else, rather than in a village or kin group. Frederico worked with us for a week, bringing us to trails local people had already cut, and bringing us to river crossing points where one could safely wade across or where the local people had stashed a balsa-log raft. One night he had us sleep in one of the huts made of bent branches that local people use as a kind of traditional motel for when one can't make it back home before dark. That evening we feasted on sweet potatoes, which the Cabécar plant near these huts so wayfarers have something to eat.

Frederico, I came to understand, led an entangled life of people, nature, and the divine. He had amazing skills in jungle-craft. Once when we were walking through some woods on a floodplain, an animal called a *tepisquintle*—a forty-pound rodent that, I discovered, tastes a lot like lamb—crossed our path. I was "el jefe" in that situation, so Frederico looked to me for permission (which felt strange, as he was probably more than twice my age). I nodded. Frederico had three of his dogs along. He pointed into the woods in the direction the *tepisquintle* had gone, and off the dogs went. Apparently, when chased, *tepisquintle* head for water, as they are excellent swimmers. The job of the dogs was partly to let Frederico know, through their barking, where the *tepisquintle* would emerge from the forest and try to dive into the river. And it was partly to drive the animal to Frederico, when it did emerge. They did their job perfectly. We raced behind Frederico, crashing through the undergrowth, and were able to watch as the *tepisquintle* shot out of the forest and ran right toward Frederico, who was standing in about a foot of water with his machete raised. One chop and we had fresh meat.

On our last day in Frederico's area, after a week together, we had to cross a high mountain pass. At the top of the pass, we came across a small lake, one of the very few lakes in the region. It may have had a glacial origin for, hot as Costa Rica is today, the Talamanca Mountains had active glaciers during the height of the Ice Age. However the lake came to be there, Frederico stopped us and said, "there is a song for this place." First starting quietly, then swelling in volume, and then ending quietly, he sang a chant-like melody in Cabécar. I don't know what the song was about, at least not specifically. He never said. Probably neither he nor I had good enough Spanish for him to communicate its precise meaning. But in one sense, I knew very much what the song was about: the presence of the divine, which he felt tangled there in that lake, and that I too was able to feel a bit through the tangle of my relationship with him.

———

An entangled view of people, the divine, and what we now often call nature—experienced with great specificity in places local to our lives, and by no means always kind and good—remains common, despite the worldwide spread of modernism. Frederico first introduced me to contemporary entangled views, but I have experienced them most deeply in the South Africa village of KuManzimdaka, guided by a remarkable man from the region, Mpumelelo Ncwadi, now one of my closest friends. Mpumelelo and I have been working together since 2009, along with an ever-widening group of colleagues, students, and villagers, on an agroecological and participatory approach to livelihood.[23] He's taught me a lot, as have the local community members.

KuManzimdaka is a village of the amaQwathi, a small subnation of the amaXhosa in South Africa's Eastern Cape Province, one of the country's poorest regions in wealth and health, home to some eight million amaXhosa.[24] Legal apartheid may be over, but economic and social apartheid continues for most of those living on these grassy plateaus, rolling up from the Indian Ocean to a height of five thousand feet.[25] The Drakensberg Mountains loom behind, part of a long wall of basalt known as the Great Escarpment, reaching to over eleven thousand feet. Given the inaccessibility and challenging topography, the environment itself serves as a means of the continued apartheid local people must contend with.[26]

Still, the area is rich in tradition, community, and a beautiful and potentially productive landscape. Most local people live in scattered settlements based on customary land rights, with no deed other than a verbal agreement with the local chief, granted to one's family through tribal membership. These rights can be pretty secure, though—in many ways more secure than land with a deed that one can buy and sell, and thus may lose when a hard period leaves one little alternative but to sell, perhaps because one does not even have enough cash to pay the taxes on the land. There are no taxes with customary land rights. Community has its benefits.[27]

Mpumelelo isn't amaQwathi, but was raised in the Eastern Cape countryside and is a member of another amaXhosa subgroup. His parents were illiterate but understood the importance of school—something at which Mpumelelo excelled, despite the ten-mile walk each way. He went on to earn a certificate in mining engineering from Witwatersrand University, a bachelor's in engineering from the University of Texas at Austin, a master's in sustainable engineering from Cambridge, and an MBA from the University of Cape Town. He had been doing consulting work on sustainable development all across Africa, but decided he needed to change his focus to the Eastern Cape, giving back to the community that launched him into such success. He saw my name on a website and sent me an email, looking for partners. I was intrigued, having once visited the region many years ago.[28] We call the collaboration that developed the LAND Project, for Livelihood, Agroecology, Nutrition, and Development.[29]

Religion is central to community strength for most people in the area. Almost 90 percent of people in the Eastern Cape reported a religious affiliation on the 2001 South African census.[30] The religion they reported was almost uniformly Christian. Only 1.1 percent indicated a religious affiliation other than Christianity, with Islam being the largest sub-fraction at 0.3 percent of Eastern Cape residents. Only 0.1 percent reported "African traditional belief." But anyone with much experience among the people of the Eastern Cape knows this to be a vast underestimate. Most people in the area practice both Christianity and traditional beliefs, to varying degrees, depending on the need and context.

I first encountered traditional beliefs when one day I noticed off in the countryside a group of young men whose skin had been splotched with white clay. Mpumelelo explained that this was part of their initiation into manhood, a ritual that includes circumcision. Most amaXhosa men from rural areas continue this traditional practice, generally in their late teens.[31] Most amaXhosa women also go through an initiation ritual in their teens (but which does not include female circumcision, as is practiced in some areas in Africa to the north, mainly in the countries ringing the Sahara). By these measures alone, the vast majority of Eastern Cape residents continue to practice traditional beliefs.

Ancestor veneration gives spirit to those practices. Everyday speech often uses the phrase "ancestor worship," but many scholars balk at that terminology because the amaXhosa do not regard their ancestors as actually taking on the status of gods. However, the amaXhosa do see their ancestors as able to intercede in the affairs of the living, for both good and ill. So the difference between "veneration" and "worship" is perhaps a matter of degree, rather than a sharp line.

The amaXhosa can be quite private about ancestor veneration. A traditional healer called an *igqirha* usually leads the rituals, which often include divination by the throwing of bones, reading the desires of the ancestors from how the bones scatter. It is not the kind of thing Westerners typically give much respect, so the amaXhosa don't advertise it much. And aside from a few quick explanations when we were working in the countryside with villagers, Mpumelelo and I hadn't talked about it.

Ancestor veneration sometimes involves agricultural concerns, particularly around livestock health, crop disease, bad weather, and other matters that we often put in the category "nature." I didn't want to intrude, but it seemed important for our work on the LAND Project. I took out some books and crawled around the web a bit. The information I found was contradictory and fragmentary. I sat there wavering. "Okay, I'm just going to call Mpumelelo," I finally decided, and I used the computer to dial his number from my home in Madison, Wisconsin.

"Hey, Mpumi," which is his nickname, "I've been reading and trying to understand about ancestor worship"—I didn't use the word "veneration"—"in the Eastern Cape. How much of it still goes on?"

I was a bit nervous and felt I had put the question awkwardly. But Mpumelelo laughed, and the line crackled. "Yes, sure. We slaughter for our ancestors."

"Really?" which was a dumb thing to say. But Mpumelelo was tolerant of my clumsiness. "When? Like, at what seasons or occasions?"

"Well, sometimes we do it if someone has a dream they're worried about. Or when someone is born, or for initiation," meaning a teenager's initiation into adulthood. Bad dreams can indicate to the amaXhosa that the ancestors feel they aren't being remembered enough, and it is similarly important to honor them at important events in the lives of the living. "Other times too. Usually we slaughter a goat. But sometimes we slaughter male cattle, what you would call an ox." He hesitated a moment. "I do it."

"You do?" I blurted, instantly regretting my tone, and hoping it didn't sound disapproving. I didn't mean to be. This was an important moment between us, and here I was still being awkward. "Wow, awesome, that's great," I followed up, maybe a little too enthusiastically. "Um, when was the last time you did it?"

"Earlier this year," said Mpumelelo, taking it all in stride. "I'll have to do it again [in a few years] when my son is ready for initiation. And I had to do it when he was born, and when my daughters were born, and for their initiations too. Actually, when my son goes for initiation, I'll have to slaughter two goats. One for my son, and one for my great-grandfather."

I've visited Mpumelelo's home. He lives in a lovely suburban neighborhood of Cape Town, with tidy yards and spacious, well-maintained houses. I was trying to imagine where the slaughtering would happen. "Where do you do it? Not inside Cape Town, do you?"

He laughed again. "No, no, not in Cape Town. I'll go to Grahamstown to my mother's place." Grahamstown is a medium-sized city at the southern end of the Eastern Cape Province. His mother lives in the countryside a few miles outside. "We do it at my mother's *kraal*," he continued, using the Afrikaans word for corral, as is commonly done in South Africa, even when speaking English. Most amaXhosa rural homesteads in the Eastern Cape have a small *kraal* to keep livestock safe at night. "You have to do it at the *kraal*. And then we hang the horns of the goat on the gate of the *kraal*."

I'd read something about this the previous day, how the sacrifices take place in the family homestead in your home village, where your ancestors' spirits are strongest. Another widespread custom is burying a newborn baby's umbilical cord in the fireplace of the hut where she or he was born, with a special ceremony. When first getting to know each other, a common question one amaXhosa person asks another, with a bit of a smile, is "where is your navel buried?" instead of "where are you from?"

But I remembered that Mpumelelo's mother didn't live in his home village. Mpumelelo's parents moved the family when Mpumelelo was seven, in part so he and his sister could more easily get to school.[32] "But your mother has moved," I said. "Don't you have to do the slaughtering where you were born, where your navel is buried?"

He chuckled at my use of the phrase. "If I wasn't born where I do the sacrifice, then I round up all the old people from my home village who share my lineage," he explained. "They come and they bless the spot to reinstall the spirit of my ancestors there. They've done that for my mother's *kraal* where she is living now. They called my great-grandfather's spirit to there. They came and blessed that spot, that *kraal*, because we all of us share a bit of that spirit."

I was struck by how locally specific the installation of spirit was, and the special rituals required to transfer it to another location. To the extent that they follow traditional beliefs, every amaXhosa person who moves away to the city therefore needs that rural connection back to the precise spot of the family *kraal*—or *ubuhlanti*, to use the isiXhosa word, which Mpumelelo taught me some time later—even those with a globalized life course. Like Mpumelelo. Through it, Mpumelelo and other amaXhosa gain a deep and unshakeable sense of home. I felt a bit envious, I came to realize afterward.

We also talked about a number of other aspects of amaXhosa ancestor veneration. The discomfort many amaXhosa feminists feel about the patrilineal character of the tradition. Ways a person can stay connected to the ancestors other than through a sacrifice at the family *kraal*. The tensions between Christianity and slaughtering for one's ancestors. How all the leading South Africa politicians with tribal heritage—Mbeki, Zuma, and Mandela (who was still alive at the time)—slaughter for their ancestors.

But what really stands out to me is what Mpumelelo said when I asked him, "So, are the spirits of one's ancestors always nice? Or do they get angry if you don't do a sacrifice?"

"Yes, yes!" he excitedly replied. "You have to sacrifice! Like people often say, if you get a family that is falling apart, it's because they don't slaughter for their ancestors. Or if you have young people that are behaving badly and getting into trouble, we say it's because they are not slaughtering for their ancestors."

To the sociologist, the wisdom here is sound. Holding a sacrifice also holds a community together. People assemble for the ritual, enjoy the feast that follows, and reinforce their fellow-feeling. When a family is not well integrated with the local community, I can well believe that both the adults and the children have more difficulties, both economically and psychologically. I've seen as much in my own local community. It takes a village to raise a child, of course, but also to raise adults back up if they fall into hard times. The spirit of community has its benefits too.

———

Ancestor veneration entangles humans with the land and the divine. The ancestors with their special powers are themselves human, and through them, humans become tightly bound to place. Perhaps we might best regard venerated ancestors as semidivine, blurring the usually sharp categorical line modern culture draws between humans and gods.

Other cultures of nature before nature experience entanglement in other ways. Consider a powerful but long-forgotten story that came to light in Iraq the evening of December 23, 1853.[33] Aided by torches, a group of rough men were digging into a fifty-foot high mound a mile long, across the Tigris River from the city of Mosul. They were not grave robbers, at least not in the conventional sense of the phrase. They were in the employ of an archaeologist from the British Museum, one Hormuzd Rassam, who had hired them to dig in the ruins of the ancient Assyrian city of Nineveh. But Rassam didn't actually have permission to dig at this mound. Those rights (such as they were) belonged to the French and the Louvre—which is why Rassam and his men were digging at night.[34]

The third night of the dig the workers' shovels banged into one of the most spectacular archaeological discoveries of the nineteenth century: the Palace of Ashurbanipal, the last great king of Assyria, who ruled from 668 BCE to 627 BCE. In the middle of the palace was a large room, fifty feet by fifteen feet.[35] The walls were covered with carved panels of King Ashurbanipal hunting lions (which, incidentally, are now extinct in the region). On the floor scattered thousands of pieces of cuneiform tablets, baked hard by the fire that burned Ashurbanipal's palace during the sacking of Nineveh in 612 BCE. Like most nineteenth-century archaeologists working for imperial powers, Rassam's main object was showy pieces like Ashurbanipal's lions. (Room 10a in the British Museum still displays the panels.) At the time, no one could read more than a few characters of this kind of cuneiform anyway.[36] Thankfully, Rassam didn't just chuck it all. When the shovels turned up bits of clay tablet, he had workers toss them into a few wooden crates, jumbling the pieces together. Eventually, the crates made it onto a boat back to the British Museum, along with the panels of lions.

Twenty years later one George Smith, a volunteer research assistant at the British Museum, figured out that there was something extraordinary to be read in these crates of fragments. Among the shards were some shattered tablets recounting part of an astonishing tale: the *Epic of Gilgamesh*. Much of the story was missing, so Smith went back to Nineveh a couple of times to find more. A few bits of other copies later turned up elsewhere.[37] We now have most of it.

This now world-famous saga recounts the adventures of Gilgamesh, king of "great-walled Uruk," an ancient Sumerian city-state in southern Iraq from which the name Iraq descends. There is a fair chance there really was a King Gilgamesh. At least the Sumerian King List—an enumeration that archaeologists have found half a dozen times or so—records a King Gilgamesh who reigned around 2600 BCE.[38] Archaeologists have also found the ruins of Uruk, which was indeed surrounded by great walls. Its main temple was dedicated to Ishtar, the goddess of love, who often appears in the epic.[39] So there is some real history in the *Epic*. There is also much real humanity, entangled with nature and the divine. Here's a digest.[40]

———

Gilgamesh is the fantastically strong King of Uruk, son of King Lugalbanda (the principal character in several other Sumerian myths). He is also the son of the goddess Ninsun, daughter of Anu, one of the Sumerian trinity of chief gods. Gilgamesh, then, is a human-god hybrid—a kind of demigod. But Gilgamesh is a bad king. He forces the young men of the city to fight him, even though they are sure to lose. And he forces the young women of the city to have sex with him. The people cry out to the gods for help.

Anu hears their plea. He asks Aruru, the goddess of creation, to create a companion for Gilgamesh who is equal to him in strength and can balance him. So Aruru creates Enkidu, a fierce wild man. Enkidu grows up alone, far from the city, with only animals for companionship. He defends wild animals from hunters, freeing them from traps and filling in hunters' pits. Hunters in the area worry about losing their livelihood, so they send word about Enkidu to Gilgamesh.

Gilgamesh agrees that Enkidu must be tamed. He sends Shamhat, a priestess at the Temple of Ishtar, to use sex to lure Enkidu into human society. In a remarkable passage for a religious myth—remarkable at least in comparison to widespread contemporary understandings of religion—they have sex continuously for a week.[41] It works. Tamed by sex, Enkidu agrees to join human society. Enkidu comes to Uruk and challenges Gilgamesh to a wrestling match. The fight shakes the very walls of the city. Gilgamesh eventually wins. However, as a result, Gilgamesh and Enkidu become the closest of companions, and set out on a series of adventures together.

In their first adventure, the two friends attack the monster Humbaba, guardian of the cedar forest that lies at the base of Cedar Mountain, dwelling place of the gods. Shamash, god of justice and the sun and one of the two friends' patron deities, sends a big wind that pins Humbaba down. The monster curses them and says the gods will be angry if they kill him—especially Enlil, another of the trinity of chief gods, who ordained Humbaba to guard the forest:

> If you kill me, you will call down the gods'
> wrath, and their judgment will be severe . . .
> I curse you both. Because you have done this,
> May Enkidu die, may he die in great pain,
> May Gilgamesh be inconsolable,
> may his merciless heart be crushed with grief.[42]

The two friends don't listen. After all, Shamash is helping them. Gilgamesh cuts off the monster's head, and Enkidu and Gilgamesh promptly chop down the entire cedar forest.

The goddess Ishtar is very impressed with their deeds—so impressed she asks Gilgamesh to marry her. He refuses, noting that Ishtar has mistreated many of her former husbands and lovers. Ishtar is furious at this insult. She gets Anu, who is her father, to send the Bull of Heaven to punish Gilgamesh. Gilgamesh and Enkidu kill the Bull of Heaven instead, and offer its heart to Shamash. Enkidu rips off the bull's hind quarter and flings it at Ishtar's face.

This is too much for the gods. Gilgamesh and Enkidu have killed both Humbaba and the Bull of Heaven, and they have insulted the goddess Ishtar. Anu and Enlil hold a council of the gods and determine that one of the two friends has to die. They settle on Enkidu. After a series of vivid and scary dreams, punctuated by Gilgamesh's efforts to console him, Enkidu does indeed die, as the gods have ordained, mollifying Ishtar and fulfilling Humbaba's curse. Gilgamesh is devastated, both at the loss of his closest friend and at the recognition that he too one day must die. For although he is a grandson of Anu, Gilgamesh is ultimately human and a mortal.

The final tablets of the epic recount Gilgamesh's search for the secret of immortality. Many incidents later he finds Utnapishtim and his wife, the only humans ever to be granted immortality. Utnapishtim explains how they gained this boon.

Long ago, led by Enlil, the gods sent a flood to cover the world and wash away its evils. But Ea, the third of the trinity of chief gods, secretly asked Utnapishtim to build a huge boat and to put his family and representatives of all the animals on board. Utnapishtim did, and waited for the flood waters to recede. He sent out first a dove, then a swallow, and then finally a raven, to look to see if there was any dry land yet. The raven found a branch, showing that land had indeed reemerged. Utnapishtim then set loose all the animals and his family. (It was the discovery of this Noah-like figure that first attracted George Smith's interest in the *Epic of Gilgamesh*.)[43] Enlil was furious, but Ea convinced Enlil that he had overreached a bit, and that Utnapishtim should be rewarded for saving life on Earth. So Enlil granted Utnapishtim and his wife immortality.

Utnapishtim tells Gilgamesh he will grant him immortality in turn—but only if he can stay awake six days and seven nights. Gilgamesh, exhausted by his travels, instantly falls asleep for the entire six days and seven nights. Nonetheless, at his wife's suggestion, Utnapishtim tells Gilgamesh how to acquire a plant that grants perpetual youth. Gilgamesh gets the plant. But before he can eat it, a serpent steals the plant, leaving behind its newly shed skin. Gilgamesh weeps because he has lost this last chance for immortality.

The epic ends with Gilgamesh's return to "great-walled Uruk," and his recognition that its marvels are the true source of any immortality he may attain.

———

The ancient Greeks and Mayans would have loved the *Epic of Gilgamesh,* for it shows a similarly immanent sensibility of humans entangled with natural and supernatural actors who are not necessarily good. I imagine the amaQwathi of KuManzimdaka would too, if they heard it. (Maybe one day I'll try it out with some of my friends there.) The two human heroes, Gilgamesh and Enkidu, are constantly in direct interaction with the gods. Although they are human, both are the offspring of the divine: Gilgamesh through his mother, the goddess Ninsun, and Enkidu through the goddess Aruru, who created him. Gilgamesh and Enkidu are also constantly implicated in various ambitions of the gods, such as Ishtar's insatiable love.

They are also entangled with nature. For example, they do battle with Humbaba, the guardian of the cedar forest, and with the Bull of Heaven. Gilgamesh loses his final chance at immortality when a snake eats the plant that will give him immortality. (In the full story, there are many more examples—a few of which I'll get to shortly.)

Plus it would be hard to consider the actions of nature and the divine in the story as wholly benign and good, at least from a human perspective. Humbaba curses Gilgamesh and Enkidu, and Ishtar furiously determines that they must be punished. The Bull of Heaven attacks Gilgamesh and Enkidu. The gods decide to kill Enkidu. We learn that earlier the gods had tried to wipe out all life on Earth with a huge flood.

And in all of this, we see a divine that is immanent in nature, embodying it and acting through it. Enlil is the god of the wind. Ea is the god of water. Anu is god of the sky.[44] This divine immanence in nature (which is equally a natural immanence in the divine) besets humans with floods and winds and vicious animals, often with reference to specific places such as Cedar Mountain, the home of the gods.

Entangled, immanent, and not necessarily good: these common nature before nature features interconnect with many others. In my reading, I've noted eleven more that follow on from these three. I'll describe them below, drawing on the extended examples of nature before nature traditions that I've given already, with some brief references from other ones around the world.

First, I am always struck by the exuberant pluralism in all these traditions. We have a long-held intellectual habit of calling them "polytheistic," in contrast to the monotheism characteristic of world religions of more recent origin.

I don't think that is the best term. Shortly I'll explain what I think is a better term. But for now, I'll just observe that it would be more accurate to refer to them as based on *poly-divinity*, not polytheism. Not all the divine agents in these traditions are understood to be full gods. Venerable ancestors, the *curetes*, the heroic twins, Gilgamesh and Enkidu, and perhaps the spirit of that lake high in the Talamancas: these are divine figures, but not gods on the level of Zeus, Ishtar, Anu, and the Mayan corn god. Nature before nature is filled with demigods, as well as (depending on the tradition) sprites, fairies, genies, nymphs, imps, elves, specters, phantoms, ghosts, wraiths, demons, monsters, and more.

Second, the divinities in these traditions are active and engaged with the world, sometimes wildly so. They have personalities and moods. They are busy about their days, full of intentions and projects. They are not abstract and distant. They are not consistent and predictable.

Third, this active, plural divine almost always has form, generally based on humans and animals or their combination, allowing for interactiveness with humans. In some tales, we also hear of the spirits of plants and rocks and objects normally considered inanimate today.[45] Such a world is deeply alive. These visions of divine form and pervasiveness of spirit resonate with a sensibility of interchange and unboundedness. The natural, the supernatural, and the human all tumble together into one entangled community, or one entangled community of communities, with all the tensions between chaos and order, conflict and cooperation, and anger and love that we know from community life.

Which leads to a fourth observation: the poly-divinities of nature before nature usually manifest not only ecological features of "nature" but also its relevance for the means of human sustenance: for hunting, for gathering, for agriculture. Divine agents often represent the forces and factors of provisioning. The Maya focused much of their worship on the corn god. Ishtar is the Assyrian goddess of fertility, including agricultural fertility, as well as of love. Demeter is the Greek goddess of the harvest. Diana is the Roman goddess of the hunt.

Fifth, in nature before nature, humans—especially heroic and divine humans—may influence the jumbled course of an entangled life. Hunahpú and Xbalanqué overcome the lords of the Mayan underworld. Local villagers help guard the baby Zeus by disguising the sound of his wailing so his father, Cronus, can't hear it. The amaXhosa ancestors shape the fortunes of weather, disease, and economy. Gilgamesh and Enkidu are able to kill the Bull of

Heaven. True, the gods have the last word, as in when they condemn Enkidu to death and deny Gilgamesh immortality, indicating the limits of human power and the importance of caution in disputing the will of the gods. This last word often takes natural form through floods, earthquakes, diseases, and other ecological calamities. But humans have some power to dispute and subvert the will of the gods. Gilgamesh refuses Ishtar's request that he marry her, speaking to her forthrightly on the matter. She gets mad, and things turn out badly for Gilgamesh in the end, and especially for Enkidu, but that's because they take things too far by killing the Bull of Heaven and throwing one of its haunches in Ishtar's face. Humans have to exercise caution in disputing the gods. Still, they often get away with it—especially with the help of other gods. Indeed, Utnapishtim got away with it spectacularly when he subverted the will of Enlil and saved representatives of all creatures from the flood, which later led to Utnapishtim and his wife being granted immortality with the help of the god Ea.

Sixth, Ishtar's desire for Gilgamesh professes a very intimate entanglement of humans and the divine. That basic passion of ecology, sex, is part of the divine in nature before nature. In addition to sex between gods, the gods can show sexual desire for humans. Sometimes they even consummate this desire. In the *Epic of Gilgamesh*, we are given a vivid and frank description of Ishtar's seduction of the gardener Ishullanu, one of her previous human loves. Mitchell perhaps takes a bit of license in his version of this passage from Tablet VI:

> "Sweet Ishullanu, let me suck your rod,
> touch my vagina, caress my jewel."[46]

But the more literal version we have from Andrew George's translation is still pretty explicit:

> "O my Ishullanu, let us taste your vigor,
> reach out your 'hand' and stroke my quim."[47]

Other traditions also speak of gods having desire for humans. Zeus has a very active sex life with humans. He partners with both women and men, including Danae, Leda, Eurymedousa, Semele, Callisto, Europa, Phthia, Thyia, Elare, and Ganymede, a beautiful prince of Troy. One accounting finds twenty-three different human sex partners of Zeus, across various Greek myths.[48] Stories of Aphrodite, the Greek goddess of love, record her as having sex with several humans as well, including Phaeton, Anchises, and Butes.

These are not all tender and loving encounters. Zeus rapes most of the humans he has sex with. Enlil rapes the demigoddess Mullitu. Aphrodite tricks Anchises into having sex with her, and Ishtar is not gentle in seeking Gilgamesh's love. I do not wish to portray these traditions as imagining a uto-pian state of happy unity between humans, ecology, and the divine. There is power. There is violence. There is loss. There is injustice. There is much that is ugly and horrible in this entangled cosmology. Indeed, this is one of the main points such a cosmology makes about the world.

Seventh, humans are not mere sexual pawns and victims. Humans can show their own sexual desire for the gods. Humans can even commit sexual violence against the gods. In another myth of Ishtar—or, more exactly, a myth of Inanna, her Sumerian name—she falls asleep in a garden and is raped by Shukaletuda, the gardener, a mortal human. But, as I say, countering the will of the gods and goddesses is hazardous. Inanna is furious when she wakes up and discovers that Shukaletuda has violated her. She searches him out and kills him.

Eighth, these stories tell of more than human intimacy with the supernat-ural. Humans have sexual encounters with nature, as much as with superna-ture—or, again, with the kinds of entities that we typically regard today as nature. Zeus seduces Leda in the form of a white swan and Eurymedousa in the form of an ant. Often this intimacy is violent. Zeus rapes Europa in the form of a white bull and Ganymede in the form of an eagle. A violent intimacy of the natural also follows from Inanna's reaction to Shukaletuda. Before she kills him, in her anger she turns water to blood, conjures damaging storms, and unleashes devastating plagues, which indiscriminately besiege the country-side. The sexual fury of the supernatural is a sexual fury of the natural as well. The lines between nature and supernature are as tangled as those between humans and supernature.

Ninth, the feminine divine rings out strongly in nature before nature.[49] A great many nature before nature divinities are female, in contrast to contem-porary world religions like Judaism, Christianity, Islam, and Buddhism in which the divine is overwhelmingly male. Moreover, in nature before nature, religious leaders are often female. Among the amaXhosa, *amagqirha* (the plural of *igqirha*, the ritual diviner I mentioned earlier) are usually women. In *Gilgamesh*, we learn of the priestess Shamhat in a strikingly sexual situation: her weeklong intimate encounter with Enkidu. But what needs equal underlining here is that Shamhat was a priestess at an important temple. Back on Crete, archaeological evidence from the famous Minoan "palaces"—which were as much religious as administrative—show that the Minoans accorded great authority to women in their worship. Some scholars of Minoan life suggest that, in fact, the head of the Minoan religion was a woman, and possibly the head of state was also often a woman.[50] Images of priestesses show up on Minoan frescoes and pottery far more commonly than images of priests. And women were often accorded great power in later Greek religion, as in the Oracles at Delphi and the priestesses of Athena at her temple in Athens.

Tenth, these traditions eroticize both the masculine and the feminine divine, not only the feminine divine. True, the Minoans and later Greeks often sexed up the images they made of goddesses and priestesses. Perhaps most striking are the open bodices and Barbie-doll figures of Minoan priestesses and goddesses, as in the famous statue of the "snake goddess" (who many scholars now think is probably actually a priestess). But, then, there are also sexed up religious images of Minoan men, such as the famous "Prince of the Lillies" fresco at Knossos, with his codpiece, bare chest, and Ken-doll figure (and which is probably actually an image of a priest or a priest-king).[51] The later Greeks and Romans also sexed up their portrayals of the male divine, as in the many man-hunk statues of Zeus or the eroticism of statues of Apollo. In *Gilgamesh*, we encounter both the eroticized femininity of Shamhat and Ishtar and the eroticized masculinity, including homoeroticism, of Gilgamesh and Enkidu.

And eleventh, the gendered associations of the divine in nature before nature often surprise, given contemporary Western perspectives. Yes, many ancient goddesses had attributes that fit modern stereotypes of femininity, such as goddesses of the hearth, health, home, childbirth, love, and fertility. But many of the attributes of ancient goddesses do not fit our stereotypes. Toward the end of *Gilgamesh,* we meet Shiduri, goddess of fermentation and tavern keeper at the Garden of the Gods. (I'll have more to say about her later.) Ishtar is Assyrian goddess of fertility, love, and sex, but she is also the goddess of war, as is her Sumerian counterpart, Inanna. In ancient Greece, Athena is also a goddess of war, as well as goddess of wisdom. Other Greek goddesses have associations that do not easily fit Western gender dichotomies: Demeter, the goddess of the harvest; Artemis, the goddess of the hunt; Eos, the goddess of the dawn; Nike, the goddess of victory; and Themis, the goddess of justice. And take Gaia, goddess of the Earth. Her association with the Earth does indeed match the conventional Western designation of the female as below, in contrast to Zeus, god of the sky, and Apollo, god of the sun, up above. But in some cultures of nature before nature, the deity of the Earth is male, not female, as in Geb, the ancient Egyptian god of the Earth. And the divine up above can be female, as in Nut, Geb's wife, goddess of the sky, and Amaterasu, the Shinto goddess of the sun.

Male and female, humans and divinities, and ecological associations all mix together in nature before nature, with muted segregations of position, power, and attribute.

————

It would not be an uncommon reaction to regard these visions of nature before nature as untrue—as mere myth, unsophisticated and unscientific, or even as heresy and blasphemy. True or not, there is a striking *realism* in their acceptance of the materialism, desire, strife, and imperfections of daily life.

This realist acceptance does not necessarily indicate approval of these troubles and the motivations behind them.[52] Rather, it represents a reckoning with the inevitable and unpredictable, and with outcomes we may influence but likely cannot fully avert. Sex happens, for good and for ill, in pleasure and in pain, as a surrender of power and as a route to power. Disorder and calamity happen too. There is much about the world that is good, but much that is not. Try as we might, pray and sacrifice as much as we might, the gods are not fully in control of the world, of each other, or of their own selves. Besides, even if you have done the right thing, quite possibly someone else in your group has not—the gardener Shukaletuda, perhaps—and the fury of divine response catches you in the bloody froth of the elements unleashed.

The divine in nature before nature is not perfect. There is conflict. There is confusion. There is unpredictability. Nor are the gods all powerful. Not only do humans not always get what they want, the gods don't either. Ishtar doesn't. Nor does Zeus. Even he cannot enforce and predict every outcome. Other gods aren't as pliable as that, and neither are ecology and the will of humans. Take this passage in the *Iliad*, commenting on how Zeus's jealous wife Hera once tricked him into oppressing his son by a human mother, Hercules (Herakles in Greek): "Even Zeus once fell into disastrous folly, he who they say is best among men and gods."[53] There is a plurality of powers in the jumbled community of humans, gods, and nature—a realist acknowledgment of limits central to what I have been calling an entangled view of existence, a view that does not recognize or even need a concept of nature.

The gods in nature before nature can be funny too. You can tell jokes about them and laugh at them. Much of this humor is sexual, like much of all humor. Because the gods have desires just as humans do, we can laugh at our own frustrations by laughing at theirs. Desire is not a sin in nature before nature's realist view. Rather, Ishtar's insatiable craving in *Gilgamesh* makes her a clown figure in the story. Ancient Assyrians must also have had many a good laugh hearing about Enkidu being lured into human society by sex. Or take Priapus, a Roman fertility god and protector of gardens, fruit, and livestock. Statues of Priapus, with a huge erect penis, sometimes half the size of the rest of his body, were common in Roman gardens, and he was often painted in frescoes. Yes, Priapus had an instrumental role in protecting crops from insects and livestock from disease, but he was also supposed to make you laugh. It is a challenge even today to look at a statue or fresco of Priapus and not chuckle.[54] We laugh because we are trying to deal with the real.

This realist grasp also gains hold through the concrete experience of place. In nature before nature, the interactiveness of humans with the divine is immanent, as I have mentioned, in the touchable of the here and now, not remote or diffuse. Heroes can have direct interaction with the gods and their ecological attributes, and ordinary people can encounter a god in the special place of that divinity or semidivinity. Pilgrims and tourists gain a sense of the presence of Zeus by visiting the Ideon Cave. Frederico experienced a specific presence in that lake in the Talamancas, and I think I felt it too, through him. My friend Mpumelelo needs to do his sacrifices at the *kraal* of his mother, now that his close relatives have installed his great-grandfather's spirit there. No other spot will do.

Through these real specificities of place, people also connect to specific communities of place: the family, the kin group, the tribe, the nation to whom the place properly belongs because of members' connections to its spirits.[55] Our spirits, our communities, our places. It would be an odd thing for me to visit Mpumelelo's mother's *kraal* and sacrifice to his ancestors—or to sacrifice to my own. It would not be my place to do so, pun intended. Only specific people in specific spots possessed by specific spirits can have these experiences. As well, a local kin group is highly real and present, right there, in your face, for they are the folks you meet with regularly and depend upon for daily needs. They are not abstract and distant, an "imagined community," in Benedict Anderson's memorable phrase (except to the extent that all human relations are imagined across a reach of space and time, however short).[56]

And there is deep realism in the acceptance of the *political* character of the world. In traditions of nature before nature, both ancient and contemporary, the gods and their ecological associations are full of politics, from petty peeves and wild mood swings to out and out warfare among each other. Humans often get caught in the divine fray. Moreover, these divine politics mix the good and the bad together. Like everyday human life, good intentions and bad intentions are often inextricably intertwined, even becoming one and the same, present in the same individual or force in our lives. Characters usually have mixed moralities—not a pure goodness or a pure badness. Early in *Gilgamesh*, Anu, the father of the gods, is in a helpful mood, and instructs Aruru to make Enkidu, so as to tame Gilgamesh. But later in the epic, Anu is in a vindictive mood, and orders that either Gilgamesh or Enkidu must die for killing Humbaba and the Bull of Heaven. Ishtar's swings are the most violent of all. She plots the downfall of Gilgamesh and Enkidu, but also professes admiration of them and even love. And the gods do not necessarily agree with each other. Although the god Enlil set Humbaba to guard the cedar forest, the god Shamash helps Gilgamesh and Enkidu by sending strong winds to control the monster Humbaba. Politics is like that, full of contradiction and confused morality, with uncertain outcomes.

Political realism likewise infuses the *Popol Vuh*. The lords of the underworld Xibalba are evil and the heroic twins and their corn god father are good, all mixed together in the same divine politics. But this is not a politics with a straight duality of good and evil. There is complexity. The twins, for all their valor, do some rather unpleasant things too. We have heard already about how they shot a hawk in the eye with their blow gun for amusement, and helped the hawk recover only when the hawk otherwise refused to deliver the message he had for them. But also, in one of their first acts, the twins turn their two older brothers into monkeys because their brothers were acting a bit jealous of them. The twins talk their brothers into climbing a tree and into loosening their breechclouts, "leaving the long ends hanging . . . from behind" like tails. Then they use magic to turn the dangling breechclout ends into monkey tails and to give the rest of their brothers' bodies the appearance of monkeys.[57] The twins thus are "trickster" figures as well as heroes, a kind of moral complexity of the political, common in cultures of nature before nature.[58]

Nature before nature also places great emphasis on the trickiest politics of all: family life. Its stories typically describe the active agents of the world as having important family and kin relations, whether those agents are human or nonhuman, divine or semidivine. Zeus has a father and a mother, brothers and sisters. He has aunts and uncles too: the Titans he and his siblings lock up in Tartarus along with his father. He has a wife, Hera, and many sons and daughters. Most of the other gods are also his relations. His days are largely taken up in dealing with all the squabbles among them. Gilgamesh is the child of Lugalbanda and Ninsun, and Ninsun is the daughter of Anu, one of the trinity of chief gods. But Ishtar is also Anu's daughter. Thus when Ishtar falls in love with Gilgamesh, she is falling in love with her nephew. And when Ishtar asks her father Anu to punish Gilgamesh with the Bull of Heaven, she is asking him to punish his own grandson. The *Epic of Gilgamesh* is not only an adventure story; it's a soap opera, full of family dynamics and the complexities and conflicts of interpersonal relationships. The *Popol Vuh* is pretty soapy too. The heroic twins are brothers, and they free their father and trick their other brothers. We also hear about the twins' mother and grandmother. Like Zeus, Hera, Gilgamesh, Anu, and Ishtar, the twins' motives are largely those of family.

Mpumelelo told me the same about his ancestors. They can be tricksters, with important implications for the micro-politics of relationships. "Sometimes they're good, and sometimes they're not," he said on a later phone call. "But either way, they are still your ancestors, and you have to deal with that." The confused politics of the personal: sounds like family to me.

————

Mpumelelo also made a request, after he had read an early version of this chapter.

"If there's one thing you can communicate, Mike, it would be great. That worshipping ancestors is not evil. It gives me a religion I can relate to. I can relate to my grandfather and great-grandfather. How can I relate to a god that I've never met?"

The divinity of relationality: that sounds like family to me too.

————

When we reflect on the beliefs people have about such fundamental matters, we should also consider the context of those beliefs. We need to think about the manners of living for which such accounts make sense. For we do not all live the same way and face the same dilemmas with the world and its contentions.

There is a word that has long been associated with these ways of looking at experience, a word that has not always been kindly meant. That word is *pagan*, which has often been intended to mark these ways as backward, delusional, improper, and immoral, identifying the holder of them as being in need of punishment, edification, or exclusion. Sometimes even death. Take the joint decree of November 14, 435, from Roman emperors Theodosius II and Valentinian III, who each controlled half the Roman Empire at the time. Not only did the decree ban the ritual practices of "all persons of pagan criminal mind" and order the destruction of "all their fanes, temples, and shrines." It also proclaimed that "all men shall know that if it should appear, by suitable proof before a competent judge, that any person has mocked this law, he shall be punished with death."[59]

But as a sociologist, I find the term "pagan" apt and descriptive, as I mentioned in the first chapter, with no necessary moral judgment. The English word "pagan" derives from the Latin *paganus*, which the *Oxford English*

Dictionary translates as meaning "of or belonging to a country community, civilian, also as noun, inhabitant of a country community, civilian."[60] The origin of *paganus* probably dates from the early fourth century, a century or so before Theodosius II and Valentinian wrote their joint decree. *Paganus* itself derived from the earlier Latin word *pagus*, meaning "country district," which in turn derived from *pangere*, meaning "to fasten" or "to plant something in the ground." *Pangere* also led to the English word "peasant" by way of the French for country and country person, as in *pays* and *paysan*.[61] Other European languages have similar terms and phrases that use rural and agricultural metonyms to reference holders of religious beliefs not accepted by Christianity and other world religions. And it is contextually accurate that they do. The kinds of orientations I have been describing originate in rural and agricultural lives—an empirical observation evidently made by the Romans long ago, even if their intent was not benign.

Those living in the countryside and trying to wrest a living directly from the ground are well aware that much happens in our ecological relations that we cannot control or anticipate. In *Gilgamesh*, we get an explanation: the politics of the gods are to blame. When Anu grants Ishtar the Bull of Heaven to punish Gilgamesh, he tells her, "But if I give you the Bull of Heaven, Uruk will have famine for seven long years."[62] And then when the Bull of Heaven descends, we hear this: "Ishtar led the Bull down to the earth, it entered and bellowed, the whole land shook, the streams and marshes dried up, the Euphrates' water level dropped by ten feet." The politics of ecology and the divine are densely entangled, and we with them, in nature before nature. What the gods are doing is what ecology does, what ecology does is what the gods are doing, and what they do together we humans must contend with.

The pagan, rural orientation of nature before nature traditions also manifests in its commonly agricultural imagery. Bulls are an especially popular theme, found in the faiths of cattle-rearing, agricultural peoples across the globe. There is the Bull of Heaven in *Gilgamesh*. The bull was also central to Minoan religion, from the myth of the Minotaur—the half-bull, half-human monster that lurked in the Labyrinth at the palace of Knossos—to a ritual that apparently involved doing a summersault over a charging bull.[63] Although the ancient Greeks saw Zeus as a sky god, he could also take the form of a bull, as he did in his rape of Europa. These divine ecologies are chaotic, unpredictable, powerful, a struggle to comprehend and control—like bulls themselves.

Cattle are not indigenous to the New World. Corn (maize) is the common agricultural theme of the original cultures from there. Many of these cultures utterly relied on corn (which, of course, originated in the New World). As with all crops, some years corn does well, and some years it doesn't. Big swings in corn yield still occur from year to year, even in the US corn belt.[64] Without today's mediating technologies and wider array of crops, groups like the ancient Maya no doubt saw even wider swings, with far less margin for adjustment. We see the concern and doubt about the corn crop in the *Popol Vuh*, as I noted earlier. The heroic twins are able to bring corn back to life from the depths of Xibalba only through trickery in the face of a precarious ecology, with its bird monsters, volcanoes, earthquakes, and fierce gods of the lower realms. Agriculture as trickery: many a farmer or gardener today would agree.

If this is your context of life—if your ways are pagan ways, closely dependent upon kin, immersed in the rhythms and needs of cultivation, securing a livelihood directly from a resistant ecology—you must hope that the heroic twins (or your own cultural parallel) win this uncertain fight every year, and that therefore the community does too. You must hope that the gods will be nice to people. You must hope that we land on the upside of the outcome of their moods, plots, and squabbles. You must hope that we make the right allies in the divine politics of the disputatious family that is the Earth.

———

But that context was beginning to change for the people of Great-Walled Uruk. A substantial portion of the local population now lived in the city, engaging in urban pursuits. Pursuits like collecting taxes for the state. Serving as record keepers to keep track of the taxes. Going to school and running schools so there would be record keepers. Building public works like roads and canals to grow the economy enough to yield sufficient taxes to support institutions like schools. Serving as soldiers to protect public works and the economic gains people had made, lest another state decide to try a faster route to building a tax base: war. Or declaring a war of your own.[65] Cities were growing, the state was growing, and the careers and ambitions they served were growing. Daily life seemed less bound by place and the local specificities of family and kin ties. It was a more transcendent, less immanent, time.

And as the context of people's lives changed, so did the questions they asked about their lives. Reading *Gilgamesh* today, one gets the feeling that people were in growing doubt about those questions. Should we venerate our ancestors? *Gilgamesh* seems to say, well, sort of: not your ancestor, but venerate the great king Gilgamesh, the ancestor of your king today. Should we continue to show our primary allegiance to our kin group? Again, *Gilgamesh* seems to say, well, sort of: consider your kin group the city-state of Uruk, with its heroic ancestor, Gilgamesh. Is our newfound ecological power, which is capable of wiping out the cedar forest and killing its guardian, good and wise? *Gilgamesh* seems to say such acts are glorious but dangerously contrary to the will of some of the gods. Should we pursue the life of glory in the first place, exercising our ambition, doing great deeds in faraway places, and gaining the immortality of notoriety? *Gilgamesh* clearly delights in Gilgamesh and Enkidu's transcendent accomplishments on their travels, but at the end of the story Gilgamesh realizes that Uruk is his home and that the true basis of contentment lies in immanence. As Shiduri, goddess of drink and the divine tavern keeper, counsels him near the end of the epic:

> Humans are born, they live, then they die,
> this is the order that the gods have decreed.
> But until the end comes, enjoy your life,
> spend it in happiness, not despair.
> Savor your food, make each of your days
> a delight, bathe and anoint yourself,
> wear bright clothes that are sparkling clean,
> let music and dancing fill your house,
> love the child who holds your hand,
> and give your wife pleasure in your embrace.
> That is the best way for a man to live.[66]

Surer solutions to these new questions—although perhaps not better solutions—would soon arise.

3

The Natural Conscience

MAYBE IT'S BECAUSE I'm a part-time musician. For me, a sound speaks the characteristics of a place. Its reverberations give the dimensions. Its timbre gives the materials. Its timing gives the rhythms of the society and the ecology of the locale. The memory of the sound retrieves not only an audio loop from somewhere in the gray, but also the context that gave it resonance.

I'm remembering a sound as I write. Nothing remarkable—just a knock, somewhat thudding and indistinct, on the front door of the farm cottage I was living in at the time in the English countryside. There was no bell on the door. The place was too small to have need of that. Nor did the cottage have central heating. The place was too humble to have benefit of that. So, in the damp of that bleak morning, I was huddled around the "electric fire," as the British call what Americans know as "space heaters." I had come to this village— Childerley, we'll call it—to study the meaning of nature in people's lives.[1] This old farm cottage was the only place available for me and my wife to stay in. We worshipped the electric fire those first few frigid months.

I opened the door, and there stood Nigel, a young man of about eighteen, son of the couple who owned the farm. Nigel's family lived a hundred yards away in the main farmhouse. The next closest house lay a quarter-mile away, up a twisty, single-track lane, walled by hedges into a sort of green tunnel. Nigel's family weren't farmers. Like most other residents of Childerley, his parents worked in the city and had bought their place because they wanted to live in the country. The family rented the fields out to a neighboring farmer.

We hadn't arranged an interview. In fact, at that point in my research, hardly anyone had yet agreed to an interview. I was starting to worry that my research wouldn't pan out (a common feeling at the beginning of ethnographic field-work). Nigel and I had spoken a bit about various things, including my project, when we occasionally bumped into each other around the farm. But he was a quiet man, and the conversations were short. Now he wanted to talk.

And talk we did. Nigel had finished his secondary schooling, and was taking a year to decide where to take his life, now that he was an adult. He needed a sounding board. We talked about Nigel's love of nature and country life. We talked about how he used to be a hunter, and would take his gun out and wander the fields and woodlands, "potting at anything that moved." We talked about his guilty feelings about his indiscriminant shooting, and how he had lately become an avid supporter of the environmental movement. Nigel had been mostly raised in the city; the family had bought their farm only a few years previous. But Nigel now intended to dedicate himself to the defense of nature. I listened in wonder and appreciation, as he had given little hint of this (or much else) in our previous conversations.

Somehow, the conversation moved from there to politics. "The Troubles" in Northern Ireland boiled with gruesome intensity at the time, and Nigel felt torn about what to think of the situation. The Protestants were regularly shooting the Catholics, and the Catholics were regularly shooting the Protestants. Both sides were taking down British security forces in the crossfire, and the security forces were doing quite a bit of shooting of their own. Children knew no other life. Both the Protestants and the Catholics had a lot to answer for, Nigel reckoned, as did the British government. Plenty of fault lay on all sides. I agreed, and told him so.

The conversation, which had been rattling on for an hour, paused. I think we sat there for over a minute, each silent in his own thoughts.

Then Nigel said, barely louder than a whisper, "That's why I think I'm interested in the environment. You *know* what's right. It's clear where one should be standing. It's never that way with politics."[2]

———

The contention that nature is a moral good, a matter of conscience, is very old—nearly as old as the very idea of nature. Some say the ancient Greeks invented the idea, but it is probably demanding too much of history to make such a claim.[3] As I'll come to later in the chapter, the ancient Chinese developed closely related thoughts, as did some thinkers elsewhere. Different peoples in similar circumstances can hit upon similar ideas, and may borrow and modify ideas from others that fit their lives. Moreover, our evidence base for so long ago is slender and fragmentary. Yet our record for the ancient Greeks is both comparatively good and very influential today, so it is worth focusing on their experience, as well as that of the Romans, their direct intellectual descendants.

The Greek word for nature is *physis* (pronounced PHU-sis). The English word for nature derives from the Latin *natura*, which we also find in words like "natural," "naturalistic," and "naturalized," as well as "unnatural" and "denatured." But we also use versions of the Greek word in English, as in "physics," "physical," "physique," "physician," and "metaphysical." It soon became a powerful word for the ancients, and a root for other powerful words. It remains so for us.

The earliest use of *physis* in Greek that scholars have turned up is in Homer.[4] In Book 10 of *The Odyssey*, the god Hermes shows up to warn Odysseus about the enchantress Circe. Hermes tells him that Circe will put a potion into the food of Odysseus's crew, turning them into swine. However, says Hermes, there is a plant that protects against the potion, a flower called moly. Odysseus later explains that Hermes "gave me the herb, drawing it from the ground, and showed me its nature. At the root it was black, but its flower was like milk."[5] The herb works, and Odysseus is able to free his crew.

This passage dates *physis* to the seventh or eighth century BCE, when most scholars think Homer lived. Here, Homer uses *physis* not as a moral good, but to refer to the essential, in-born, permanent qualities by which one can be sure to know what something really is—in this case, black at the root with a milk-white flower. Nature before nature had become what I like to call *first nature*, since nature's first use was to describe the material first-ness of things—how something is before and apart from any later manipulation or disguise—a use to which we still often put the word "nature."

The etymological origin of *physis* reflects this first use. *Physis* derives from *phyein*, which in (even more) ancient Greek meant "to give birth," and itself derives from *phy*, meaning "to be."[6] *Physis*, then, was the way something first came into the world, its material origin, unadulterated by later layers and designs: the way it truly was. When Roman philosophers subsequently translated *physis*, they were good scholars and followed a similar etymology in Latin. They derived *natura* from *nat-*, the Latin past participle stem of *nasci*, which meant "to be born," and which also survives in English in words like "natal," "native," and "nativity." They combined *nat-* with *-ure*, a suffix meaning "the result of," yielding "the result of having been born."[7] Rather clever, actually.

In the two centuries following Homer, *physis* took a huge conceptual step. First nature quickly gained the possibility of a second major use, what I like to call *second nature*: nature as a moral good. By the fifth century BCE, Greek authors had taken to contrasting *physis*, the way things truly were, with *nomos*, the ancient Greek for "convention," "custom," "culture," and "law."[8] *Nomos* itself derived from *nim*, a very ancient word that goes back to the Proto-Indo-Europeans. For the PIE people, *nim* meant to "deal," "distribute," "hold," or "manage."[9] In other words, *nomos* meant that which people had manipulated for their own reasons. It is also easy to hear in *nomos* a suspicion that maybe the outcome of our dealing, distributing, holding, and managing—our conventions, customs, cultures, and laws—gave advantage to some over others. *Physis* seemed right and just, and *nomos* did not. The unmanipulated firstness of *physis* had taken on a second basic meaning. Not only was nature first, it was therefore good.

This second nature turned out to be extremely useful, and has become central to our understanding of a vast expanse of endeavor. As the sociologist Raymond Williams once noted, "'nature' is perhaps the most complex word in the English language," and presumably so for many other languages as well.[10] Conceiving nature as unmanipulated and thus good raises some huge issues with the idea, powerful as it is, and has led to much of this complexity, as we shall see. But let us first look at the circumstances of Greek life in the fifth and fourth centuries BCE, circumstances that led philosophers to craft this most wild and civilized of ideas.

———

It's 388 BCE, the final day of Dionysia, the annual drama competition in honor of the god Dionysus. You and your husband are racing around your *oikos*, your house, getting ready to go to the competition's last play. In keeping with tradition, the last play is going to be a comedy and staged at the Theatre of Dionysus Eleuthereus, set into the hillside on the south slope of Athens's Acropolis. The previous four comedies in the competition—*Admetus* by Aristomenes, *Adonis* by Nicophon, *Pasiphae* by Alcaeus, and *The Laconians* by Nicochares—had all been good, and a welcome point of emotional balance with the tragedies. But there was no tragedy on the schedule for today—just the final comedy, plus the end of the dithyramb competition.

Funny word, dithyramb. And such a weird dramatic form: Big teams of men or boys, singing and doing wild dances to honor Dionysus. It's exciting, but why do we have to turn all drama into competitions? That's Athens, you sigh. A team from each of Athens's ten tribes will sing and dance a dithyramb today, accompanied by *aulos*, the double-reeded pipe that sounds so uplifting.

Unfortunately, rumors murmur that your tribe's team isn't very good this year. So you are skipping the dithyramb competition, and hoping to time things right to arrive at the theater for the start of the final comedy.[11] This year's final comedy was written by the most famous playwright alive, Aristophanes, sixty years old and still going strong. But Aristophanes had declared that this new play would be the last one he would also direct. You don't want to miss it.

"Eirene," you call from the ramshackle balcony overlooking the tiny court-yard of your *oikos*, "where are you?" Eirene is the new slave. With her easy laugh, saucy tongue, gentle looks, and aristocratic upbringing, she has quickly become your favorite of the household's three. True, her work ethic isn't the best, but she is still recovering from the shock of losing her family and being taken as a slave during an Athenian naval expedition earlier that year.

"Here, madam," calls Eirene from behind you, coming out of the *gynaikon*, the special room for women on the second floor, common even in modest homes like yours. "I found the right color thread." The left shoulder tape on your best *peplos*, the green one with the embroidered flowers, had pulled loose when you stepped on the bottom hem going upstairs. Fortunately, the fabric hadn't ripped—just the shoulder tape. It should be an easy fix. It had better be. There aren't many *drachmas* left in your money pouch, and now there's another mouth to feed. Slaves are cheap to buy but expensive to maintain.

"Excellent, Eirene. Thanks. You're such a dear. Do you know if my husband is ready?"

"The gray goat?" (There's Eirene's cheeky confidence that you like so much.) "Yes, he's in the *andron*," the room for men and their affairs on the first floor. "I think he's talking to Thraix," the male slave in charge of the family's twelve-acre farm a short distance out of Athens.

"The goat talking to the goatherd," you say, and you both laugh.

You and your husband arrive at the theater in good time. It was only a fifteen-minute walk through the maze of streets from Melite, your neighbor-hood, to the theater district, lying on the far side of the Acropolis. "What a wonder and a comfort," you think, to be able to walk so far and still be safe within Athens's sturdy walls. The wars with Sparta have gone on for as long as you can remember.[12] But the average free person must bear the burden of paying for all the military construction projects, and for the upkeep of the soldiers.[13] It seems like the tax collectors come by every month, nowadays. As well, prices are horribly high. The military's appetite for food and goods competes with the needs of everyone else in the city. Plus the weather has been so terribly dry, lowering yields. That's the farmer's perpetual problem: When prices are good, it seems like you never have a lot to sell. And when you've got lots to sell, prices immediately start dropping. Either way, you don't make much money.[14]

Anyway, this is not a time to worry about walls and wars and taxes and the struggle to make a decent living. This is a time to laugh. The ten thousand or so others in the theater, ranged out on the rows of wooden benches layering up from the orchestra at the bottom, clearly agree. They are already in a grand mood as they watch the last of the dithyramb performances—nearly fifty dancers in a great circle, singing, stamping, and acrobatically hurtling into and off of each other. It must be the dithyramb team from one of the wealthier tribes, the Aegeïs from the look of their costumes.

The audience is almost all men, and you get a chorus of hoots and catcalls as you and your husband make your way toward empty seats. Unpleasant and unwanted, but not unexpected. You love drama and are determined to attend anyway.

"Do they think that women actually like this? The pigs!" you say with exasperation to your husband.

"They hoot to please themselves, not you," replies your husband, a man of few but trenchant words. You have always loved that in him.

You take seats along the edge about halfway up the rows. The first rows are reserved for the judges, the priests, and the leading aristocratic families, sitting on cushions in special stone seats shaped like thrones. A few empty seats beckon from closer to the middle, but much higher up and further away from the orchestra. You'd rather hear better and see the actors' masks better than take in the full sweep of the action. Aristophanes's recent plays have been more about words than action, anyway.

You remember his last one, *A Parliament of Women*, in which women take over the government and ban private property. It had that new, more intimate style, a kind of comedy of manners and less about slapstick (although there was still plenty of that). Some found it dull. Others it irritated, particularly men, whom the play lampooned. That meant the play put off pretty much the entire audience. It didn't win the comedy competition. But you quite liked it, both the content and the subtler approach.

"I just love how Aristophanes points out the absurdity of all our conventions," you remember telling Eirene this morning. "Why shouldn't women be in government? And why shouldn't we all just share things?"

"It's just politics, madam, men's politics," she had replied. "The *agora* is really just a big *andron*."

You'd laughed loud and long at that. Eirene was so right. In fact, that's why you love your garden at the farm, you found yourself thinking—a chance to escape the wearisome politics of the *agora* and the *andron*. Yes, the work is hard sometimes. But out there, among the plants and the soil, the sun and the wind, away from the city, you feel free. You feel like yourself. There is no arguing with the sun and the wind. There is no arguing with plants and the soil. They just are. And so are you, immersed in—what is it that the philosophers have started calling it? That's right, *physis*, another funny-sounding word.

And it's also because of politics that Aristophanes almost never wins competitions, despite his thirty-seven previous plays. His work is usually too shocking for the generally conservative, male judges. He has no fear about toying with the raw nerves of Athenian society. No strata are safe from his barbs, bottom to top. His savaging of Cleon, the Athenian politician and general who ran a network of informants throughout the city, led to Aristophanes being put on trial for slander, you remember. The city council let him off, fortunately. This new play, titled simply *Wealth*, also seems likely to spawn consternation.

The last dithyramb ends, with much applause. People stir in the seats, get up for stretches and trips to the latrine and to haggle with the food vendors making their way through the crowd. Meanwhile, stagehands roll out a painted scene of a street on the edge of Athens, with a farmhouse in the background, and hang it from the *skene*, the stone façade behind the orchestra. Aristophanes himself comes out, cracks a few jokes, and announces the start of *Wealth*. People settle back into their seats.

———

An old man in rags, apparently blind, enters the stage, groping his way across. Is this the start of the play, you wonder? Yes, it seems to be. An elderly Athenian citizen follows—the character Chremylus, it turns out, who owns the farmhouse in the painted scene. He is accompanied by his slave, Cario, who wails, "Zeus and all you gods, what a ghastly thing it is to be the slave of a master who is out of his mind!"

The crowd guffaws. After a few more disses of his master, Cario turns to Chremylus and says, "Now then, there is no way I'm going to keep quiet if you don't tell me, master, why on earth we're following after this man," indicating the ragged, blind figure on the far side of the stage.

In the story that unfolds, it emerges that Chremylus has just returned from the Oracle of Delphi, where he went for advice about his son. Chremylus is a humble farmer—you like that!—and has struggled to make a living all his life. So Chremylus wanted to know from the Oracle whether to advise his son to be virtuous or a villain, for it seems plain that villains are the ones who usually do well in life. "I've been a pious and honest man," Chremylus says, "and I've done badly in life and been poor . . . while other people were rich—crooked politicians, informers and all sorts of villains."

The Oracle does not answer Chremylus directly. Rather, the Oracle tells him to follow the first person he meets—who turns out to be the poor old blind man they are tailing. But it doesn't make sense. Chremylus and Cario decide they had better ask the blind man who he is, in order to figure out the Oracle's meaning. At first the blind man refuses to tell them, but then he confesses "what I had intended to keep a secret. I am Plutus."

The crowd roars at this ridiculous pronouncement because Plutus is the Greek god of wealth. He shouldn't be in rags, let alone blind. It's another of Aristophanes's characteristic power reversals. You start to shush the two drunken men next to you, but your husband catches your hand. You stop, but not without a glare because you can barely hear what Chremylus says in response: "You, Plutus, and in this piteous guise! Oh, Phoebus Apollo! Oh, ye gods of heaven and hell! Oh, Zeus! Is it really and truly as you say?"

Apparently it is. Plutus's divine responsibility is supposed to be to reward the good and virtuous with wealth. But Plutus explains that Zeus, in one of the fits of perverse pique for which he is infamous, made him blind. So Plutus can't tell who is deserving of wealth and who is not. As a result, Greece society shows no relationship between whether someone is wealthy and whether someone is good.

Chremylus sees an opportunity, and he comes up with a plan to get Plutus his sight back. That way he can reward the virtuous instead, including Chremylus. The plan is very simple: to take Plutus to the sanctuary of the god of health, Asclepius, and ask for a cure.

But Plutus is afraid to offend Zeus. Chremylus and Cario try to convince Plutus not to worry about retribution from Zeus. Since every want and need depends upon having money, Plutus is actually the most powerful of all the gods, they tell him. Even Zeus is subordinate to Plutus. If there were no wealth, Zeus would get no sacrifices from people and would soon become poor himself.

You love this scene, with its fast and witty dialogue.

PLUTUS: So it's because of me that sacrifices are offered to [Zeus]?
CHREMYLUS: Most assuredly. Whatever is dazzling, beautiful, or charming in the eyes of mankind, comes from you. Does not everything depend on wealth?
CARIO: I myself was bought for a few coins. If I'm a slave, it's only because I was not rich [and could not pay my debts].

CHREMYLUS: And what of the Corinthian whores? If a poor man offers them proposals, they do not listen. But if it be a rich one, instantly they turn their arses to him.

CARIO: It's the same with the lads [the male whores]. They care not for love, to them money means everything. . . .

CHREMYLUS: It is in you that every art, all human inventions, have had their origin. It is through you that one man sits cutting leather in his shop.

CARIO: That another fashions iron or wood.

CHREMYLUS: That yet another chases the gold he has received from you.

CARIO: That one is a [cloth maker].

CHREMYLUS: That the other washes wool.

CARIO: That this one is a tanner.

CHREMYLUS: And that other sells onions.

CARIO: And if the adulterer, caught red-handed, [gets a shaved head instead of paying a fine], it's on account of you.

PLUTUS: Oh! great gods! I knew naught of all this! . . .

CARIO: It is not because of you that Agyrrhius [the new general of Athens] farts so loudly [demonstrating his pride and power]?

CHREMYLUS: [. . . And] that troops are sent to [save] the Egyptians? . . . In short, Plutus, it is through you that everything is done. You must realize that you are the sole cause both of good and evil.

CARIO: In war, it's the flag under which you serve that victory favors.

PLUTUS: What! I can do so many things by myself and unaided?

CHREMYLUS: And many others besides. Wherefore men are never tired of your gifts. They get weary of all else. Of love . . .

CARIO: Bread.

CHREMYLUS: Music.

CARIO: Sweetmeats.

CHREMYLUS: Honors.

CARIO: Cakes.

CHREMYLUS: Battles.

CARIO: Figs.

CHREMYLUS: Ambition.

CARIO: Gruel.

CHREMYLUS: Military advancement.

CARIO: Lentil soup.

CHREMYLUS: But of you they never tire.

Before Chremylus and Cario can take Plutus to the Sanctuary of Asclepius to get cured, however, an ugly, withered old woman appears. She turns out to be Penia, the goddess of poverty. Penia tries to convince Chremylus that, if she is banished, society would soon be a shambles. No one would be willing to work, and so no work would get done. Nothing would get cleaned. Nothing would get cooked. Nothing would get made. There would be no beds, blankets, clothes, fancy oils, perfumes.

"And really," Penia argues, "what's the good of being rich when you're lacking all these things? From me, on the other hand, all these things that you want are available in ample supply, because I sit over the craftsman as a mistress sits over her slaves, compelling him through need and penury to seek a means of getting a livelihood."

Chremylus dismisses Penia's arguments. "The way life is arranged at present for us humans, who would not regard it as sheer insanity and, even more, sheer wretchedness?" he asks. "Many men are wealthy who are wicked, having amassed it by crime. And many who are very virtuous are in a bad way."

Chremylus sends Penia away. He and Cario take Plutus to Asclepius, who does indeed cure Plutus's blindness. The effect on the world is immediate and transformative. The virtuous become wealthy, beginning with Chremylus and his fellow farmers. Those who are not virtuous discover that they need to change if they are to be wealthy too. The rich and powerful discover they can no longer hold others in thrall—although they need a bit of time to figure that out, as a series of walk-on characters show. An informer becomes suddenly poor, while an honest man becomes suddenly wealthy. A wealthy old woman who had romanced a young man with gifts discovers her strategy no longer works because the young man already has enough money.

Aristophanes isn't done. The god Hermes shows up, followed by a priest of Zeus. They both complain that sacrifices have stopped. People are doing so well, they don't need to ask for favors from the gods. So the gods have become poor, hungry, and powerless.

"Since Plutus began to be able to see once again," Hermes complains, "no one sacrifices any more to us gods—no incense, no laurel, no ground-cakes, no animals, no nothing! . . . I'm completely ruined and done for! . . . Now I just rest with my feet up and starve."

The play ends with Hermes becoming a servant of Chremylus, and the whole company taking Plutus to the Parthenon to install him as the new chief god.

The cheering is thunderous. Many in the audience stand on the wooden benches and throw money toward the stage, pelting the actors (who quickly run for cover). Having exhausted their coins (or not having any to begin with), some men start tearing the benches apart and throwing chunks of wood. Left-over food flies through the air, too. It's supposed to be in good fun, but it's chaos, and you and your husband quickly leave, thankful that you chose seats close to the side.

"A marvelous vision," you say to your husband when you get to the street, thinking of your own family's struggles to maintain a decent life in the city, based on the meager profits from the farm.

"Too bad this could never happen," he replies.

"Yes, and too bad that Aristophanes, once again, won't win the comedy competition," you answer, a touch exasperated.

You look at each other and nod. *Wealth* is a fantasy that is all too true.[15]

———

A major change was under way in Athenian society and Aristophanes had his finger on the pulse of it: a sharp increase in both vertical and horizontal inequalities, in social class and in rural-urban differences. It would be simplistic to read *Wealth* as a plea for equality. The play is full of ambivalence, questioning the structure of society, not resolving its problems. Ambivalence is Aristophanes's most consistent strength as an author (and is the strength of comedy more generally). Was Aristophanes telling his audience to deal with each other more virtuously, so that a good life would be possible for everyone? Or was he suggesting that equality itself is a fantasy because not everyone is in fact virtuous, and the fortunes of wealth indeed are blind to who is virtuous and who is not? Was Aristophanes anticipating Karl Marx's line about the opiate of the masses and arguing that a just society would have no need for religion? Or was he saying that money is the real basis of the divine for us? Was, perhaps, Aristophanes anticipating Thomas Jefferson and suggesting that struggling farmers like Chremylus are the true source of virtue in Greek society, as they live more in tune with nature and its goodness? Or was he saying that the city will corrupt even them, and that humble folk advocate for equality only because it is their best argument for getting ahead themselves?

With any of these readings, though, *Wealth* is plain in pointing out the rising inequality at the heart of the Athenian social order, even if Aristophanes does not suggest a clear guide to possible alternatives.

Aristophanes also brings out Athenian society's utter dependence on slavery. He portrays Cario as quick-witted and capable, not a lower order of person, therefore somehow deserving of being a slave. We learn in the middle of the play that Cario is a slave only because he couldn't pay his debts (or so

Aristophanes implies). But having pointed out this injustice, Aristophanes goes on to suggest that Athenians would never willingly give up their slaves anyway. Here is the exchange between Penia, goddess of poverty, and Chremylus, after she ticks off her list of the unpleasant work that wouldn't be done if Plutus were able to see again:

> CHREMYLUS: All those laborious jobs you just listed, the slaves will do them for us.
> PENIA: So where are you going to get slaves from?
> CHREMYLUS: We'll buy them with money, of course!
> PENIA: But who's there going to be to sell them in the first place, when he's got money too?
> CHREMYLUS: Oh, some trader wanting to make a profit, coming from Thessaly where all the kidnappers are.
> PENIA: . . . Who, if he's rich, will want to risk his own life doing that?

Chremylus's only response is to curse Penia.

> CHREMYLUS: May those words be on your head!

Although we often regard Athenian society as one of democracy's birthplaces, somewhere around a quarter to a third of the population of the Athenian city-state were slaves—roughly the same proportion of slaves as in the southern states of the United States in the years just before the US Civil War.[16] Almost all households headed by free people owned slaves, even an ordinary farming family like the one I have described. Probably most of the farm labor was done by slaves. Some were captured in war, some were kidnapped by slave traders, and some fell into slavery when they couldn't pay off their debts. Apparently, slaves were so cheap to buy that few families raised new slaves from the children of their current ones. It made more economic sense to buy slaves who were already old enough to work.[17]

Athens was also sharply divided between citizens and *metics*—free men born of Athenian citizens versus free men born of non-Athenian citizens, many of them non-Greek. Citizens could vote and citizens could own land; metics could do neither. About a third of free men were metics.[18] Many had come to Athens for its economic opportunities, both from other Greek city-states and from other lands entirely. Some metics, however, were former slaves who had been freed by their masters or had bought their own freedom. Slaves sometimes received wages, giving them the chance to save. (Paying slaves may seem an economically unnecessary arrangement, but it meant that owners did not have to spend for the upkeep of their slaves, who would then live in separate households on their earnings, making do as best they could on their meager wages.) Slaves could also borrow money. Either through saving or borrowing, slaves sometimes could amass enough money to convince their masters to let them go. But they could not become citizens.

Wealth inequality among the free was also on the rise. Compared with the Roman Empire, the distribution of wealth in Athens was relatively flat. An aristocrat like Alcibiades, an Athenian statesman and general in the Peloponnesian War with Sparta, owned only about seventy acres of farmland, still the main source of income in classical times.[19] Most landowners had less than fifteen acres, though, and a fifth to a quarter of Athenian citizens owned no land at all.[20] But some were starting to amass quite significant holdings. For example, when he died in 330 BCE, we know that a wealthy man named Phainippos owned about 850 acres.[21]

The growth of Athens led to a great profusion of new economic opportunities, from small-scale artisans to large-scale operations, making a wide variety of goods for sale. Some families farmed along with running small home workshops, especially peasant farmers. And some of the wealthy—many of whom were metics, not citizens—had operations large enough that we almost could call them factories. A metic named Lysias ran a shield workshop that seems to have been big enough for that word. He owned 120 slaves, most of whom probably worked in the shield-making operation, and he kept an inventory of seven hundred shields on hand.[22] (As Aristophanes observed with his crack about why soldiers were being sent to Egypt, war could be a great way to make money.) Demosthenes, a famous Athenian politician, reports that his father ran a couch-making workshop with twenty employees and had a knife-making facility with over thirty employees, most of whom were probably slaves. Another Athenian politician, Nikias, had a thousand slaves working the Athenian silver mines, which he leased from the state.[23] Plainly, a few men were becoming very rich, while most men were struggling hard.

And I do mean men. Athenian society was strongly patriarchal, as I tried to bring out in my story of the woman attending the first performance of *Wealth*.[24] Women had few rights. Women could own, inherit, and pass on property, and they continued to own their dowry when they married. But husbands controlled the property of wives, although they did not own it. Women's freedom of movement in public life was also highly curtailed. It's actually not certain that they could attend the drama festivals, even in the company of a male relative, such as my little story describes—although scholars are divided on this point.[25] And they could not vote.[26] Aristophanes pointed out these injustices too (in his characteristically ambivalent way) in *A Parliament of Women* and, most famously, in *Lysistrata*, a play written at the height of the Peloponnesian War in which Athenian women get men to give up their war-making by refusing them sex. We cannot doubt that women's lack of social and political status was closely connected with the restraints on their economic status.

In short, as Aristophanes pointed out in *Wealth*, Athens had become a world of money. Older forms of social connection and stratification were fading. Hereditary ties still existed—your clan and tribe still mattered, and so did aristocratic birth—but were far less important. As Chremylus says to Plutus, "Does not everything depend on wealth?"

But as well, Athens had become a world of voting rights and equality under the law, what ancient Greeks called *isonomia*. Around 507 BCE, a remarkable politician named Cleisthenes had reorganized Athens's political order, based on some earlier reforms by the equally remarkable Solon around 590 BCE. Solon had abolished political privilege based on birth, and replaced it with privileges based on four classes of wealth. The poorest class, the *thetes*, could vote but they couldn't hold office. It was a compromise. The aristocrats still had privilege because of their preexisting wealth, but now had to share some control. The poor got a bit of power, but they didn't get the land redistribution they had called for. It turned out to be an awkward compromise. Much turmoil followed, in large part because of continued clan and tribe conflict.

So Cleisthenes came up with a radical and unprecedented move. He abolished the traditional Athenian tribes and replaced them with ten new ones, based on locality instead of heredity. Each of these non-heritage-based tribes chose fifty citizens by lottery to represent them for a year on the "Council of Five Hundred," the main legislative body of Athens. And to prevent the gerrymandering of interests and the emergence of local patronage systems, Cleisthenes divided the region around Athens into 139 neighborhoods called *demoi*—"demes" in English—with about a third each demes from the city, the coast, and the hinterland. Each individual tribe in turn was composed of roughly a third demes from each kind of region, carefully selected to balance interests.[27] In the singular, *demos*, the word came to mean the people common to an area. They called this form of government by a new word, *demokratía*, rule by the people—the people being itself composed of many peoples, many demes, carefully balanced to ensure that minority voices could still be heard. It was raucous. It was problematic. It was full of tensions. And it largely worked, then as now.

In other words, democracy developed as a response to wealth inequality. But people had noticed (again, then as now) that despite these efforts at *isonomia*, the wealthy had a lot more political power than the poor, and often used that power to increase their wealth even further. So they laughed at *Wealth*. It turned out to be Aristophanes's most popular play—so popular that we have over 150 surviving manuscripts of it.[28] Apparently, even the judges laughed at *Wealth*. Scholars think it actually did win the comedy prize in 388 BCE.[29]

———

Although they laughed at *Wealth*, people had doubts about this churning up of the old that was taking place in the *polis*, the Greek word for a city-state like Athens.[30] They had doubts about living what I will refer to as *bourgeois* lives: that is, living not in a kinship-based society, but in a society dominated by the social relations of class. The word "bourgeois" comes to English via French, which got it from the Latin *bourg*, meaning a town big enough to rate a defensive wall. So it is apt to call this class society a bourgeois manner of living, for it arises with the growth of cities and their need for division of labor, record keeping, and an increased centralization of authority and the means of violence, all of which enable differential accumulation of wealth and protect it behind walls of many kinds.

It is also apt to call these class-based ways bourgeois because they are closely associated with another characteristic of city life: politics, a word whose very origin is the word *polis*. Contending with interests and their many conflicts— politics—was by no means new to human affairs.[31] But in a social context in which a person's life chances and social relations were so much more fluid, the significance of politics in the gaining of those chances and relations grew mightily. For the principles of legitimate contention (grounded, as they are, in the social) seemed equally fluid. And we must note too that the bourgeois life turned out to be markedly less fluid than it appeared to promise. The settling out of distinct layers in the liquid of social opportunity is, after all, what we mean by class. Politics can shake some turbidity into these layers, but it is also the main source of their viscosity.

Political economists have long used a similar term, the bourgeoisie, and I'm aware that my usage might be confusing. By the bourgeoisie, political economists usually mean to refer to the rich, the owners, those who control the means of production. These writers often use a separate term for the poor, the owers, those who actually do the producing: the proletariat. Here I use the term "bourgeois" for both rich and poor, owner and ower, as well as for all the other motivations of social class that came along with city life. I don't mean to deny the conventional usage. Rather, I mean to point out that there has long been another basic economic inequality in social life, indeed one that is in some ways prior to that between the urban rich and the urban poor, for it provided the initial accumulation of riches behind the walls of the *bourg*: the inequality of city and countryside, what I am calling bourgeois and pagan. Both axes of inequality—the vertical inequality of bourgeoisie and proletariat, and the horizontal inequality of bourgeois and pagan—interact, each feeding the other: a *double conflict*.

Although they originate with the expansion of cities about this time, these inequalities and the cultural orientations associated with them are no longer so spatially confined, as I will be emphasizing later in the book. But they are still with us. As well, both axes continue to present deep political questions of legitimation and justice.

———

An immensely powerful means for trying to settle either kind of question—questions of legitimating these inequalities or of challenging their justice—turned out to be the idea of nature. For nature provided a different manner of conscience, of moral thinking, that many came to feel lay beyond accusation, beyond the interests of politics.

The poet Theocritus was one who felt the attraction of this new manner of conscience. He liked nothing better than to wander in the back country, far from the city, among the pastures, glades, leys, grottos, and tumbling fountains of clear-flowing streams that he found there, overflowing in abundance, at least in his imagination. Sometime in the middle of the third century BCE, Theocritus and two friends headed out for a ramble on Kos, a small island that lies just off the Asia Minor mainland. As was his custom, he later set down a few reflections in a form of poem he called an *eidullion*—a term that meant "little picture," and which led in time to the English word "idyll." Scholars call this particular *eidullion* his "Seventh Idyll," and sometimes add a more colorful descriptor like "Harvest Home" or "Thanksgiving Festival." (Theocritus himself didn't bother with titles.)

"Once on a time," writes Theocritus in the Seventh Idyll, "Eucritus and I (with us Amyntas)" did "steal from the City" in order to attend a festival in honor of Demeter, goddess of the harvest.[32] On the way, they encounter a *boukolos*—a herder—named Lycidas. Theocritus challenges Lycidas to a singing match. Each acquits himself well in the competition, with a long song apiece about the captivating glories of food, love, wildlife, and the scenery

of the countryside. Lycidas gives Theocritus his crook as a present and departs, and Theocritus and his friends continue on to the harvest festival. They
find a nice spot to lie down, soaking up the gaiety and the charms of country
life:

> . . . there we lay
> Half-buried in a couch of fragrant reed
> And fresh-cut vineleaves, who so glad as we?
> A wealth of elm and poplar shook o'erhead;
> Hard by, a sacred spring flowed gurgling on
> From the Nymphs' grot, and in the sombre boughs
> The sweet cicada chirped laboriously.
> Hid in the thick thorn-bushes far away
> The treefrog's note was heard; the crested lark
> Sang with the goldfinch; turtles made their moan,
> And o'er the fountain hung the gilded bee.
> All of rich summer smacked, of autumn all:
> Pears at our feet, and apples at our side
> Rolled in luxuriance; branches on the ground
> Sprawled, overweighed with damsons; while we brushed
> From the cask's head the crust of four long years.

Four-year-old wine. Damson plum trees overweighed with fruit. Pears and
apples rolling at their feet. Larks, goldfinches, and turtles (that would be turtle
doves, not amphibian turtles) singing and moaning, and cicadas and tree frogs
too. A gurgling spring. Fresh-cut vine leaves. Fragrant leaves. The shade of the
elm and the poplar. Glorious.

If you can tolerate the gooey sentimentality, that is—especially as passed
through the pen of this high-Victorian translation by C. S. Calverley, from
1869. I confess I do like it, even though it is (or maybe because it is) so plainly
over the top. The modern reader may laugh a bit at lines like "turtles made
their moan," but we readily see the attraction of the world Theocritus portrays
in his "little pictures." Here is nature, painted in unflaggingly positive, naturalistic, and innocent terms, implicitly contrasted with the city. Theocritus's
countryside suffers no conflict—other than a gentle contest over who is the
best singer. And Lycidas is unperturbed by the lack of an obvious victor. He
even gives Theocritus a gift, so much does he admire his opponent's music.
Nor does anyone seem to have to work. Nature yields sustenance without the
force of labor. No money changes hands. The wealthy and powerful do not

receive fealty. Rather, honor lies with the *boukolos*, and especially one who is also a good musician.

The central moral is that the idyllic world of the Seventh Idyll, immersed in nature and a giving agriculture, has no politics. There is no conflict, no contention, no wrestling for hierarchical advantage in the pursuit of interests. And it is therefore good. That is what is idyllic about the idyllic. It is a place of imagined remove from the polluted bourgeois norms of the *polis*.

Theocritus launched an enduring genre. We call it bucolic writing, after Theocritus's favorite stock character, the *boukolos*. But for all its rural innocence, politics persist in the bucolic vision. Its very nonpolitical stance has meaning for us precisely because we bourgeois souls know the reality of politics in our lives.

As well, bucolic innocence can usefully cloak a secret political motive. In the case of the Seventh Idyll, scholars are pretty well convinced that the people in the poem are real, albeit disguised with pseudonyms. Scholars have wondered about one reference in particular: the appeal to a mythical goat-herd and poet, Cometas, that Theocritus puts into Lycidas's song.

> Happy Cometas, this sweet lot was thine!
> Thee the chest prisoned, for thee the honey-bees
> Toiled, as thou slavedst out the mellowing year . . .

In the normal telling of this ancient myth, Cometas's master gets mad at him and locks him in a cedar chest for three months to see if the Muses will save him because of his poetry. They don't. In Theocritus's telling, though, the Muses come through, sending honey bees to feed Cometas until his master releases him.

> . . . the round-faced bees,
> Lured from their meadow by the cedar-smell,
> Fed him with daintiest flowers, because the Muse
> Had made his throat a well-spring of sweet song.

Some scholars suspect that Theocritus included the reference to this myth to mourn the murder of his friend, the poet Sotades, who had written a salacious poem to protest the emperor Ptolemy's incestuous marriage to his sister.[33] (It was a rather ripe topic, and the poem did not hold back.)[34] Ptolemy had him imprisoned, but Sotades escaped. Unfortunately, he was recaptured, locked in a lead chest, and thrown into the sea to drown. By telling the story of Cometas being locked in a chest, but with a happier ending, saved by the

Muses, Theocritus seems to be saying that Sotades would not be forgotten—all the while protecting himself from the wrath of Ptolemy through the bucolic innocence of a world with no politics. Only music, leisure, and vine leaves.

And love. Theocritus, like all the bucolic poets, loved love. He has Lycidas sing to his love, Mitylene, hoping that "from Love's furnace she will rescue me, for Lycidas is parched with hot desire." Theocritus's own song in response tells of the woes of his friend Aratus, who "pines for one who loves him not." He calls on the gods to shoot love arrows "and strike that fair one . . . strike the ill-starred damsel who disdains my friend."

Theocritus had a broader understanding of love than some in our own day, we should note. The C. S. Calverley translation that I have been quoting actively suppresses the homoerotic in the Seventh Idyll. In a later translation by J. M. Edmonds, Theocritus writes that although he himself "loves a lass," his "dear'st Aratus sighs for a lad"—not merely "one who loves him not," as the Calverley translation has it. Theocritus does not disapprove of his friend's homosexuality. Rather, in the Edmonds translation (and similarly in all subsequent translations), Theocritus asks the gods to use their love arrows and "come shoot the fair Philinus, shoot me the silly boy [not a 'damsel'] that flouts my friend!" All our loves are equally innocent for Theocritus, here in the countryside, far from the city.

But Theocritus is a transitional figure. His idylls remain partially nature before nature, not yet fully second nature, nor even first nature. We see throughout his writings references to what we today easily put in the category nature: the sights and sounds and foods of the wild and gently cultivated. He also references gods and demigods that fit what we now call nature and the rural. Pan, the god of shepherds and wild things. Demeter, the goddess of the harvest. Apollo, the god of the sun. The centaur Chiron, a great healer and hunter. And the Nymphs, beautiful female spirits of waters, hills, trees, and woodlands. But the word *physis* does not appear in Theocritus's work.[35] There is no nature here. Not yet. We know philosophers had taken up the word a century before, making the firstness of things into a secondness, a moral good. That was in Athens, though—not remote Kos. Evidently, the term had not then become popular in Kos, even among the educated like Theocritus. Yet the need for nature's potential moral help he plainly felt.

So he paints his little pictures with the moral resources he did have: those of nature before nature. We discover in Theocritus an exuberant pluralism of the divine. We see interactiveness between humans and the divine. We hear a blending of the natural and the supernatural. We find a frank and diverse

accounting of the sexual. And it is all told through a deep immanence in specific places that touch us through sight, sound, texture, taste, smell, and spirit.
But unlike the nature before nature of *Gilgamesh*, African ancestor veneration,
the *Popol Vuh*, and the Greek gods as Homer understood them, this nature
before nature is purely good. It is a refuge from the political, not a product of it.

This distinctive formulation of the early bucolic writers—perhaps we could
call it second nature before second nature—soon moved on. (In fact, given
what we know about the talk among the philosophers in Athens a century
before, it had already begun to move on.) From Theocritus, it was a short
step, and a giant leap, to link such a picture of rural innocence to nature and
the conscience it can provide.

———

Pan the camera now to Rome a couple of centuries later, where the old gods
seemed to have had less and less relevance for an increasingly urban people,
at least among the elites. The inequality already evident in ancient Greek
society widened greatly with the coming of the Roman Empire. Roman militarism, slavery, and market development, assisted by improved technology,
led to extremes of wealth and poverty not unlike our own today. The houses
of the Roman middle and upper classes were large and well fitted with the
conveniences of the day. Better lamps brought good lighting in the evening.
Aqueducts brought water for fountains, showers, and flushing toilets. Drains
took rainwater and wastewater away. You could relax and clean yourself in
vast, heated bath-house complexes. The wealthiest even had a form of central
heating, plus private baths. Food and imported luxuries regularly came in from
thousands of miles away. Life was less and less local, less and less tribal, less
and less uncomfortable, and less and less rural and agricultural—at least for
the better-off classes of people within the growing cities.

And these are precisely the people who had the time and schooling to write
their thoughts and arts down. One among them was the Roman poet Horace,
scratching out his verses on a waxed tablet while luxuriating in his rural villa
in the Sabine Hills above Rome. By that time, the late first century BCE, the
old gods have pretty much disappeared for a well-off intellectual like him.
Instead, Horace is all about *natura*. In his Tenth Epistle, he tells his friend
Fuscus back in Rome that "life in harmony with Nature is a primal law."[36] He
warns Fuscus that if we try to "Push out Nature with a pitchfork, she'll always
come back, and our stupid contempt somehow falls on its face before her." In
place of the "city pleasures" Fuscus enjoys, Horace enthuses about his home in
the "blissful country" with its breezes, fragrant grass, and "lovely rural rivers,

and trees, and moss-grown rocks." The gods are reduced to a mention of a "crumbling shrine" to a disappearing cult, which Horace only includes as a landmark.

And he has a new concern that rarely made it into the old tales of the gods, goddesses, and demigods: concern about greed, wealth, and ambition. Horace is deeply disturbed by the dangers of "piled up gold" and the way it can distort one's priorities. Theocritus definitely had this worry as well, but not so explicitly as in a line like this from Horace to Fuscus: "Never let me be busy gathering in more than I need, restlessly, endlessly."

Because, Horace says, you are only setting yourself up for disappointment. Free yourself from money, he advises his urban friend, Fuscus:

> If Fortune's been kind–
> Too kind!—loss will seem more than loss, will seem
> Catastrophe. Whatever you like is the hardest of all
> To lose. Try for nothing grand: kings and the friends of kings
> Can be excelled, even under a humble roof.

Horace also worries about the kind of issues we would today call "pollution": the ill effects of pursuing our ambitions with little regard for our health and the health of the environment. "Is your water as clear and sweet, there in its leaden pipes," he asks Fuscus, "as here, tumbling, singing along hilly slopes?" Horace could not have been referring to the effects of lead poisoning, which were not understood at the time. But we can well imagine how fetid and stale that water must have been after miles of lead-lined Roman aqueducts, and the final stretch of lead piping to bring it to a Roman home.

After it left Roman homes, the water was ranker yet. Rome had grown to a vast scale, likely approaching (and perhaps exceeding) a million inhabitants. No city would again reach that size until London in 1800. A million people means a lot of effluent, so, following the old out-of-sight-is-out-of-mind school of environmental relations, the Romans built a Roman-scale system of drains to carry it all away. The largest such drain, the *cloaca maxima*, still runs under Rome today, helping drain the Forum. But all that waste water had to go someplace, and the pollution in the River Tiber was probably also unequalled until nineteenth-century London and the poor River Thames.

Thus, Horace favors the simple country life, close to Nature's primal law—but also as a refuge from pollution of a moral kind. "Where can we sleep safer from biting envy?" he asks. This is why Horace says, "I run looking for good plain bread, just crusty bread, no honeyed confections, dripping sweet," like one gets in town. He likens civilization and its ambitions to a bridled horse, racing against the stag of nature.

> There was a stag, once, who could always defeat a stallion
> And drive him out of their pasture, until, tired of losing,
> The horse begged help of man, and got a bridle in return.
> He beat the stag, all right, and he laughed—but then the rider
> Stayed on his back, and the bit stayed in his mouth.

So refuse the bit of civilization with all its class competitiveness, Horace advises Fuscus. It's slavery for all who take it up. Don't.

> Give up your freedom, more worried about poverty than something
> Greater than any sum of gold, and become a slave and stay
> A slave forever, unable to live on only enough.

Seek instead a different conscience and basis for motivation: the conscience provided by harmony with Nature's primal law.

————

Half a world away, in the area we now call China, a calm, peaceful man was having similar thoughts. His given name was Li Ehr, but hardly anyone recalls that now. He served as government historian for the state of Zhao, one of the main powers struggling to rule China during the Warring States period. The Zhao nearly won. But in 221 BCE, after a roughly 250-year-long struggle, the state of Qin wound up on top—which is why today we call China China, after the Qin (which is more or less pronounced "chin"). Otherwise, we might well call that most populous of countries Zhao.

Li Ehr lived during the early part of the war, probably in the late 400s BCE, about the same time that the ancient Greeks were extending first nature into second nature, making nature a form of the good. He became a teacher of moral value, in addition to holding his position as court historian. He hated all the fighting—as well as all the infighting among local elites, trying to use the war to promote their own ambitions. Li Ehr taught a different way of being, a way that he simply called the *Way*, the *dao*. Some listened avidly to Li Ehr, and grew to calling him Laozi, meaning "Old Master"—the name by which he is most remembered today in English (or by the variants Lao Tzu and Lao-Tze). But still the war went on. Disgusted, he put a pack on his back with a few possessions and took the road over a mountain pass out of Zhao. A Chinese historian from the first century BCE tells the story like this:

When he reached the Pass, the Keeper there was pleased and said to him, "As you are about to leave the world behind, could you write a book for my sake?" As a result, Lao Tzu wrote a work in two books, setting out the meaning of the way and virtue in some five thousand characters, and then departed. None knew where he went in the end.[37]

Two very short books. Five thousand Chinese characters works out to roughly three thousand words in English, or about twelve pages of doubled-spaced text. The first book was the *Daojing*, which focuses on the character of *dao*, the Way. The second book was the *Dejing*, which focuses on the meaning of a Chinese term that has long confounded translators: *de*, which means something like virtue or integrity, but is really much more than that.[38] Today we call those two books together the *Dao De Jing*, meaning, roughly, "the classic work on the Way and on integrity." Surely, no work of a mere three thousand words has influenced so many for so long.

In the words of the twentieth-century Chinese philosopher Fung Yu-Lan, Laozi saw *dao* as "the all-embracing first principle of things . . . the unitary first 'that' from which all things in the universe come to be."[39] *Dao*, then, is very much a first nature kind of idea. But *Dao* also extends first nature to second nature. Laozi makes plain his sense that the *dao* is not just a firstness but it is also morally good—albeit with a note of caution. Laozi harbors a constant wariness of distinctions, especially ones that might tempt us into exalting ourselves for being better than others:

> Everybody knowing
> that goodness is good
> makes wickedness.[40]

So the *Dao De Jing* generally doesn't use terms that easily translate into the English word good. But Laozi plainly thinks that following the *dao* leads us to what is right for ourselves and for others. We get no sense in the *Dao De Jing* of a nature-before-nature political struggle in the deeper powers of existence. Rather, the *dao* is free from the desire, manipulation, ambition, and inequality Laozi saw all around in Zhou society.

> The Way of heaven
> is like a bow bent to shoot:
> its top end brought down,
> its lower end raised up.
> It brings the high down

lifts the low,
takes from those who have,
gives to those who have not . . .
Not so the human way:
it takes from those who have not
to fill up those who have.[41]

Laozi connects the ambitions of inequality to the human habit of giving things names. The *dao* does not name or categorize. Names and categories stem from human intentions and therefore, ultimately, the conflicts of human politics. The true *dao* is peaceful, nameless, and simple, says Laozi, like an uncarved block of wood:

The nameless uncarved block
Is but freedom from desire,
And if I cease to desire and remain still,
The empire will be at peace of its own accord.[42]

In short, the *dao* is beyond politics. And the way to follow it is to learn to act without intention, and thus without politics. Laozi termed this way of acting *wu wei*, which literally means "without action." He contrasted it with acting deliberately, what he termed *yu wei*, or, literally, "with action." He advised us to *wei wu wei*, to act without action, as in this passage.

Do without doing
Act without action.
. . . the wise soul
by never dealing with great things,
gets great things done.
Now, since taking things too lightly makes them worthless
and taking things too easy makes them hard
the wise soul,
by treating the easy as hard,
doesn't find anything hard.

Act without acting? Treat the easy as hard? Do great things by not doing great things? Laozi loved to teach through paradox, I think to try to shock us out of our conventionalized lives. In the second book of the *Dao De Jing*, the *Dejing*, from which the quotation above comes (the others were from the first book, the *Daojing*), he tries to help us find our elusive *de*. Everything has a *de*, its individual essential quality, integral to someone or something. To follow one's *de* is to experience a very encompassing form of integrity, the virtue of being what and who one ought to be. A *de* comes from the *dao*. Acting in accordance with our *de* is how we manifest the *dao* in our own lives, and experience the rightness of our existence. We do so through acting *wu wei*, without intention, without effort, without doing.

> In the pursuit of learning, one knows more every day;
> in the pursuit of the Way one does less every day.
> One does less and less until one does nothing at all,
> and when one does nothing at all there is nothing that
> is undone.[43]

Or as another Daoist master, Zhuangzi, put it sometime during the final decades of the Warring States period,

> Fishes are born in water
> A person is born in Dao.
> If fishes, born in water,
> Seek the deep shadow
> Of pond and pool,
> All their needs
> Are satisfied.
> If a person, born in Dao,
> Sinks into the deep shadow
> Of non-action
> To forget aggression and concern,
> Nothing lacks
> And life is secure.
> Moral: "all the fish needs
> Is to get lost in water.
> All a person needs is to get lost
> In Dao."[44]

———

Not every Greek and Roman saw things as Horace did, nor all Chinese from the Warring States period as Laozi and Zhuangzi did. Nor every intellectual—probably not even most of them, or Horace and the Daoists would not have felt need to make their arguments. Horace's contemporary Virgil certainly did not see things Horace's way (even though Virgil and Horace were reputed to have been friends and colleagues). The *Eclogues*, which Virgil modeled closely on Theocritus's *Idylls*, do not mention *natura* a single time. His other works only occasionally mention *natura*, and only in a first nature sense—not nature as a moral good beyond politics.[45] The other of the three greats of Roman poetry, Ovid, reads like a splitting of the philosophical difference. His vast *Metamorphoses* traces the history of the world, from its creation to the murder of Julius Caesar. *Metamorphoses* is our main source on Roman myths about the gods, but the word *natura* also appears thirty-four times.[46] For Ovid, nature precedes the gods, intertwines with them, and is "more powerful than them all."[47] But Ovid isn't clear about whether nature is good or not.

Horace is plenty clear. For him, not only is nature a moral good, a second nature, we are good to the extent that we follow nature. Plus Horace seeks not only second nature but a different kind of self that comes from living in tune with nature's rhythms—a self that is free of envy, greed, ambition, and the inevitable disappointments of desire for more and more and more, desires that he associates with urban life. Laozi frames the matter a bit differently, but he looks for and finds much the same resolution to the grievances of bourgeois living. Thoreau in his shack by the shores of Walden Pond would have understood immediately. So would my young friend Nigel. Thoreau quite possibly had even read Horace, given the importance of the classics in nineteenth century education, and maybe even Laozi.[48] I'm pretty sure Nigel hadn't read either. But we don't have to have read Horace or Laozi or Zhuangzi to get the point, weary and wary as we are of the striving ways of our fellow bourgeois humans. We get it because we have sensed these striving ways in our own selves.

As have many before us. Ever since urbanism and the expansion of the economies of empire and capital accumulation that fed urban growth, these themes have run through our literatures, from the Daoists to the Buddhists, from the middle East to the middle West, from Horace to Thoreau, from then until now. I call it the discovery of a *natural conscience*, a basis for moral thinking we believe to be free of society and all its politics and constant play of interests and ambitions. I use this phrase in part to compare it with what the sociologist Émile Durkheim described as the *collective conscience* that comes from social life.[49] The natural conscience comes from social life too, although we do not experience it as doing so. And we use the natural conscience as a direct response to social life and its troubles.

I find it helpful to think of the natural conscience as emerging from the interaction of a sense of *natural other* and a sense of *natural me* that the natural other sees and condones. We imagine a natural other as lying beyond the reach of human politics and its manipulations. It is other, separate and pure, real and true. We imagine a natural me as that the self that comes from the nonpolitical other—that it creates, sees, and potentially guides. Thus, we feel the natural me as a more authentic and valid self than what society creates, sees, and guides. The natural me, then, we imagine as a nonpolitical self, as opposed to the self that emerges from society's constant tussle and scuffle of interests and ambitions. It is a second self that comes from second nature.

By using the terms "natural other" and "natural me," I am trying to draw another comparison with another famous theory. The great social psychologist George Herbert Mead used to say that our sense of *me* comes about through learning to imagine how others see us. He called it "taking the role" of others. Mead argued that, in time, we generalize our imagination of specific others like our mother, father, brother, sister, friend, or other associates. We come to an overall sense of "them" he called the *generalized other*. The me imagines the generalized other's response to us, which simultaneously shapes what our sense of me is to begin with.

Think of Mead's dynamic of generalized other and me as a kind of mental personification of what Durkheim described: the collective conscience as built from the interaction of the generalized other and me. Think of what I'm talking about as a kind of parallel moral structure: the natural conscience, with its dynamic of natural other and natural me.[50] But this parallel moral structure we see as coming from beyond the social and its politics—even though it does not—and as being a more sure basis for the moral for precisely that reason.

Mead and Durkheim didn't discuss the existence of this parallel conscience. They saw the development of a collective conscience as pretty much trouble-free. We just take it in, without much fuss or gripe, they felt. They presumed that sociality is so fundamental to our being that we readily embrace its ways. I agree that sociality is fundamental. But in certain times and situations, we find ourselves disputing our sociality and the forms of self it encourages. We doubt the motives of the generalized other, and we even doubt the me that it calls forth from us. We doubt "the human way" that "takes from those who have not to fill up those who have," as Laozi put it. We worry that we are being led astray by the bit of civilization, busy gathering in more than we need, "restlessly, endlessly," as Horace described it. We come to sense that the generalized other is full of manipulation and ambition, and that the me it tries to create in us serves society's dominant interests and purposes, not ours.

This is a very troubling realization to come to. For if our interests and purposes really come from society with all of its politics, and if these politics serve certain others and not us, then what should our own interests and purposes be? What is moral? What is right to do? Is there a truer source upon which to base the self?

Horace said, yes, there is a truer source: the nature he found in the countryside. Thoreau also said, yes, there is: the nature he found in the "subtile magnetism" of the wild. Laozi and Zhuangzi said as well, yes, there is: the nature to be found from following the Way without effort, abandoning ambition and desire, for these are merely social. As the chapters to come will describe, the divine can equally yield this sense of a truer source, free of the "lust of domination" that comes from "liv[ing] by man's standards," in the words of Augustine—a divine natural other, emancipated from the manipulative powers of human politics.

From these natural others, each felt one could gain a more authentic self, a natural me whose morals and motives lie beyond the corrupting influence of the political. Horace felt it in his sense that country life, closer to nature, allowed him to refuse the bit of civilization and how it turns us into slaves of money and status. Thoreau felt it his sense that living in tune with nature's rhythms granted him "absolute Freedom" from "man and his affairs . . . even politics, the most alarming of them all," whereby he might learn his true "savage name."[51] Laozi and Zhaungzi felt it in their sense that we all have a *de* that we can manifest by allowing ourselves to "get lost in *dao*," like a fish in water. Augustine felt it in the words of Paul and his advice to "put on the armor of light" that comes from embracing the Lord Jesus Christ. They each discovered thereby a rock of self in a roiling sea of turmoil, a source of morally secure motivation in a storm of self-serving desires, clashing and dashing against each other, like waves from a hundred hurricanes.

Many others have found this second self in many other ways, both in nature and in the divine. But the natural conscience is not a nonsocial conscience. These are very human concerns. They are concerns of humans about humans. These sages were not escaping the city. They were rebuilding it.

———

I'm remembering another sound. We call it "chuckling"—the sound of the waves rippling up the lapstrake sides of a Saint Lawrence skiff. A lapstrake boat like a skiff has a wooden hull set with overlapping planks, making for a kind of cedar washboard for the flow of the water. The wind has to be just right, not too strong and not too calm. The angle of the boat has to be right too, roughly forty-five degrees off the wind. And you need to be rowing at a fair clip. A motor won't do. You wouldn't hear the chuckling reverberating through the cedar.

It's a musical and calming sound, an arpeggio of water chimes. We love it. We even put it into a song that we sing every summer when we return to the Thousand Islands section of the Saint Lawrence River for family vacation.[52]

The oars rise up, the oars dip down
And I hear a chuck-a-ling sound
As I row this golden river skiff
Up to Rockport town

A branch of my mother's family were among the first European settlers of these islands. First Nations folk already lived here, and the story of how the settlers pushed them out isn't pretty. But that was a long time ago, and we don't often remember it. Rather, we remember our family's two-hundred-year history in the area, some of which is now a Canadian national park. We and various families of our cousins still own cottages on the islands. Hardly anyone lives on the islands year-round now, but we reconstitute the old community every summer.

To have a summer place is, I recognize, rather bourgeois. I confess one must possess considerable class privilege for even a jointly owned family vacation cottage on an island. But that's not the story we tell ourselves, just as we don't often speak of the long-ago theft from the First Nations. Instead, we think of the Thousand Islands as a place of release from these and other politics. This is no place of urban wiles (or at least not so much, for we do bring our laptops). Nor is it nature before nature, full of pagan contest and ambivalence (or at least not so much, for we do still tell some of the old stories). For us (at least in the main) this is a place of nature, of conscience, of the good and true, of the solid and conflict-free, undefiled by hierarchical ambition.

"Going up to the islands again this summer to escape the real world?" friends sometimes say, inquiring about my summer plans.

"No," I like to reply. "That *is* the real world."

Sometimes I find myself in a *daoist* mood—without trying, of course. I take the skiff out into the main channel. I ship the oars, and just let the boat drift. Sometimes I even lay on the bottom, looking up at the sky, the sides of the boat obscuring my view of where we're headed, the skiff and I. No needs. No intentions. No politics. Pure *wu wei*. Complete peace with my savage name. We like to sing another song about that.[53]

> *Put me in a boat in the water*
> *Let the current take me where it will*
> *As I drift through the tree-green islands I love*
> *I will know I am near to my home*

I cannot be a sociologist only. Even though I can be quite analytical about this kind of experience (if nothing else, this book should show that) I still feel these matters deeply. For me, as for so many others of similar times and places, second nature has become second nature.

4

Pagan Monotheism and the Two Evils

"DAD, LET'S STOP READING THIS," said my daughter, then eleven. "I don't think I'm old enough yet."

The work in question was the Bible. I had taken to reading it to Eleanor as a bedtime book. Whatever religious import one may or may not take from it, the Bible brims with great stories—way more compelling than your average preteen novel, at least to an academic father in his fifties. It is, of course, a major work of world literature. Contemporary culture references the "Good Book" constantly. I thought Eleanor should know more about it. I hoped as well she'd have a more informed basis for coming to her own view of the Bible's theological significance.

So we had been reading the Bible, right from the beginning, every evening for some weeks. It was slow going, with lots of pauses for questions and discussion. Eventually, we got through Genesis—albeit not without a few complaints about the sections she said had given her nightmares. We got stuck for a bit early on when we hit the story of Cain murdering his brother Abel because he was jealous that the Lord preferred Abel's offering of lamb to Cain's offering of vegetables. We made a few jokes about the Lord seeming to prefer meat to a vegetarian diet, and that helped. But soon after that we got to the story of the Lord's anger over the "wickedness of humankind" and his resolution to bring about a huge flood to "blot out from the earth the human beings I have created—people together with animals and creeping things and birds of the air, for I am sorry that I have made them."[1] That passage was pretty hard for Eleanor to process. The Lord being sorry for making humans and other living creatures? What about being a loving god? And how could he have messed up to begin with? Isn't God supposed to be all-powerful and all-knowing?

Eleanor was also troubled by the Lord's testing of Abraham to the brink of sacrificing his son, and by his odd treatment of Ishmael. Rebekah's scheme for her son Jacob—a deception that leads Esau to lose his firstborn right to inherit Isaac's wealth and position—led to another long talk. Most disturbing was the story of Lot, supposedly a righteous man, trying to protect two angels sheltering in his house by offering a mob at his door that they take his "two daughters who have not known a man" to "do to them as you please."[2] Rape. Murder. Jealousy. Plagues. Famine. Annihilation of whole cities by a rain of "sulfur and fire from the Lord out of heaven."[3] Genesis is not a gentle book. I hadn't read it with any care in some time. I'd forgotten how much shocking stuff it contains.

We probably should have stopped there (if not earlier). But Eleanor insisted we continue. Genesis often horrified her but also fascinated her. Reluctantly, I agreed, and we started in on Exodus.

It went reasonably well at first. Eleanor knew the general outlines of the escape from Egypt and the Passover story. So she was prepared for all the carnage there—Moses's murder of an Egyptian who was beating a Hebrew, the slaying of the firstborn, and the drowning of Pharaoh's army in the Red Sea— although Exodus was more direct and matter-of-fact about the bloodshed than she had expected or I had remembered. She positively liked the Lord wrapping Mount Sinai in smoke and fire, blasting his trumpet, and answering Moses through thunder, although it did seem to her a bit much to decree that "any who touch the mountain shall be put to death."[4] The giving of the Ten Commandments was fine too. But Eleanor puzzled over the subsequent passages. About when and when not it is appropriate to buy or sell a slave.[5] About the need to maintain the "food, clothing, and marital rights" of the first wife if a man takes a second one.[6] About the Lord's very specific requirements for how to worship and obey him—from not boiling a kid in its mother's milk, to the layout and furnishings of his Tabernacle, to the vestments that his priests should wear, to the proper way for performing animal sacrifices. About how if an owner strikes a slave so hard that the slave dies immediately, the owner is to be punished, "but if the slave survives a day or two, there is no punishment; for the slave is the owner's property."[7] About how "whoever strikes father or mother" or "curses father or mother shall be put to death."[8] About how "whoever does any work on the sabbath day shall be put to death" as well.[9]

This was scary and strange enough. Then we got to the section where the Lord fumes over the casting of the Golden Calf, and the passages that immediately follow. "I have seen this people, how stiff-necked they are," the Lord tells Moses. "Now let me alone, so that my wrath may burn hot against them and I may consume them."[10]

Moses does his best to calm the Lord down, and asks, "O Lord, why does your wrath burn hot against your people, whom you brought out of the land of Egypt with great power and with a mighty hand?" Moses points out that it would look pretty bad. "Why should the Egyptians say, 'It was with evil intent that he brought them out to kill them in the mountains, and to consume them from the face of the earth'?" And he implores the Lord to "Turn from your fierce wrath; change your mind and do not bring disaster on your people."[11]

Remarkably, for arguing with God is not commonly advised, Exodus reports "the Lord changed his mind about the disaster that he planned to bring on his people."[12] Eleanor cheered at that.

But then Moses loses his own temper. He heads down the mountain with the Ten Commandments carved onto two stone tablets, sees the people dancing around the Golden Calf, and infamously dashes the tablets on the ground, breaking them. Eleanor knew that part. She didn't know what happens next. First Moses grinds up the Golden Calf, scatters the powder into water, and makes everyone drink it. Alarmed, his brother Aaron tries to settle Moses down. Moses ignores him, goes over to the gate of the Israelites' camp, and shouts, "Who is on the Lord's side? Come to me!"[13] Here's what ensues:

And all the sons of Levi gathered around him. He said to them, "Thus says the Lord, the God of Israel, 'Put your sword on your side, each of you! Go back and forth from gate to gate throughout the camp, and each of you kill your brother, your friend, and your neighbor.'" The sons of Levi did as Moses commanded, and about three thousand of the people fell on that day. Moses said, "Today you have ordained yourselves for the service of the Lord, each one at the cost of a son or a brother, and so have brought a blessing on yourselves this day."[14]

After this slaughter, Moses then goes back up the mountain to plead the Israelites' case with the Lord. The Lord tells Moses not to worry. He is content, and tells Moses to "lead the people to the place about which I have spoken to you; see, my angel shall go in front of you."[15] Even so, the Lord sends a plague on the remaining Israelites before they depart—not because they killed three thousand of their brothers, friends, and neighbors, but "because they made the calf."[16]

That was it. Eleanor was done. The Bible may be the Good Book, but it's not a bedtime story.

————

The tough-guy god of the Old Testament, full of pride, resentment, anger, and callous violence even against his own followers, jars pretty strongly with the common contemporary image of the divine as kindly, loving, and good. The god of the good, like the goodness of nature, would develop eventually. But the inspiration for these passages was both older and different. The context of life for the overwhelming majority of Israelites at the time was not Athens. It was not Rome. It was not the life of the elites of the Chinese state of Zhou. It was not New York, Berlin, Johannesburg, Buenos Aires, Moscow, Tehran, or Beijing. Understanding the ancient Israelite context, though, has much to show us about why the Old Testament, especially the early books, now frequently feels odd, and even immoral.

Because of this oddness, religious leaders in the Abrahamic traditions—the largest being Judaism, Christianity, and Islam—usually clean up the Old Testament stories, or simply skip over the stranger passages. It is a rare pulpit that thunders with Bible quotes like "whoever does any work on the sabbath day shall be put to death." Many traditions counsel their faithful to take a day every week for rest, reflection, devotion, and communion with one another. But death if you don't? Few highlight that line today.

Of course, most followers of the Abrahamic traditions—even the devout—haven't read the Bible with much thoroughness. People are busy, and the Bible is long and often dull. In 2014, some 19 percent of Americans reported reading the Bible at least four times a week, and some 45 percent reported reading the Bible at least once a month.[17] But most return again and again to their favorite passages. Americans report to survey researchers that they gain feelings of peace, encouragement, hope, direction, and happiness when they read the Bible.[18] Likely not from reading about the sons of Levi murdering three thousand of their friends and kin, and winning the blessing of the Lord for doing so.

More thorough reading practices confront one with a wide range of other oddities as well—oddities that provide important clues as to how the ancient Israelites encountered the divine in their lives. Take its occasional polytheistic and poly-divine description of divinity.[19] The Old Testament frequently rails against polytheism, as we might expect for a work that urges the acceptance of a monotheistic conception of the divine. So it comes as some surprise to encounter passages like these from Genesis, Deuteronomy, and Psalms:

> Then the Lord God said, "See, the man has become like one of us, knowing good and evil."[20]

> When the Most High apportioned the nations,
> when he divided humankind,
> he fixed the boundaries of the peoples
> according to the number of the gods;
> the Lord's own portion was his people,
> Jacob his allotted share.[21]

> God has taken his place in the divine council;
> in the midst of the gods he holds judgment . . .[22]

One of us. According to the number of the gods. The divine council. Maybe in that first quote from Genesis the Lord speaks in the "royal we," referring to his singular self in the plural, and does not intend to imply that he is only one of many gods. But the line about "the number of the gods" is a little harder to pass by so quickly. It comes from a famous passage in Deuteronomy known as the "Song of Moses." Moses sings this song to an assembly of the entire people of Israel just before ascending Mount Nebo, looking on the promised land that he himself would never enter, and dying. Scholars have long remarked on these lines. The passage seems to contrast a deity called "the Most High" with a "number" of other gods, one of whom is "the Lord." The original Hebrew makes the contrast between different gods clearer. "The Most High" is the traditional translation for a deity named *Elyon* or *El Elyon*, and "the Lord" is the traditional translation for a deity whose name is spelled יהוה, which is roughly equivalent to *YHWH* in English.[23] In this passage, *Elyon* sounds like a chief god, sort of a Zeus figure, presiding over a group of less powerful gods like *YHWH*, each of whom *Elyon* assigns to the job of taking care of a specific group of people.[24] *YHWH*'s assignment, his "own portion," is the people descended from Jacob, the Israelites.

The third quote—the "divine council" passage (which is from Psalms)—continues the holy board of directors theme. It concerns a deity called "God," which is the traditional translation for *Elohim* in the original Hebrew. And it describes how *Elohim* is but one member of a group of gods who regularly get together to deliberate on the problems of the world. Moreover, the very word

Elohim is the plural form of the name *El*—another term for the divine in the Bible, and perhaps the oldest—although the biblical text treats *Elohim* as if it were a grammatically singular name, making for an entity who is both plural and one.[25]

None of which sounds terrifically monotheistic. Let me put it this way: If you read the Bible in English, you might well accept the varying terms like "Most High," "the Lord," and "God" as literary license for the same powerful divinity. But if you go back to the original Hebrew for these terms, and ponder the lines where they appear just a minute more, you'll find yourself pondering them for quite a bit longer as well.[26]

————

The Old Testament has plenty more to puzzle the attentive reader, providing more clues about the context of ancient Israel.

Take the transcendence of God, one of the hallmarks of common contemporary understandings of the divine. The Old Testament God can be transcendent but is also often very much here, bound in the real, present in daily life, a god of places, immanent in them. True, the Old Testament God is none too fond of idols. But there he is walking around the Garden of Eden. There he is in the burning bush.[27] There he is in the pillar of fire and the pillar of smoke, leading the Israelites along and throwing the Egyptian army into confusion.[28] He doesn't just send the pillar of fire and the pillar of smoke; he's actually in them.

> The Lord went in front of them in a pillar of cloud by day, to lead them along the way, and in a pillar of fire by night, to give them light, so that they might travel by day and by night.[29]

And there he is, right at the top of Mount Sinai, summoning Moses up to talk to him and establishing that stern guideline about putting to death anyone other than Moses who touches the mountain, thus offending God's presence by coming closer than he allows. There he is once again in the fire and the cloud after all the conflict over the Golden Calf, when the Israelites have finally constructed the Tabernacle—a kind of special tent that could be packed up and moved around—to his specifications. "My presence will go with you," he promises, once Moses "did everything just as the Lord commanded him."[30] True to his word,

> Then the cloud covered the tent of meeting, and the glory of the Lord filled the tabernacle . . . the cloud of the Lord was on the tabernacle by day, and

fire was in the cloud by night, before the eyes of all the house of Israel at each stage of their journey.[31]

Much later on, Solomon finally replaces the Tabernacle. No more movable tent of meeting. Solomon builds a true temple out of stone and wood in Jerusalem, and the presence of God enters in the form of a cloud again. His cloud descends right after the priests finish transferring all the holy vessels and the two tablets of the Ten Commandants out of the now unneeded Tabernacle and into the inner sanctuary of "the house of the Lord" that Solomon commanded to be built.[32] Then,

> a cloud filled the house of the Lord, so that the priests could not stand to minister because of the cloud; for the glory of the Lord filled the house of the Lord. Then Solomon said, "The Lord has said that he would dwell in thick darkness. I have built you an exalted house, a place for you to dwell in forever."[33]

In short, the "house of the Lord" really is his house. He lives there. It's where God "dwells," back there in the "thick darkness" of the inner sanctuary. It's where he is present and where the faithful can encounter him. There is no idol, however. God does not inhabit a statue, such as one quite likely would have encountered for Ishtar in her temple at Uruk in the time of Gilgamesh. But he is present, right there, nonetheless—just as he had been present, right there, in the Tabernacle. Indeed, the ancient Hebrew word for Tabernacle, *mishkan*, means a "dwelling place."

———

A quick recap. The Old Testament's portrayal of the divine seems out of step with contemporary notions in several ways. Instead of being a god of the good, the Old Testament god is often violent and scary. Instead of monotheism, the Old Testament often seems to describe a polytheistic divine. Instead of just transcendence, we read a lot of discussion of God as a concrete and immanent presence.

Plus there's more to puzzle over.

Consider how the Old Testament god is also often a god of what we today consider attributes of nature. That is, he is a god of nature before nature—literally, for the word nature does not ever appear in the Old Testament.[34] God is not over and above nature. He *is* nature, an immanent part of it—especially some attributes of nature common to many nature before nature divinities. Like Zeus and other commanding figures that people have seen in the heavens, the Old Testament god is a storm god, ready to fire away with his thunderbolts at humans he judges need a little disciplining. Take this passage from Job:

> See, he scatters his lightning around him
> and covers the roots of the sea.
> For by these he governs peoples;
> he gives food in abundance.
> He covers his hands with the lightning,
> and commands it to strike the mark.
> Its crashing tells about him;
> he is jealous with anger against iniquity.
>
> At this also my heart trembles,
> and leaps out of its place.
> Listen, listen to the thunder of his voice
> and the rumbling that comes from his mouth.
> Under the whole heaven he lets it loose,
> and his lightning to the corners of the earth.
> After it his voice roars;
> he thunders with his majestic voice
> and he does not restrain the lightnings when his voice is heard.
> God thunders wondrously with his voice;
> he does great things that we cannot comprehend.[35]

This passage also connects the Old Testament god to another characteristic of nature before nature: to sustenance needs and the rhythms of agricultural prosperity. By his lightning and, we presume, his rain, God "gives food in abundance." God can also give "a fine flaky substance, as fine as frost on the ground . . . like coriander seed, white" and with a taste "like wafers made with honey." That sweet substance is the manna, the "bread from heaven" he provides the Israelites in the wilderness.[36]

God does not only provide, however. He also punishes those he finds wicked by attacking their sustenance capabilities. When God wants to free his people from Egypt, he sends the Ten Plagues, most of which directly undermine the ability of Egyptians to provide for themselves. He turns water into blood so that the Nile is undrinkable and its fish die. He sends frogs, gnats, and boils that torment humans and animals alike. He sends livestock disease, hail, and locusts that kill cattle and damage crops. For the ninth plague, he sends darkness so thick no one can see to move and do what needs to be done to sustain their livelihoods. And the most fearsome, the tenth plague, the slaying of the firstborn, God applies to humans and livestock alike.

God not only punishes foreign powers through undermining ecology and agriculture. He also disciplines the Israelites with ecological and agricultural threats.

> But if you will not obey me, and do not observe all these commandments, if you spurn my statutes, and abhor my ordinances, so that you will not observe all my commandments, and you break my covenant, I in turn will do this to you: I will bring terror on you; consumption and fever that waste the eyes and cause life to pine away.... I will break your proud glory, and I will make your sky like iron and your earth like copper. Your strength shall be spent to no purpose: your land shall not yield its produce, and the trees of the land shall not yield their fruit.[37]

Terror. Consumption. Fever. Broken pride. Land which no longer produces. Trees which do not yield. Tough words from a tough God—even toward his own people.

Happier connections to sustenance are the Old Testament god's directives for ensuring agricultural sustainability through rest. His injunction to "remember the sabbath day, and keep it holy" includes livestock "so that your ox and your donkey may have relief."[38] Even happier, it also includes required rest for slaves and "resident aliens." But not only a sabbath day: God directs the Israelites to have a sabbath year for the land, presumably in rotation, field by field—a *shmita*, as the Israelites called it, derived from the Hebrew word for "release."

> Six years you shall sow your field, and six years you shall prune your vineyard, and gather in their yield; but in the seventh year there shall be a sabbath of complete rest for the land, a sabbath for the Lord: you shall not sow your field or prune your vineyard. You shall not reap the aftergrowth of your harvest or gather the grapes of your unpruned vine: it shall be a year of complete rest for the land.[39]

Rotating a period of rest for one's land is sound agronomic advice. But the *shmita* also promoted economic and ecologic justice, for God remembers both the needs of wildlife and of the poor—which, frankly, I think is pretty cool.

For six years you shall sow your land and gather in its yield; but the seventh year you shall let it rest and lie fallow, so that the poor of your people may eat; and what they leave the wild animals may eat. You shall do the same with your vineyard, and with your olive orchard.[40]

God also organizes three agricultural harvest holidays: the festivals of Pesach, Shavuot, and Sukkot. The climate of the Mideast leads to quite a different pattern of agriculture than in more temperate regions, and three periods of harvest were the norm in biblical times. Many Jews today still honor these festivals—especially Pesach, better known today as Passover—although with little of their original agricultural meaning. Pesach is the early spring festival of unleavened bread, today widely celebrated as a freedom holiday focused on the Exodus story. (Increasingly, some Christians also celebrate a version of Pesach.) In an earlier day, Jews also appreciated Pesach as a metaphor for release from winter and the re-leavening of the world with the return of warmth and plant growth. Central to Pesach was the ritual of the Cutting of the First Sheaf, a sheaf of barley—which is a winter crop in these regions—indicating the barley was ripe and ready for harvest, and that spring had arrived.[41] Shavuot is a late spring holiday, originally focused around the wheat harvest. And Sukkot is a fall holiday, originally focused around the harvesting of tree and fruit crops like olives and grapes.

All three were major festivals during biblical times, not only Pesach. At each of these holidays, every Jewish male in the land was even expected to make a pilgrimage to Jerusalem, fulfilling God's commandment that "Three times in the year all your males shall appear before the Lord God" at his house, the Temple.[42] If we blink over this practice's sexism for a moment, it is also pretty cool: everyone (every man, that is) coming together in one place three times a year to celebrate their connections with each other through agriculture.[43]

Although there is a certain romantic appeal to these agricultural rituals of social and ecological unity, archaeologists doubt that most ordinary Israelites actually did all the things the Old Testament demanded of them—which is likely much of why the Old Testament writers felt they had to make those demands.[44] Plus the sociological economist would be right to point out that no one was supposed to arrive at the Temple empty-handed. Everyone was supposed to bring a substantial offering from the season's harvest. These offerings weren't all burned up on the Temple's altars. Only a small amount was, for ceremonial purposes. The city folk, even though they were few, needed to eat too. More on that later: For now, I want to emphasize a different implication. These were offerings to a God of what we today call nature and of our agricultural connections to ecology.

————

The Old Testament's accounts of God's personality offer more clues about the context of ancient Israel and its people's understandings of the divine.

First, you can argue with the Old Testament god. Consider the story of Moses arguing with God and convincing him not to obliterate the Israelites for being a "stiff-necked people" and casting the Golden Calf. The Lord listens and changes his mind.

Plus the Lord makes mistakes and has regrets. He is not omniscient, infallible, and omnipotent, as Eleanor noted concerning the story of Noah's ark when God confesses that "I am sorry that I have made" human beings and decides to clean the slate with a huge flood. God goofed and felt the world needed a reset. Another example is when God makes Saul the first king of the Israelites, but he doesn't turn out so well, in the Lord's view. (Saul refuses to "utterly destroy" the Amalekites, as the Lord commanded, and spares their king and the best of their sheep and cattle.) The Lord goes to Samuel and says "I regret that I made Saul king, for he has turned back from following me, and has not carried out my commands."[45] He does a reset on that one too, and brings in David to be king.

The Old Testament god is capable of apology, too, telling Jeremiah to tell the people that "I am sorry for the disaster that I have brought upon you," meaning the destruction of Jerusalem and the Temple by the Babylonians in 587 BCE.[46] That was quite a major misstep as it devastated not only his "own portion," his people, but even his own house, the Temple. And God is remorseful.

As well, the Old Testament god can be quite emotional. His most common emotional response, though, is what my daughter called his "anger management problem" when we were reading the Bible together. The Lord spends quite a bit of the Old Testament in a very sour mood, taking great offense at the Israelites' transgressions of the covenant he established with them to follow his laws. He frequently thunders at the Israelites that "I the Lord your God am a jealous God."[47] He's not often given to forgiveness either. As Joshua warns the Israelites, "He is a jealous God; he will not forgive your transgressions or your sins."[48] You might even call "Jealous" another of his names, suggests Moses to the Israelites in this passage: "You shall worship no other god, because the Lord, whose name is Jealous, is a jealous God."[49]

These characteristics manifest a much more interactive conception of the divine than Abrahamic tradition generally promotes today. The interactiveness of the Old Testament divine with humans even extends to sexual relations, as the divine does in *Gilgamesh* and in ancient Greek and Roman religion. Genesis and some of the Apocrypha speak of the "sons of God" (contrary to the New Testament's description of Jesus as God's "only son").[50] God's sons lust after human women and descend to the Earth to take them as wives and have intercourse with them, leading to a race of semidivine superheroes called the Nephilim.[51] Here's the passage from Genesis. It's short and often overlooked, but pretty striking if you slow your eye for a moment and take it in:

> When people began to multiply on the face of the ground, and daughters were born to them, the sons of God saw that they were fair; and they took wives for themselves of all that they chose. Then the Lord said, "My spirit shall not abide in mortals forever, for they are flesh; their days shall be one hundred twenty years." The Nephilim were on the earth in those days— and also afterward—when the sons of God went in to the daughters of humans, who bore children to them. These were the heroes that were of old, warriors of renown.[52]

Plural, immanent, concrete, bound to place, immersed in ecology and sustenance needs, fallible, emotional, violent, interactive, and sexual: the Old Testament divine is a very human divine.

––––––

These characteristics all sound very much like the pagan, nature before nature deities of Greece, Mesopotamia, and the *Popol Vuh*, as well as the semidivinities of ancestor veneration in South Africa. But there is much that differs as well. The Old Testament God occasionally has his transcendent moments, like when he speaks the world into existence from the formless void. Even though some poly-divine passages remain, *YHWH* generally strongly opposes the thought that one might worship other gods. While not all-powerful and all-knowing, he is certainly extremely powerful and very knowing. Although there are hints of divine sex in the Old Testament, they don't directly involve *YHWH*.

Scholars sometimes call the Old Testament's not-quite-full-on monotheism *monolatry*—the idea that you ought to worship one god but don't necessarily discount the possibility of other gods out there that you or others might worship.[53] Jacob is the allotted share of *YHWH*, but other gods have other peoples to look after. Think of it as a kind of football coach vision of the divine: Each people has their own god to lead them, and for whom that god is responsible, as they are responsible to Him or Her. (Some monolatrous beliefs focus on a female divine.) Then we all have it out on the field of human struggle and combat, and we see whose god is better and stronger by who wins.

Yet monolatry does not exactly fit the Old Testament god, as least in most of the Bible.[54] No doubt many peoples in biblical times had such views. The Old Testament also shows considerable awareness that other groups worship other gods. And there are definite hints of the divine coach vision of *YHWH* in the passage from the Song of Moses with the line about *YHWH*'s "allotted share," and in a few other spots. But far more common is a distinctive theological innovation: The Old Testament contention that when Israel loses to another army it is not because *YHWH* wasn't as strong as the god or gods of that other people. It is because *YHWH* is mad at the Israelites for not keeping his covenants and for worshiping other gods. Like the Golden Calf. Or perhaps the god Ba'al or the goddess Asherah, two other divinities the Old Testament often rails against. Therefore *YHWH* decides to punish the Israelites by having them lose in warfare, even to the point of causing the Babylonians to destroy Jerusalem and the Temple, God's own home, leading to the exile of the Jews to Babylon, even though he later regrets instituting such a hard punishment on the Israelites. *YHWH* is so powerful, so much in control, he can as easily tip the scales so that the Israelites lose as he can ensure their victory. This is a thoroughly transcendent move, however unpleasant.

This is also a move that speaks to the overriding moral message of the Old Testament. It would be hard to characterize the Old Testament god as good—powerful and scary, jealous and angry, a deity to fear, but really not especially good—and the Old Testament doesn't much try to make such a case, at least in the early books.[55] It's not where its main concerns lie. Rather, its primary moral principle is loyalty, and, correspondingly, its main notion of evil is *disloyalty*. The Lord has established a covenant with the Israelites, and they had better stick to it. He is their god now, and they are his chosen people. Don't try to get out of it. The costs will be huge.

Take the time when the wandering Israelites sojourn in Shittim, a city in Moab, the kingdom across the Dead Sea from the Promised Land. "The people" fall for some Moabite women and for the main Moabite god, the Ba'al of Pe'or—Pe'or being a mountain in Moab revered locally as Ba'al's home.[56] The Lord is not happy, and the consequences are gruesome.

While Israel was staying at Shittim, the people began to have sexual relations with the women of Moab. These invited the people to the sacrifices
of their gods, and the people ate and bowed down to their gods. Thus Israel
yoked itself to the Ba'al of Pe'or, and the Lord's anger was kindled against
Israel. The Lord said to Moses, "Take all the chiefs of the people, and im-
pale them in the sun before the Lord, in order that the fierce anger of the
Lord may turn away from Israel." And Moses said to the judges of Israel,
"Each of you shall kill any of your people who have yoked themselves to the
Ba'al of Pe'or."[57]

The Lord ordering the impalement of the chiefs of the Jews—and Moses following up with ordering the killing of anyone who worshipped Ba'al of Pe'or,
not just the chiefs. I'm glad Eleanor already had had enough of the Old Testament before this story appears.

Note the framing of disloyalty in this story. The Old Testament here and
many other places ties disloyalty to god with disloyalty to the group, and
vice versa. The crime at Shittim was not just following the Ba'al of Pe'or, the
Moabite god. It was also having sex with Moabite women, who in turn induce
the Israelites to make sacrifices to the Ba'al of Pe'or. The god of the group
dictates the group of the god. And if you forget, your own people will come
against you. Foreign armies will come against you. Storms, drought, and pestilence will come against you.

Disloyalty is not the only basic evil that the Old Testament discusses. The
Old Testament also takes up the evil of *desire* that so concerned the ancient
Greek, Roman, and Chinese writers from about the fifth century BCE on, and
which we will shortly hear much more about in this book. Our moralities suggest to us the dangers of *two basic evils*, disloyalty and desire, the one focused
on the integrity of the group and the other on the integrity of the individual.
But it is the former that most concerns the Old Testament—another important clue to the context of life in ancient Israel.

I find it telling that the order of the Ten Commandments resonates with
the priority the Old Testament lays on the problem of disloyalty. The first five
of the Big Ten are concerned with various forms of disloyalty, while the second five weigh in on the many problems of desire.

Here's a reminder of the first five, in order:

You shall have no other gods before me.
You shall not make for yourself an idol.
You shall not make wrongful use of the name of the Lord your God.

Remember the sabbath day, and keep it holy.
Honor your father and your mother.

The first four commandments all focus explicitly on loyalty to God, while the fifth focuses on loyalty to one's parents and kin. The fifth also ties the reasoning back to loyalty to God if we look at the full commandment, which reads: "Honor your father and your mother, so that your days may be long in the land that the Lord your God is giving you." Note here, too, the appeal to the Israelite's self-interest in showing commitment to the group and its kin relations, as well as to God, for that commitment is the basis of your right to land.

Here's a reminder of the second five:

You shall not murder.
You shall not commit adultery.
You shall not steal.
You shall not bear false witness against your neighbor.
You shall not covet anything that belongs to your neighbor.

In these commandments, the focus is on bad things that untempered desire can lead to: murder, illegitimate sex, theft, lying, and jealousy. Given the opening five commandments, I find myself hearing an echo of the problem of disloyalty even in the second five: that these interpersonal issues might sow discord in the group. The god of the Old Testament repeatedly frames the problem of their violation as a challenge of loyalty to him and his covenant with Israel, as when the Israelite men have sex with the Moabite women, not as a problem of desire in and of itself.

Eleanor was puzzled by this ordering. After I read through the Ten Commandments section of Exodus—we never got to the section in Deuteronomy where the Ten Commandments get a repeat—Eleanor asked, "So why isn't 'thou shalt not murder' the first commandment? Murder seems like the biggest sin to me. A lot bigger than making idols or working on the sabbath."

Apparently not to the god of the Old Testament.

———

So what is going on here? Why would disloyalty be the bigger evil? And why is there such a pagan, nature before nature vibe in the Old Testament?

I often found myself telling Eleanor that "It's a very old book. Times have changed a lot." But that is true only as far as it goes. These notes of the Old Testament divine show a difference in instrumentation, key, and variations, but not in the basic melody of human affairs: our preoccupation with politics.

Politics is one of the central concerns of the Old Testament. From when Cain kills Abel in the fourth chapter of Genesis, hardly a page goes by without mention of a righteous conflict between different human interests. One could argue that the politics start even earlier, in the garden of Eden, with the conflict of Adam with Eve—not to mention the conflict of Adam and Eve with the serpent, and the conflict of God with Adam and Eve. These politics are not easy to sort out, though. Literally thousands of scholars in our universities and seminaries have worked on the problem, looking for hints in the Bible and other ancient Israelite texts, in the texts of nearby peoples like the Mesopotamians and Egyptians, and in the archaeological record. Based on this work, we can piece together something like the following general history, and its associated political challenges.[58]

The Old Testament describes a religious tradition in transition, associated with a people in transition. A nature before nature world was beginning to split nature from supernature, and to split them both from the human community. The ancient triangle was beginning to form, although it had not yet fully taken shape. Conceptual gulfs were forming and widening as the Israelites struggled to shift from a kin-based, tribal, and agrarian society to a small state and empire with significant growth of cities. Nature still did not exist as a concept. (As I noted earlier in passing, the word nature does not ever appear in the Old Testament in the original Greek and Hebrew.) And a fully transcendent concept of the divine, abstracted and removed from the human, had not yet developed. But the ancient triangle began to divide as soon as it began to form. It began to divide because of attempts to unify—as I'll describe.

Scholars argue over how much we can trust the Bible's political history, sometimes calling each other biblical "maximalists" or biblical "minimalists," not altogether kindly. The biblical maximalists say we can trust the Bible a lot, and the biblical minimalists say we can't trust it very much at all, and ask us to look more toward the archaeological evidence.[59] Yet there seems to be consensus on a few basic points about the transition that was under way, and the political debates that ensued.

Here's one: For a thousand years or more, this little corner of the world found itself pinched between one empire after another, rising and falling on one side or the other. The Egyptians to the southwest. The Assyrians, Babylonians, and Persians to the East. The Hittites, Greeks, and finally the Romans to the north. Meanwhile, the Israelites harbored imperial ambitions of their own, and at various times achieved some small success—generally to be followed shortly afterward by disaster at the hands and swords of their bigger neighbors, or due to the casualties of their own infighting. And some of both.

Another point of consensus is that the early Israelites, both in the Old Testament and in the archaeological record, are a more agrarian and pastoral people, little urbanized at first, but gradually developing villages, small towns, and eventually small cities.[60] Researchers dispute when and how that settling down happened, and the reliability of the Bible's account of it. For example, archaeology shows that Jericho was unoccupied around 1200 BCE, the time the Old Testament says Joshua and the Israelites attacked it.[61] Some scholars have even proposed that rather than the Israelites taking over and absorbing the Canaanites, the historical flow went more the other way.[62] Instead of being conquered, the Canaanites may have actually developed into the Israelites, more or less in place. Careful study of Canaanite religion—which we know a fair bit about, principally from cuneiform tablets discovered in the ruins the Canaanite city of Ugarit, as well as other sources—actually shows few significant differences from early Israelite religion.[63] But scholars agree that the early Israelites were mainly farmers and pastoralists, not urbanites.

One possible exception to the dominance of rural livelihoods in the lives of ancient Israelites was their sojourn in Egypt, and their later Exodus—if and how that even happened. If it did happen, some of the distinctive features of ancient Israelite worship, especially its largely monotheistic take on a mainly nature before nature orientation, possibly developed at this time. Here we enter very contested scholarly terrain. First, let's consider what we know pretty much for sure.

There is a striking archaeological coincidence with the Exodus story. The timing the Bible gives for the Israelites' exit from Egypt corresponds closely with one of the most dire moments in human history: the Bronze Age collapse around 1200 BCE. Urbanism had already begun in the bronze age, as I discussed in chapter 2 concerning the rise of Mesopotamian civilizations like that of the Sumerians, and their passion for the story of Gilgamesh, king of great-walled Uruk. Plus the Egyptians, Minoans, Mycenaeans, Hittites, Mittani, Aramaeans, Amorites, and more, including the Canaanites, were all having an early try at building cities and states. But most of these urbanizing civilizations wink out within a few short decades of 1200 BCE, and apparently with special force in the year 1177 BCE, the culmination of a series of coastal attacks by the mysterious "sea peoples," who seem to have been displaced from further west.[64] Abandoned and burnt cities show up about this time in the archaeological record all around the eastern coast of the Mediterranean. We even have preserved in cuneiform a desperate letter from the king of Ugarit to the king of Cyprus asking for help fending off the sea peoples. "My father," he writes, using a term of honor, one king to another,

> now the ships of the enemy have come. They have been setting fire to my cities and have done harm to the land. Doesn't my father know that all of my infantry and chariotry are stationed in Khatte, and that all of my ships are stationed in the land of Lukka? They have not arrived back yet.[65]

The king of Cyprus didn't send help in time, apparently, for this letter was discovered in the burnt ruins of Ugarit. Because of the burning, this letter and thousands of the city's other cuneiform tablets were unintentionally fired from clay into something hard enough to last until archaeologists could dig them up, adding greatly to our understanding of Canaanite culture and society. Either what we have is a copy of the letter or, quite possibly, the city was attacked before the king of Ugarit could even send it.

Who were the "sea peoples," and are they really to blame for the Bronze Age collapse? Now the uncertainty dials up many notches. Many archaeologists now suspect that the collapse may have had as much to do with climate change, famine, and economic collapse as direct attacks by displaced peoples—a "perfect storm of calamities," as the historian Eric Cline puts it.[66] But it does seem that there was a significant opening for new groups like the Israelites to arise. The Philistines also suddenly appear in the archaeological record at this time, establishing a string of small cities along the coast of what is now Israel. In fact, many archaeologists suspect that the Philistines may have been one of the "sea peoples."[67]

Most archaeologists think the Israelites weren't, however. Perhaps aside from an absence of pig bones, the Israelites' archaeological traces seem little different from those of the earlier Canaanites, who were also a Semitic group.[68] The earliest inscription to mention a people called "Israel"—the Merneptah Stele, which records a series of victories of the Pharaoh Merneptah over the sea peoples and others around 1208—appears to regard the Israelites as different from the sea peoples, and perhaps as related to the Canaanites.[69] Plus we do know a significant population of Semitic peoples lived in Egypt before the Bronze Age collapse and before the rough timing of the Exodus story. There isn't a shred of bona fide evidence of the Exodus itself.[70] Many have searched for old encampments in the Sinai, or for evidence of a large battle in the right place and time, and have found nothing that professional archaeologists can accept. But Semites were definitely in Egypt, as well as in many other areas of the Mideast. Semites were not a new group in the region, like the Philistines. The archaeological record is definitive on that score.

In fact, Semites ruled much of Egypt for a while. This was during what archaeologists call the "Intermediate Period" that followed the "Middle Kingdom," stretching from roughly 1800 BCE until Pharaoh Ahmose I restored the traditional royal lineage around 1539, ushering in the "New Kingdom." Elites with Semitic names continued to have prominent positions in Egypt as late as Pharaoh Amenhotep IV, the pharaoh who imposed a controversial and short-lived new religion based on worship of one god, the sun god Aten, and changed his own name to Ahkenaten, meaning "beloved of Aten." A man named Aper-el, whose name contained the name of the god El—much as do Old Testament names like Israel, Daniel, Samuel, Raphael, and my own name, Michael—served as Ahkenaten's vizier for a while. But when Ahkenaten died in 1336 BCE, leaving his nine-year-old son Tutankhaten as pharaoh, Atenism rapidly collapsed. Elites led a successful countermovement—elites who likely were allied with the political forces that lost out during Atenism. These elites ran the show during Tutankhaten's reign. They even changed the young monarch's name to what is surely the best known of all pharaoh names: Tutankamun, changing the Aten to Amun, a deity in the older tradition of Egyptian religion.

The timing of the Exodus story seems to land right about then, or shortly afterward. Did a group of Semites leave Egypt during this period of political turmoil, seeking to rejoin their Canaanite kin, perhaps led by a Semitic former high official in Ahkenaten's administration or a high priest of Atenism? Did the story of Moses and the tale that he spoke Hebrew poorly because of a speech impediment from eating a hot coal as an infant somehow loosely derive from having a Semitic leader who was from the Egyptian elite and a nonnative speaker of Hebrew?[71] Were most Egyptian Semites oppressed following the coming of the New Kingdom and the restoration of the traditional royal lineage, including being made into slaves? Did many Semites embrace Atenism during its short tenure, perhaps in hopes of regaining royal favor? Did these Semites retain a few monotheistic ideas from Atenism after its fall? Did they drift around for a time, from community to community, generally on the outskirts, looking for the right political opportunity to win some land for themselves? Like the Bronze Age collapse?

It's conceivable—or some now much-muddled version of all of this. But if so, it's more likely that it was a small group that left, a few hundred at most, too small to leave an archaeological trace of their departure, not the 603,550 enumerated in Exodus and Numbers.[72] And it is more likely that they were driven out, heretics and outcasts, rather than escaping. The story later became more glorious in generations of retelling.

———

But I'm being wildly speculative, joining the cacophony of many centuries of conjecture on these matters. Let's go back to what we actually know.

First, as I discussed earlier, there's a long history in this area—the coastal lands of the southeast corner of the Mediterranean—of efforts to create and maintain states and governments, while being squeezed between much bigger imperial players. Second, whatever the connection to the Bronze Age collapse, scholars agree that the peoples of the region were, from around 1100 BCE, coming together into ever bigger settlements. Archaeologists have done a staggering amount of work on the history of urbanization in biblical times, in part because of the region's unusual cultural importance. Literally thousands of biblical sites have felt the archaeologists' trowel, sieve, and horsehair brush. As a result, we can make pretty good assessments of population numbers.[73] Archaeologists currently estimate that Bronze Age Jerusalem was only about eleven or twelve acres and perhaps five to seven hundred people—a largish village. Following the Bronze Age, it began to grow, but not very fast. Between the tenth and the eighth centuries BCE, around the time the Bible says Kings Saul, David, and Solomon ruled and continuing on for another century or so, Jerusalem grew to about forty acres and roughly two thousand people. By the end of the sixth century BCE, Jerusalem had grown to a fairly substantial hundred sixty acres and six to eight thousand people, and an attractive prize for the imperial ambitions of others.[74] Nonetheless, the bulk of the population remained rural. Some 75 percent lived in settlements of three hundred people or fewer, or singly or in tiny hamlets in the countryside. Twenty percent lived in settlements of three hundred to a thousand people, and only 5 percent lived in settlements of a thousand or more.[75]

Here's the third point of scholarly consensus: The people the Bible calls the Israelites used to be two separate but closely aligned kingdoms, not just one state. To the north was the Kingdom of Israel with its capital at Samaria, and to the south was the Kingdom of Judah with its capital at Jerusalem.[76] (The word "Judaism" derives from the name Judah.) The Bible describes a unified monarchy of both under kings Saul, David, and Solomon, ruled from Jerusalem, and lasting through to Solomon's death around 931 BCE. Biblical maximalists generally accept the existence and timing of the united monarchy as largely true. The minimalists can't see this in the archaeological record so they don't trust this description.[77] It could well be a myth, they suggest, invented later to legitimate claiming both territories as one.[78] Minimalists contend that, in fact, the Bible in general should be largely read as an exercise in the political creation of a cultural tradition with a sense of a common past, rather than as a work of history as we understand that term today.[79] But everyone agrees that at one time there were two separate kingdoms. The Bible talks extensively about the two kingdoms, we can see it in the archaeological record, and there is independent textual confirmation in the records we have from Mesopotamia— although many minimalists think the Kingdom of Judah was far smaller, more agrarian, and less consequential than the Bible describes it.[80]

The Kingdom of Israel had a harder time of things, however. If you are a king from Mesopotamia and you march your army northwest up the Euphrates River valley—where there is a continual water supply and a green thread of farmers' fields to raid to keep your forces going—and then turn south when you get close to the Mediterranean coast, you could reach Israel without having to deal with much desert. Go a little further south, and you'll march into Judah too. But you'll hit Israel first. And as an Egyptian pharaoh coming up from the south, you'll have to get your army around the Sinai desert. You can do it, but you won't find any farms along the way to raid for provisions for your army. So you'll have to get your supply lines worked out pretty carefully. As a result, the Kingdom of Judah enjoyed some geographic protection from the major powers of the time. Israel and its capital Samaria fell first.[81] The Assyrian king Shalmaneser V laid siege to Samaria for three years, finally taking it in 722 BCE. Shalmaneser V died that year, and his successor, Sargon II, immediately followed up on his predecessor's victory and consolidated the conquest, deporting the elites back to his own capital, as was commonly done.

A century later, in 605 BCE, the Assyrians themselves were vanquished by an alliance of the Babylonians and the Medians, who ran a huge empire of their own for a while, covering most of what is now Iran and Afghanistan. The Babylonians didn't waste much time and seized the opportunity to claim the territory that the Assyrians had controlled, and to push the borders a bit further. The Judeans tried to hold the Babylonians off with a series of alliances with Egypt (albeit largely forced on them by the Egyptians). Then in 599 BCE the Babylonians invaded, led by King Nebuchadnezzar II. In 597 BCE, the Babylonians conquered Jerusalem but—probably hoping to gain a nice stream of taxes from a functioning economy—did not destroy it. As Shalmaneser V had earlier done with the elites of Israel, Nebuchadnezzar deported the elites of Judah to his capital, Babylon, in order to clear the stage for the puppet government he thought he had established.[82] The puppets later tried to rebel, so Nebuchadnezzar laid siege to Jerusalem once again. It fell for the second time in 587 BCE. After this, the Babylonians took no chances and totally devastated the city and the Temple, such that no unambiguous trace of the temple Solomon is reputed to have built remains to this day.

Then in 539 BCE, just forty-eight years later, the Babylonians themselves fell when the Persians, led by Cyrus the Great, defeated them at the Battle of Opis. Cyrus allowed the Jewish elites to return, as long as they respected the Persian Empire (including paying taxes). A great many did return, and they promptly rebuilt the Temple, what has come to be called the Second Temple. Many Jews today believe the Wailing Wall in Jerusalem was part of the foundation of this Second Temple.

The Jews spent the next six hundred years trying to put their unified state of Israel and Judea back together—if it ever really existed, some minimalists would insist—amid the constantly changing tidal forces of one empire and warring party after another. Alexander the Great's empire. The wars between Alexander's generals when he died in 323 BCE. The battles between the Seleucid Empire to the East (named for one of Alexander's generals, Seleucus) and the Ptolemaic Empire to the West (named for another of Alexander's generals, Ptolemy), with Judea in between.[83] Meanwhile, an even mightier empire was growing. By the middle of the second century BCE, the Romans were putting a lot of pressure on the Seleucids, who then controlled Judea. The Jews seized this moment of Seleucid weakness, and between 167 and 160 BCE launched the Maccabean Revolt. Although the Seleucids eventually put down the revolt, the resulting politics nevertheless worked out such that, starting around 140 BCE, the Jews finally once again enjoyed a Jewish-controlled kingdom. It was led by the Hasmonean Dynasty of Jewish monarchs (about whom we'll hear more in the next chapter).

The Roman Senate even officially recognized Jewish control in 139 BCE. But the Romans were biding their time, and took over Judea in 63 BCE during a moment of political instability. The Jews fought the Romans on and off for another two hundred years, without much success. The final blow was the Roman defeat in 135 CE of the revolt led by Simon Bar Kokhba and his short-lived independent Jewish state, leading the Romans to ban Jews from Jerusalem.

It's dizzyingly complex stuff—even at the level of detail we're sure about—like human politics generally are. But now let's imagine the situation of the leadership of this querulous bunch of tribes and descendants of tribes, trying to create a bulwark against the constant wash of empire and ambition on all sides. Likely the leadership wanted not only to protect the Israelites but also to advance its own interests. (Leaders can be like that today, and I very much doubt it's a new motive.) With either goal in mind, a theology of unity would be mightily attractive. The biblical historian Tamara Prosic describes this attractive theology as based on the unity of "three great unities, one people, one god, one temple."[84] Getting people to commit to one god for all—and to downplay the localized household and tribal poly-divinities that the Old Testament lambastes and that archaeology shows people at the time did indeed follow—would be a tradition worth the hard, hard work of establishing.[85] Theological concern for the evil of disloyalty has obvious political advantages in such circumstances.

————

Biblical scholars have long picked up on some striking textual evidence of this drive for unity. For example, the early books of the Old Testament frequently give two versions of the same story, what scholars call "doublets," sometimes with substantial differences. (There are even a few triplets.) Many scholars argue that the two (and sometimes three) versions reflect an effort to patch together different traditions and their peoples.

Consider the account of creation at the beginning of Genesis. In chapter 1, a transcendent God speaks the world into existence from out of the void over the course of six days. "God said," we read, "and it was so." Day by day creation unfolds: light and darkness; water and sky; land and vegetation; the sun and moon; the animals of water and air; and then, finally, land animals, including humans. This famous account is immediately followed by a second creation story, starting at Genesis 2:4, in which a much more immanent and embodied God—a God who walks around in the Garden of Eden and interacts directly with humans, forming Adam out of dust and breathing into his nostrils—appears to create everything on a single day.[86] The passage is worth quoting in full:

> In the day that the Lord God made the earth and the heavens, when no plant of the field was yet in the earth and no herb of the field had yet sprung up—for the Lord God had not caused it to rain upon the earth, and there was no one to till the ground; but a stream would rise from the earth, and water the whole face of the ground—then the Lord God formed man from the dust of the ground, and breathed into his nostrils the breath of life; and the man became a living being.[87]

"In the day" that the Lord God made the earth and the heavens: Is Genesis just taking a bit of literary license with itself? Maybe, but there's more. Since the eighteenth century, Old Testament scholars have painstakingly tracked how writing style, narrative continuity, consistency of content, stage in the historical development of Hebrew, and even the names used to refer to God all change together, discrete passage to discrete passage.[88] They have identified five main "voices" in the early books, what scholars call the *Yahwist voice*, the *Elohist voice*, the *Priestly voice*, the *Deuteronomist voice*, and the *Redactors voice*, often abbreviated as simply the J, E, P, D, and R voices. The Yahwist (as in *YHWH*) or J voice ("J" because the German transliteration of *YHWH* begins with a "J") pretty much always calls the divine *YHWH* and clearly represents the concerns of Jerusalem and the Kingdom of Judah. The Elohist or E voice pretty much always calls the divine *Elohim* and represents the concerns of the Kingdom of Israel, which even contains a version of Elohim in its name: *Yisra-el*, meaning "ruled by El." These are the oldest voices, perhaps dating from around 900 to 700 BCE, but based on far older materials.[89] The Priests, the reformers associated with Deuteronomy (which means "second law"), and the Redactors (meaning "editors")—the P, D, and R voices—all come later.[90]

The five voices present compelling evidence of a long-standing effort to bring the two kingdoms of Judah and Israel and their different traditions together, and to keep that solidarity going through the vicissitudes of invasions and deportations, with the constant thunder of divine jealousy as the connecting electricity. Take the opening, six-day account of creation again. Scholars identify it with the Priestly voice.[91] As fits the interests of the priests in a centralized religion, God in this account is abstract and transcendent, and thus hard for adherents to encounter on their own, concretely in their own localities. The second account—the one-day version—is in the J voice.[92] It gives a much more immanent and embodied vision of the divine, walking in the garden and talking directly to Adam and Eve, and seems to be a more popular version of creation that resonated with the experiences of the agrarian majority, less attracted to an abstract and transcendent rendering of the divine. The priests and other editors apparently felt they needed to include the second account to win the allegiance of the masses, although they gave it second billing.

Intriguingly, the name for the divine suddenly changes when the second creation story begins. At Genesis 2.4, God's name shifts from *Elohim*, usually translated into English as "God," to *YHWH Elohim*, usually translated into English as "the Lord God," combining the name preferred by the people of the northern Kingdom of Israel with that of the southern Kingdom of Judah. The second story is otherwise in the J voice, however. What scholars think is that a later editor inserted *Elohim* immediately after every appearance of *YHWH*, creating the construction *YHWH Elohim*.[93] There is no third creation story in the E voice—at least in the versions of the Bible that have come down to us. Nonetheless, this merging of *YHWH* and *Elohim* in the more popular version of the creation story gave everyone, north and south, an immanent god with whom they could identify from their own traditions.

For in order to bind people into a state, it is best to appeal to their values and beliefs, instead of relying only on force—if I may say, instead of relying on thugs like the sons of Levi, as Moses did. If nothing else, it's just plain easier for the powers that be. The Old Testament has to tread a fine moral line to do so. At least initially, most people's lives remained driven by the rhythms of agrarian subsistence. Most still lived by what they grew. Theirs was a nature before nature world for whom an abstract and distant god likely made little intuitive sense. Monotheism in itself does not answer the great questions of agrarian life—Why don't we have any rain? Why are pests eating up our crops? And how can we ensure that neighbors and kin help each other through these troubles? An abstract god likely made both political and personal sense to the priests and other elites living in town. After all, they relied on an expansive sense of the divine to ensure their livelihoods—a territorial expansiveness that resonated with a transcendent god, unconfined to a particular locality—to ensure that people paid their taxes and brought in produce and animals for sacrifices, which the priests, scribes, and other elites later ate and used to build their wealth. The elites are the people who wrote down the biblical texts, after all. They would have wanted what they wrote to reflect their beliefs and needs. But there were very few urban folk like themselves, at least in the early centuries of biblical times. There had to be ways to appeal to the agrarian situation of the vast majority during ceremonies and readings from the book of their traditions.

So make it a unity of four great unities, not just three: one people, one god, one temple, one state. If there is a single god, and that god resides in his special temple in the capital city, built for him by the monarch, then the people must come to the state to worship. Even better from the point of view of the state, if there is only one god anywhere for anyone, then the state is morally free to consider its borders as wherever it thinks it can get away with putting them—a point I will revisit in chapters to come.

The result was a blended divine, a divine with agrarian powers that spoke to the daily concerns of Jews in the countryside but also a divine with a transcendent reach. The Old Testament gives a distinctive twist to these powers, however. In most nature before nature faiths, politics among the gods commonly explains why the rains haven't come and why pests have invaded the crops. A monotheistic, universal god can't have politics with other gods, though, because there aren't any other gods. But he—and I do mean he— can have politics with humans.[94] He can have conflict with his stiff-necked mortal subjects. And the Old Testament god does, frequently, especially over their commitment to him. The same divine explanation for why the Israelites win or lose in war the Old Testament also applies to the sustenance troubles of agrarian life: disloyalty. The three harvest festivals give people a clear way to show that loyalty: by sending the men on a pilgrimage to God's Temple in Jerusalem, his only house, bearing offerings of grain, fruit, and animals.

This is theological brilliance.[95] It gives agrarian people an explanation for their woes, and a way to resolve them, while at the same time centralizing political control—and ensuring that the people of the city get fed.

———

Notably, then, the Old Testament god is not beyond or above politics. He makes little attempt to establish what in the previous chapter I called a "natural conscience"—a sense of the good that is beyond politics and the play of interests. Such a sense of the nonpolitical good would in time come to have many bases, including both the natural and the supernatural. But, as I also noted earlier, in the period of the Old Testament, nature does not yet exist as a concept. The divine does exist, but this is a divine that is still very human and still largely immanent within what we would come to call nature. The ancient triangle is stretching out and taking shape, but has yet to stabilize into distinct points. It is the notion of the goodness of nonpolitical absolutes that eventually would do that. But there is no nonpolitical absolute here. Rather, the Old Testament god is a supremely political god. He has an agenda. He has projects he is struggling to accomplish in a resisting world, for he is not all-powerful and all-knowing. But that struggle is only with humans, not also other gods. And that struggle is mainly over securing human loyalty to him and his statutes. His techniques include shaping the vicissitudes of both war and ecology.

It was definitely a struggle, though. The archaeological evidence for continued Israelite allegiance to a pagan, poly-divine theology makes plain the ideological foot-dragging. The Temple-based, urban religion of the one God with many names—*YHWH, El, Elohim, YHWH Elohim, Adonoi, El Shadai*, and more—was not immediately to everyone's liking.[96] For example, archaeologists have dug up from the homes of ordinary Hebrews over three thousand terracotta statues of the goddess Asherah, the local version of a mother goddess widespread in ancient Middle Eastern cultures.[97] The lack of success is plain in the Old Testament too.[98] Why else would the one God so continually complain that the Hebrews aren't being loyal to him, except that they aren't?

Consider this passage from Second Kings, describing some of the reforms instituted by King Josiah, whom the Bible records as monarch of Judah shortly before the Babylonian invasion:

> The king commanded the high priest Hilkiah, the priests of the second order, and the guardians of the threshold, to bring out of the temple of the Lord all the vessels made for Ba'al, for Asherah, and for all the host of heaven; he burned them outside Jerusalem in the fields of the Kidron, and carried their ashes to Bethel. He deposed the idolatrous priests whom the kings of Judah had ordained to make offerings in the high places at the cities of Judah and around Jerusalem; those also who made offerings to Ba'al, to the sun, the moon, the constellations, and all the host of the heavens. He brought out the image of Asherah from the house of the Lord, outside Jerusalem, to the Wadi Kidron, burned it at the Wadi Kidron, beat it to dust and threw the dust of it upon the graves of the common people.[99]

The strong implication here is that earlier religious leaders—the "kings of Judah"—brought pagan practices right into the Temple itself, likely in an effort to secure the allegiance of the great bulk of Hebrews. The god Ba'al was being worshipped there. The goddess Asherah was being worshipped there. The "sun, the moon, the constellations, and all the host of the heavens" were being worshipped there. (Indeed, a minimalist might suggest that maybe it had even been that way since the Temple was constructed—that the Temple was originally built as a center of poly-divine worship—even though the passage implies that previous kings of Judah had corrupted an originally monotheistic religion.)[100] And throughout much of the Old Testament, we hear other complaints about people's immanent worship of idols and the local sacred spots this passage calls the "high places."

But maybe the tactic of centralizing the pagan poly-divine wasn't working very well. Maybe it allowed for too much fragmentation, too much local control. Or maybe poly-divinity really did seem morally wrong to Josiah, a member of the urban elite, in comparison to ideas derived from Atenism, more monotheistic visions of *YHWH* and *Elohim,* and other sources.[101] So he ground up the image of Asherah, and threw "the dust of it upon the graves of the common people," making plain the association between pagan belief and agrarian non-elites.

This passage also highlights another transformation that the monotheistic centralizers of the Old Testament sought, a point I alluded to earlier: masculinizing the divine. If you are going to have one god, you are faced with three choices on the question of the god's gender. That one god could be male, female, or neither. The priests of the Temple went with the first option. There can be no doubt but that ancient Israelite society was highly patriarchal. Plus the Jewish state was assembled and maintained through warfare, like all states at the time, and I suspect the men trying to establish a new monotheistic centralized religion felt that a masculine god resonated with the aggressive tone they found helpful for sanctioning militarism and male dominance.[102]

Couldn't such an aggressive masculine god have a wife? Or couldn't a female god have a warlike husband? Or, given the sexual variety in pagan traditions, couldn't either a female or a male god have a same-sex or sexually diverse partner as long as one of the partners was combative and bellicose? Couldn't there be a duotheism, based around a divine couple? Apparently, yes. Duotheism seems to have been more than a theological possibility. There is good archaeological evidence, and some strong hints in the Bible itself, that Asherah was God's divine consort for a time during the development of Old Testament religion.[103] But it didn't last. If there is to be single god, and moreover a single god who is male and powerful—a patriarchal god for a patriarchal time—evidently he had best be maritally single too, with no partner who might have her, his, or their own ideas and powers. Thus divine sexuality went by the wayside too, apart from a few curious stories, as monotheism masculinized.

The result of all this? A *pagan monotheism*—a monotheism that continues to speak, in the main, to the ecological and local concerns of an agrarian majority, while also struggling to bind them into a unified state, capable of collecting taxes and supporting a small urban elite, and marshaling an army in times of need and imperial ambition.

———

There was some ideological trouble, though, with such a vision of pagan monotheism. Brilliant it may have been, but not brilliant enough. For a great transition in social life was still under way. This jealous and violent concept of god really doesn't make for good stories for middle-class city children going to bed, or for other folks in need of comfort. It doesn't now, and it didn't then.

The moral questions that people increasingly faced—questions about a different sense of evil, as states and cities expanded and as different concerns about life arose—led them to seek a more comforting and stable divine. Something else was needed, a different form of conscience, if the one god everywhere was to actually have an appeal as wide as his realm.

In the first century CE, a figure arose on the Israelite landscape who seemed to many to provide exactly that needed something else.

The Bourgeois

5

Why Jesus Never Talked about Farming

"MIKE . . . MIKE . . . MIKE! Wake up," said my wife Diane.

"Whaaa . . . I . . . I'm not sleeping. Just thinking with my eyes closed."

"Looked like sleeping to me."

"Well, maybe I sort of was." In fact, I didn't have a thought in my mind. But a mood, yes, definitely a mood—a mood of peace and goodness, as I sat alone in one of the front pews of Notre Dame des Doms, the twelfth-century cathedral that stands beside the Palais des Papes, on the shoulder of the highest hill in Avignon, France, where we'd been living the past two months during a sabbatical. I rubbed my neck. A touch stiff. Maybe I really had nodded off. But it felt like I'd been pulled out of some special zone of consciousness, not sleep exactly. A gentle place between all other states of mind is the best I can describe it.

"Come on. The kids are outside. We've been waiting there for five minutes at least. We thought you'd gone out already."

"Oh, sorry, sorry. Okay. I'm coming now."

I stood up and stretched. My eye fastened momentarily on the small golden cross in front. The Avignon cathedral is rather small, as cathedrals go, so it seemed appropriate that the cross is not a large one. It's rather dark inside, too, but the cross's gold seemed to glow with its own light out of the gloom.

We emerged from the cathedral, blinking, into full sunlight blazing from the blue. Sam and Eleanor were chatting away, soaking each other up like the sunlight, enjoying Sam's visit from the United States, where he continued in graduate school while we were living in Avignon. They were standing beside the huge statue of Jesus's crucifixion that stands just outside the Notre Dame des Doms's front door, dark iron spikes poking through his white marble hands and feet, an iron rendition of the crown of thorns on his marble head.

"Hey, where were you? We looked all over."

"Oh, just sitting inside, thinking. But I guess the thinking turned into a bit of sleep-sitting!"

They laughed, and went back to their conversation, Diane joining in with them now. I was still feeling a bit dazed and retreated into my own thoughts. I looked up at Jesus, hanging here. It's a powerful statue, especially viewed from its base, tracing with your eye the marble's reach into a high sky. I took out my camera and clicked off several pictures, trying to get the best angle. But I couldn't get the whole statue into the frame from where we stood. I tried several different positions and then abandoned the effort. It just wouldn't fit. Plus my neck was getting stiff again, this time from stretching up instead of down.

It's not easy to fit Jesus into any frame. His story is profound, as profound as any. So are its contradictions. So are ours.

————

Dick Thompson was one of the most impressive people that I, and many others, have ever met.[1] Over the years, some ten thousand or so people came to visit him and his family on their cattle and grain farm just outside Boone, Iowa. (At least that's how many signed the farm's visitors books.) They came to see and hear about the remarkable transformation that he and his wife Sharon Thompson undertook on their three hundred acres—a small place by the standards of central Iowa, where one- to two-thousand-acre farms are more the norm for grain production. In 1968, they abandoned the big-chemical, big-iron way of farming that focuses on yields, yields, and yields, with little regard for any other consequence. They adopted and concocted other techniques for ensuring weed control, nutrient availability, and soil that didn't pour off the farm and into the creek—techniques like long crop rotations, cover crops, integrated animal and crop agriculture, and a little-used form of cultivation called ridge tilling.

Though lots of other farmers have since picked up on these ideas and developed them further, few people used them then. Dick and Sharon never held back what they had learned. Rather, they worked with other farmers to do their own comparative research on how to perfect these and many other techniques. At the time, what Dick and Sharon came up with didn't really have a name. Today we call approaches like this "sustainable agriculture," "agroecology," and "organic agriculture." Actually, Dick and Sharon deliberately never certified their farm as organic, believing that a farmer should be able to use chemicals as an occasional tool if things get out of hand. (After 1968, that happened only once on Dick and Sharon's farm.) Plus they felt that they should be able to make a good living on three hundred acres without the price bump that comes from being certified organic—and without farm subsidies, which they refused to accept. And they did make a good living, maintaining a modest, tidy, comfortable home. They liked to call their approach "practical agriculture" and, in 1985, they helped set up an organization of like-minded farmers called Practical Farmers of Iowa (PFI). Dick was the first president. With twenty-five hundred members, PFI is still going strong.

Dick did most of the talking when people came to visit the farm. Sharon was a bit shy. Dick was the public figure. And he would say to anyone who asked—he usually didn't offer this up without a direction question—that it was not him and Sharon who were behind these remarkable changes. It was, they felt, Jesus.

Rates of religiosity are quite high among America's farmers, almost all of whom are Christians. With few exceptions, America's true pagans—that is to say, America's country people—are no longer pagans. But not many have as powerful a story as Dick of what I'll be arguing is a fundamentally urban, bourgeois conception of the divine. In the estimation of believers, that conception centers on a god of the good—a god who provides a difference conscience, a natural conscience, a conscience beyond desire and its conflicts and politics. In the late 1990s, I heard of the impact of this conscience while sitting in Dick and Sharon's machine shed with about another seventy-five people, come to hear the story of their farm's transformation.

Dick had just given us a half-hour overview of their farming techniques, including a few handmade charts and a visit to the ridge-till planter at the far end of the barn, his handheld microphone snaking over there on a long cable. Now we were back in our plastic folding chairs. Q and A time. Someone asked how it was that he and Sharon came to change their farm practices, especially given that all their neighbors were continuing their big, bigger, biggest ways.

"Now this is something that is hard to be explained," Dick said, his voice dropping and his microphone lowering. "I've never done this before at a field day."[2]

We in the crowd exchanged looks. Where was Dick going with this?

"In January of 1968, while chopping stalks in field number six, going north, I was—" Dick's voice trailed off. Then he looked up, raising microphone and voice. "I'd had it. All the work. The pigs were sick. My cattle were sick. I hollered 'help.' That's about the only way I know how to explain this. But some things started to happen."

He paused again. This was hard.

"And a lot of things that happened seem to happen early in the morning. That thoughts come into my mind that I know that are not mine."

Dick later told me about this in more detail, one on one, when I didn't have a recorder with me. One early morning in 1968, out in the pasture, he said he heard one of his cows talking to him, without sound, straight into his mind. He could only understand it as being the voice of the divine. But he didn't mention the soundless voice of the cow to the crowd in the shed. Too much.

"So I want to share this," he continued to the crowd. "The creator wants to put a receiver, a still small voice, way down deep inside each one of us, for communication. It's our choice. It's not forced on us. If you want it, you can have it. If man can send pictures through the air to our TV, in our houses, and if man can send voices through the air from one cell phone to another, it shouldn't be too hard to understand how the maker of mankind can do the same, and much more. A personal communication. No hackers. No one to hone in. There's much that's new about the Internet and the World Wide Web, and all this information. That's good. It can be confusing. But I want you to remember that the Internet is a tool, not the toolbox. It's not the source. Don't let WWW be a substitute for the still, small voice."

Dick and Sharon used to put out a two-hundred-page report about their farm, which they would update every year. They called it *Alternatives in Agriculture*. Right in the first chapter they explained their experience of the still, small voice this way:

> The real change started taking place in 1967, when we began learning about the Holy Spirit. This is when Dick realized that he was caught up with things, building a kingdom with sheds, silos, cement floors and more land. Enough was never enough. We were to the place where we were looking for something better. The livestock were always sick with one disease or another. Sickness was the rule and health was the exception. A word came to us in a supernatural way, through the gifts of the Holy Spirit, the word being that God was going to teach us how to farm.[3]

Caught up in things. Enough was never enough. Sickness, and most fundamentally a sickness of craving more and more. God was going to teach them another way to farm, a way that was unforced, unhacked, and unhooked from the treadmills of desire.

But Jesus, the Good Shepherd, never talked about farming.

————

There seems little reason to doubt that Jesus was a historical figure.[4] We have a couple of independent Roman accounts—the works of the early historians Josephus and Tacitus—from a half century or so after he likely lived. They give just short, offhand mentions, not the panegyrics of advocates (although part of Josephus's discussion was clearly later supplemented by an overeager Christian scribe).[5] Josephus and Tacitus mention Jesus without fanfare, and move on. Maybe they thought Jesus unimportant, at least in those still-early years of the growth of Christianity. Maybe they were worried by Jesus's followers and didn't want to give the movement much credit. (Tacitus's writings make it plain that he was not a fan of Christians.) Nonetheless, they seem to have felt obligated, as historians, to at least note in passing "Jesus, who was called Christ," in the words of Josephus.[6]

Rather more far-fetched evidence are several ossuaries—stone boxes for the bones of the dead, typical of Jewish burials during the first century CE—inscribed with "Jesus son of Joseph," "James, son of Joseph, brother of Jesus," and "Judah son of Jesus." The ossuaries seem real enough, but debate shouts about whether recent forgers chiseled in new inscriptions and whether Jesus could have had a son.[7] Others question whether we can find much significance here even if the inscriptions are as old as the ossuaries, given how common all these names were. Jesus is a variant of Joshua—or, more accurately, Yeshua is a variant of Yehoshua, which is how Jesus and Joshua would have been pronounced at the time. Lots of people back then had these names.

To the sociologist and historian, the authenticity of the ossuaries and the brevity of Josephus and Tacitus hardly matters. We have more solid evidence from the plain fact that accounts of a man named Jesus (or Yeshua) spurred a vast and varied religious literature. At the core of that literature stands the New Testament of the Christian Bible.[8] But we also have many early religious writings about Jesus that didn't make it into the Christian canon. (I'll discuss some of them in the next chapter.) This corpus is filled with inconsistencies and disagreements, to the puzzlement of many a Christian and to the delight of many a Christian detractor.[9] Many of the details seem messy and awkward, like Mary becoming pregnant with Jesus before marrying her husband Joseph.[10] It just doesn't read like a carefully crafted setup job. It reads like somebody named

Jesus, with a real history of circumstance and happenstance, had a big impact on his contemporaries.

But evidently his impact was not due to what he said about farming and the challenges of rural life. At least, those aren't the bits of his life and sayings that anyone at the time took much notice of, or anyone later bothered to write down, if he indeed spoke about them. Take the four books of the Gospels: Matthew, Mark, Luke, and John. Jesus basically never discusses farming, neither its ecological challenges nor its social and economic rhythms. The word "farmer" doesn't even appear in the Gospels.[11]

Jesus does, however, draw extensively on agricultural themes as a source of metaphors—as a source of earthy truths that his audience would readily understand. For example, Jesus often uses the metaphor of shepherd and flock. The word "shepherd" occurs seventeen times in the Gospels, as when Jesus proclaims in John that "I am the good shepherd. The good shepherd lays down his life for the sheep."[12] Also in John, Jesus declares that "I am the true vine, and my Father is the vinegrower."[13] Many of Jesus's parables, like the Parable of the Sower, use agricultural metaphors.[14] The Gospels also sometimes combine agricultural metaphors, as in this passage in Matthew that moves quickly from Jesus as shepherd to the work of the church as harvesting:

> When he saw the crowds, he had compassion for them, because they were harassed and helpless, like sheep without a shepherd. Then he said to his disciples, "The harvest is plentiful, but the laborers are few; therefore ask the Lord of the harvest to send out laborers into his harvest."[15]

These are beautiful lines, but they do not discuss agriculture and sustenance needs themselves. The Gospels proclaim that Jesus has a mission to change things that aren't right. But that mission does not include a reformulation of agriculture and its social and ecological relations. He proposes no new agricultural festivals. He does not lament mistreatment of animals. He offers no explanation for the great agrarian questions of why the rains have not come and pests and diseases have. He does not critique Judeans for insufficient attention to stewardship of the land. He does not comment on the *shmita*, and he does not seem to regard Passover—a central event in his life, for the Last Supper was a Passover feast—as an agricultural holiday. He often quotes the Old Testament, but not the agricultural and ecological passages, and he offers no new grand agricultural and ecological stories, like the Garden of Eden or Noah's flood.

Indeed, Jesus even advises people to abandon farming and follow him instead. "No one who puts a hand to the plow and looks back," Jesus tells a man he meets on the road between villages, "is fit for the kingdom of God."[16] Abandon the fields, Jesus proclaims.[17] Believe in me and you will be fed, for "I am the bread of life. Whoever comes to me will never be hungry, and whoever believes in me will never be thirsty."[18] As he tells his disciples, "do not worry about your life, what you will eat, or about your body, what you will wear. For life is more than food, and the body more than clothing. . . . Instead, strive for [God's] kingdom, and these things will be given to you as well."[19]

Be fed by faith. That would be hard advice for a peasant to swallow, if I may put it that way, at least without a radical and difficult reconfiguration of his or her life.

————

A radical and difficult reconfiguration of life is exactly what Jesus was asking for. Jesus's message was not merely spiritual. It was also social and political. Although widely revered as standing apart from the social and political, Jesus demanded a reordering of human interaction and the institutions that pattern it, proclaiming that spiritual fulfillment was not possible without major change in how people get along. What made such change difficult was exactly the principle source of the troubles: the Roman Empire and the motivations that fueled it.

The scholar trying to understand the context of Christianity must take into account the timing and setting of the appearance of a figure like Jesus.[20] The area the Romans called the Province of Judea was a constant source of turmoil, struggle, and imperial irritation. The Romans had grabbed control of the area in 63 BCE during a civil war between the sons of Queen Salome Alexandra, the last great monarch of the Hasmonean Dynasty. After a millennium-long struggle against the various larger empires washing over it from all sides, the Jews had finally achieved their own state again, ruled by the Hasmoneans— until Rome ended that, as I described in the previous chapter. Nevertheless, the Jews remained fiercely nationalistic, and retained their commitment to their distinctive religious tradition, centered on the Temple, God's house, in Jerusalem.

The Romans first tried ruling the region with a Hasmonean puppet, Hyrcanus II, while giving the real power to a man named Antipater, who had helped the Romans take control of Judea.[21] The politics got messy when Caesar was murdered in 44 BCE. Antipater was murdered the next year, poisoned by one of Hyrcanus's cupbearers. But in the chaotic aftermath, it was actually one of Antipater's sons who wound up on top: Herod, one of history's most ruthless and extravagant monarchs. Herod had managed to sneak away to Rome where he presented himself to the Senate, swearing allegiance to the empire. The Romans knew they had their man and proclaimed him king of the Jews in 40 BCE. And so he was, at least in name, until 4 BCE.[22]

Herod pretty much immediately set about clearing the decks of the remaining Hasmonean nobility, cleverly claiming to align himself with them before finding each individually guilty of some capital offense. Herod also set about on a massive building campaign, fueled by equally massive tax increases. He built a gorgeous new seaside capital, Caesarea Maritima, named to honor his Roman patrons, including a lavish palace. (The remains are now a popular Israeli national park.) He was more than a bit paranoid, though. So he also ordered the building of two remarkable fortresses, in case of need: the Herodium and the plateau-top fortress of Masada. Herod planned the former to double as his mausoleum. He had it erected on a huge artificial hill, making the Herodium to this day the highest point in the Judean desert. It was basically a kind of pyramid topped by a fortress. But what a fortress: inside were a bath complex, banquet halls, courtyards, and a 450-seat theater, all guarded with a massive wall and four security towers, each seven stories high. Masada—later the site of a tragic Roman siege of a party of radical Jews during the Jewish Revolt some seventy-five years after Herod's death—was another staggering feat of ancient engineering. Herod ordered it built on top of a mesa surrounded by cliffs up to thirteen hundred feet high, making it nearly inaccessible. Herod edged the top with a thirteen-foot-high wall, fortified its access paths, and erected barracks, storerooms, administration buildings, cisterns, a bathhouse, and two palaces.

Needless to say, with such self-centered and expensive excesses, Herod was not a widely liked monarch, especially among the common people of Judea. So Herod also set about on a more popular project: a massive expansion of the Temple in Jerusalem, the temple that Jews refer to as the Second Temple, which had been built when Cyrus the Great gave the Jewish elite permission to leave Babylon and return to Judea. By the time Herod got done with it, the Second Temple was virtually an entirely new building, often referred to by historians as the Herodian Temple. It didn't last long, though. The Romans leveled it in 70 CE during the Jewish Revolt, leaving only the huge platform on which it was built, including the supporting wall that Jews today call the Wailing Wall, now widely considered the holiest place in Judaism. The site is also widely revered as the third holiest place in Islam, commemorated by the Dome of the Rock and the Al-Aqsa Mosque, from which Muslims hold that the prophet Muhammad ascended to Heaven one evening to meet with God and the earlier prophets.

In rebuilding the Second Temple, Herod was doing more than wowing the masses with grand architecture. He was also following a basic formula of the day: a strong centralized state needs a strong centralized religion. Not everyone appreciated this formula, though. There was much about such an imagination of governance, as well as such an imagination of the divine, that didn't fit with the dreams and experience of people in their daily lives.

But before we get to that, let me describe another set of tensions that had emerged in those dreams and in that experience.

––––––

Around 700 BCE, or possibly a bit earlier, the Kingdom of Aegina, a small Mediterranean island south of Greece, hit upon an amazing and transformative idea: minted money. Stamped with a turtle, the drachma of Aegina was the first true coin ever produced, as far as we know. Initially the idea spread slowly, turtle-like. Then around 600 BCE, the Lydians produced their own coin, stamped with the head of a lion, and the idea soon roared across the kingdoms and empires of the world.

Earlier, people had mainly traded or paid taxes using commodities.[23] Recall those three annual Old Testament harvest festivals, when a man from every household was expected to head to Jerusalem for celebration and sacrifice— which meant bringing the products of the harvest into that central institution of the state, the central temple. Today, we don't think of harvest festivals like Thanksgiving as an exercise in paying taxes, but that is, in large measure, what they were for agrarian civilizations. The trouble is a chicken or a goat doesn't store very easily. They have to be housed, fed, and bred to last. A bag of wheat does better in a well-maintained granary, but still not longer than a few years, and it can easily spoil if it isn't stored properly. Commodity-based trade and tax collecting made it hard to amass wealth because the riches could easily either die on you or just rot away.

Plus there were troubles with standardizing weights and volumes of commodities, and debating what and how much of any commodity was equivalent to another. You could easily get cheated. People started using stable commodities of known volumes or weights, like a shekel of silver—which was about eleven grams. That was better, but it was hard to know if the shekel being offered to you really was silver, and if it really was eleven grams. The minted coin took away much of the uncertainty by backing up the unit of money with a royal imprint, making it easier for people to treat the metal in the coin as actually being what it purported to be. Not everyone had access to a mint, after all, so it wasn't easy to counterfeit coins by mixing in lower value metals and stamping them with unauthorized images of the king's head or symbol. Plus coins were indeed very convenient, and you could make change, vastly easing commercial transactions. You no longer had to trade things. You could just sell them.

A few centuries earlier than the rise of minted money, the Phoenicians hit on another amazingly transformative idea: the alphabet. Dozens of other societies in the Iron Age soon made their own versions, generally based on the Phoenician model. Now you only had to learn a couple of dozen signs to be able to read and write, instead of thousands of hieroglyphics or hundreds of cuneiform signs. And other societies came up with nonalphabetic writing improvements, such as the Demotic script for writing Egyptian hieroglyphics.[24] Easier reading and writing made for a greater spread in literacy, and thus better record keeping. Combined with the way coins made money more abstract and numeric, rather than a matter of commodity exchange, better record keeping in turn made it far easier to keep track of who owed how much to whom.

We are also, by this point, solidly in the Iron Age, which archaeologists date to about 1200 BCE, immediately after the Bronze Age collapse. People had figured out how to do iron smelting at least a thousand years earlier. But the early iron tools were actually softer than bronze ones. They were cheap to make, but wore out quickly. Eventually, though, smiths figured out that adding a bit of carbon turned iron to steel and made much stronger tools, including lighter weapons that really held an edge. That was the transformative change, not the use of iron itself. (Perhaps the Iron Age really should be termed the Steel Age.) So it became much easier to defend your riches and raid the riches of others.

Together, coins, better writing, and steel tools made it possible to concentrate wealth like never before—and not just for individuals. The state found it much easier to collect taxes, to record who had paid and who hadn't, and to store up the results. It also made it easier to convince people to do the state's bidding, through either enticing them or forcing them. With a stock of coins, the state could more easily pay people to build a new city wall or a new palace for the elites, or to fight in armies to defend those walls and palaces. Plus it takes arms and armor to make an army (armies being made up of those who are armed and armored), and cheaper, stronger, lighter arms and armor made it easier to compel people to do that building and to pay the taxes the state said they owed. And similarly the state could more easily entice and force people to carry out the wide range of tasks necessary to its structure and governance. Consequently, state power and the number of those who worked for it expanded considerably, allowing it to concentrate even more wealth. But not only state wealth. Much of what state power did was protect merchants and their commerce—as remains true today—which in turn built up more wealth for the state to tax.

Cities long predate coins, better writing, and steel tools, of course. But these technologies of inequality and the social formations that accompanied and grew along with them decisively changed urban life, and widened the gulf between the rural and the urban. Aristocrats like Herod were no longer the only ones living lavishly, as had been the case with the early cities of the Bronze Age. In contrast to the Iron Age cities of empires like Rome, archaeological excavations of Bronze Age cities generally show little spatial differentiation and segregation of housing size and type by wealth and class. Instead, the Mesopotamian archaeologists Elizabeth Stone and Paul Zimansky note, "group formation tends to be based on kinship, occupation, ethnicity, or some other non-class basis, with the result that all residential districts contain both elites and commoners" in a Bronze Age city.[25] Similarly, in the early Iron Age cities of Israel—still a dominantly pagan and agrarian context—"differences of social class were not particularly marked by the architecture," notes the biblical archaeologist Volkmar Fritz.[26]

Of course, there was indeed inequality in these early cities. But rather than a pyramid of wealth distribution, such as is familiar to class society, it was more of a flagpole. The number of the elite was proportionately much smaller, and their spatial distribution was either largely confined to the temple and palace districts or distributed relatively evenly through the residential areas.

Yet in Iron Age cities, many more citizens found they too could gather together fortunes, "restlessly, endlessly," as Horace put it in 20 BCE.[27] The middle classes expanded rapidly as well, through employment with the state and through trade. The archaeological record of Roman cities shows the change, with a wide variety of size and grandeur of housing types becoming the norm, from villas for the second assistant tax collector and the merchant whose ship had just come in to simpler houses for shopkeepers, potters, knife sharpeners, brewers, weavers, soldiers, masons, and more. As well, cities began to spatially divide into different districts for the rich, the poor, and the in-between.

Not only could you now more easily amass wealth, you could also lose it like never before. Instead of a group having to mount a raiding party to make off with your cattle or your grain stores, someone could just rob your wallet full of coins, at steel dagger point. Or someone could swindle away your money with some complex scheme you signed your name to on a piece of papyrus. It was a lot easier to make a large and foolish economic choice, get yourself in debt, and be stuck paying back loans at interest that you couldn't afford, perhaps even requiring you to sell your land or even to sell yourself or a family member into slavery.[28]

Difference was rising along another axis too. Before the rise of social class, ancient agrarian civilizations saw little distinction in culture or kinship between rural and urban people. Pretty much everyone was at least a part-time farmer, whether or not their home lay in relative security within city walls. Cities were agrarian too. That is, they were mainly populated by farmers, albeit ones who likely had an economic sideline associated with urban life, such as a trade like pottery-making or leather goods. As the art historian Lothar von Falkenhausen notes concerning ancient Chinese agrarian cities, "there is no indication that they stood culturally apart from the surrounding rural areas, which were populated, as far as we know, by members of the same group that inhabited the urban sites."[29]

Indeed, it seems that many ancient civilizations did not even have a comparable word for the modern notion of a city as a place of high population density. The Yoruba of West Africa defined city—the *ilú*—by the location of the ruler's palace.[30] Similarly, rather than a "city" in the modern sense, the Maya spoke of the *cacab*, meaning the area controlled by the ruler, including any densely populated districts as well as the countryside.[31] For the most part, farming was the main employment of the population of both rural and urban areas. So ancient agrarian peoples saw little need to remark on what would later become not only a spatial category but also a social and economic category: whether or not one lived in a city.

But that homogeneity was changing. Through the workings of these three transformative ideas (coins, better writing, and steel) along these two axes of difference (richer and poorer within the city, and the general wealth of the city versus the general poverty of the countryside), the Iron Age cities of Rome and other empires of the time manifested a dramatic rise in social inequality. Cities were no longer agrarian, no longer population centers of farmers plus a few aristocrats and priests. They were becoming too big for that, and too differentiated for that. Cities were becoming bourgeois, the nexus points of both vertical and horizontal economic inequality.

It took a while for these gaps to develop. We start to see them in ancient Greek society, as chapter 3 describes. With Roman culture, though, bourgeois life expanded mightily, and social and economic gaps with them. People could see the wider gaps plainly, and it caused moral tensions for everyone. For the urban and rural poor, the question that probably occurred to pretty much everyone was this: Why should I give up the product of my hard work to support their villas, parties, and wars—except that I don't have much choice? For those on the upside of bourgeois life, the moral issue was no less intense: What right do I have to be better off than all those complaining about my richer status?

After all the gilding was scraped away, it was increasingly hard to escape the same dirty answer: politics.

————

"Descendez, s'il vous plaît, monsieur."

Monsieur? Did she mean me? I was standing on a partially reconstructed wall at Glanum, a vast Roman archaeological site just south of Saint-Rémy-de-Provence, where Van Gogh had lived for a time in a sanatorium, and where he had painted some of his best-known paintings, including *Starry Night*. Glanum nestles at the base of the Alpilles Massif, and at one time was a small fortified city, famous for its sacred well. We had traveled down for the day from Avignon during my sabbatical there. At that moment, my daughter Eleanor lay down below, sprawled out in a glorious bed of wildflowers that had grown up in the ruins of one of the rooms of Glanum's Roman bathhouse. The sun was shining, and so was everything else. Eleanor looked fit for a magazine cover, and I was trying to get a photo.

"C'est interdit," the guard at the archaeological park continued. She looked me over. American, clearly. "It's forbidden," she repeated in English.

"Okay. Sorry. I'm done anyway." I don't have much French. "Excusez-moi," I tried with a smile. The guard frowned back, but walked away after I jumped down. It was then I noticed the small sign in both French and English saying that you weren't supposed to climb on the walls. Fair enough.

Glanum is definitely worth a visit, if one is ever in the area. The setting is spectacular, as are the ruins. Just outside of the town's front gate a two-thousand-year-old triumphal arch still stands, as does a mausoleum that is even older and must be over fifty feet high. Both are in remarkably good shape. Proceed into the ancient town and, after passing the site's museum and ticket office, a huge expanse of excavated area opens up, mainly along the main street where the shops would have been, with villas immediately behind on both sides. If you keep going up the main street, you'll come to a bathhouse, the market place, the sacred well, the forum, and the famous "twin temples," a few Corinthian columns of which yet remain. It's a vast site.

But what really caught my eye at Glanum is the spatial layout of the residences for the townsfolk. In the center, safely within the walls, are the villas, each built as a two-story square of buildings surrounding a courtyard, or in some cases two adjoining squares with two courtyards. Only the bases of the walls remain, but there is clear evidence that the villas had running water, with several ruined fountains and drain openings in the courtyards. An upper-middle-class person today would have found any one of these villas spacious and comfortable.[32]

Keep going up the main street, though, out through the back gate in the southern rampart, the more humble entrance to Glanum. There, just outside the city wall, are the ruins of a small sacred spring (not to be confused with the sacred well inside the walls) and a couple of tiny temples, cheek by jowl on the left-hand side. And even more cheek by jowl on the right are the ruins of a series of tiny houses built into the side of the hill, with little twisting passageways and stairways to get to one or the other. No courtyards here. No fountains. No drains.

If you could, it would be instructive to proceed farther down the old main street through what used to be the second southern gate, out into the countryside. But you'll just have to look at the lovely miniature reconstruction of the full landscape setting of Glanum in the site's museum, or to look at the excellent relief map of the site, which includes little drawings of all the buildings. There are no nearby ruins of rural Roman homes to visit—but not because there weren't any. Rather, Roman rural houses were mostly scattered small huts and shacks, although some of the wealthy maintained sumptuous villas and estates in the countryside, like that of Horace.[33] Archaeologists can find evidence of these huts and shacks, but their traces are now mainly reduced to a few stones and discolorations in the soil. They aren't the kind of thing most people would pay €9.50 a ticket to see.[34]

All evidence of that widespread characteristic of Roman society: the bourgeois life of social class and rural-urban differences.

———

What did the rise of bourgeois life in the empires of the Iron Age mean for religion in the Middle East? Although some people benefited from the rise in social inequality, many did not. That's what we mean by a rise in social inequality, after all: gains are not evenly distributed. The new social order that went with the new economy and the politics behind it clearly troubled a Jewish man who was probably born in 4 BCE, the same year that Herod died: Jesus of Nazareth.[35] (The monk who established the starting point of the Common Era, thinking it to be the birth year of Jesus, made a calculation error.)

The politics remained pretty intense after Herod's death. But eventually things settled a bit through the institution of the Tetrarchy: a division of Herod's kingdom into three parts (despite the four implied by the prefix *tetra-*), one for each of his sons, all of them confusingly also named Herod. The biggest chunk went to Herod Archelaus, who got Judea, Samaria, and Idumea. Herod Antipas got Galilee and a stretch of land just north of the Dead Sea called Perea, which was actually not contiguous with Galilee. The third brother, Herod Phillip, got the land in between Galilee and Perea—the Golan Heights and the area behind it to the northeast.

Rome wasn't too happy with the job Herod Archelaus did, though. After a few years, they removed him and reorganized his area as a Roman province, meaning it would be run by a governor sent from Rome, not a local king. The Romans called it the Province of Judea, even though it also included Samaria and Idumea.[36]

Thus Jesus, although a Jew, was not actually raised in Judea, the ancient heartland of the Jewish people. He was supposedly born there, in the Judean town of Bethlehem—or so some of the Gospels recount. But he was not raised there. His parents had been living in Nazareth, a midsized town in Galilee, but they traveled to Bethlehem for his birth, later returning to Nazareth.[37] Because of the Tetrarchy, Galilee at that time was part of a separate, although largely Jewish, kingdom. Rome was a mighty influence on the government of Galilee, and Herod Antipas had to rule with Rome very much in mind, but Rome did not govern the area directly.

Consequently, Galilee enjoyed a measure of political remove from Rome. Plus Galilee is a rough and rocky area, with many mountains. Its rugged topography gave it some additional physical separation from Judea, and thus from Rome as well—which made Galilee an apt place to try to organize a Jewish resistance movement against the Roman Empire and the ways of life the empire encouraged.[38] Since the local people were mainly Jews, they were no doubt plenty upset that the Romans had politically separated them from the Temple back in Judea's capital, Jerusalem, the focal point of their sense of faith and nation. And yet they were nicely sheltered by geography and political lines from the great eye and hand of Rome.

Was Jesus, then, the leader of a Jewish nationalist movement, bent on recovering the Jewish state and shaking off Roman control? It seems pretty plain that, however Jesus understood his message, many of his followers and detractors saw him that way: a Jewish leader of a Jewish movement in a time of Jewish oppression. "Where is the child who has been born king of the Jews?" ask the three wise men from the east at his birth.[39] Yes, that phrase could be understood as meaning the theological king of the Jews, and not the political king of the Jews. Okay, sure. But more likely, that potential second reading was something of a cover for the nationalist dimension of what historians sometimes term the "Jesus movement."[40] (Historians call it that because Christianity did not then exist, and all of Jesus's contemporary followers were Jews, just as Jesus was a Jew.) At least the writers of the Gospels seem very intent on not giving a definitive answer to the question of whether Jesus is king of the Jews, whether understood politically or theologically. Matthew, Mark, and Luke all report Jesus himself as refusing to answer one way or the other.[41]

Yet the Gospels are also quite intent on establishing that Jesus was descended from the house of David, the traditional line of the Jewish monarchy.[42] Routinely, the Gospels report local people calling Jesus the "Son of David." As well, the Old Testament reports King David as coming from Bethlehem, and predicts that the Messiah—the Jewish king who is supposed to usher in an age of world peace and harmony at the end of time—will also come from Bethlehem. It is a central tenet of Christianity, of course, that Jesus is the Messiah, fulfilling this passage from Micah:

> But you, O Bethlehem of Ephrathah,
> who are one of the little clans of Judah,
> from you shall come forth for me
> one who is to rule in Israel,
> whose origin is from of old, from ancient days . . .
> he shall be great
> to the ends of the earth;
> and he shall be the one of peace.[43]

Many have speculated that this is why Matthew and Luke report Jesus as being born in Bethlehem, based on what skeptics even in New Testament times found to be an awkward and inconsistent story.[44] Skeptics also like to point to another awkwardness. Jesus's claim to descent from David is via his father "Joseph, of the house of David," as Luke describes him.[45] But the Gospels famously describe Jesus's father as actually being God, not Joseph. Direct descent from God would appear to preclude direct descent from David. Of course, his descent from David could be via his mother Mary. But Mary is never described in the Gospels as being of the house of David—only Joseph.

Whatever the actual history, this much is sure: the Gospels clearly want to make the case for Jesus's descent from the Jewish royal house, thus amplifying the image of him as a rightful national leader.

Plus the whole arc of Jesus's life reads as a steadily building confrontation with Rome, from the swelling crowds that follow him in small Galilean towns and villages to his eventual crossing into Judea and entrance into Jerusalem, with all the tragic events that took place there, leading up to his crucifixion. As the sociologist Reza Aslan notes in his much discussed book about Jesus, the Romans used to reserve the punishment of crucifixion for political crimes.[46] Again, however Jesus saw himself, it is clear that a good many others understood him as a nationalist figure.

————

But it was not only the nationalist implications of his teachings that attracted so many followers. It was also how Jesus articulated what the moral problems were with the current Roman social order.

> Do not store up for yourselves treasures on earth, where moth and rust consume and where thieves break in and steal; but store up for yourselves treasures in heaven, where neither moth nor rust consumes and where thieves do not break in and steal.[47]

> No one can serve two masters; for a slave will either hate the one and love the other, or be devoted to the one and despise the other. You cannot serve God and wealth.[48]

> If you wish to be perfect, go, sell your possessions, and give the money to the poor, and you will have treasure in heaven; then come, follow me.[49]

> . . . [I]t is easier for a camel to go through the eye of a needle than for someone who is rich to enter the kingdom of God.[50]

These quotes are all from the Gospel of Matthew, and the first two are from the famous Sermon on the Mount, one of history's most vigorous complaints about the troubles of economic inequality. These are hard-hitting lines. You can't take it with you. Sell all your possessions. Besides, it's basically impossible for a rich person to be part of God's kingdom. All three of the first Gospels— Matthew, Mark, and Luke, what are often called the "synoptic Gospels"

because of their similarities—are quite critical of economic inequality, especially Matthew and Luke. The camel and eye of the needle line shows up in
all three of them.[51] All three similarly report Jesus advising people to sell all
they own and give it to the poor.[52] The Gospel of John doesn't bother much
with direct critique of inequality, but is very keen to emphasize Jesus's own
humble background. "How does this man have such learning, when he has
never been taught?" John reports Jews as wondering about Jesus, implying
that he was not even literate. John also describes Jesus as entering Jerusalem
on a young donkey, as opposed to a horse, and as washing others' feet—a deep
statement of humility in the culture of that time, usually associated with the
lowest of the low.[53]

Doubt about the morality of wealth and inequality has ever since been
a central theme of Christianity. Here is the well-spring of monastic vows of
poverty and other forms of Christian asceticism. Here is the touchstone of
St. Augustine's concern about the "lust for domination" and the problem of desire.[54] The Gospels also report Jesus as having a fair bit to say about desire in
the sexual sense. He strongly inveighs several times against adultery, and he is
plainly against divorce. But his greater concern—at least in terms of number of
times and ways he speaks about it—is the problem of desire for material gain.

This is a different kind of teaching for sure, a different kind of teaching for a
different time. The early books of the Hebrew Bible show almost no concern
about wealth accumulation. That concern does make increasing appearance
in some of the later books, in tune with the steady rise of class differences and
urban and rural differences as cities grew in size and wealth. But it doesn't hit
with anything like the force of Jesus's sharp words on the subject—words that
evidently resonated strongly with his audience of Jews suffering under the lash
of the Roman Empire. A new vision of evil was plainly growing in people's
minds, waiting to be articulated by a powerful voice. Disloyalty—horizontal
evil, the problem of maintaining the integrity of the group—was still a great
concern, and I'll have more to say about that in a moment. Desire—vertical
evil, the problem of maintaining the integrity of each self—was now equally
plain as a great issue for human society, and perhaps even the greater one.

Jesus, or the writers of the Gospels, evidently had noticed that the Ten
Commandments don't exactly put it that way. The ten Mosaic laws foremost
stress loyalty to the god of the group and the group of the god, and put the five
more desire-oriented commandments further down the list, as I discussed in
chapter 4. But the Gospels recount Jesus as completely skipping the first four

when asked about the commandments—the four that are most strongly about loyalty to the group and the group's god. Here's the relevant passage in Mark.[55]

> As he was setting out on a journey, a man ran up and knelt before him, and asked him, "Good Teacher, what must I do to inherit eternal life?" Jesus said to him, "Why do you call me good? No one is good but God alone. You know the commandments: 'You shall not murder; You shall not commit adultery; You shall not steal; You shall not bear false witness; You shall not defraud; Honor your father and mother.' "

If order indicates priority, the injunction against murder is now the top commandment (as my daughter thought it should be). Jesus does retain one of the loyalty commandments, number five, about honoring one's father and mother, listed last here. And he also adds a sixth commandment, placed in the fifth position, about not defrauding—another statement of the vertical problem of desire. Jesus drops entirely the injunctions about no other god before me, no idols, no taking the Lord's name in vain, and remembering the Sabbath day. He doesn't specifically reject them. He just passes over them.

The Gospels of Luke and Matthew contain similar passages that list just five or six commandments, focused on issues of desire.[56] And in Matthew the parallel passage makes a striking addition at the end of the list: that "also, You shall love your neighbor as yourself." Here is a version of the famous "golden rule," a powerful statement about controlling one's hierarchical desires. A little later on in Matthew, Jesus gets it down to just two commandments.[57]

> " 'You shall love the Lord your God with all your heart, and with all your soul, and with all your mind.' This is the greatest and first commandment. And a second is like it: 'You shall love your neighbor as yourself.' On these two commandments hang all the law and the prophets."

Here we find a repeat of the anti-desire, anti-hierarchy golden rule about loving one's neighbor as oneself. But now Jesus gives primary footing to loving "your God," a mighty command for loyalty to the God to whom you belong.

Is concern for loyalty, then, actually number one for Jesus? Perhaps. Yet overall Jesus gives a lot more attention to the problem of desire than did the Hebrew Bible. A case could be made that he is actually giving equal priority to addressing both disloyalty and desire. The "second is like" the first, he says, and maybe the message here is that each of the two commandments supports the other. Anti-desire prevents discord of one person against another, helping prevent the group from splitting apart. And mutual loyalty to the group gives a person confidence that one's fair treatment of another will be returned in kind. It's an interactive matter. If you treat someone well, there is a better chance they will be loyal to you—and vice versa.

Whether or not Jesus and the Gospels intended this message, on the whole such an interactive materiality is a pretty decent way to lead your life.[58]

————

It's also a pretty good recipe for running a powerful social movement. Jesus is rather top-down about it, though—even authoritarian. He demands loyalty, telling his followers to "make disciples of all nations" and to teach them "to obey everything that I have commanded you."[59] And Jesus can be rather threatening about disloyalty, too, saying, "Whoever believes in the Son has eternal life; whoever disobeys the Son will not see life, but must endure God's wrath."[60] But alongside this obey theme is a theme of abundance for his followers—"fed by faith," as I put it earlier—appealing to people's material needs. Take the miracles of the loaves and fishes. First, he feeds five thousand people with just five loaves and two fishes, breaking them into small pieces and having his disciplines distribute them to the crowd.[61] Then shortly afterward he does it again, almost as efficiently, this time feeding four thousand people with seven loaves "and a few small fish."[62] This is therefore clearly someone worth following, the Gospels suggest, even to very radical ends.

Yet at the same time that the Jesus movement had radical ambitions, it also had conservative concerns. I've already described the concerns about the justice of class hierarchy. But class isn't only a matter of how wealthy you are. It's also a matter of what social ties you have, and what social ties you can safely reject. Class is as much about the kind of claims of obligation you can make on others, and the ability to ignore some claims of obligation others might request or expect of you. Think of the resumes and letters of reference of today. Credentials and a good word from a teacher mattered a lot in early class societies too, and represented claims made and—for those who didn't get the position—claims denied. In pagan, kinship-based society, claims of obligation flow along lines of kin and clan, not credentials and references. Your kin lines are your bank account in times of trouble, just as you are part of the bank account of help for others of your kin when they in turn have need. So kin can be a mighty help. But also a mighty hindrance. Family obligation has long been two-edged. When you don't have much else to rely on, though, you go with it, despite the second edge.

Increasingly, some people found they did not have to rely on family ties, or at least not so much. Class-based ties have long been in tension with kin-based ties, as they remain today, even in settings where nuclear family structures dominate. For people in the countryside, where the Jesus movement began, that tension no doubt rankled those who found their expectations of mutual aid disrupted by class's increasing power—perhaps even expectations for aid from close family members who had found a way to start climbing the ladder of class, in place of carrying assistance back and forth along the footbridge of kinship. Class disrupts kinship. That's part of its point.

There's something else that powerfully disrupts our lines of obligation and expectation: sex. It has long been the case that we experience sexual union as more than a pleasure of intimate communion with another—or find ourselves constrained to experience it as more than that. For there is commonly much resistance to the redrawing of social ties and boundaries that intimate pleasures so often imply. Does it have to be that way? Maybe not.[63] But sex's compulsions have long proved a fruitful way to get others to accept constraints, applying the simple maxim that disallowing some sex allows other sex. Here's how you can have sex, we say in effect: by honoring a particular set of social obligations. And don't tangle the whole complicated web by crossing the lines. Don't commit adultery. Don't violate the calculations of financial exchange and mutual obligation that others have made through arranging your marital match. Don't mess up the deal. Honor your father and your mother, and all they represent concerning your and their kin and livelihood. And therefore expect that any children—a common outcome of sex, after all—will do the same for you.[64]

Of course, people have long routinely ignored sexual injunctions and what they mean for our social abilities and disabilities. Sometimes they have done so for love. Sometimes they have done so for lust. Sometimes they have done so because they saw some social or financial gain in the scrambling of the lines of obligation and expectation—always a delicate matter, and one that oft goes awry. And perhaps most usually, all three motives have often been at work in some combination or another. However, the point is, like class, sex has enormous disruptive power for social life, sometimes creative and sometimes destructive, largely depending on where you stand and therefore on your point of view and nexus of needs. Sex too is a political act.

The disruptions presented by sex and class interwove in ancient times, as they continue to do today. By challenging kinship and its lines of obligation and expectation, the rise of social class revolutionized sex and its intimate politics. Sex, after all, is central to kinship. By revolutionizing sex, bourgeois life gave kin-based society a second political challenge, equal to, and compounded with, the challenge represented by social class.

Rural, agrarian life too has its potential for disrupting the expected lines of sexual obligation and pleasure. But sexual disruption in rural life is harder to disguise. Although one can easily overstate the matter, in rural life fewer people constitute the significance of one's days, and those fewer typically know each other better—in part because they watch each more, having fewer to watch at all. This doesn't necessarily mean that community life is stronger in a village, as legions of rural sociologists have documented.[65] It may mean just the reverse. Visibility can give occasion for as much suspicion as confidence, divisiveness as unity. But it is a plain fact of life in the Roman Empire that the brothels and bars were mostly in town. So were the marketplaces and shops and workshops. So were the service businesses like laundries, tailors, barbers, and doctors. So were the temples and government offices. So were the baths. So were most of the places where partners could meet and discretely arrange the love, lust, and gain of sex, outside the confines of kinship and the sexual bargains it imposed.

Moreover, class society and the bourgeois sexual revolution promoted each other. By challenging kin ties, what we might term *bourgeois sex* gave greater weight to one's class power. And by promoting urban society and urban form, class gave longer leash to sex's disruptive potentials.

Plus more than that: by stimulating the mobility of people and capital through trade and coinage, and by accentuating inequality, class society encouraged and facilitated the commodification of sex. Ancient pagan life knew of sex as a commodity, but to nothing like the same extent as the class life of ancient bourgeois cities. Take Pompeii, a city of some ten to twelve thousand souls, the Roman city we know best because of its spectacular misfortune to be suddenly buried by a volcanic eruption. It had forty-one brothels, according to one detailed study, mostly staffed by slaves selling sex for as low as one Roman *as*, or about a dollar or two in today's money, as well as more expensive sexual services for the elite.[66] If we assume that about four thousand of that population were sexually mature men (recalling that a large proportion of the inhabitants would have been children, and roughly half would have been female), that's about one brothel and perhaps ten prostitutes for every hundred or so adult male residents.[67] Of course, many of the clients were visitors from the countryside—but that was exactly part of the concern that many had about the city, and still do: the city as reputedly the principal site of sin, vice, and ethical corruption.

As well, many wealthy people imposed sex on their family slaves. Not all bourgeois sex was sex as property, but much of it was, then as now. Bourgeois sex had its freedoms and its lack of freedoms. It had disruptive potential but also oppressive potential.

In the face of these ambivalences, Jesus and his movement tried to reckon with the two basic imaginations of evil, disloyalty and desire, finding them connected. For both material and sexual desire lead easily to disloyalty, and thereby to new loyalties, loyalties that often prove stronger. In a time of weakening kin ties, concern nettled about all potential sources of that weakness, especially among those who found themselves disadvantaged by the changes.

In the chapters to come, we will see the same increased concern about material and sexual desire associated with the rise of other religious movements that react to the coming of bourgeois society.

———

Recognizing the troubles facing kin obligations as class society developed allows us to see a special attraction in the way Jesus described and organized the movement he was trying to incite. Throughout the Gospels, and continuing on with the letters of Paul and others, we see a constant exhortation to recognize a new form of kinship: a *quasi-kinship* of faith, connecting the divine and the human into a community of the good—into what the New Testament calls "a holy nation, God's own people."[68]

We can see the rise of quasi-kinship in the changing names for the divine in the Bible. In the New Testament, God is no longer *YHWH*. He is no longer *El, Elyon, Elohim, YHWH Elohim, El Shaddai,* or *Adonoi*—the Most High, the Master, the Lord God, or the Lord God Almighty. He is *Kyrios,* Greek for "Lord" or "Master," a term the New Testament also often uses for Jesus. Or he is *Theos,* the Greek word for God, and another variant on the PIE people's term for the head god, Dyeus—the word that was also the basis for Zeus and Jupiter. These new names largely keep company with the older forms, albeit in Greek tones, reflecting the respect for Greek culture throughout the Roman Empire. But now God is also often *Pateras,* Greek for father, yet given in the New Testament as a title: a divine Father. God had been occasionally described as a father in the Hebrew Bible, but only as a metaphor, not father as a title. Romans came closer to using father as a title in the name Jupiter, which, as I mentioned in chapter 2, is a contraction of Dyeus and *pater,* meaning father god. And maybe there was a little Roman influence going on here. More likely, though, most adherents of Roman religion did not recognize the etymological roots of the name Jupiter. Romans did not place anything like as much emphasis on divine fatherhood that the Jesus movement did, and as Christianity has since done.

Plus there is not only the divine Father in the New Testament. Now there is also the divine Son. Jesus is everywhere described as the Son. He is the Son of God, of course, but also the Son of Man and the Son of David. And Jesus constantly speaks of carrying out the will of his Father. The image of Jesus as Son is central to the New Testament.

The New Testament doesn't carry this divine kinship through to Jesus's mother Mary, however. Christians today often speak of the "Holy Family" of Jesus, Joseph, and Mary, continuing the family language of divine kinship. But "Holy Family" is not a phrase from the New Testament. (Nor is the phrase "Virgin Mary," for that matter, although Mary is described as being a virgin at Jesus's birth.) Mary is now venerated as a saint, as is Joseph. But she is not herself divine. The New Testament is plain on that, and she gets left out of what Christians eventually (for it too is not a term used in the New Testament) came to call the Trinity, the idea that the divine manifests as three consubstantial persons: the Father, the Son, and the Holy Spirit.

Many have felt some sexism at work here, as the Trinity does not represent the basic triad of kinship: Father-Mother-Child. That's as may be. But because she is not divine—or not fully divine, perhaps a semidivinity—Jesus is able to use Mary to develop the human side of Christian quasi-kinship.

For example, Jesus often exhorts his followers to think of themselves as brothers and sisters, and to abandon their birth families. His followers are to think of each other as their true kin, not the families they were born into. In Matthew, Jesus even says that he no longer recognizes his own mother and brothers as kin.

> While he was still speaking to the crowds, his mother and his brothers were standing outside, wanting to speak to him. Someone told him, "Look, your mother and your brothers are standing outside, wanting to speak to you." But to the one who had told him this, Jesus replied, "Who is my mother, and who are my brothers?" And pointing to his disciples, he said, "Here are my mother and my brothers! For whoever does the will of my Father in heaven is my brother and sister and mother."[69]

Such hard treatment of his birth family would be difficult to sustain if Mary were divine, at least divine at the level of God, the Son, and the Holy Spirit. Plus, because Mary is human, Jesus is human while still being fully divine. And as a human, Jesus can welcome other humans as quasi-kin, despite his status as a divinity. In this way, the quasi-kinship of faith links the divine to the human, sanctified by the former and put into practice by the latter.

Such hard treatment of one's birth family must also have been difficult for Jesus's followers to sustain. Giving up on their families also meant giving up on that bank account of kinship—as well as the pleasures of fellowship that family can provide. But Jesus promises great rewards for joining this new quasi-kinship, not just material sustenance but the transcendent hope of life everlasting. As he says, "everyone who has left houses or brothers or sisters or father or mother or children or fields, for my name's sake, will receive a hundredfold, and will inherit eternal life."[70]

For the pagan, blood ties are the main source of transcendence, granting a sense of progeny continuing on afterward in the undying body of descendants. For most of us today, the blood ties of kin can still grant a feeling of transcendence (and perhaps to at least that extent, we yet retain some pagan sensibilities—a point I will expand on in later chapters). Paganism's ancestor veneration gives a divine spark to this everlasting remembrance of blood. Jesus's divine quasi-kinship provides this spark as well, amplified through the communion ritual of bread and wine he introduces at the Last Supper, here described in the Gospel of John.

> So Jesus said to them, "Very truly, I tell you, unless you eat the flesh of the Son of Man and drink his blood, you have no life in you. Those who eat my flesh and drink my blood have eternal life, and I will raise them up on the last day; for my flesh is true food and my blood is true drink. Those who eat my flesh and drink my blood abide in me, and I in them. Just as the living Father sent me, and I live because of the Father, so whoever eats me will live because of me."[71]

The quasi-kinship of faith was a welcome service for a disoriented people in a troubled time, giving them a new basis for transcendent social ties when those they thought they could expect were fraying. For part of the Roman game plan for subjugation was to give people a different basis for social relations than that of their local kin. Rome generally hired local people to staff the government apparatus of its various provinces, and welcomed efforts to expand local market activity and to export goods throughout the empire. Getting people hooked on class meant getting them hooked on Rome. The quasi-kinship of the Jesus movement gave people a way to reengage with one another, but not along the lines of Roman class and not along the lines of kin that Roman society had already frayed for many.

Plus it helped build the Jesus movement. Whether or not Jesus himself was actually trying to revive the Jewish nation, he certainly used the Jewish confrontation with Roman society and the Roman state to provide edge and impetus to assembling his collectivity. As Jesus is reported saying in John, in one of the most controversial passages in the New Testament,

> Do you think that I have come to bring peace to the earth? No, I tell you, but rather division! From now on five in one household will be divided, three against two and two against three; they will be divided:
>
> > father against son
> > and son against father,
> > mother against daughter
> > and daughter against mother,
> > mother-in-law against her daughter-in-law
> > and daughter-in-law against mother-in-law.[72]

Even more controversial is the parallel passage in Matthew:

> Do not think that I have come to bring peace to the earth; I have not come to bring peace, but a sword.[73]

For all his universalism—"My house shall be called a house of prayer for all the nations"—Jesus also starkly sets out the deep question of any profession of community: that of the boundary.[74] Where it lies. How firm it is. And what you do with it.

————

Yet despite all the evident political implications of what Jesus asks of his followers—even to the point of rejecting peace and taking up arms against one's own kin, kin who may have been enchanted by the seductions of class and Roman life—the Gospels are at pains to present Jesus as nonpolitical. And because he is nonpolitical, he is good. He is a natural other, a basis for a natural conscience.

Or perhaps we could say he is a supernatural other, a basis for a supernatural conscience. But let's not have too many terms. The world has an abundance already. Plus, I think having the same terminology for describing the moral transformation of what we have come to call nature (as I have earlier described) and for the moral transformation of faith helps us see their historical and social parallels. So I will call Jesus's nonpolitical standing a basis for a natural conscience—even though, as we've seen, he had very little to say about ecology and agronomy. There are more bases for a natural conscience than nature.

The Gospels establish Jesus's nonpolitical character in several ways. One is through externalization of motive. Jesus doesn't act on his own ambitions, say the Gospels. He acts on those of God the Father in heaven. "My teaching is not mine but his who sent me," says Jesus.[75] What is key about God the Father, the one who sent Jesus, is that he is not human, and therefore has no stake in human politics. So when Jesus acts or judges something, he does so unaffected and uninfluenced by human machinations and intrigues. As John reports Jesus saying,

> I can do nothing on my own. As I hear, I judge; and my judgment is just, because I seek to do not my own will but the will of him who sent me.[76]

As a result, both God the Father and Jesus are impartial. Mark reports (and there is a similar passage in Matthew) that some Israelites admired Jesus because "we know that you are sincere, and show deference to no one; for you do not regard people with partiality, but teach the way of God in accordance with truth."[77] Paul similarly states that "God shows no partiality" and "judges all people impartially according to their deeds."[78] God and Jesus are politically neutral and therefore represent the truth.

Plus the New Testament is clearly trying to argue that God the Father is the only god there is. It is maybe not always 100 percent effective at making this case, but that's definitely where the New Testament is headed. Take the phrase "You shall love the Lord your God with all your heart." The implication of "the Lord your God" perhaps could be taken to mean that others have their own gods, an echo of the monolatry we sometimes see in the Hebrew Bible. Similarly, the Gospels sometimes portrays Jesus as speaking on behalf of the condition of Jews, implying that *Pateras* is the god for the Jews. But overall—and this is a point that the letters of Paul and much later Christian exegesis make a huge effort to establish—the New Testament presents *Pateras* as the only god there is anywhere for anyone. God the Father doesn't have to argue or compete with other gods because there aren't any. He has no divine politics.

Here the New Testament is very much in keeping with the Old Testament. *YHWH* in the Hebrew Bible also doesn't have divine politics—as I discuss in chapter 4, he does not have politics with other gods because the Old Testament also contends that there are no other gods. *YHWH* is plenty political, but his conflicts are with "stiff-necked" humans. What is distinctive in the New Testament about God the Father is that he doesn't have politics with humans either. You can't influence *Pateras*. You can't argue with him, like Moses does with *YHWH*. And *Pateras* is ordinarily so transcendent and abstract you can't even interact with him, at least not directly. He has no house. He doesn't have a garden. He doesn't walk around. He doesn't pervade a pillar of smoke or a pillar of fire. You don't see him on the Earth, although occasionally you do hear his rumblings from on high. And when he gets involved in something as intimate as sexual reproduction, he appears as the Holy Spirit, not as a concrete presence, and sends the angel Gabriel to explain to Mary what is happening to her.[79] A transcendent, abstract, and non-interactive god is a nonpolitical god.

Jesus, however, is an immanent, concrete, and interactive presence, all of which are crucial to his appeal. But although he satisfies and inspires in these ways familiar to the pagan divine, it would serve only to annoy Christians to classify Jesus as a pagan god. For equally crucial to Jesus's appeal is that he follows the will of the Father, and therefore does not practice the two evils, as pagan gods routinely do. He is unflinchingly loyal to the Father, and to the followers of the Father—even to the point of antagonizing disbelievers and the Roman state into crucifying him. And he does not commit the characteristic bourgeois sin, that of desire. He is humble from humble origins. He does not seek wealth or glory. "I do not accept glory from human beings," he says.[80] "If I glorify myself, my glory is nothing. It is my Father who glorifies me."[81] Thus, no one will be able to manipulate him for political gain, enticing Jesus into acts of partiality to glorify himself or his followers, as politicians have long done.

Nor does Jesus have a sexual partner, at least in the accounts of the Gospels—although some have long murmured about whether another New Testament Mary, Mary Magdalene, was a love interest of Jesus, and others have enjoyed speculating about the "Judas, son of Jesus" ossuary.[82] Indeed, he was even born without an act of sex, the Gospels relate, via immaculate conception between God the Father and his mother Mary, via the Holy Spirit. Therefore we can expect no scrambling of the lines of quasi-kinship from Jesus. We can trust that he will not show partiality on sexual grounds either. For, the Gospels claim, Jesus is beyond the politics of sex.

Jesus also distances his movement from the state and economy, the basic political drivers of the two evils. "Give to the emperor the things that are the emperor's, and to God the things that are God's," he says.[83] And in one his few flashes of emotion in the Gospels, he loses his temper when he encounters "my Father's house"—the Temple, lapsing here briefly into an Old Testament vision of an immanent divine—turned into a marketplace, with "people selling cattle, sheep, and doves, and the money changers seated at their tables."[84] What was being sold were sacrificial animals, required to pay homage at the Temple and necessary probably for an urban person who did not farm. Also on hand were people to make change to facilitate the transaction, ultimately supporting this central institution of the state. But Jesus wants a religion that is separate from the state and economy. Plus the vision he proclaims is of a God who can't be influenced by currying favor with a sacrifice. Unlike Zeus or Jupiter, God the Father does not rely on sacrifices to pile up riches, such as Aristophanes described in his play *Wealth*. God the Father has no need for such a human motive. You can't influence him. So Jesus famously makes a "whip of cords," drives out the sellers, and overturns the tables of the money changers.[85]

Impartial. Loyal. Free of material and sexual desire. Separate from the state and economy. And—most fundamentally, for this is the claim underlying all of these—nonpolitical. As with God the Father, Jesus presents a concept of divinity that is profoundly different from the pagan divine: a nonpolitical divine.

And because they are nonpolitical, with no disloyalty or desire, Jesus and the Father are everywhere described as good, in contrast to *YHWH*'s violence and what my daughter called his "anger management problem."[86] Jesus constantly proclaims the "good news of the kingdom" and the "good news of God," and he exhorts his disciples to "go into all the world and proclaim the good news to the whole creation."[87] The phrase "good news" appears twenty-four times in the Gospels. Indeed, the very word "Gospel" derives from the Old English for "good news," *godspel*, just as the term "evangelist" derives from the Greek for "good news," *euangelion*. Jesus himself is the "good shepherd." He is also the "good teacher." Jesus's followers are to "let love be genuine; hate what is evil, hold fast to what is good."[88] They are to "guard the good treasure entrusted to you."[89] They are to "share in suffering like a good soldier of Christ Jesus."[90] And they are to "live as children of light—for the fruit of the light is found in all that is good and right and true."[91]

Upon this foundation of nonpolitical goodness, upon the moral strength of this supernatural natural other, the Christian can gain a feeling of a different self, a good self, a self apart from the machinations of the social: a natural me, as I earlier called it. "Set your minds on things that are above, not on things that are on earth," the Apostle Paul counsels. When you "put to death, therefore, whatever in you is earthly" you will see that "you have stripped off the old self with its practices and have clothed yourselves with the new self."[92] No longer rooted in the social, this new self can grow resiliently, protected by righteousness from criticism. As Jesus promises in the Sermon on the Mount, "Blessed are you when people revile you and persecute you and utter all kinds of evil against you falsely on my account."[93] Cleansed of the social, this self gains a childlike innocence, maintained by faith in Jesus as thee, a natural other.[94] "Abide in me as I abide in you," Jesus says.[95]

This natural me gains greater strength and power through its connection to what I'll term a *natural we*, a sense of a nonpolitical community derived from a natural other—the natural we of Christian quasi-kinship.[96] This we is a good community for it is a community of the good, divinely sanctioned. "We are justified by faith," Paul declares.[97] "We, who are many, are one body in Christ, and individually we are members one of another."[98] Indeed, there is even no partiality in joining this community—no political intent in acting with good intent—for it is not the believer who chooses the divine. Rather, the divine chooses the believer. "As God's chosen ones," Paul writes,

> holy and beloved, clothe yourselves with compassion, kindness, humility, meekness, and patience. . . . Above all, clothe yourselves with love, which binds everything together in perfect harmony. And let the peace of Christ rule in your hearts, to which indeed you were called in the one body.[99]

Billions have been moved by this understanding of nonpolitical goodness, a sociological trinity of thee, me, and we.

———

But in this divine goodness of the nonpolitical one can also hear the metallic ring of authoritarianism: the emphasis on obeying that I mentioned earlier. For all the love, kindness, and impartiality that is part of the New Testament vision of God and the good, we also often hear that the good cannot be debated. God the Father is not described as a gentle figure who, trying to do his best to be even-handed in dealing with the various disputes and wrong-doings of his children, recognizes that he doesn't necessarily know the full context and therefore encourages dialogue and discussion in case he missed something. This is not your modern, softball-playing dad. This Father only plays hardball. You are not supposed to argue or debate. You aren't supposed to try to influence him. Instead, "blessed rather are those who hear the word of God and obey it."[100] You're not supposed to argue or debate with Jesus either, or to doubt or deny him, as Peter and Thomas infamously do in the Gospels. As the Gospel of John opines, "whoever disobeys the Son will not see life, but must endure God's wrath."[101]

More tough words, but tough words framed as being the authority of God, who is beyond politics, and therefore good nevertheless. The result is not just goodness. It is absolute goodness—the *summum bonum*, a supernatural natural other for establishing a conscience that many experience as innocent of politics.

So why such a commanding God? Perhaps because this conscience is not as innocent as it often appears. As Acts reports the disciples discussing, "We must obey God rather than any human authority."[102] The absolute goodness of the nonpolitical thus affords goodness to political absolutes. In uncertain times, that affordance can be a great comfort—however illusory that comfort may oftentimes ultimately be.

————

The rural, pagan trust in birth-based kinship does not center around the goodness of the divine. It has less need for such a logic. Birth-based kinship gives one far more certainty about the patterns of relations upon which one can rely, and therefore about one's identity, than does social class.[103] You can lose your social class, but your parents and kin will always be your parents and kin. Of course, life for the pagan does not necessarily always work out happily. The pagan explanation for our troubles is straightforward: the divine is not beyond politics, and consequently is by no means necessarily good. No natural conscience here, as conscious of what we now call nature pagan faiths all are.

The New Testament does not totally ignore what we now call nature, however. I want to be clear about that. The term "nature" even shows up in the New Testament, its earliest versions being written in Greek with many indications that its writers were quite conversant in Greek philosophy, as I'll discuss in the next chapter. The terms *physis* (nature) or *physikos* (natural) show up seventeen times, although never in the Gospels—only the later sections.[104] It appears in a first nature sense of something's essential and defining characteristics, as in Paul's description in Romans of God's "eternal power and divine nature."[105] And it also appears in a second nature sense as a moral good, as in Paul's complaint about homosexuality a short while later in Romans, where he writes that many "women exchanged natural intercourse for unnatural, and in the same way also the men, giving up natural intercourse with women, were consumed with passion for one another."[106] But the New Testament writers do not seem concerned to help followers with the pagan challenges of wresting a living from an oftentimes resistant ecology. Rather, the main way they consider ecological matters is to demonstrate that Jesus is very, very, powerful—that he is *super*natural, above and able to control nature.

Look, there is the Star of Bethlehem, appearing at Jesus's birth. Look, there is Jesus at the Sea of Galilee, walking on water. Look, there is Jesus feeding thousands with just a few fish and loaves of bread. Look, there is Jesus "rebuk-ing" the wind and the sea, turning a tempest into a dead flat calm. Onlookers "were afraid and amazed, and said to one another, 'Who then is this, that he commands even the winds and the water, and they obey him?' "[107] Plus Jesus has power over disease and even over life itself, curing the crippled and with-ered, causing the dead to rise again. And, of course, Jesus himself rises from the dead. But Jesus is not immanent *in* nature. The wind and the waves are not material manifestations of him, in the manner of the pagan divine. Rather, he transcends and directs nature.

We do get a bit of divine immanence in nature in New Testament descrip-tions of God the Father. *Pateras* sometimes speaks from heaven, as I noted above, and sometimes flashes heavenly lights, storm-god style. For example, when Jesus arrives in Jerusalem for the final showdown with the authorities, he strikes up a divine conversation with God the Father.

> "Now my soul is troubled. And what should I say—'Father, save me from this hour'? No, it is for this reason that I have come to this hour. Father, glorify your name." Then a voice came from heaven, "I have glorified it, and I will glorify it again." The crowd standing there heard it and said that it was thunder. Others said, "An angel has spoken to him." Jesus answered, "This voice has come for your sake, not for mine. Now is the judgment of this world; now the ruler of this world will be driven out."[108]

Justice thundering down from the skies. Later, after he has died and risen into heaven, Jesus himself gets some storm-like powers, as when he challenges Paul (who was then still named Saul) on the road to Damascus and convinces him to become one of his followers.

> Now as he [Saul/Paul] was going along and approaching Damascus, sud-denly a light from heaven flashed around him. He fell to the ground and heard a voice saying to him, "Saul, Saul, why do you persecute me?" He asked, "Who are you, Lord?" The reply came, "I am Jesus, whom you are persecuting. But get up and enter the city, and you will be told what you are to do."[109]

This is universal immanence, however, not place-based immanence in the manner familiar to pagan thought. God the Father is everywhere, not here or there in a certain spot—and, after he rises to heaven, the same for Jesus. Neither are confined by human form. Moreover, God the Father no longer lives in his house, the Temple, in Jerusalem (despite the story of Jesus and the money changers). As we hear in Acts, God "does not dwell in houses made with human hands."[110] The New Testament divine is usually too abstract, too non-material, too powerful for that.

Which is another reason why God the Father does not require sacrifices— not just because he is beyond the politics of influence, but because part of what sets God the Father beyond influence is that he does not have human needs. He doesn't need food. He doesn't need wealth. He doesn't need a house. Everything comes from him anyhow, through his control of the material world. As Acts later elaborates,

> The God who made the world and everything in it, he who is Lord of heaven and earth, does not live in shrines made by human hands, nor is he served by human hands, as though he needed anything, since he himself gives to all mortals life and breath and all things.[111]

The demonstration of extreme power through control of nature amplifies the divine's absoluteness and status as the definer of the good. But nature in the New Testament also begins to take on another meaning: the negative, problematic moral load that bourgeois cultures have often laid upon it, even while cherishing nature in other ways. The morally negative use of nature stems from the difficulty humans have in controlling it, unlike *Pateras* and Jesus. In this view nature beats with a wild, two-chambered, demon heart: our desires and how they scramble our loyalties. This third basic use of the concept of nature seems to have developed third in intellectual history, after the notion of nature as a moral good. So we might term it *third nature*: nature as a moral bad, as the seat of desire and thus of politics.

The true divine does not suffer from such a demon pulse. After he is baptized by John, Jesus is "led up by the Spirit into the wilderness to be tempted by the devil."[112] There in this state of pure nature, he fasts for forty days, showing his ability to even overcome the bodily desire for food. Then the devil shows up and tells Jesus, if he is hungry and divine, to turn stones into bread and eat them. Jesus refuses and famously replies, "It is written, 'One does not live by bread alone.'"[113] The devil then tests Jesus's loyalty to God by asking him to test God's loyalty to him, jumping from a pinnacle and seeing if God will send his angels to save him. Jesus again refuses, saying, "Again it is written, 'Do not put the Lord your God to the test.'"[114] Finally, the devil tests Jesus's desire for material power, telling him that Jesus can have "all the kingdoms of the world and their splendor" if he agrees to worship the devil instead of God. "Away with you, Satan!" Jesus responds, and the devil vanishes.[115]

In the centuries to come, the imagination of the devil as nature, and nature as the devil, would only grow in Christian tradition. Christian images of the devil took on a strongly animalistic quality, and not the features of animals that people typically admire. Horns. Hooves. Bat wings. Goat legs. Fangs. A hairless tail. And the devil became characteristically red, the animalistic red of desire and vanity. Weak humans may struggle against these wild sensibilities, but Jesus and the Father are unaffected by them. Jesus and the Father are not controlled by nature, the damning seat of our desires. Rather, they control nature. Therefore, they have no desires and thus no politics.

So are we supposed to follow nature or not? Do we let ourselves be directed by second nature or third? Should we strive only to commit "natural" acts, or should we resist demon nature? And how do either relate to the first nature of God's essential divinity and supreme power? Are we part of the divine at least in some small way, for the divine does, after all, sometimes take human form? Are we part of nature in some big way, or are we to overcome our nature and its politics through our faith in the divine?

The New Testament seems to ask these questions more than it resolves them. They all confront the adherent to this day. Maybe that's their moral point. But the sociologist wants to underline something else that is going on here: Distinctions are forming and widening. Just as supernature was becoming more distinct from the human, so supernature was also becoming more distinct from nature, in turn demonstrating supernature's distinction from the human community. The human relation to nature was now also very much at issue, clearly having a first nature but caught in ambivalence between second and third nature. And overlaid with a second ambivalence: both second and third nature imply our separation from nature, either as a Thoreauvian failing or an Augustinian aspiration, just as first nature implies our unavoidable connection.

The ancient triangle forms and immediately begins to split apart. Indeed, it seemingly forms in order to split apart.

––––––––

The New Testament case, then, is not for a pagan monotheism. Its case is for a *bourgeois monotheism*, responding to the context of an increasingly bourgeois society of class, city, state, and empire. It speaks little to the pagan's concrete concerns for ecological sustenance, and offers an abstract sustenance by faith in its place. It shows great concern for inequalities of wealth and how they scramble age-old social ties of obligation and trust. It is also deeply suspicious of sexuality and its own great power to scramble social ties, and to upend the economics of arranged marriages. It attempts to institute a new manner of social ties, a quasi-kinship of faith, that cuts across the contentiousness of class and the frayed pagan commitments of birth-based kinship. In these ways, it shows largely equal concern for both of the two evils, disloyalty and desire, and their politics, and tries to offer a resolution to them. And it offers a new vision of the divine, a divine that is beyond these politics because it is unitary, universal, and uninfluenced; because it is nonhuman and has no interest in material or sexual desire; because it is transcendent and in control of nature; and because it is therefore good, absolutely good. It is a natural conscience without nature, for its innocence ultimately lies in being not just beyond politics but beyond what it sees as the very origin of politics: our desirous natures.

A curiosity of the history of the Christian formulation of a bourgeois divine, however, is that its initial followers were themselves largely country people from a largely country district—Galilee in the first century CE. Some of Jesus's first followers were from the elite of local villages and towns: a tax collector, a scribe, a member of council, a soldier, a rich man, to list some of their descriptions in the Gospels. But his first followers also included rural people with more characteristically humble rural employment, including four fishermen among his twelve disciples: Peter, Andrew, James, and John. Whether from village, town, or open countryside, and whether from among the humble or the local elite, Jesus's first followers were mainly rural people, and not from the larger cities of the time. Some historians have even argued that the Jesus movement was largely a peasant movement, and there is some evidence— even if much of it is circumstantial—to make that case.[116]

That too is as may be. What is more certain is that most rural folk quickly lost interest in Jesus after his disastrous encounter with the Roman state, resulting in his execution. The theology of bourgeois monotheism was likely a bit of a stretch for most of them anyway. No doubt people with pagan circumstances appreciated Jesus challenging their ambitious city cousins, and no doubt they appreciated him challenging the Roman Empire, whose taxes were the cause of so much complaint and misery. They also probably applauded his argument that the Temple shouldn't be taking money either. For many years, everyone had been paying a high "Temple tax"—even after Galilee and other areas had been split from what had become the Roman Province of Judea, home of Jerusalem and the Temple. But sustenance by faith? And replacing birth-based kinship with the quasi-kinship of faith? Sure, birth-based kinship was being eroded by class, but it probably still seemed to most rural people a trustier thing than the kinship of strangers. Plus, if you were very poor, the anti-wealth argument perhaps seemed rather overdrawn. Wealth, after all, is what the poor generally feel they need most. And this abstract, distant notion of the divine? Maybe that worked when Jesus was around to balance the Father's transcendence with his own immanent presence. But after he was gone? And after crucifixion's bitter reminder of what happens if the Romans are pushed too hard? It had all seemed more promising in the isolation of Galilee. The quiet life in the countryside, for all its troubles, apparently came to seem as good a circumstance as rural people were likely to have.

The Jesus movement was clearly in crisis in the 30s and 40s CE, following the execution of Jesus. His remaining followers were thinking diverse thoughts about what could be made of the aftermath. Should we keep the movement a Jewish undertaking, and use our remembrance of Jesus and his words to keep the fires of nationalism going? That appears to have been the take of the Apostle Peter, as well as his colleague James, often considered to have been one of Jesus's brothers. (The idea that Jesus had a brother is hotly disputed by those who hold to the doctrine of Mary's perpetual virginity, despite the New Testament language that describes Jesus as having four brothers—James, Joseph, Simon, and Judas—as well as some sisters.)[117] And indeed, Jewish resistance to Rome continued for another century, although it was ultimately crushed.

A Roman Jew and bourgeois intellectual, the Apostle Paul, had quite a different view—probably because he came from quite a different background than the other Apostles. He was raised in the city, for one thing; the others all appear to have been from the countryside. Paul had also received a thorough classical education. It's entirely plausible that the other apostles could neither read nor write. Plus Paul was not among the first group of Jesus's followers. Whatever the reasons, the New Testament is quite explicit that Paul did not get along very well with the other early leaders of the remnant Jesus movement, and that he saw other significance and political possibilities in its theology.[118]

Paul seems to have taken an especially hard look at the likely results of continuing Jesus's direct confrontation with Rome. And he seems to have considered carefully the long-term likelihood of a movement based on poor Jewish peasants. Moreover, as an urban person himself, he had urban concerns, and probably had fewer social skills for motivating rural people. So he took his evangelism to the city, setting up a series of churches in cities around the eastern rim of the Mediterranean, with a coordinated and increasingly centralized structure. Under his leadership, what was starting to be called "Christianity" began to rapidly spread through the cities of the Roman Empire.[119] But perhaps Paul's most distinctive move was to say that everyone could, and everyone should, become a "Christian"—and that men would not need to be circumcised to join the church, as is required to be a Jew. Indeed, he liked to call himself "an apostle to the Gentiles," meaning non-Jews.[120]

As well, Paul and others likely did some selecting and shaping of Jesus's message to fit more closely with the moral concerns of a dominantly bourgeois audience, an audience that was proving remarkably receptive. After all, no one disputes that Jesus did not write down the Gospels himself, nor any other book in the New Testament. Paul was among those seeking to give Christianity a written scripture—he was a brilliant writer—which was in itself much more appealing to urban people, who were far more likely to be literate. And he played up strongly the quasi-kinship side of Christianity, which was probably especially attractive to those who experienced the greatest weakening of birth-based kinship: urban folks, living the life of class. His church was almost a new ethnicity, but an ethnicity without birth-based borders. And it soon had a centralized authority not unlike a state or empire, but a state or empire without military-based borders. It was brilliant and it was hugely successful.

The Romans fought it for a good long while. Yet eventually, the Roman Empire too came to see the appeal of a bourgeois religion for a bourgeois time.

———

There's an island in the Rhône that gives a great panorama of Avignon.[121] The walls. The towers. The spires. The fourteenth-century bridge, subject of the famous children's song.[122] ("Sur le pont d'Avignon. . . .") And, on top of the highest hill, the Palais des Papes—the Palace of the Popes—adjacent to Notre Dame des Doms, where I had my sleep-sitting episode. You're looking east, so sunset puts the whole city aglow. That's when I was there, taking a stroll in the park at the river's edge along with hundreds of others—families, lovers, loners, shutter bugs like me—come to admire one of the best views in southern France. Gorgeous.

In a way, though, the building of Avignon began well before the fourteenth century. In 325 CE, at the Council of Nicaea, the Emperor Constantine reversed three centuries of on-and-off Christian persecution. But Christianity was not yet declared the state religion of the Roman Empire. On February 27, 380 CE, the joint Edict of Thessalonica of the Emperors Theodosius I, Gratian, and Valentinian II made the declaration complete:

We authorize the followers of this law to assume the title of Catholic Christians; but as for the others, since, in our judgment they are foolish madmen, we decree that they shall be branded with the ignominious name of heretics, and shall not presume to give to their conventicles the name of churches. They will suffer in the first place the chastisement of the divine condemnation and in the second the punishment of our authority which in accordance with the will of Heaven we shall decide to inflict.[123]

This close relationship of state and religion doesn't seem to have been what Jesus had in mind. It was probably closer to the hopes of Paul. Either way, it certainly helped spread the faith. There is nothing like a big and strong empire to spread a religion far and wide. Indeed, all the large world religions today— Christianity, Islam, Buddhism, Hinduism—have experienced such a boost, as I'll discuss in the next two chapters. The Edict of Thessalonica didn't establish a complete unity of religion and state, though. The Romans kept Christianity at a slight remove from the state, essential to the new notion of a nonpolitical divine and its goodness. It was also essential to the ability of state and religion to support each other. If the two were just branches of a single entity, as had been the case with pagan monotheism and with Roman paganism, they wouldn't have a point of difference across which to offer mutual support. So the Romans really couldn't make them one and the same.

The slight remove between state and religion was not only conceptual. It was also spatial. After the edict, the Roman state carried on from its various new capitals scattered across the empire, most importantly Constantinople. Meanwhile, the leadership of the Christian church—the Papacy—set up a base of operations in what was formerly the sole capital, Rome. In 1054, Eastern Orthodox Christians split from Roman Catholics, but Roman Catholics continued (as their name implies) to center their organization in Rome.

Except from 1309 to 1377, when the Papacy moved to Avignon. It moved because the remove between state and religion really was only rather slight, and pretty much everybody knew it. Around 1300, the Papacy and the French Crown got into a huge tiff over who had the right to rule in "temporal matters"—that is to say, day-to-day life. Not surprisingly, a lot of the fight had to do with who could collect taxes from whom. Plus a fair bit of French and Italian nationalism was involved. In a memorable line, the French king called the pope (who was Italian) "your venerable conceitedness."[124] (One can imagine the pope's consternation when the wax seal was removed from that particular missive.) Finally, the French were able to get their own man elected pope in 1305: Clement V, from southern France. And in 1309, Clement V moved the Papacy to Avignon, where he and the next six popes—all of whom happened to be French—resided.

In 1378, though, the Avignon Papacy degenerated into the Western Schism when the Italians put forward one Bartolomeo Prignano to be Pope Urban VI, and the French put forward one Robert of Geneva to be Pope Clement VII. Things got even messier for a while with three different men claiming to be pope. Finally, the Italians got their way at the Council of Constance in 1417, resulting in an Italian, Otto Colonna, being accepted as the one pope, Pope Martin V. That was the end of popes living in Avignon.

But you never know what's coming next in the colorful world of papal succession. So the Papacy in Rome held on to their holdings in Avignon as long as they could. The Palais des Papes is a bit of a misnomer. More accurate would be "Fort des Papes," given the structure's twelve defensive towers and walls seventeen feet thick. It looks a lot more like a castle than a palace. Surrounding this massive edifice are the city walls of Avignon, nearly three miles in circumference, twenty-five feet high, with eighty-five more towers. The city walls also used to be surrounded by a moat. The Papacy kept it all—just in case. As a result, Avignon remained part of Rome, not France, until the French Revolution.[125]

I'm reflecting on the paradoxes of this history, as I amble down the riverside path in the park across from Avignon. How a rural religious movement became an urban religious movement. How a faith that began by contesting state and empire became a creature of state and empire. How a religion that professes itself to be about peace and universal love could lead to so much conflict. I pause for a few photos.

I'm also reflecting on the spectacular natural setting. The Rhône is a mighty work of nature, five hundred miles long, flowing down from the Alps. At this great bend in the river, there happened to be a hundred-foot-high limestone massif, now capped by the golden stone of the Palais des Papes, and ringed by Avignon's walls, still essentially complete seven hundred years after they were first built. Nature, faith, and the human community all come together here—and come apart. Walls, whether physical or conceptual, do that. For they manifest and create the very thing they seek to keep out: politics.

6

Great Departures

I'M PRETTY SURE I've got an old picture of it somewhere. I've been through our old photo albums from the days before we started taking digital photos. But I can't find it. (Maybe in one of those shoe boxes never opened since our last move?) Nonetheless, the photo is in my mind. It's me at a garden on the shore of West Lake, Hangzhou, China, one of the most compelling places in one of the world's most compelling countries. It's 1999, and I'm there on a US Agency for International Development trip to work on rural democratization in China. (We didn't have much effect, I fear.) I've slipped away from my group for the day to walk around West Lake, headed for Lingyin, the Temple of the Soul's Retreat, across the water from Hangzhou's seven million residents. In the photo, I have my arm around a pearl diver. He's got one arm around me while his other arm holds out an oyster shell, opened to reveal a huge pearl shining from its nest in the muscle.

Just before the photo, the pearl diver swam out into the lake to retrieve a bunch of oysters from a kind of fence structure in the water, where they were being cultivated. He opened them one by one in front of the crowd of tourists, all Chinese, except for me. (West Lake is immensely popular among the Chinese.) I fell immediately in love with that huge pearl, but the Chinese tourists apparently weren't interested. Surprised, I stepped forward and started to pull some yuan out of my wallet. The pearl diver waved me off. The pearl was misshapen and therefore worthless, he said through someone in the crowd who could translate. I thought the misshapenness made it more interesting and more valuable, and told him that through the friendly man who was translating. I began again to take out some yuan. No, he said. You can have it. Keep it as a memory of China. I did, passing my camera to a tourist to take my now-lost photo.

Delighted, I continued my walk around West Lake to the road up to Ling-yin Temple. I had a map, but hardly needed it. The people were all streaming that way. I took the turnoff to the right, flowing along in a human river as I would do many years later when I visited the Vatican. The road was lined with vendors. Most of their wares were the kind of plastic tourist junk that China makes for the world, but also for its own tourist sites. Mixed in were open-air tea roasters, stirring and sifting mounds of dragon well tea by hand in huge bronze woks. The original dragon well tea comes from a village in the next valley over, so is famous to the area. Its sweetness scented the crowd.

Lingyin lived up to the hype, despite the overabundance of souls seeking retreat. The Grand Hall of the Great Sage was stunning, with an eighty-one-foot-tall wooden statue of a seated Buddha covered in gold leaf. I tried to get a picture, but like the statue of Jesus outside Notre Dame des Doms in Avignon, it was very hard to get in one frame. I leaned against the far corner of the back wall. Not enough. I took off my backpack to get a few more inches. Still not enough, but all I was going to get. I snapped what I could, and headed off to see some of the other sights.

I was particularly taken by the statue of the Laughing Buddha, carved into a grotto right into the rock of a nearby cliff face. I found myself laughing along with him. There is such a release in that image. I sometimes think of it today if my mood sours or if I have to put up with something like a flu shot. It helps.

But hang on! Where's my backpack? Must still be in the Grand Hall. Damn! I think I even left my wallet in it. And the pearl. Idiot!

I went racing back, which took about five minutes of dodging through the crowd. I hurdled up the steps, ducked in, and veered to the corner. There it was! I picked up my backpack. I looked through. Everything was in it. The pearl and the wallet, still stuffed with yuan. I smiled and looked up. A man was looking at me. He smiled back. I think he understood what had just happened. My backpack had been sitting there on the floor of that temple for almost an hour. Hundreds of people must have walked by. In the steady gaze of that statue, no one touched it.

The pulsations of material desire clearly course through the veins of Chinese society, as they do my own American society. It doesn't take a visitor with a shrewd eye to pick up on that. But this doesn't mean Chinese people are entirely comfortable with their surging acquisitiveness and class hierarchy. This, perhaps, is the main retreat they seek for the soul at Lingyin: release from desire, as the Buddha advised, including desire for a tourist's forgotten backpack.

Although I've lost the photo with the pearl diver, I still have the pearl. I keep it in a little embroidered cloth box I bought in China. I just went downstairs to get it from the knickknack shelf. I took out the pearl and fingered its lustrous smoothness in contentment. Now it's sitting beside the computer as I type this sentence. I think again of the diver. Did our encounter serve as his own moment of release from desire? So it seemed. I guess, though, still pearl-smacked, I need to work more on my own.

————

What I find most significant here about these encounters with desire in China—including my desire for the pearl, a reminder of the many material lusts I must confess I feel—is that I am not alone in being troubled by such thoughts. I am not alone in my own country. I am not alone across the world. I am not alone up and down the ladder of time. So many faith traditions have provided solace to so many through their help in guiding people through these doubts. We heard from Christianity in the previous chapter. In this chapter we hear from six more traditions and their many resonances of concern: Buddhism, Zoroastrianism, Jainism, Platonism, New Judaism (or what is more commonly called Rabbinic Judaism), and Gnosticism. In the next chapter, we'll hear from two more: Hinduism and Islam.

As we listen to these resonances, we will also see striking commonalities in the shapes of their moral instruments, even if the techniques for playing them vary considerably. Played together, they yield a massive key change. As with the rise of Christianity, what we will find in these shifts is a transition from the kin-based societies of pagan life to the class-based sensibilities of bourgeois life made possible by mounting urban wealth and widening separation in rural and urban ways. The root note of that moral key change is the desire for a manner of conscience—of other, self, and us—beyond politics: a desire not to desire.

The change is nowhere smooth nor complete. It always seems to jangle on in the ear, a tinnitus of discontent. By the end of this book, I hope to have pointed to a more consonant way.

————

Siddhartha Gautama was one who heard this key change early. Wealth, we are often told, is what we want. And twenty-five hundred years or so ago, Siddhartha had it all, and all that comes with having it all. Nonetheless, he chucked splendor aside and walked out the door, leaving his comfortable life of luxury behind—what Buddhists call the "Great Departure."

Historians can't be sure the stories about the man who was born Prince Siddhartha Gautama are based on a real person. They probably are. He is at least as likely to have been a real person as Jesus. But as with Jesus, people were either very impressed by the things that a real person did, or impressed by things they wished a real person did. That much we know for sure.

As amazed as we are today that a prince would walk out on his riches, and instead lead a simple and plain life devoted to teaching others how to avoid and resolve suffering, people of the time were equally amazed. They passed on his teachings orally for hundreds of years, and eventually wrote them down in a corpus of holy writings that is many times larger than those of either Judaism, Christianity, or Islam. Evidently, by the fourth and fifth centuries BCE, when most scholars believe Siddhartha Gautama likely lived, people already had need of the messages they took from his story—messages that were strikingly similar to messages that the peoples of the Mediterranean region were also increasingly responding to.[1] They were hearing the key change too.

Those messages had many facets, as I'll come to, but the central one people took from the story of this remarkable man was that the root of people's troubles lay inside themselves, in their wanting. Don't go looking for wealth, for wealth actually makes you poor, he taught. That is to say, what you desire makes you poor, because you always feel a lack. It is wanting that leads to want—that leads to the suffering of lack.[2] The same is true for all our desires and attachments, not just for wealth, explained this deeply centered man that people came to call the Buddha, the "awakened one." Extinguish the flame of those desires, he taught, and you will be released from the suffering that comes from not attaining and holding on to them.

People found this message relevant because of a major transition taking place in north Indian society, and the society of the region we now call Nepal, where Siddhartha likely was born. While we don't know the details of the political history of the time, we do know that the region saw rapid growth in the century before Siddhartha. New and larger kingdoms—*mahajanapadas*—were forming out of the tribally based city-states of the past. *Jana* meant tribe in Sanskrit, and *janapada* meant the "foothold" of that tribe, where it had settled down and established a permanent city-state out of the seminomadic life characteristic of the earlier time that historians call the Vedic period. A *mahajanapada* was an aggregation of these city-states into something approaching what we would call a state today. Some sixteen *mahajanapadas* had formed by the sixth century BCE, each a substantial region.

Then as now a larger state both facilitates and depends upon the expansion of bourgeois society. To have a state, there have to be people to collect taxes, to keep records of who paid, to discipline those who didn't pay, and to trade the production of one region with that of another so as to hopefully attain enough surplus to pay those taxes. And there have to be people to train those people, house and furnish those people, and feed those people with the production from the land that they have little time to manage themselves. Plus when a few smaller regions come together into something larger, the choice of who will lead this centralized authority is seldom settled purely by reasoned discussion. Rather, it is generally settled by force or the threat of force—that is, by who has the strongest military. In short, there need to be soldiers. It helps if at least some of those soldiers are permanent, an employed class, and not occasional conscripts from the countryside.

How, then, is a society going to keep all of these social classes coordinated together underneath a centralized authority? Through cities, the most powerful organizing tool ever invented. And indeed, this was a time of widespread urban growth in the Indian subcontinent. With that urban growth came bourgeois society, and with bourgeois society came more urban growth, and all the troubles and accomplishments of individualism, careerism, and new inequalities.[3]

Central to those conflicts in the Indian subcontinent was the development of castes, a particularly hardened form of hierarchy in which class position is inherited and marriage is endogenous—that is, limited to within it. Class and kinship go together in caste hierarchies, rather than colliding in the provision and denial of material security and social power. By the time of Siddhartha, the four basic *varna* or "colors" of caste were already firmly in place. Then as now there were three upper castes: the *Brahmins*—the priests, teachers, scribes, and record keepers; the *Kshatriyas*—the rulers and soldiers; and the *Vaishyas*—the merchants, landowners, and bankers. But by far the largest group, composing about 85 percent of all caste members, was the lower caste: the *Shudras*—the laborers and servants. There was also a fifth group, not even defined as a caste, but kept out of the system of advantage and thus becoming the most disadvantaged of all: those who have come to be called the *Dalits*, and more widely known in English as the Untouchables, expected to do the very worst work. Each caste was further divided by *jatis* or sub-castes that followed the same pattern of inherited and endogenous class.

Such an approach, however, did not resolve the new tensions of an increasingly centralized and bourgeois life. Growing disparities in wealth only exaggerated the conflicts, including among those in the upper castes. Centralization of wealth followed on from centralization of religion, government, and settlement, advantaging Brahmin, Kshatriya, and Vaishya in various complex and often contradictory ways.

An idea that vastly promoted the formation of bourgeois society elsewhere also occurred to the newly emerging *mahajanapadas* in northern India: the issuing of minted coins. Like in Europe and the Middle East, minted coins took off in the sixth century BCE. Commodity exchange through commodity money (like a standardized weight of silver) and through barter was still the major part of the economy. But coins came on strong at this time, beginning with the *purana*.[4] It was a heady period, full of new wealth but also its many conflicts, as social inequality expanded with the new ease of accumulating riches.

Perhaps it was the Brahmins that were doing best out of all this. The historical record isn't certain. But what is certain is that Siddhartha was not Brahmin. He was a prince, and thus Kshatriya. And going along with his concern about wealth, he was strongly anti-caste. It also seems that he and his followers were especially concerned about the growing power of Brahmins in particular—a point I'll pick up on later, especially in the next chapter when I discuss Hinduism.

———

Wealth was not the only form of desire that Siddhartha walked out on in his Great Departure, however. The extremes in its distribution seem to have been central to his imagination of our troubles, and has ever been a central metaphor of his life. But he also left behind sex and family: his harem, his wife Yasodhara, and his new son Rahula. The Buddhist canon is often quite vivid in its description of Siddhartha's earlier attachments to sexuality, noting that in his palace he was "constantly attended by entrancingly beautiful women who danced, sang, and played instruments" in order to "amuse, delight, and seduce him."[5] Endogenous marriage within castes may have been a response to the rise of bourgeois sex that challenged kinship lines, but it didn't prevent deep concern about sex and its transgressive powers.

The ancient sources also relate that Siddhartha was born of a kind of immaculate conception, without sex—a theme common to the birth stories of Jesus and important figures in several other bourgeois faiths, as I'll come to.[6] In the case of Siddhartha, his mother, the beautiful Queen Maya, had made a vow of celibacy, swearing off sex's disruptive potential. She "never desired any man whomsoever," and despite her beauty "neither did any man feel lust in [her] presence."[7] As well, "she was untroubled by attachment, anger, or delusion."[8] One night, the future Buddha decided it was time for his final rebirth. He had a look down at the Earth, and he observed that Queen Maya was "not lustful, or corrupt as to drink."[9] Therefore he chose her to be his mother, and he descended into her womb in the form of a six-tusked elephant, entering her right side. Ten months later, he emerged from her right side, as Queen Maya stood holding the branch of a *sala* tree.

But not only did Siddhartha overcome the desires of sex, wealth, and status. His Great Departure was also a great awakening about the woes of the world. Because of a prophecy made at his birth, Siddhartha's father, King Suddhodana, tried to shield his son from knowing about the everyday troubles that beset us all. Yet, in the end, the king's efforts failed. The reasons why make for one of the key narratives of Buddhist tradition.

After Siddhartha's birth, King Suddhodana invited eight Brahmin wise men to predict the future of the new baby.[10] All eight said that he would become either a great king or a great holy man. One wise man, though, went so far as to predict that Siddhartha would grow to be the Buddha—and therefore to renounce his wealth, position, and family. Alarmed, the king resolved to protect the young Siddhartha from all knowledge of suffering, surrounding him with every pleasure, including three palaces and the harem, in addition to arranging his marriage to the beautiful Yasodhara.[11]

It worked until, finally, at the age of twenty-nine, Siddhartha figured out how to elude his father's protections. On a series of trips out of the palace, he encountered four people who changed his impression of life: a person who was sick, a person who was old, a person who had just died, and a traveling ascetic who lived in poverty. Shocked to discover that there was suffering in the world, one night Siddhartha made his Great Departure and left the palace permanently, renouncing the pleasures and ties that had formerly held him, including his wife and son, in order to seek better answers.

He began by experimenting with extreme poverty and austerity. He resolved to only eat "one sesame seed, one grain of rice, one jujube [a kind of date], one pulse pod [meaning a lentil pod], and one bean" per day, and to sleep outdoors on *darbha* grass (which is not noted for its relative comfort).[12] He also practiced self-mortification. After six years of these austerities, Siddhartha nearly died. Weak and emaciated, he accepted a meal of milk and rice pudding from a local village girl, and decided that such a path of extreme rejection and denial was no more correct than the wealth and indulgence of his former life.

So he sat under a tree, a *bhodi* tree, and meditated, resolving to find the truth.

He meditated for forty-nine days, seeking the true character of the good. As Siddhartha sat there, cross-legged in the posture that is now world-famous, his awakening as the Buddha steadily developed.

But then the demon Mara, the "Evil One," approached him and asked "who is your witness" of your supposed Buddha-hood, with all the good deeds of your past lives. According to tradition, Siddhartha replied "the earth is my witness."[13] The Earth Goddess appeared and confirmed this truth. Then Mara sent his "three daughters, Lust, Desire, and Passion. With their young intoxicatingly attractive bodies, bedecked in divine garments, they stood in front of [Siddhartha] and began to display their feminine charms." But Siddhartha used his emerging magical abilities to deny their transgressive power, and turned them into old hags. Next Mara sent thirty-six million demons to attack Siddhartha with lances and spears and arrows. Siddhartha did not counterattack. Rather, he meditated on tranquility and *metta*, or loving-kindness, "and all those weapons were transformed into beautiful blue, red, yellow, and white lotus flowers and fell around him."[14] Thus Mara was defeated, and Siddhartha was transformed into the Buddha. He awoke from his meditation truly awake in the deepest possible way.

The Buddha began traveling the countryside giving sermons on what he had learned. Most famous is his "Sermon at Benares," the Indian holy city on the Ganges River—which is roughly the equivalent to Jerusalem for the Brahmanic faiths, as it is holy to Buddhists, Hindus, and Jains alike. The principles he articulated there remain the core of Buddhist thought today.

The first is the principle that the Buddha called the "middle way." This idea is easy to state but great in significance for Buddhists. The middle way is simply the idea of avoiding extremes, such as wealth or austerity, which are themselves each forms of desire, the Buddha taught. Buddhism is sometimes believed by Westerners to be an ascetic tradition of denial. But severe renunciation was not the Buddha's message.

The second principle is the "four noble truths." The first is the truth that *dukkha*, or suffering, exists. This was the truth the Buddha had realized when, as Siddhartha, he left his father's palaces and saw old age, disease, death, and poverty. But suffering also includes the loss of our happiness through lamentation, pain, and grief over others, the Buddha taught. As well, it includes separation from what one likes and association with what one does not like. Plus suffering can also be the pain of not getting what one wants.

The second noble truth is that the cause of suffering is, most fundamentally, our desires and the attachments they create—our desires to be rich and our desires for sex, as well as our attachments to others and the world that these desires create. The material world—the aspects of existence that the West often calls nature—is the source of our troubles and the origin of our wants, the Buddha taught, articulating a third nature view of materiality as the origin of our politics of wanting. The inability to overcome these politics is what leads to yet another round of reincarnation through the continuance of *samsara*, the continuous flow of birth, death, and rebirth. Like other Brahmanic traditions, Buddhism does not see reincarnation as a good thing—another common point of misunderstanding in the West. It does not see reincarnation as a way to beat the sting of death. Rather, reincarnation means subjecting yourself to another round of the suffering and suffocating politics that constitute the nature of material life.

The third noble truth is that we can end our suffering and suffocating by "blowing out" our desires, like the extinguishing of a candle. When we do, we enter *Nirvana*—which means, quite literally, "blowing out." With no desires and attachments, no effort to gain what we want or to hold on to what we have, *Nirvana* also means the blowing out of politics. Here we exist as a consciousness without object and desire in which the distinction between body and mind, self and other, is finally fully transcended. There is no class or caste. There is no pull of sex and its aspirations and obligations. There is no nature.

The fourth noble truth is the path of action the Buddha called "skillful," a path that will enable one to blow out desire and end the cycle of *samsara* so we may reach *Nirvana*: the "eightfold path." These eight components are right views, right intention, right speech, right action, right livelihood, right effort, right mindfulness, and right concentration.

The eightfold path is itself the third major principle of Buddhism, and is often visualized as an eight-spoked "wheel of *dharma*." In its most general sense, *dharma* means what one ought to do to uphold rightness. And it also can mean the body of teachings about rightness taught by the Buddha—what Buddhists will sometimes call *The Dharma* or *Buddhadharma* to distinguish it from *dharma* in the more general sense.

Dharma is closely related to *karma*, the universe's measure of a sentient being's intended actions in relationship to *dharma*. In the briefest terms, *dharma* is what we ought to do; *karma* results from what we actually do. The relationship of *karma* to *dharma* determines one's progress along *samsara*'s flow of reincarnation toward attainment of enlightenment, escape from materiality, and entry into *Nirvana*.

Herein lies the Buddhist natural conscience. It is not a natural conscience based on nature, though. It makes no second nature argument for a first nature that is beyond politics and therefore good. Although Westerners sometimes today look to Buddhism as a basis for environmental ethics, it offers no "unified vision of the sanctity of the natural world," at least in the original texts, the Buddhist scholar Malcolm David Eckel has observed. Rather, notes Eckel, "if anything, there is the opposite," the view that I have been calling third nature: nature as the morally problematic origin of our political desires.[15] Instead, it is *dharma* that gives a natural other, a standard that is beyond human politics. And it is *karma* that reckons with the natural me—with the human struggle to enact that standard beyond politics.[16]

Although the eightfold path might seem rather individualistic in its orientation, the Buddha stressed the importance of understanding what he called *anatman,* or no-self, in which the distinction between self and others collapses. The natural me merges into the natural we. As a consequence, "a person who loves the self should not harm the self of others," for they are one and the same—the Buddha's version of the golden rule.[17]

Tradition says that the Buddha delayed his ascent into Nirvana so he could help others discover the four holy truths and the natural conscience of the eightfold path. He spent the next forty-five years traveling and developing his *dharma*—his teachings about what people ought to do—and developing the Buddhist *sangha,* or community. Give up your ties of class and caste, of sex and kinship, and reground yourself in the natural we of the Buddhist family, he taught. He was a fabulous organizer and developer of what in the previous chapter I called the quasi-kinship of faith, a community of the Buddhist good. He set up a system of monasteries supported by the giving of *dāna,* or alms, by which lay people could gain good *karma* and a sense of commitment to the *sangha,* becoming good by doing good. (Monasteries remain central to Buddhist practice today.) Finally, at age eighty, the Buddha announced that he would die and pass on to Nirvana. He urged his followers not to be sad about his passing. He took off his robe, lay down, and said "do not break into lamentations after I am gone, for all karmically constituted things pass away. Seek your own liberation with diligence."[18] And then he died.

In the aftermath, the Buddha's relics were distributed around and became sites of pilgrimage, and remain so to this day.

———

It's a compelling history, and hundreds of millions today continue to find great truth and release in the natural conscience it provides. Buddhism ranks as the fourth largest religion in the world, after Christianity, Islam, and Hinduism, with roughly five hundred million adherents, mainly in Nepal, China, Japan, Korea, Southeast Asia, and Sri Lanka. (There are only a few Buddhists in India today.) As of 2010, Buddhism also numbers as the third largest religion in the United States, after Christianity and Judaism, with nearly four million people identifying as Buddhists, as well as the third largest in Europe, after Christianity and Islam, with another million or so Buddhists.[19]

In addition, various aspects of Buddhism are widely practiced by those of other faiths. Take for example mindfulness-based stress reduction, or MBSR, for which you can actually get a prescription from your doctor in many places, including in my own city of Madison. As of 2016, some 36 million Americans, or 11 percent of the adult population, practice yoga and some 28 percent of Americans report having taken at least one yoga class.[20] (Yoga in America mainly draws from Hinduism. But it is in part Buddhist.)[21] A number of faiths have also emerged that blend Buddhism and other traditions together, most notably Bahá'í, Unitarian Universalism, and the various New Age religions. It is not uncommon to hear some quote from the Buddha mentioned on a popular website. Even without including the quoting of Buddha, one could probably make a reasonable case that roughly a third of the US adult population has practiced some aspect of Buddhism.

Some of what makes Buddhism so attractive to a dominantly Christian country like the United States are the striking parallels between the story of Jesus and the story of the Buddha, giving an intuitive appeal or resonance to their blending. Consider the list in Table 6.1, and the parallels in their life histories, personal characters, and teachings—and the parallels in what they didn't teach. It's really a very long list. And there are more than what I include in the table.[22] Of course, there are also some striking differences. But given this list, some have wondered if maybe there is some syncretism at work here—that Christianity incorporated elements of the older faith, Buddhism, or was at least influenced by it, and that Buddhism in time came to be influenced by Christianity. And possibly so, at least to some degree. We can't say for sure that there was any direct borrowing. But we do know that Buddhist ideas were around and about throughout the eastern Mediterranean in the centuries before the time of Jesus. And we know that peoples from the eastern Mediterranean were around and about in India well before the time of Jesus as well.

———

Two great figures of antiquity worked to ensure this encounter of traditions. A century or so after the death of Siddhartha Gautama, another remarkable prince was born in south Asia: Prince Ashoka, who was emperor of the Mauryan Empire at the time of its greatest extent. His grandfather, Chandragupta Maurya, had conquered nearly the entire Indian sub-continent, putting almost all the *mahajanapadas* into one political unit. Ashoka finished the job shortly

TABLE 6.1. Parallels between Jesus and the Buddha

Parallels in their life stories

Each had an immaculate conception that required no sexual act.

Each had wise men attend their birth.

Each lived a life of poverty, but not asceticism.

Each walked out on family life and its ties.

Each is presented as being beyond sexual desire.

Each was tempted alone in the wild by a devil figure.

Each has an immaculate death, which he faces without fear, and asks his followers not to lament his passing, for he is going to a better place where he is ordained to go.

Each is associated with a prophecy of a return one day of a messiah figure who will bring enlightenment and goodness to the world at the end of time—although in the case of Buddhism, that figure, called the *Maitreya*, will be another Buddha, not Siddhartha Gautama himself.

Parallels in their personal characters

Each occasionally displayed miraculous powers, including healing powers.

Each traveled around giving sermons with wise sayings, and is presented as a monological figure of authority who has unique insight far beyond that of anyone else.

Each is shown learning but never actually making a mistake and virtually never having his mind changed by others through argumentation.

Each is a figure who is divine but has a human form that can and does die, and provides an immanent presence in relics and places one can still visit, yet all the while representing and communicating universal, transcendent, and absolute themes.

Each is male.

Parallels in their teachings

Each strongly articulated a natural conscience, a vision of goodness derived from motives claimed to be free of human politics.

Each warned of the troubles of material and sexual desire.

Each asked his core followers to give up wealth and sex and to leave their families behind.

Each articulated a natural we via an ethics of faith-based quasi-kinship and religious community.

Each established monastic orders, separated by gender.

Each established a tradition that often had things to say about women and gender relations that many today would regard as unsympathetic and discriminatory.

Each articulated a version of the golden rule.

Parallels in what they didn't talk much about

Each had very little to say about nature in the ways we understand it today, at least not directly, and is not portrayed as an embodied presence in nature. Indeed, nature is often described as the source of our desires, and as something to be overcome.

Each had little to say about our ecological needs for sustenance.

after taking the throne in 269 BCE.[23] Ashoka became a key figure in the spread of Buddhism to the south, north, east, and west—even as far as the Mediterranean region.

According to the stories that have come down to us, Ashoka wasn't a very nice fellow, at least not at first. He had an infamously bad temper. He was renowned for "Ashoka's Hell," a series of torture chambers he had built disguised as a beautiful palace. He was renowned as well for murdering ninety-nine of his hundred brothers (his father, the Mauryan emperor Bindusara, had a lot of wives), including tricking his father's chosen successor into walking into a pit of live coals. And he was renowned for pursuing a war against Kalinga, a small kingdom of fertile land on India's eastern coast, roughly the area of the state of Odisha today. By the end of it, some hundred thousand had been killed and some hundred fifty thousand deported as slaves.[24] Plus there was widespread burning and looting of towns and villages. The carnage was apparently so great that it gave pause to even a hardhearted, ambitious, maniac for power like Ashoka. For the legends say that, after touring the aftermath of the war, he cried out,

> What have I done? If this is a victory, what's a defeat then? . . . Is it valor to kill innocent children and women? Do I do it to widen the empire and for prosperity or to destroy the other's kingdom and splendor?[25]

So great was Ashoka's remorse that he sought refuge and release in the teachings of Siddhartha, the Buddha, and the notion of *dharma* and its rules of right conduct. The sense of peace he gained was worth urging upon his entire empire, he felt. So he set about commissioning the carving of the "Edicts of Ashoka" into rock walls, caves, and specially built pillars—edicts that basically ordered people to follow his own idea of *dharma*. (That may not sound very Buddhist, but emperors can be like that.) Some forty-nine of the edicts still survive. The edicts often read a bit like a political ad campaign, promoting the benevolence and goodness of Ashoka himself. Alongside telling readers about the *dharma*, they explain that "I have had banyan trees planted so that they can give shade to animals and men" and have had "wells dug, rest-homes built, and in various places I have had watering-places made for the use of animals and men."[26] His religious convictions may well have been sincere, but Ashoka also seems to have found some propaganda value in a universal religion of the good. A religion that applied to everyone, and that made Ashoka appear motivated by beneficence and not by politics, likely served him as rhetorical tools for holding an empire together.

Whatever his motivations, Ashoka didn't stop with having edicts carved in his own territories. He sent emissaries south into Sri Lanka, east into Myanmar, north into China, and west as far away as Greece. Their efforts took significant hold in some places. Sri Lanka, Burma, and China are all Buddhist to this day. Buddhist ideas didn't take so strongly in the Mediterranean countries, and were later overwhelmed by Christianity. But there were some successes there too, in part because of the other great figure of antiquity I have in mind.

Fifty years before Ashoka reached out to the West, the West had already come to India. In 326 BCE, Alexander the Great crossed the Jhelum River into the Punjab at the head of an army of thirty thousand, drawn from Macedonian Greeks that had been with him for ten years—especially the *Hetairoi*, the elite cavalry who were sworn lifelong companions of Alexander—and supplemented with soldiers from the regions he had earlier conquered.[27] Alexander's army had been battling their way across Asia for eight of those ten years, after first consolidating Alexander's hold on Greece and the Balkans, following the assassination of his father, King Philip (who was possibly killed at Alexander's direction).[28] They started with the Persian Empire, taking Anatolia (modern-day Turkey) from the Persians. Then they headed on down the eastern coast of the Mediterranean, conquering Syria, Judea, Egypt, and other lands that the Persians had held. In 331 BCE, Alexander turned his army east, headed for the heartland of the Persian Empire, what is now Iraq and Iran. After several dramatic battles, and some ugly politics, the Persian Empire fell completely into Alexander's hands in 328 BCE. The next year, Alexander headed for India, threading his forces through the Hindu Kush Mountains in a bloody effort to conquer the entire known world. In 326 BCE, they arrived and accomplished yet another of Alexander's amazing victories against a much larger army.

It was as far as he would go. The Macedonians in Alexander's army had been away from home for eight years. They refused to budge further east. Reluctantly, Alexander agreed and turned his army back west—only to die three years later in Babylon of a fever following a night of drinking with a friend, perhaps brought on by a viral or bacterial infection, but maybe instead by poison in the wine. (Hardly a year passes without another new theory of his cause of death.) What followed was another incredible mess of politics, with forty years of war and murder. By the end of it, Alexander's three wives, his son, his mother, and his uncle had all been murdered, and many others too. It was a true *Game of Thrones* affair. Although still often admired today, more than two millennia later, Alexander was one of the great monsters of history, and created conditions that inspired the monster in many others. He was the cause of a staggering amount of bloodshed. People at the time greatly esteemed his character, finding him noble, modest, generous, honest, and sympathetic. "Yet the fact is," as one ancient chronicler of his life put it, "that in battle he was a berserker, as addicted to glory as men are to any other overmastering passion."[29] And violence typically leads to more violence.

Eventually, by about 275 BCE, Alexander's short-lived empire had sort of stabilized into three main chunks. A much reduced Macedonian Empire controlled Greece and some surrounding areas. The Ptolemaic Empire, named after Ptolemy, one of Alexander's generals, held the pharaoh's flail and crook over Egypt and its surrounding lands, including Judea. And the Seleucid Empire, named after Seleucus, another of Alexander's generals, had sway over the rest clear across to India.

In the process, several hybrid forms of culture emerged which we can track in the historical and archaeological record. Greco-Bactrian. Greco-Indian. Even Greco-Buddhist. All of which Alexander would have applauded. Despite his remarkable appetite for violence, he was apparently fascinated by the different peoples and social customs of the places he conquered. He sought not only to unify the world politically but also culturally, so as to promote greater world harmony—a more pleasant side effect of his megalomania, perhaps. As he urged in his will, read to his soldiers upon his death, his followers should seek the "transplant of populations from Asia to Europe and in the opposite direction from Europe to Asia, in order to bring the largest continent to common unity and to friendship."[30]

In short, there was plenty of opportunity for Christianity and Buddhism to influence each other.[31]

———

But to the sociologist, establishing historical precedence and cultural connection is potentially beside the point. We don't want to turn the history of religion into a game of gotcha—that what you thought was an idea original to your faith really came from elsewhere. If you hear an idea that sounds good to you, what the sociologist most wants to know is not where the idea came from but why it sounded so good. For most seeds fall on infertile and unwelcoming soil.[32] That's why plants make so many of them. It is indeed illuminating to know the original plant, and how the seeds dispersed. But it is the context of their quickening that is the most decisive for growth.

The sociologist, then, is less concerned about proving the existence of syncretism between different faiths. Besides, with the sparse evidence that over two thousand years of historical accident has allowed to survive, proof of syncretism is challenging to establish to the satisfaction of a reluctant jurist—an adherent of a demonstrably younger faith, perhaps. Making a case for *contextual parallels* in religious form and religious situation is enough for the argument I am trying to make here. Any borrowing, and any directionality to that borrowing, for sure is interesting, but less important. Moreover, you probably can't have syncretism without parallels of context, or any syncretic ideas would not be welcomed. But given human creativity in the face of need, similarities may well emerge without syncretism, if the context urges it. So contextual parallels are more decisive.

What we should be noting foremost, then, are the parallels between the European and India contexts during these centuries, and placing the parallels in religious ideas within those commonalities. There are four pretty striking ones:

1. The growth of massive empires emanating out of both Europe and India
2. The development of urban centers for administering them and allocating their riches
3. The dividing of society into vertical and horizontal inequalities, a double conflict that assured taxes would be paid, armies provisioned, peasants disempowered, and elites rewarded for their allegiance to the central state
4. The relative decline in the power of tribal-based kinship

Europe and India were not the first regions to experience large empires, though. Nor were they the first to see great departures in religious ideas—departures toward faiths that emphasized a unified god of the good for everyone, with strong cautions about the presence of desire and politics in human affairs.

Zoroastrianism—or, as its adherents sometimes prefer to call it, *Mazdayasna*—is one that predates both Christianity and Buddhism.[33] Scholars aren't certain exactly how old Zoroastrianism is. Our earliest accounts date from Herodotus's writings in the fifth century BCE, but there is indirect evidence that Zoroastrianism had been going for some time by then—maybe since the tenth century BCE, if not earlier.[34] It was once one of the world's largest religions, and is still practiced by two hundred thousand to two million or so faithful (estimates vary widely) mainly in India, Pakistan, Iran, and the United States. Probably the best known Zoroastrian in the West was Freddie Mercury, lead singer of the rock group Queen. Its main symbol is a guardian angel figure embedded in a sun with wings, called the *faravahar*.

The name Zoroastrianism derives from Zoroaster, the Greek form of the name Zarathustra, a prophet from ancient Persia who had some revolutionary revelations. Zoroastrianism is sometimes regarded as the oldest monotheistic religion, but that's probably not quite right. As I discussed in chapter 4, the short-lived veneration of Aten in Egypt in the fourteenth century BCE very well may predate Zoroastrianism on that score, depending on when Zoroaster actually lived. No, what is the most remarkable innovation is Zoroaster's sense that this one god—a god Zoroaster called *Ahura Mazda*, or the "wise being"—was a god of the good. As far as we know, no religion had had such a vision before.

The term Mazdayasna means the worship of Ahura Mazda, an uncreated creator who has no form. In English, we generally call Ahura Mazda a "he." But as Ahura Mazda has no form, gendering isn't theologically accurate. Still, Zoroastrians describe Ahura Mazda as "fathering" six physical emanations, the "divine sparks" or *Amesha Spenta* who assist Ahura Mazda in creating and maintaining order in the world. Three of the Amesha Spenta are male, and three are female. Together with Ahura Mazda, they form a Holy Heptad.

Zoroastrians envision a constant divine battle between order and truth, called *asha*, and disorder and falsehood, called *druj*. This battle takes place between Ahura Mazda and an evil spirit of disorder and falsehood, *Angra Mainyu*, who was also uncreated. Ahura Mazda has the Amesha Spenta on his side, and Angra Mainyu gets help from a large group of violent evil spirits. But humans can support Ahura Mazda through acting on three moral principles: *Humata*, *Hukhta*, and *Huvarshta*—Good Thoughts, Good Words, and Good Deeds. If we do, Zoroastrians say, eventually Ahura Mazda will prevail over Angra Mainyu. Then time will end and the dead will be revived. All souls will be cleansed and united with the divine. This final moment of cosmic reunification and renovation will be heralded by the arrival of the *Saoshyant*, the agent on Earth of Ahura Mazda. Born immaculately from his virgin mother, *Eredat-Fedhri*, when she enters a lake to bathe—a lake that preserves the semen of Zoroaster—the *Saoshyant* brings about the final victory.

It is not hard to see some strong parallels here with Buddhism and, even more strongly, with Christianity. A transcendent god of the good who has physical children who do his good work. A constant divine battle with a figure of evil. The prophecy of an end time when good wins over evil, and the dead rise and join with the divine. The end time ushered in by a messiah-like figure born of a virgin mother.[35] There are also parallels with Judaism, which like Christianity and Buddhism stresses that a divine savior will arrive one day to usher in a time of unity and goodness (although Christians believe this arrival will also be a return).

Zoroastrianism isn't the same as Buddhism, Christianity, and Judaism. It has plenty of differences. For example, we could say that Zoroastrianism isn't really monotheistic, given the Amesha Spenta. But, then again, the Amesha Spenta are only manifestations of the one transcendent divine, Ahura Mazda. And besides, when you think about it, Buddhism and Christianity aren't all that strict about their monotheism either. Consider the Trinity and the many semidivine saints in Christianity, and the many *bodhisattvas*—semidivine humans who have reached enlightenment but hold off their entry into *Nirvana* so they can help others—in some forms of Buddhism.[36]

A more telling difference, I think, is that Zoroastrians see each Amesha Spenta as being responsible for a different ecological factor: plants, animals, water, fire, earth, and minerals. There is a place for the female divine as well; the Amesha Spenta for earth, water, and plants are all regarded as female. Plus Zoroastrianism shows less concern with issues of wealth and sexual desire. Zoroaster's focus was more on peace and ending warfare with other Persian tribes, a loyalty theme, useful for building a state out of a tribal society. And in Zoroastrianism, the divine is definitely not all powerful. The divine needs our help.

But it is hard not to suspect some syncretism, given how similar many of these notions are to both the Brahmanic and the Abrahamic faiths. And once again, there was plenty of opportunity for these ideas to spread around. Darius I, the Persian emperor who followed shortly after Cyrus the Great, was an ardent Zoroastrianism follower. Zoroastrianism remained the main faith of the Persian state until the time of Darius III, when Alexander the Great conquered Persia. Although the Jews had mostly returned to Judea by that time, and had rebuilt the Temple, they were still part of the Persian Empire. The Jewish elites had to have heard of Zoroastrianism and its religious innovations. No doubt they had heard of it long before the Babylonian exile as well. Given the power of Persia throughout the first millennium BCE, we can well believe that many Jews during these times were impressed by Zoroastrianism's association with political success. And indeed, the latter books of the Old Testament—especially Isaiah, Jeremiah, and Ezekiel, which were written between the eighth and sixth centuries BCE, and likely revised and edited for hundreds of years onward—make similar prophecies about the end time, prophecies that many Christians and Jews believe a messiah will one day fulfill.

Plus the New Testament makes a striking allusion to Zoroastrianism: Matthew's description of the "three wise men from the East" who come looking for "the child who has been born king of the Jews."[37] The original Greek for the "wise men" is μάγοι, sometimes translated into English using the Latin, which is *magi*. Starting with the Greek historian Herodotus in the fifth century BCE, the term μάγοι or *magi* was widely used to refer to Zoroastrian priests. The term soon evolved a parallel use to mean the kinds of acts and rites that μάγοι or *magi* did: which is to say magic (μαγικός in Greek and *magicus* in Latin). But the usage here in Matthew seems pretty clearly to describe a blessing from Zoroastrian priests "from the East" at Jesus's birth.

Still, the evidence for Christian, Jewish, and Buddhist syncretism with Zoroastrianism is mainly circumstantial. Which is exactly how we should treat it. It is the parallels and differences in the context, the *circumstances*, of these ideas that should catch our eye most. Zoroastrianism arises in a more pagan society, struggling to centralize, and speaks to pagan concerns from a bourgeois center, much as does the Old Testament. In short, Zoroastrianism too is a pagan monotheism, but with a more developed natural conscience than early Judaism.

————

Others were to take these and similar ideas further, perhaps developing and expanding from Zoroaster's insights, or reinventing them on their own.

One such thinker was Vardhamana or, as he later came to be known, Mahāvīra, which means "Great Hero" in Sanskrit.[38] Vardhamana was born in 497 BCE, a few decades before Siddhartha Gautama. Like Siddhartha, he was also a prince, a *Kshatriya*, and he also came to doubt the princely life of luxury, wealth, and bourgeois excess. He left it all behind at age thirty—almost exactly the same age, twenty-nine, when Siddhartha left his family and palace. In fact, wealthy men leaving it all behind to become wandering ascetics was pretty common at the time. *Shramanas*, people called them, "strivers" for enlightenment. The ascetic that Siddhartha saw on his fourth trip out of the palace sounds like one such *shramana*.

Just as Siddhartha was later to do, Vardhamma strived unusually strongly for enlightenment. He became chaste, practiced meditation, and abstained as much as he could from food. He abandoned all forms of wealth, even clothing, and went about naked. After twelve and a half years, Vardhamma succeeded in reaching enlightenment, say ancient sources. (Siddhartha took only six years, the Buddhist canon reports. We may perhaps sense here a Buddhist claim of precociousness, like having Siddhartha's great departure at twenty-nine instead of thirty.)[39] Vardhamma's moment of realization came while sitting under a tree—a *sala* tree instead of a *bodhi* tree like Siddhartha. (But Siddhartha's mother gave birth to him under a *sala* tree, say the Buddhist sources, perhaps symbolizing that his teachings supplant Vardhamma's.)[40] For the next thirty years, the one we should now call Mahāvīra traveled across South Asia, counseling that our problems start with attachment and desire, establishing a community of followers—a quasi-kinship of faith in the good—and, like the Buddha, founding orders of monks and nuns. (The Buddha traveled around preaching and organizing for forty-five years.)

With his teachings, Mahāvīra crystalized the natural conscience of the tradition we now call Jainism, from the Sanskrit word *jina*, meaning conqueror. But a Jain does not try to conquer others. A Jain tries to conquer the inner self, and the desires and attachments that lead us astray, and thereby develop a natural me. The six million or so Jains of today are guided by three main principles, derived from Mahāvīra's teachings. Rather than orienting faith toward the gods and their needs for ritual and sacrifice, Mahāvīra focused on *Ahimsa* (non-violence), *Aparigraha* (non-possessiveness), and *Anekantavada* (non-absolutism)—that is, welcoming multiple perspectives on all matters of importance. Jains are also known for their belief in the presence of varying degrees of *jiva*, or life, in all matter, including matter most Westerners would regard as inanimate. Here Jains come the closest of all bourgeois traditions to a second nature sense of the goodness of first nature. Most Jains practice strict vegetarianism and are concerned not to harm even insect life, because of their view that all life is bound together through mutual support and interdependence. Jain monks and nuns sometimes carry a broom and sweep the ground ahead of them as they walk, so as not to step on any insects. Jains also revere *Brahmacharya* or abstinence, including both abstinence of sexual thoughts and thoughts about material desire—thoughts that they argue are connected to sexual thoughts, as both Buddhism and Christianity also often argue. For lay Jains, this means practicing chastity outside of marriage, and for Jain monks and nuns this means practicing celibacy, much as with Christianity and Buddhism today.

Mahāvīra had a more ascetic take on the question of desire than did the Buddha, however. Although Jains do revere *jiva*, Mahāvīra took with staggering seriousness the goal of conquering third nature too—conquering the materiality of our desires—and thereby finally escaping *samsara*, the cycle of reincarnation. In 425 BCE, at the age of seventy-two, he achieved complete liberation from desire by freeing himself of even the need to eat, and eventually died of starvation. Jains do not counsel such a route to liberation for everyone—only for those suffering from a terrible disease or who are clearly approaching the end of their lives, and also for those rare few who are ready across the span of their own passage through *samsara* to attempt such an escape from it. This sounds a lot like suicide to many observers, but Jains don't see it that way, regarding it more as an ethic of self-dignity.

To the Buddha—who surely knew about Jainism, for it was already in widespread practice among the urban classes of his time—such strong asceticism apparently was a bit much. The Buddha seems to have formed his notion of the "middle way" in direct contrast to Jainism. Many other elites during the Buddha's time evidently agreed with him. At least, Jainism never received anything like the imperial support that Buddhism received from both the Mauryan and Greek empires.

But like Buddhism, Jainism does not speak much to the agroecological concerns for sustenance of villagers laboring in the fields, who can little afford such caution about animal lives lost through the struggle to get a crop out of the ground. To this day it remains dominantly an urban religion of the middle and upper classes, providing a natural conscience of other, self, and community—of thee, me, and we—that adherents view as beyond politics.[41] It is a dominantly bourgeois tradition with some hints of pagan sensibilities, such as the notion of *jiva*.

And like Buddhism, from the start it staunchly opposed the caste system and the power of Brahmin priests—a conflict I will return to in the next chapter.

———

Two or three years before the death of Mahāvīra (historians aren't completely sure of the dates) another aristocrat was born who would have a huge impact, but in this case on the thought of the peoples of the Mediterranean. In fact, his name was Aristocles—about as aristocratic a name as one could imagine—a descendent of a king of Athens. He was an excellent wrestler as a young man, something that was highly honored in ancient Greek elite society. Because of his wide frame and ability to use it in pinning opponents, his coach nicknamed him Plato, meaning wide and plate-like. The nickname stuck and even became the professional name that he used in writing his famous letters and dialogues based on the character of his philosophy teacher, Socrates.

Plato in time came to run his own school of philosophy, set up in an olive grove on the outskirts of Athens. People called the grove *Akademia* for Academus, an Athenian hero buried there, from which we get the English words "academe," "academic," and "academy." But Plato's school was not merely academic. He was deeply involved in politics. He once even got sold into slavery because of his politics, only to later get bought out of slavery by an admirer—again because of his politics.[42] (The winds of the political were as shifty then as now.)

All of this got him thinking deeply about the good. Athens was a huge city, the biggest in the world at the time, with something like a quarter of a million people, the fruit of finally beating Sparta in 387 BCE—the year after Aristophanes's premiered his play *Wealth* (which I discussed at some length in chapter 3). The Athenians promptly set up the Second Athenian League of city-states, a kind of re-creation of the old Delian League, an association of about two hundred city-states convened to fight off the Persians but also to stimulate trade. The Delian League had essentially been an Athenian empire, with Athens using the league's navy to pursue its own agenda. Eventually, other Greek city-states came to resent Athens's power and wealth, leading to the two big wars with Sparta: the Peloponnesian War (431–404 BCE), which Sparta won, and the Corinthian War (395–387 BCE), which Athens won. The Second Athenian League was set up so Athens would not have as much control as before, but nonetheless the money and people were once again pouring into the city, resulting in some of the most wonderful art, architecture, and philosophy ever conceived.[43] The money also led to much competition and manipulation. Plato saw politics, politics, and politics everywhere, and went looking for an alternative foundation for motivation and truth—for his own vision of a supernatural basis for a natural conscience. Upon this foundation, he hoped to design a society of the good and thus a good society.

His solution was to reject the nature-before-nature poly-divinity of the ancient Greek myths and to propose a new kind of god, not just a god of the good but a god who simply *is* the good. Had he picked up the idea from the Zoroastrianism of the Persians, or from Buddhism somehow? Maybe. There were certainly some marked similarities. Like *dharma* and Ahura Mazda, Plato's divinity of the good had no material manifestation—no shape, no gender. Yet from it came all material manifestations through the crafting of the world to emulate what Plato called the "forms" of the good. The forms for Plato were sort of blueprints of the perfect, and he regarded these as eternal and a higher reality than the passing world of the material we take to be real, a notion that bears more than a passing resemblance to the Buddha's conception of *dharma*—albeit with a more dualist flair, the ideal versus the material.[44] Taken together, the forms gave a deep logic or *logos* to the world, a kind of divine language of the perfect. (Indeed, the word *logos* meant "word" or "speech" when not used in this special philosophical sense.)

Depending on how you read Plato in his dialogue *Timaeus*—he was not altogether clear on this point—the good itself had no cause. Perhaps Plato worried that if the good had cause, it would have intention and thus the beginning of politics. But the good led to cause by emanating what Plato called the *demiurge*, the architect or divine craftsman (usually described as male) who fashioned the material world according to the forms. It was a pretty similar idea to the uncreated creator envisioned by Zoroaster who emanated other divinities to do the actual material work of creating.[45] More syncretism? We'll probably never know. And it doesn't matter. We know the parallels of context were strong: growing urbanism and inequality—based on both class and rural-urban differences—in an imperial society.

And we know that the parallels of context were strong with Christianity, which, in turn, has some marked similarities with Plato's ideas. Here historians are pretty sure the similarities in ideas stem not only from parallels of context but also from actual syncretism. It's quite clear that many of the elites who were centrally involved in shaping Christianity—Paul, Ignatius, Irenaeus, Athanasius, Augustine, and others—had been schooled in the Greek philosophers.[46] They sometimes even say so.[47] The writings of the ancient Greeks were deemed central to education throughout this period. Plato's *Timaeus* circulated widely. Many found compelling its conception of a fundamental good behind and above everything, giving a divine logic to our lives.

The New Testament suggests syncretism most prominently in the Gospel of John, which repeatedly uses the word *logos* in the original Greek. The usual translation in English, though, is "the word," as in the famous opening of John, "In the beginning was the Word, and the Word was with God, and the Word was God," and his later declaration that with the coming of Jesus "the Word became flesh and lived among us."[48] At the very least, the concept of Jesus as a kind of emanation or personification of the divine good of *logos* parallels Plato's concept of a demiurge—not to mention Zoroastrianism.

———

But whether or not we are seeing syncretism here, syncretism won't happen if the ideas don't make contextual sense. Common ideas make sense in common situations, whether or not they arose independently or were brought by a traveler from afar. It's not a matter of syncretism versus contextualism.

Plus there were several other major new religious movements about that time in the Mediterranean region, movements that made great philosophical departures closely related to what became Christianity. Many, many people were having the same kinds of concerns as were Jesus, his followers, and those who developed Christianity afterward. Many were seeking release into the innocence and confidence they found in a supernatural manner of natural conscience.

Prominent among those concerned were the rest of the Jews—the ones who did not become Christians. The Jesus movement was far from Judea's only religious movement with political overtones and undertones. There was plenty of politics at the time. And they did not all lead to what we now call Christianity.

In fact, we learn from the Roman historian Flavius Josephus that the Jews had divided into at least four main political factions, with different stances toward the Roman occupation and its puppet kings: the Zealots, the Pharisees, the Sadducees, and Essenes, a spectrum from confrontation to quiet distaste to accommodation to withdrawal.[49] The Zealots preached armed rebellion against the Romans. The Zealots also had a particularly militant branch known as the Sicarii, the "dagger-men," who were even willing to assassinate other Jews for cooperating with the Romans.[50] The Essenes, at the other end of the spectrum, were communalists who withdrew from Roman Jewish society. The Zealots don't make much appearance in the New Testament, except for two quick, tantalizing mentions that one of Jesus's twelve apostles, Simon, was a Zealot. No mention of the Essenes is made at all.

But there is a lot of Biblical talk about the Sadducees and the Pharisees, who were sharply divided. On the one side were the supporters of the Hasmonean Dynasty and of King Herod, advocates of a centralized Temple for a centralized Jewish state. These were the Sadducees, and included mostly the wealthy and aristocratic, as well as many priests. They were elites, and they emphasized a literal reading of the Old Testament—a literalism whose interpretation was under their control.[51]

On the other side were the Pharisees, who felt less commitment to the Temple, the state, and the priestly interpretation of biblical law, and who ranged up and down the class ladder, from elites to those but a small remove from the pagan life of the peasant. The Pharisees briefly took control of the Temple and served as its main priests under Queen Salome Alexandra during her nine-year reign from 76 to 67 BCE. But that had been a century ago. Herod put the Sadducees back in power in the Temple, and there they remained, albeit much constrained by the Romans.

In place of the biblical literalism of the Sadducees, the Pharisees pointed to a different, popular body of law they called the "Oral Torah." When God gave

Moses the Torah on Mount Sinai, the Pharisees argued that he also gave Moses a wealth of interpretation which was never written down but rather transmitted by word of mouth, along with interpretation added by the wise through the generations. They still read the Torah, the Jewish term for the Five Books of Moses, the Old Testament's first five books. But they looked to the Oral Torah for interpreting the written Torah, not to the priests in the Temple. In this task, the Pharisees were helped by local religious leaders they called *rabbis*—a term still familiar to us since the Judaism of today directly descends from the tradition of Pharisees, what is often called *Rabbinic Judaism* by scholars. It might also be termed the *New Judaism*, even though it is now two thousand years old, to remind us of how very different it is from the centralized Judaism the Sadducees advocated and that the Old Testament describes.

Crucially, this New Judaism was a far more immanent and localized understanding of faith, brought directly to people's lives through the debates of local religious leaders about the Oral Torah, as opposed to the universal pronouncements of the priests in the Temple. Jews needed a vision like this. The Temple based religious structures of the Sadducees simply couldn't work, for there no longer was a Temple, the Romans having utterly destroyed it in 70 CE. Thereafter, the Romans pretty much (although not entirely) drove the Jews out of Judea after the failed Bar Kokhba Revolt, the last act in the Jewish-Roman Wars from 66 to 135 CE. The Romans also gave the region a new official name: Palestina, which derived from an older term that loosely encompassed many of the small territories surrounding Judea. The resulting diaspora spread Jews into hundreds of communities scattered around the Mediterranean, and eventually the world. In such circumstances, a decentralized religion led by local leaders made practical sense.

But at the same time, this New Judaism was a faith based on a vision of God as good—as a supernatural basis for a natural conscience. Eventually, around the second century CE, the Oral Torah was written down and combined with later commentaries on it to create the *Talmud*—a book as significant to Jews as the New Testament is to Christians. The *Talmud* is a very different book than the New Testament. Its focus is on laws and customs, with little in the way of stories and history. But it parallels the New Testament in representing a major liturgical development beyond the Old Testament—a great departure that equally downplays a scary image of the divine, and that focuses instead on the idea of divine goodness and the troubles that come from our desires.

———

Indeed, it could be said that Christianity is a branch of these same trends in Judaism—albeit a highly successful branch. Jesus was a Jew. All early Christians were Jews. The political context of Christianity's emergence was a Jewish context. Central to that context was the same tension over centralization of state and religion versus a more localized approach that distances itself from the center, the tension of Sadducee versus Pharisee. We even have it on Paul's own authority that he was a Pharisee.[52] And Jesus is often referred to in the Gospels as a rabbi, and thus by implication a Pharisee.[53] In its early years, Christianity was a New Judaism too.

Plus, as Christianity began to develop into a religious tradition in its own right, no longer a faith tradition of Jews and former Jews alone, it did so with great diversity. There are many, many different Christianities now, and there were many, many different Christianities then. Although the New Testament makes a strong effort to give a sense of a tradition that began in considerable unity, impressions of what to make of, and to take from, the teaching of Jesus varied very widely—I may say very, *very* widely—in the first centuries of the Common Era. Most Christians have heard little about this variety because it was actively suppressed by the Roman state, once the decision was made to make a centralized and unified Christianity its new state religion. "Lost Christianities" some scholars call this suppressed variety.[54]

Scholars wouldn't know much about these lost Christianities except for a chance discovery in 1945. At base of the cliffs that overlook the Upper Nile the lucky peasant can sometimes find a nitrogen-rich layer in the soil. Local people call it *sabakh*, and it makes a fine fertilizer. In December of that year, seven *fellahin*—a North African term for peasants—set out with their camels and mattocks to look for *sabakh* in the cliffs behind their little hamlet of al-Qasr, a small cluster of houses across the Nile from the town of Nag Hammadi. They hobbled their camels at the base of the cliff and began hacking the ground with their mattocks. One of them hit a human skeleton. Intrigued, they all started digging around near the skeleton. And then the mattock of one Abu al-Magd hit another surprise: the top of what turned out to be a huge clay jar, sealed with bitumen, containing twelve papyrus books and a few pages of a thirteenth, all written in the Coptic Egyptian alphabet.

Most of the men were frightened, afraid that they had unleashed a genie. But one of them—a man named Muhammad Ali, as it happens, and the older brother of Abu al-Magd—took the books home anyway, thinking they might be worth something. They were. The books were a collection of scriptures once held divine by a loose-knit variety of early Christianity called *Gnosticism*.

Scholars knew of these scriptures mostly only from references in the works of other early Christians, who mainly cited them to complain about them, often with considerable distortion. Now scholars had many of the actual original texts.

A huge storm of scholarly debate has since whirled up over the meaning of these texts, and why we almost lost them. The second point of debate turns out to have a lot to do with the first.

————

Imagine the scene. It's the late fourth century CE, probably the late spring or early summer of 367 CE, and a couple of monks are lugging a three-foot-high clay jar to the base of a cliff. Another couple of monks are just finishing digging a hole. The area is an ancient cemetery, across the river from their monastery in Nag Hammadi. No one pays much notice to the monks, figuring perhaps that they are burying a dead child in the jar. A burial is the sort of thing monks do.

But the monks are nervous and work quickly, for what is in the jar is no dead child. Rather, it is a collection of texts they hope to keep alive, even though they are in direct conflict with the Easter letter sent out a few months ago by Athanasius, the Christian archbishop of Alexandria, downriver at the mouth of the Nile, 450 miles away. In his *39th Festal Letter*, Athanasius gave a long list of religious texts he deemed "lying and contemptible" and ordered immediately destroyed.[55] The jar the monks carry is filled with over twelve hundred pages of these heretical texts. There are fifty-two separate works in the jar with titles like *The Gospel of Thomas, The Gospel of Philip, The Gospel of Truth, The Secret Book of John, On the Origin of the World*, and *Thunder, Perfect Mind*.[56] Not just any works: these are works that present radically different understandings from the twenty-seven books that Athanasius declared holy and legitimate. It is a defining moment in Christian history, for those twenty-seven books were what we know today as the twenty-seven books of the New Testament. Athanasius's *39th Festal Letter* is the New Testament's first table of contents.

The monks have every reason to be cautious.[57] Athanasius is a powerful, controversial, and occasionally ruthless fellow. The monks know well of his deep involvement in the Council of Nicaea, the gathering of bishops from all over the Christian world called by the Emperor Constantine in 325 CE to sort out a centralized and unified version of Christianity for a centralized and unified Roman Empire.[58] One of the big points of contention at the Council of Nicaea had been *trinitarianism*—the idea that God consists of three co-equal, co-eternal, and consubstantial divine persons: the Father, the Son, and the Holy Ghost. Athanasius won over the council against the advocates of what was called *Arianism*, led by the theologian Arius, who said the three persons were not all of the same order and that Jesus was subordinate to God the Father. Athanasius even got Arius excommunicated. Arius waited for an opportunity for revenge, and ten years later convinced the emperor to exile Athanasius. The next year, Arius suddenly died while out walking in the street—rumored to have been poisoned at the command of Athanasius and his supporters.

So the monks know that crossing Athanasius is hazardous. Many have tried. He is now bishop again, despite having been exiled four more times by four different emperors. He's a survivor and no stranger to the politics of bitter theological fights—and the theological fights of bitter politics. And now Athanasius apparently thinks that the moment has arrived when he can safely settle not only the matter of Arianism but also the matter of Gnosticism.

So the monks handle their clay jar with both care and speed. Their monastery in Nag Hammadi is one of many that reveres these diverse Gnostic texts, and had even lovingly translated them into Coptic, the common tongue of Egypt, so that others could gain their benefit. Alas, they never were able to get ahold of two important Gnostic texts, the *Gospel of Mary* and the *Gospel of Judas*.[59] But their local abbot's wish is to protect the ones they do have, burying them in the cemetery until the political winds change. The monks nervously agree. So into the hole the monks lower the jar, sealing its opening with bitumen and a smaller upside down jar, placing a boulder on top of it, and covering it all with dirt and many a prayer.

Those winds do not soon change, however, and the monks never come back.

———

Winds seem to be more in favor of Gnosticism now. Once seen as heresy, and later as a kind of odd variant of early Christianity mostly founded on rejecting the material world, scholars are reassessing Gnosticism, and some Christians are trying to revive it.[60] The year 2003 even saw the publication of *The Gnostic Bible*, a compendium of Gnostic writings, including both the contents of the Nag Hammadi jar as well as many other allied and long-neglected writings that survived Roman censorship in other ways.

It is difficult to speak in broad brush about any faith tradition, but maybe especially so Gnosticism, as our knowledge of it remains pretty fragmentary and it actually encompasses a wide range of traditions, and not only Christian ones.[61] But four ideas seem central to most of the writings gathered together under this term:

- One, that *YHWH* is not good and is not the real god, meaning that Jews and Christians have been worshipping the wrong god
- Two, that there is a real god of the good behind *YHWH*
- Three, that divinity is not only masculine
- Four, that divine truth or *gnosis* is to be found by looking in, not out

Gnostics—who initially included both bourgeois Jews and those who were starting to call themselves Christians—embraced the bourgeois sense that the one true divine must be good. But the Gnostics were more troubled by *YHWH*'s thundering ways than other Jews and Christians. If God is good, then *YHWH* can't be God, they reasoned. They agreed that *YHWH* was the creator of the material world, as the Old Testament says. And they agreed that *YHWH* quite evidently thinks he is the one true divine. But he was wrong, according to Gnostics. Rather, *YHWH* was a flawed emanation of the one true divine, the supremely good Single Principle behind everything. Which was why the world wasn't all good: *YHWH* wasn't all good.

In this way, the Gnostics grappled with a problem that has long beset traditions of natural conscience based on a vision of divine goodness: how to explain the presence of evil. The problem of theodicy, as scholars call it, is the moral need to account for why an all-powerful, all-knowing, and all-good god would allow evil to exist. Why would God allow a third nature? A common answer Judeo-Christian traditions give is that we cannot know the mind of God, and therefore what appears to be evil must not be. But that answer is often hard for a seemingly random victim of disaster or disease to accept. Another explanation is that God is testing us to determine who will be eligible for eternal life in heaven. But if God is all-knowing, God must already know who is worthy and should have no need to test us. Besides, a loving and all-powerful god of the good would want to prevent the evil in us to begin with, or so many have pondered.

The Gnostic view side-stepped these problems of theodicy. Since *YHWH* is flawed, so is the material world. The Single Principle is perfect goodness, but because of *YHWH*'s imperfections much about the material world is not good. If this sounds a lot like Plato's idea of a demiurge, a creator god that emanates from something deeper, that's probably because it largely is, most scholars agree—although with the important distinction that the Gnostic demiurge isn't fully good.

Gnostics also embraced the idea of many other emanations of the divine. In the vision of Valentinian, a Gnostic thinker that started a tradition well represented in the Nag Hammadi jar, dozens of divine beings issued from the Single Principle. First in time and foremost in power are thirty *Aeons*, which the Single Principle established in fifteen pairs or *syzygies*, one male and one female. (Other Gnostic systems have different numbers of Aeons.) Together, the Aeons exist not as bodies but as immaterial forms that manifest the *pleroma*, the fullness of the divine, and exist in a region of light which lies just above the darkness of the material world. The Single Principle itself has no form at all, not even an immaterial form, and thus no gender. The striking man-in-the-sky masculinism of most natural conscience faith traditions does not sit well with many who are concerned about gender equity, especially in recent decades. Gnosticism's embrace of female divinity provides a potential alternative, some contend.[62]

For Christian Gnostics, Jesus was a human emanation of the Single Principle, sent to explain the deep truth of the real. The most important truth is that genuine knowledge of the divine—the knowledge that Gnostics called *gnosis*, which simply means "knowledge" in Greek—can be found only by looking into one's inner being, where the spark of the Single Principle yet remains in all people. True gnosis does not come from books or religious authorities. You can only find it in and through yourself.

Like New Judaism, Gnosticism seems to have shared a suspicion of centralized religion, and its close alliance with the state. If a claim of natural we is coextensive with a state or empire, it can be hard to avoid detecting a sour stench of politics in that we. Gnosis is clearly more compatible with a more localized faith tradition. This is no doubt much of the reason that the Roman state and its new centralized vision of Christianity as a state religion had little patience for the books in the Nag Hammadi jar.

But despite Roman suspicion, Gnosticism—or, rather, the many Gnosticisms—represented a tradition that spoke to the issues its adherents experienced in their place and time. Those adherents were not pagan. Like New Judaism and New Testament Christianity, like Buddhism and Jainism, and like Platonism, Gnosticism spoke to bourgeois concerns about issues of desire and its inequalities. Like those traditions, Gnosticism spoke strongly to those who worried about religious centralization and its political implications. And like them again, Gnostic texts did not speak to concerns of ecology and agricultural sustenance. Although Gnosticism's veneration of Aeons lends it a poly-divine energy, unlike pagan traditions its many divinities are not immanent in the forces of sustenance and what we have come to call nature. There is no Aeon of rain, no Aeon of fertility, no Aeon of hunting. Rather, the Aeons manifest transcendent abstractions. The Aeon Nous represents mind. The Aeon Alethia (the female half of a syzygy with Nous) represents truth. And so it goes with the other syzygies. Sermo and Vita: word and life. Anthropos and Ecclesia: humans and church. Bythios and Mixis: profundity and mixtures. Paracletus and Pistus: comfort and faith.[63]

Gnosticism, then, is also bourgeois—but a bourgeois polytheism.

———

Nineteen ninety-nine was a year for great departures of my own. A few months after my visit to China, Lingyin, and West Lake, where I picked up that beautiful pearl, I also got to travel to South Korea, where I'd been invited to a conference on environment and consumption. The conference was held at Jeju National University, which is in Jeju-shi, the capital city of Jeju Island, which lies off the southern coast of South Korea. It was another wonderful trip that got me thinking. I didn't bring home another pearl, though. Instead I came back with a plain wooden dipper. It still hangs in our bathroom at home. I use it to rinse after brushing my teeth, or for a little drink of water now and again. The handle has a couple of symbols in Korean script carved into it. I can't read what they say. At least what they were intended to say: I can read what they say to me.

I remember well the afternoon I got the dipper. I'd just arrived on Jeju Island. The conference was to begin in a couple of days, so I had time to look around. After my host dropped me off at my hotel, I decided to take a bus out to Sanbangsan, a volcano that spurted out a million years ago right on the edge of the southwest coast of Jeju. It turned out to be an excellent choice. Sanbangsan is about twelve hundred feet high, and rears straight up out of a flat strip of coastal land. It looks twice as high as it is. Plus it has a lovely Buddhist temple, with a fabulous bell at the top, rung by a massive log like a battering ram that swings into it from chains hung from the roof of the bell tower. I had a great walk along the beach below and met a couple of Jeju's famous women shell divers, wading out into the rocks and waves. One of the women sold me a huge, fresh oyster, slathered with chili paste. It didn't have a pearl, but it wasn't supposed to. And it was delicious. We chatted delightedly for about fifteen minutes, she entirely in Korean and I entirely in English, with lots of laughter and pointing. I didn't understand a word of it.

But it didn't matter. I understood the all of it—or so it seemed in that bright moment. For after visiting the temple, and before heading down to the beach,

I had taken the stairs up to a cave a good ways up the mountain. A Buddhist monk lived there a thousand years ago, they say. Inside the cave is a statue of the Buddha and a series of pools filled by a constant drip of healing water from the ceiling. "The tears of the Buddha," people call the drips. On the way up the long course of steps, a Korean craftsman sold me my wooden dipper so I could have a drink of the tears. I entered the cave mouth and waited for my eyes to adjust. Another flight of stairs led up and into the cave, with the statue of the Buddha at the top. I climbed up to the highest pool, just beneath the Buddha. That day the tears were vigorously streaming into the pool from the cave roof, not just drips but a shower of purity. Perhaps it had rained recently.

I dunked in my dipper. I hesitated. Would the water taste foul or strange?—strange to an urban American, and a non-Buddhist? I brought it to my lips and tipped the dipper toward me. The sip was utterly clear. And utterly familiar. Because, I now realize, I had had such water before. Many, many, many times.

7

Electrum Faiths

THIS PICTURE I DID FIND. Or, rather, I happened on it while I was unsuccessfully looking for the one of me and the pearl diver. It's the neighborhood Halloween parade. My daughter Eleanor, then seven years old, is dressed as a panda. (She's always loved pandas.) To her right is my wife Diane, dressed as a witch. To her left is Ursina, the teenaged daughter of a Swiss friend who was living with us for a few months to work on her English, dressed as a peasant woman. I'm dressed as a wizard, but I'm out of the picture holding the camera, except for my wizard's staff, which Diane is carrying at the moment. And just as I snap the photo, another father in the parade, wearing an exceptionally compelling vampire costume with fangs and bloody lips, leans into the frame with a frightening gape to his mouth, as if to bite, sweeping back his high-collared black cloak, lined in red velvet to go with his red shoes. His timing was perfect. We laughed hysterically, and we had another good chuckle when we later looked at the picture at home.

It was all pretty pagan stuff. My daughter dressed like an animal. Ursina dressed as a peasant. My wife and I dressed as beings capable of working magic. The interloping father dressed as a blood-sucking spirit of evil. The couple of hundred other folks from the neighborhood dressed in all manner of the out-of-the-ordinary for bourgeois souls from a bourgeois neighborhood, led by the neighborhood brass band, in costume, playing "Have You Seen the Ghost of John?," the theme from *The Addams Family*, and other spooky music.

A wonderfully fun and family way to celebrate a Christian holiday. Yes, Christian. Although rarely acknowledged nowadays, Halloween actually marks the celebration of All Hallows Eve, the evening before All Saints Day, which is the day before All Souls Day. Together, they make up the three-day Christian holiday of Allhallowtide. The practice of traveling door to door in costumes, asking for treats, derives from "souling"—a Medieval custom in which the poor visited the houses of the rich, with candles lit inside carved out turnips, demanding food in return for offering prayers to the family's dead.[1] Historically, Halloween was also a harvest festival, landing almost exactly between the fall equinox and the winter solstice, and lining up with the ancient Celtic harvest festival of Samhain.[2] (The pumpkin is pretty clearly a harvest symbol, if you think about it for half a second.) And not only in Europe. The end of the growing season powerfully symbolizes a time to honor the dead in Mexico, too. The wildly popular Day of the Dead festival is a three-day Mexican holiday (despite the singular "day" in its name) that corresponds exactly with Allhallowtide. It began as an Aztec harvest festival. Today, celebrants in Mexico embrace the Day of the Dead as a jointly Christian and traditional event, a time for remembrance as we thankfully store away food from dead plants.

We're not used to thinking about Christianity as having pagan elements, of course, and these associations can make some Christians feel uncomfortable. But they're not accidental. Christian leaders have long been interested in building the flock of followers, of course, and having Christian holidays correspond with what people are already celebrating makes a lot of sense for getting people to join up. All Saints Day was originally celebrated on May 13 in the fourth century CE. But by the ninth century, the church had shifted it to November 1, where it could resonate better with older pagan traditions.[3]

Or take Jesus's birthday. The New Testament never says when he was born, and initially Christians celebrated Christmas on January 6. Eastern Orthodox Christianity still celebrates Christmas close to this date. (Because of how it syncs its calendar with the calendar the Romans used, the Eastern Orthodox church now celebrates Christmas on January 7.) Roman church leaders later switched Christmas to December 25, the date of the solstice on the Julian calendar, which was the calendar then in use. The solstice, of course, has long been a deeply meaningful occasion in pagan thought. It was also the birthday of *Sol Invictus*, the "invincible sun," a solar god of Persian origin who had a strong following in Rome at the time, especially among soldiers. As well, it was the birthday of Mithras, a Jesus-like divinity also of Persian origin, also widely venerated by Roman soldiers. (We don't understand the relationship between Sol Invictus and Mithras, although it seems probable that there was one.) The solstice later moved to December 21 when authorities readjusted and recalibrated the calendar to better handle the fact that the year is actually a few minutes shorter than 365 and a quarter days: 365.2425 days, to be precise.

This is all very controversial, especially the question of which religious tradition first venerated December 25.[4] Nonetheless, the controversy tells us something important about Christianity: it remains uncomfortable with paganism, despite some quiet accommodation of it. Judaism isn't exactly wild about pagan traditions either, although it does give more opportunity for expressing pagan sentiments as legitimate aspects of faith than Christianity typically does. For example, although it is a rare Jew who appreciates the agrarian origin of Passover as a springtime celebration of the re-leavening of the world, all practicing Jews understand Sukkot as a harvest festival. But Sukkot is a minor holiday, and only recently has there been much effort to welcome the many other pagan possibilities of the Old Testament into the Jewish traditions of today.[5] The pumpkin isn't any more of a Jewish symbol than a Christian one.

Buddhism can be pretty shy about its pagan elements as well, especially in what some scholars call "Buddhist modernism," the dominant form of Buddhism in the West and among the educated urbanites of Asia.[6] But alongside bourgeois worries about desire and how it prevents one from following *dharma*, Buddhism in much of Asia flourishes in part by discretely welcoming pagan concerns, and even by incorporating some worship of a region's traditional pagan divinities.[7] Thus many in Japan, for example, follow both Buddhism and Shinto, venerating ancestors and ecological spirits in all their wildness as well as the Buddha in all his calmness. The Dalai Lama doesn't talk about this much when he visits the West, though, nor when he speaks with the middle and upper classes in the East. Many major English-language sources on Buddhist history and practice barely mention Buddhism's pagan facets either, if at all.[8]

My point is this. Traditions in Christianity, Judaism, and Buddhism are heavily weighted toward bourgeois concerns.[9] Their focus has long been on the establishment of a supernatural basis for a natural conscience, and on the freedom from the moral pollution of politics and desire that such a conscience promises. But some faiths have sought more of a balance between the pagan and the bourgeois, developing compound traditions. Ancient jewelers liked to combine gold and silver together into a light yellow melding called electrum. So we might call these traditions *electrum faiths*: faiths that have forged alloys of bourgeois gold with varying admixtures of pagan silver. Such faiths emerged in contexts that experienced a less complete bourgeois revolution of increased urbanism, wealth concentration, and expansion of state and empire. I'll consider two in this chapter: Hinduism and Islam.[10]

Turn, go not farther on your way: visit us, O ye Wealthy Ones.
Agni and Soma, ye who bring riches again, secure us wealth.
Make these return to us again, bring them beside us once again . . .
I offer you on every side butter and milk and strengthening food.
May all the Holy Deities pour down on us a flood of wealth. . . .[11]

Then was not non-existent nor existent: there was no realm of air, no
 sky beyond it . . .
All that existed then was void and formless:
by the great power of Warmth was born that Unit.
Thereafter rose Desire in the beginning, Desire, the primal seed and
 germ of Spirit.[12]

These lines of scripture reach out from some of the most ancient religious texts we have. They come down to us from the traditions of Hinduism, what is sometimes called the "oldest religion."[13] Hindu scripture includes both very ancient writings and writings that are, well, merely ancient—pre-1000 BCE through to writings from the first centuries of the Common Era—as well as writings from more recent centuries that many Hindus deeply prize. The *Vedas*, the "works of knowledge," are the very earliest. These particular verses come from the oldest of the *Vedas*, the *Rig Veda*, or "verses of knowledge," which likely dates from around 1500 to 1200 BCE, drawing on traditions that are far older (as does all human knowledge).

Researchers think the *Vedas* reflect the combined wisdoms of two peoples who came together over hundreds of years. One group was the Indus Valley Civilization who had developed a substantial society of riverside agrarian cities. These cities mysteriously began to fade away beginning around 1900 BCE.[14] Speculation has roamed through a wide variety of causes, from climate change to shifting rivers to disease to mismanaged agriculture to overextended trade economies to some kind of combination of these.[15] For many years, the most popular explanation for the decline was depredations from the second group: a flood of people from the Eurasian steppes, warriors on horseback, known as the Aryans. The trouble is, no one has found any archaeological evidence that there was a military takeover: no signs of battle or of an uptick in violence, as far as archaeologists can detect.[16] Archaeologists agree that the Aryans appear in the region at this time, and maybe even earlier.[17] Yet despite the war-like reputation of the Aryans, it seems they steadily blended with the indigenous Indus Valley peoples over hundreds of years. Together they came to constitute the Vedic Civilization, a largely agrarian people.

We can immediately hear in these passages orientations to the world that would feel familiar to any nature before nature folk. The first passage speaks clearly to an agrarian concern for sustenance and ecological abundance. "I offer you on every side butter and milk and strengthening food," it reads. It also shows no doubt about the value of securing wealth and riches. The prayer asks for the "wealthy ones" to "bring riches again, secure us wealth." One of those wealthy ones is Agni, the god of fire and of wisdom, and the chief terrestrial deity in the *Rig Veda*. The other wealthy one is Soma—a god who takes the form of an intoxicating ritual drink often mentioned in the *Rig Veda*, made from the juice of plant stalks. (Alas, it is no longer known what plant.) The praise of intoxication as a divine source of riches and success is hardly a bourgeois religious sentiment.

The second passage shows no doubt about desire either. Indeed, it even praises desire as the creative force behind the whole world, calling desire "the primal seed and germ of Spirit." This is far from Laozi's vision of the *dao*, and its path of acting without intention. Nor does it sound like the Buddha's vision of *Nirvana* as a blowing out of desire and attachment, nor Plato's concept of a primal good that has no cause, nor the biblical vision of an impartial divine, nor the Gnostic faith in the goodness of the Single Principle. There is no effort in the *Rig Veda* to escape politics and discover a natural conscience.

But a thousand years later, the peoples of the Indian subcontinent were increasingly having quite different concerns than those that the *Rig Veda* addresses. The insights of Vardhama and Siddhartha Gautama in the fifth century BCE spoke to the new issues faced by the people who would come to call themselves Jains and Buddhists—the issues of a bourgeois life and its politics of status. Many then and now have found great comfort in the beauty of their teachings.

But the hierarchies of *varna*, of caste, meant that only about 15 to 20 percent of caste members experienced the social rhythms of the urban and bourgeois. The Brahmin priests and teachers, the Kshatriya rulers and soldiers, and the Vaishya merchants and landowners all found much in Jainism and Buddhism that spoke to them. Yet the Shudra still lived mainly agrarian lives, as did the Panchama, now called the Dalits, the fifth group not even considered a part of the caste system. Vardhama's and Siddhartha's advice that one ought to give up on material desire and gain a deeper peace really didn't have a lot to offer to those who had nearly nothing to begin with—the lower castes and out-castes—and the questions that daily confronted them. The questions of those with little were not more materialist than those of the upper castes. But they sprang from a different material situation: a materialism of overcoming lack more than a materialism of justifying excess. Nor were they less idealist.[18] Rather, their ideals formed in response to different conceptions and motivations of other, self, and us: the pleasures and obligations of kinship more than the aspirations and satisfactions of class and caste.

Plus, a sharp conflict among the upper castes shouts out from the annals of the period. It seems pretty plain that the Brahmins and the Kshatriyas, the two topmost castes, were not very happy with each other. Why should the priests be more important than the rulers, the Kshatriya seemed to have been asking? Why should they control religion and the income from sacrifices? Besides, the state and the increase in commerce associated with coined money, empire building, and better record keeping was leading to new bases of wealth largely controlled by the Kshatriyas and Vaishyas. The power of the Brahmins was growing increasingly shaky.

At least, it is hard to account any other way for the fact that both Vardhama and Siddhartha were Kshatriyas, and that their teachings directly confront Brahmin power. They advocate against sacrifices. They deemphasize the worship of the traditional Vedic divinities. They speak strongly against caste privilege. Which opens up another potential reading of Ashoka's astonishingly forceful embrace of the sanctity of Buddhist *dharma*: Ashoka, too, was not a Brahmin, for he was an emperor, not a priest.[19] Advocating for Buddhism (or at least his own vision of Buddhism) would have helped him centralize authority by stripping the Brahmins of their religious privilege, and a major source of their income.

Brahmins of the time certainly must have noticed that, in the minds of some, they were, well, on notice.

———

Whether or not he had these politics in mind, a thinker who seems to have lived in the third century BCE—one century after Ashoka, and two centuries after Vardhama and Siddhartha—had some religious insights that spoke strongly to the concerns of Brahmins, while not neglecting the concerns of the other upper castes as well as those of the great mass of people still living agrarian lives.[20] Vyasa was his name. He was more of a traditionalist than Vardhamma and Siddhartha, and he sought a way to reframe Vedic ideas to respond to the new concerns that many people were increasingly worried about, without losing touch with the concerns of the agrarian majority. The result was one of the central texts of the exuberant religious tradition we have come to call Hinduism: the *Mahabharata*, an epic epic—a poem with over two hundred thousand verses, about four times as long as the Bible. Vyasa appears to have begun it in about 300 BCE, and others developed and refined it through to about 300 CE.[21]

The historicity of Vyasa is pretty uncertain. The *Mahabharata* itself is the main source we have on him. We have no independent records. Vyasa shows up as a character in the epic, the grandfather of two of the main protagonists. The *Mahabharata* also attributes its composition to him. But the *Mahabharata* says he isn't the one who wrote it down. Rather, Vyasa dictated it to the god Ganesha.[22] It may seem odd that a god would serve as Vyasa's scribe, but the *Mahabharata* also describes Vyasa as an incarnation of the god Krishna. Here we encounter a prominent characteristic of Hindu traditions: delight in a highly fluid and interactive conception of the relationship between the human and the divine.

As a result, Vyasa comes down to us shrouded in some mystery. It is generally difficult to divine a historical figure from religious accounts, as with the Buddha and with Jesus, due to a lack of much in the way of independent sources. But most observers have felt that the *Mahabharata* does describe a main author who actually lived, at about the time linguistic and historical evidence suggests the *Mahabharata* began to be composed.

And what a life. Take the *Mahabharata*'s wild account of Vyasa's birth—an account that resonates well with the theological content of the epic, and its social circumstances. Vyasa's father, we are told, is Parasara, a great Brahmin sage to whom is attributed a work of astrology that remains part of the Hindu canon today.[23] But his mother, we are also told, is Satyavati, the daughter of a fisherman and therefore a Shudra, the lowest caste. Except she wasn't. And she was a virgin mother. Except she wasn't. The *Mahabharata* is like that.

Here's the story. A king goes out hunting one day at the command of the spirits of his ancestors. He is annoyed by this command, as his wife has just finished her menstrual course and so is "now in her season."[24] But he goes anyway, for one should not disobey the ancestors. He sees a beautiful tree in the forest and it reminds him of his beautiful wife. He masturbates and asks a hawk to carry his semen back to his wife. But the hawk drops some of the semen into a river where a female demon, who had been transformed into a fish, swallows it. A fisherman, who is also the local chief, catches the fish demon, cuts her open, and finds Satyavati—Vyasa's mother—and her twin brother inside. He brings them both to the king, who adopts the boy (who is actually the king's son) and gives Satyavati (who is actually the king's daughter) to the fisherman to adopt. The fisherman raises her, and Satyavati grows up into a beautiful woman—although she smells badly of fish.

Then one day, the sage Parasara travels through the area, sees Satyavati, and is instantly consumed with lust for her. Satyavati is interested in having sex with Parasara, but she worries about the consequences for her reputation. So she agrees only if no one sees and only if Parasara uses his special powers as a rishi to restore her virginity—and to cure her fishy smell. Parasara assents to these requirements. Satyavati instantly becomes sweet smelling, and they go out to an island in the river, which Parasara obscures with a great fog. They have sex, Parasara restores Satyavati's virginity, and later that day, while still out on the island, she gives birth to Vyasa.[25]

This is a story with many sides, to say the least—and with many crossings. Male and female cross. Lust and chastity cross. People and animals cross. Animals and demons cross. Humans and divinities cross. Upper caste and lower caste cross, each sanctifying the other. Plus, as if to drive the point metaphorically home, Vyasa is conceived and born on an island, a place in the middle of this constantly flowing story with its many shores and borders, a nexus between them all.[26]

The messy entanglement of nature, faith, and the human. A frank accounting of sexual desire and its own messy entanglements. Equal honoring of the lofty and the lowly, with no evident concern for the problems of wealth inequality. In short, we are not yet in a bourgeois zone of faith.

———

Many, many more crossings follow. Vyasa's birth is only one small, early episode in his monumental saga: just forty-seven verses in the first of eighteen books. The full sweep of the *Mahabharata* recounts the story of the war between two groups of cousins, the Kauravas and Pandavas. Both vied for the leadership of the ancient Vedic kingdom of Kuru, a major political power around 1000 BCE. Some historians regard Kuru as the first true state in the Indian sub-continent—the first true *mahajanapada*—and not just a city-state like the power centers of the Indus Valley Civilization. Its territory lay in the north-central zone of the Indo-Gangetic Plain, with its capital near present-day Delhi.

By the time Vyasa wrote, Kuru had declined considerably in importance. But tales of this epic conflict persisted in part because similar politics persisted. Although Kuru itself had diminished, the development of city-states into genuine states into massive empires continued on, driven by militarism and accumulation. Coined money had reached the Indian subcontinent by the 5th century BCE. The fortunes of fortunes rose and fell, as they do, but on the whole steadily rose. The conflicts of wealth, caste, kin, and sex that troubled

Siddhartha and Mahavira burned hotter and hotter. But rather than seeking a wholesale revamp of the moral vocabulary of tradition, as the Buddhists and Jains were attempting, Vyasa apparently saw the continuing currency of these old tales as a potentially more popular way to speak to the big questions of his day, most compellingly in a seven-hundred-verse section of the *Mahabharata* called the *Bhagavad Gita*, the "Song of the Lord," that occurs just as the war between the Kauravas and Pandavas begins.

A game of dice gone bad sets the war into motion. There's a lurid backstory, though, that carries on from Vyasa's birth. Vyasa's mother Satyavati never tells anyone about him, and, her virginity restored, she later marries the king of Kuru after he visits the region on a hunting trip and is overcome by her newly sweet scent. The king dies and their son (that would be Vyasa's half-brother) becomes king. But the son quickly dies too, without an heir, although he did have two wives. So Satyavati calls on her secret son Vyasa to perform *niyoga*—designated sex with a woman whose husband has died without a child, or can't conceive—with her other son's two wives. Vyasa complies. Then he uses his special powers as a yogi to transfer the paternity of the two resulting sons to his dead half-brother, making them the legitimate heirs to the kingdom of Kuru. The older son is Dhritarashtra, progenitor of the Kauravas, and the younger is Pandu, from whom descend the Pandavas.

Still with me? We're getting closer to the dice game that started the war.

The trouble is, Dhritarashtra is blind, so he agrees that his younger brother Pandu ought to become king, the better to lead the armies of Kuru. But one day, the new King Pandu is out hunting in the forest and he accidently shoots a rishi and his wife while they are having sex, mistaking them for deer. The dying rishi curses Pandu, declaring that he will die if he ever tries to have sex. Pandu is full of remorse, so he gives up his crown to Dhritarashtra, despite his blindness. Pandu lives in exile as a traveling ascetic—along with his two wives, Kunti and Madri, swearing off sex because of the curse, even though he does not yet have any children.

A sage grants Kunti a boon, however. She asks to have it fulfilled by giving birth to three sons, without an act of sex. She also extends her boon to Madri, who has two more sons, also without sex. Together, the five immaculately conceived sons are the Pandava princes. Pandu then dies when he forgets himself and tries to have sex with Madri.

The dice game? Coming right up now.

So then the five Pandava brothers decide they've had enough of exile and come back to Kuru to reclaim their royal rights from their uncle, the blind King

Dhritarashtra. Tensions are high. King Dhritarashtra decides to divide the kingdom in two, giving one half to the eldest Pandava brother, Yudhishthira, to rule. Yudhishthira has a fondness for gambling, though, so Dhritarashtra challenges him to a game of dice in which each bets their half of the kingdom. Yudhishthira loses, and the Pandava princes are left with nothing.

It all goes downhill from there. Not even the peacemaking efforts of Lord Krishna, the avatar of Vishnu, god of preservation, can bring the two sides together. War is inevitable. Krishna offers to help both sides, saying they can choose either his personal help or the help of his army. The Kauravas choose Krishna's army, while the Pandavas choose Krishna himself. Then the war—and the *Bhagavad Gita*, the most famous section of the *Mahabharata*, its bourgeois core—begins.

———

And then the war almost immediately stops. On the first day of fighting, the *Bhagavad Gita* creates a moment of considerable moral power when the Kauravas and Pandavas approach each other on the field of battle. As the two sides grow near enough to recognize each other's faces, one of the Pandava princes feels a pang of doubt. Arjuna is his name, and he is a great and famous archer. One of the main tactics of fighting at the time was to put your best archers in a chariot where they could stand several feet above the opposition and shoot down into their advancing infantry. Arjuna is so good that he has the privilege of riding in the bright white chariot of Lord Krishna himself, with all his protective powers.

So the pang of doubt that Arjuna feels is not about winning or not. His doubt is his recognition that the men are the other side are men just like him. He sees that they are "teachers, fathers, and grandfathers, sons and grandsons, uncles, fathers-in-law, brothers-in-law, and other relatives."[27] They are even his cousins. He feels he cannot fight them and asks Lord Krishna to stop the battle before it begins:

> Ah, my Lord! I crave not for victory, nor for kingdom, nor for pleasure. What were a kingdom or happiness or life to me, when those for whose sake I desire these things stand here about to sacrifice their property and their lives. . . . We are worthy of a nobler feat than to slaughter our relatives. . . . Lord! how can we be happy if we kill our kinsmen? Although these men, blinded by greed, see no guilt in destroying their kin or fighting against their friends, should not we, whose eyes are open, who consider it to be wrong to annihilate our house, turn away from so great a crime?[28]

So Krishna moves his white chariot between the armies to stop the fighting. Arjuna drops his bow and a high bourgeois moment begins. As the armies wait, Krishna and Arjuna discuss the nature of the good. Krishna explains to Arjuna about the dangers of desire:

> He attains peace who, giving up desire, moves through the world without aspiration, possessing nothing which he can call his own, and free from pride.[29]

In place of the attachments of desire that come from our senses and the material world, Krishna explains that Arjuna should practice attachments of a very different sort. He should "yoke" himself to right action, to devotion, to knowledge, and to meditation, four forms of the disciplining of the self known as *yoga*, which means "yoking." Yoking to right action is *karma yoga*:

> All honor to him whose mind controls his senses; for he is thereby beginning to practice Karma Yoga, the Path of Right Action, keeping himself always unattached [to the world of senses].[30]

Plus there is *bhakti yoga*, the yoga of devotion; *jnana yoga*, the yoga of knowledge; and *raja yoga*, the yoga of meditation. In this way, Arjuna can discover the righteous order and law that it is his duty to follow: *dharma*. If he practices it well enough, the measure of his intentions and actions—his *karma*—might be good enough to escape *samsara*, the cycle of reincarnation. Arjuna will then finally be able to unite his soul, his *atman*, with *brahman*—the all-pervading reality that lies behind material nature, *prakrti*, which we experience through the desires of our senses. He might thereby escape *prakrti*'s third nature hold on his ambitions, the source of politics, and experience only the pure, egoless consciousness the *Bhagavad Gita* calls *purusha*.

What is Arjuna's duty to *dharma*? He is an archer, a soldier. So his duty is to fight—not for personal gain or glory, but because of his yoking to his position in society. Yet, importantly, this yoking is not to his position within his lines of kinship. Indeed, Krishna's whole explanation of *karma* and *dharma* comes in response to Arjuna's doubt about whether he should fight against his relatives. Rather, it is his skill and his training as a Kshatriya—his skill and position in relationship to caste, class, state, and empire—that it is his duty to follow. But most especially his duty is to his skill and position in relationship to caste, which leads to his duty to class, state, and empire. As Lord Krishna says in the *Bhagavad Gita*'s most controversial passage, caste is a divine injunction. It is not an injunction made up by human society and all its politics, he maintains.

The system of four castes was created by Me,
According to the distribution of the qualities and their acts.
Although I am the creator of this,
Know Me to be the eternal non-doer.[31]

Caste, then, is not political, Lord Krishna relates. Is it not political because
Krishna is not political. He does not do things. He is eternal, and he has no
desires, no intentions, no taint of action. Thus neither will Arjuna, if he follows
what Krishna says.

Actions do not taint Me;
I have no desire for the fruit of action;
Thus he who comprehends Me
Is not bound by actions.[32]

The essential thing, Krishna explains, is for Arjuna to give up desire and
thereby learn to act without politics, reaching perfection: a natural conscience
of other, self, and community—of thee, me, and we.

Relinquishing egotism, force, arrogance,
Danger, anger, and possession of property;
Unselfish, tranquil,
He is fit for oneness with Brahman.[33]

And Arjuna replies,

My delusion is destroyed and I have gained wisdom
Through Your grace, Krishna.
My doubts are gone.
I shall do as You command.[34]

The *Bhagavad Gita* ends. Arjuna rejoins the war. The battle restarts.

————

The bourgeois vision of the *Bhagavad Gita*, then, is broadly similar to Buddhism, especially its focus on *dharma* and *karma*; on release from the cycle of
samara through disciplined practice, thereby escaping the third nature pain
of our ambitions; and on overcoming the commitments of kin ties. For both
Buddhism and Hinduism, release from *samsara* is release from politics into
the innocence of a natural conscience, finding the natural other in *dharma*,
the natural me in *karma*, and the natural we in the social duties of disciplined

practice. All one's politics thereby become nonpolitical, for they are guided by that which is beyond politics.

They have important differences too, of course. Hinduism weights the political rightness of *dharma* more in terms of one's moral and social duty, meaning what constitutes the right action of *karma* depends more heavily on one's social position. Buddhism tends to see *karma* as being the same for everyone. In Hinduism, the sufferings of our position in life are mainly a matter of punishment for misdeeds in our past lives, which also prevent us from release from *samsara*. In Buddhism, the suffering we face in this life is more a matter of the enlightenment we have not yet achieved concerning release from desire, keeping us in the cycle of samsara. At the risk of oversimplification, we could say that *samsara* is more a stick in Hinduism and more a carrot in Buddhism— punishment to be avoided versus enlightenment to be gained. Still, this is all comfortably bourgeois, claiming the absolute good of the nonpolitical.

There is a lot more to Hinduism than the *Bhagavad Gita*, though. Its many traditions contain many surprises—what we might call *bourgeois surprises*, for they are only surprising from a bourgeois point of view. Hinduism's many crossings of people, animals, spirits, gods, genders, emotions, and social statuses; its pleasure in stories that astonish with their complex plots and messy outcomes; and its frank and welcoming attitude toward sexual pleasure: these rhythms of the sacred jostle and ruffle against the more settled accounts of, say, Christianity or Buddhism. Hinduism is also famously polytheistic and poly-divine, while at same time finding a unity through all this diversity in the notion of *brahman*, the holistic spirit of the universe that runs within and behind everything, including the gods themselves. And as is typical of pagan, nature-before-nature traditions, there is a vibrant pluralism of the divine and semidivine that clangs and jangles with the difficulties of kin ties—even as Krishna recommends a non-kin-based path of *karma* and *dharma* for Arjuna. The Hindu gods are not isolated entities, with separate origins, unrelated to each other and to humans. They have families, with all the contentments and troubles that families give.

Take Ganesha, one of the most popular divinities in Hinduism today. Hindus turn to Ganesha for his special powers in helping people remove obstacles and make good beginnings, for his patronage of science and the arts, and for his role as god of wisdom and intellect. His life has had its share of tragedy, including death and resurrection. He is also the son of the supreme god Shiva, according to many Hindus, as well as also being born through an immaculate conception with no act of sex. To this extent, Ganesha fits within a broadly bourgeois religious imagination, resonating with the life stories of Jesus and the Buddha—albeit a polytheistic and poly-divine bourgeois imagination.

But there are plenty of surprises, too. Most obviously for anyone who knows his famous image, Ganesha has the head of an elephant, immediately attesting to a religious vision that crosses the natural and supernatural. He gets it shortly after his birth.[35] The goddess Parvati takes a bath and asks her husband's bull to make sure no one disturbs her. Yet when her husband Shiva comes home, the bull fails to stop him from intruding. So Parvati wipes some turmeric paste from her body, which she had been using to clean herself, and breathes life into it, creating Ganesha, so she can have someone more loyal guard her bath. Shiva is furious when he comes home during her next bath and Ganesha doesn't let him pass. They fight and Shiva slices off Ganesha's head, killing him. It is Parvati's turn to be furious, and she begins to destroy all of creation in her anger. At this, Shiva relents and asks the god Brahma (not to be confused with brahman) to go get a replacement head. Brahma comes back with the head of the first being he happens to encounter: an elephant. Shiva puts it on Ganesha's body, restores him to life, and declares him to be officially his son. Her son restored, Parvati stops destroying creation.

In addition to the crossing of nature and supernature, Ganesha's birth story illustrates other nature-before-nature sensibilities in Hindu traditions. The gods are emotional and often caught up in the conflicts of domestic and sexual politics. And the gods are both male and female. Hindus generally revere a divine trinity, again somewhat like Christianity, known as the trimurti, the "three forms." But most Hindus understand the three forms to be manifested by three male-female pairs of divinities: Brahma and Saraswati, the creators; Vishnu and Lakshmi, the preservers; and Shiva and Parvati, the destroyers and transformers. Some Hindu traditions emphasize the male manifestations more, as in Vaishnavism's celebration of the power of Vishnu or as in Shaivism's central worship of Shiva. But Shaktism, one of the largest branches of Hinduism, focuses most of all on the female manifestations, seeing them all as different forms of Devi, the great mother goddess. Smartism, the fourth major branch of Hinduism, more or less worships them all equally, while also elevating Ganesha and the sun god Surya to the same highest level of the divine, expanding the trimurti into five forms of the divine known as the panchayatana puja.[36]

Hindu gods are often imperfect, another bourgeois surprise. Ganesha has a broken tusk, for example. He broke it off to serve as a pen when he wrote down the Mahabharata for Vyasa. Ganesha is also fat and jolly and loves to dance. Plus he's funny looking—and there is nothing irreverent in saying so. Hindu tradition has no trouble laughing at, and with, the gods. A little laughter helps Hindus deal with what they see as an evident observation about the world: The gods are not necessarily good. Although the gods are often heroic and helpful—and some gods particularly so, like Vishnu, especially his avatars Krishna and Rama—many of them are as flawed and political as we humans are. The gods are just massively more powerful.

For Hindus, the divine also embodies and intervenes in nature and our ecological relations. The sun is the god Surya, riding across the sky in a chariot pulled by seven celestial horses, one for each color in the rainbow. Indra is the bellicose god of rain and thunder, and his bow is said to be the rainbow itself. Most Hindu gods have a *vahana*, or mount, that transports them wherever they need to go, and that they have special powers to control. Ganesha rides a rat, which he keeps in control with a snake. Shiva and Parvati ride Shiva's bull. Lakshmi rides an elephant, and sometimes an owl. Ushas, the goddess of the dawn, rides a chariot pulled by seven red cows. It is not hard to see here a divine agroecology, controlling the forces of sustenance with which every farmer must daily contend.

Controversially, many Hindus maintain another tradition familiar to pagan, nature-before-nature religions: animal sacrifice, especially agricultural animals. Siddhartha, Mahavira, and Jesus banned animal sacrifice among their followers, and it disappeared from Judaism after the diaspora. But animal sacrifice continues today in some branches of Hinduism, especially in Nepal and Bali. Hindu worshippers typically sacrifice farm livestock such as buffalo, bulls, goats, and chickens. At Nepal's vast festival for Gadhimai, the goddess of power, which takes place every five years, devotees slaughter thousands of animals—reputedly some quarter million or so at the 2009 festival, including about ten thousand water buffalo, which are widely domesticated in Asia.[37] Many Hindus disagree with these practices, and animal rights activists campaign strongly against them. Most devout Hindus also engage in uncontroversial forms of sacrifice as part of their daily rituals: the practice of giving *tarpana*, a small offering to the gods and to one's ancestors. Typical forms of *tarpana* include cow's milk mixed with spices, a spoonful of sesame seeds, or even just a bit of water.

————————

Hinduism, then, is a complex and varied religious tradition. Some have even argued that we would do better to speak of Hinduisms in the plural, rather than in the singular. Despite this complexity and variety, Hindus have long maintained a strong sense of unified identity across their many traditions, and their many manners of living, from agrarian to urban, pagan to bourgeois.[38] Consider India, which has the largest population of Hindus. Some four hundred million people live in India's cities. By no means do they all lead middle-class lives, but twenty-two million of them own cars, as of 2013, and several times more than that live in households that own cars. That's a lot of people with access to private cars, roughly as many as in France. Meanwhile, some eight hundred million people in India continue to live agrarian lives, living mainly from subsistence agriculture. A notable achievement of Vyasa and other Hindu sages has been to divine a religious tradition that speaks across this variety, forging an alloy of the pagan and bourgeois.

By contrast, the Buddha himself and the initial forms that Buddhism took had little to say about this broader sweep of the human condition, contributing to its eventual decline in India. As Buddhism developed, it did find some ways—often, as I put it earlier, rather "shy" ways—to connect with pagan concerns and lives. Buddhism in some parts of Asia includes significant elements of polytheism, poly-divinity, and sustenance rituals, and also embraces side-by-side practice with more pagan and agrarian traditions, such as Shinto in Japan, as I mentioned.[39] But this broader connection came a bit late, and remains not as strong as in Hinduism. Pagan practices like ancestor veneration and animal sacrifice do not easily fit in a purely Buddhist frame.

Meanwhile, Hinduism "shyly" took on some elements of Buddhism, even coming to regard the Buddha as another incarnation of the Hindu god Vishnu.[40] Consequently, notes Peter Harvey, there was "a dilution of the distinctiveness of Buddhism relative to the rising power of Hinduism."[41] Plus the implications of Hinduism's greater comfort with caste hierarchy cannot have been missed by those in a position to be advantaged by it—and who were also those in a better position to shape its canon. Combined with the vagaries of elite politics over the millennia and Buddhist regions being more in the path of the twelfth-century Muslim invasions, Hinduism's earlier and greater electrum appeal steadily edged Buddhism out in India.[42]

Hinduism is indeed a complex and varied tradition. It is a complex and varied tradition for a complex and varied people.

———

"What the heck is this, Daddy?" Eleanor asked.

We were riding side by side on a plane from Chicago to Paris, a bourgeois moment (as all air travel is) amplified in this case by the privilege of Delta's "economy comfort" seats. But although we had sprung an extra hundred bucks or so per seat for a bit of additional legroom, that privilege apparently didn't apply to having an actual working video screen for Eleanor. No matter what she did, it persisted in showing the same movie.

"I don't know, but it looks like fun."

It was, even without sound. By comparing with my screen (which did work) we eventually figured out that we were watching *Bajrangi Bhaijaana*, a 2015 Bollywood movie with Bollywood's biggest star, Salman Khan, in the lead role. The color and excitement of all the dance scenes was enough to hold our attention, despite the lack of music and dialogue. And it had English subtitles, so we were able to follow the plot.

A devout Brahmin man played by Khan gets unwillingly befriended by a six-year-old girl who cannot speak. Although he initially tries to avoid the girl, he eventually takes a shine to her, in part because he suspects she must also be a Brahmin, given her lighter brown skin tone. Khan's character semi-adopts the girl while he tries to figure out who her parents are, despite the fact that she cannot speak and has no identity papers. Along the way, the movie finds occasion for one amazing scene after another of crowds dancing in the street to the Hindu gods, impelled by what we imagined were the catchy tunes and rhythms of Bollywood music. But eventually it emerges that the girl must be a Muslim from Pakistan. The characters watch a televised sports match between Pakistan and India, and the girl starts cheering for Pakistan. And she happily wanders off into nearby Muslim homes a couple of times, leading Khan's character to panic until he finds her. All this is a shock to Khan and his friends. Undaunted, he decides to try to take her back to Pakistan to find her mother, which in the end he does, despite many misadventures. Eventually he comes to be seen as a hero to both Pakistan and India.

In real life, Khan himself has a Muslim father and a Hindu mother, and often describes himself as both Hindu and Muslim. Pretty much everyone in South Asia knows this, and it helps the film ask its viewers to reflect on some important basic facts of social life. There may be almost no Buddhists in India today, but there are a huge number of Muslims—enough that India ranks as the third largest Muslim country in the world. India's neighbors to the east and west, Bangladesh and Pakistan, are dominantly Muslim but have two of the world's largest populations of Hindus. Bangladesh has the third largest, and Pakistan has the fifth largest. There have been long-standing tensions between and within these three countries over this. Let's overcome it all, is the movie's point.

For sure.

Besides, for all their differences, Islam and Hinduism have a similarly electrum sheen. Islam's alloy, though, was forged in a remarkably short period of time in the midst of a striking social and political opening.

The early seventh century CE was not a calm time to be living in the Arabian Peninsula. The Sasanian Empire to the east clashed its ambitions against the Byzantine Empire to the west, with Arabia caught in between. It was an old fight. The Sasanians were the descendants of the Persian Empire and the Byzantines the Roman, and they had been at each other's throats on and off for hundreds of years. The period between 602 and 628 was particularly bloody, both on the battlefield and in the golden halls of the elite. Murders. Executions. Breakaway factions. Armies and navies sweeping this way and that. Finally, in 628, both sides collapsed in mutual exhaustion, destruction, and impoverishment.

The peoples of the Arabian Peninsula didn't know which way to turn. They enjoyed a measure of independence from both Byzantium and the Sasanians, but only by means of careful diplomacy, aided by their protective shield of sand and water on most sides. The various Arabian tribes were guessing differently about the constantly changing best bets as to whom to side with, and often guessing wrong. They weren't getting along very well with each other, either. There was no central authority over the Arabian Peninsula's roughly one million square miles. Plus the tribes were constantly on the move, hunting water and forage for their sheep and their camels. Misunderstandings and conflicts were common. It didn't help that the tribes also made it a point of pride and wealth to raid each other's livestock.[43]

Another source of conflict was also on the rise: social class. It takes special skills to navigate the sands of the Mideast deserts. One could move the increasing flow of commerce between east and west through the oceans, but the boats of the time were small, slow, and hard to control. One could attempt a northern land route, but Pakistan, Afghanistan, and Iran are really quite staggeringly mountainous. And one could use the old solution of countless armies and follow the Euphrates to where it nearly meets with the Mediterranean, but that took a long time and meant having to pass right through the zone of Byzantine and Sasanian conflict, presenting a dicey challenge to the merchant eager to avoid local taxes, bandits, and half-starved armies. Another common means, then, was to draw on those special desert skills and sell through the Arabians, with their caravans of camels. The result was that Arabia's few urban centers were flush and flourishing, especially Mecca, the center of the caravan trade. Inequality was rising dramatically. The carefully crafted ties of kin and tribe, always at issue, were fraying even more.

One Meccan man was particularly troubled by the consequences for Arabian society. He was a well-regarded merchant himself. He had been orphaned at a young age and so didn't get much starter capital from his own family. But people admired his trustworthy character, rather rare for the caravan trade. He became particularly established in the trade route to the Mediterranean Sea, where he came into closer contact with the cultures of that region. A wealthy widow named Khadija learned of his reputation and hired him to run her caravan business.[44] He turned out to be very good at it. They also turned out to be very good for each other, and after a short time they married. Most sources say she proposed to him, rather than the other way around.[45] After all he was just twenty-five at the time and she was forty, in addition to her being his boss. Plus this was her third marriage. Khadija already had three children, and the two of them went on to have six more together. All the sources agree that Khadija and her new husband, who was named Muhammad, loved each other very dearly.

But although his own life was good, Muhammad found the times disturbing. He had been having a lot of perplexing dreams and had taken to climbing a mountain just outside of Mecca, praying alone in a small cave about a third of the way up, hoping to clear his mind and gain perspective on the many tensions of life in Mecca. One night in 610 CE, he reported having a remarkable experience. The angel Gabriel suddenly appeared in the cave and said to him, "Recite!"[46] The startled Muhammad replied that he didn't know what to recite. The angel repeated the command two more times, until finally Muhammad found himself speaking the lines now included as Sura 96—the 96th chapter—in the Qur'an, Islam's holiest scripture (also sometimes rendered in English as the Koran or the Quran). Indeed, the name Qur'an means "the recitation."

At first Muhammad thought he must be going crazy, or that he was possessed by a demon. The angel Gabriel reappeared and told him, no, he had been chosen to be God's messenger in these troubled times. Muhammad talked to Khadija about it. She reassured him that he really had been visited by the angel Gabriel. Tradition therefore considers her the first convert to the religion that Muhammad found himself articulating, the religion of Islam, those who "submit" to the will of God. They then went to see Khadija's cousin Waraqa—a Christian, in fact. He agreed that Muhammad's recitations really were divinely inspired.[47] Slowly at first, others came to agree as well. Now a billion and a half do, making Islam the second largest religion in the world, after Christianity.

Muhammad's religious vision differed dramatically from that of most Arabs of the time, although we don't know many details of those older customs. Early adherents to Islam thoroughly destroyed most of the evidence, from texts to temples. Scholars have sorted through a few hints and stories in the Qur'an and other sources, especially *The Book of the Idols*, a manuscript by the early Arabian historian Hisham Ibn Al-Kalbi, written about 800 CE. *The Book of Idols* barely survived. A century ago, a collector picked up the only known full copy at an auction in Damascus. It's treasure for the historian, but tarnished treasure, for its standards of history aren't exactly those of today. So there's plenty of disagreement about the finer points of what people believed and practiced during the period Muslims call *Jahiliyah*, meaning the "days of ignorance." Still, we have a rough idea.

Not surprisingly, given their manner of life, the Arabian tribes mainly followed a range of nature-before-nature traditions. I say "mainly followed" because several of the tribes were Jewish, and Judaism by that time had already changed greatly from the pagan monotheism of the Hebrew Bible. Muhammad even had a Jewish wife, Safiyya—daughter of the chief of the Banu Nadir, one of the three known Jewish Arabian tribes—who converted to Islam. I'm getting ahead of the story a bit, but after Khadija died at about age sixty-five, concluding her twenty-five-year monogamous marriage to Muhammad, he married many other women, polygyny being customary for male leaders of the time. Accounts of the number of Muhammad's wives vary from eleven all the way up to nineteen.[48] (Part of the disagreement is what constituted a wife versus a concubine, and how that distinction relates to contemporary understandings of marriage.) Another of Muhammad's wives or concubines (depending on your point of view) was Maria, an Egyptian Christian, who also converted to Islam.

But although some were Jews and Christians, most of the Arab tribes had a polytheistic, poly-divine vision of a spirited world, moved by many gods, both male and female, as well as genies and ancestors, immanent in specific places and objects, and manifesting the uncertain and vital powers of ecological sustenance and what we now typically call nature. The tribes often diverged on the specifics, though. They were neither a politically nor religiously unified people. Given the mere shards of history that have come down to us, much of the scholarly confusion about pre-Islamic religious practices among the Arabs reflects this variation. Indeed, the notion of a unified and unchanging faith is anachronistic. It's something we bourgeois moderns often search for among pagan peoples and peoples of the past, feeling that a religious mentality always strives for systematic coherence, because ours does.

One point of confusion is over who was the lead god for most of the pre-Islamic Arab tribes: Allah or Hubal. In Muhammad's time, Hubal had pride of place inside the Masjid al-Haram, the Great Mosque of Mecca, where worshippers would cast his seven divination arrows to make difficult and important decisions.[49] At the center of the Great Mosque is a small cubic building, roughly forty feet on a side, built of dark granite blocks, and covered with a rich dark cloth. Muslims call it the Kaaba, and it is reputed to have been built by Abraham and his son Ishmael on the precise spot where Adam and Eve themselves had built the very first shrine to God. Some believe the Gates of Heaven lie in the sky directly above the Kaaba. Ishmael and his mother Hagar are said to be buried there. It's the holiest spot in Islam. But the Kaaba, which had been built several centuries before Muhammad's day, was then the shrine to Hubal. His idol stood inside, carved of red agate with a gold right hand. The Quraysh, the wealthiest Arab tribe, had placed the statue there.[50] Outside the Kaaba stood idols to many other divinities, apparently less powerful ones—as many as 360.[51] One of those idols was for the divinity called Allah, whose name simply means "the God."[52]

But some sources describe Allah as head of the pantheon, and more important than Hubal, even though Hubal's idol was inside the Kaaba. Certainly, the name "the God" seems rather maximally grand. As well, The Book of Idols and other records describe Allah as having three daughters during the Jahiliyah days, all of whom had idols at the Kaaba, and all of whom had popular shrines of their own: Manah, Allat, and Al-'Uzza. Manah seems to have been some kind of sea goddess, and her shrine at the coastline was a popular pilgrimage site.[53] Allat's shrine, on the other hand, was at Ta'if, a city in the mountains east of Mecca, where she was worshipped in the form of a cubic rock, tended by a Jewish priest who used to make a barley porridge in her honor.[54] (Some Arab Jews evidently did not observe a sharp line between monotheistic and polytheistic practice.) Perhaps Allat was an agricultural goddess, given the ritual of barley porridge. We don't really know. Her name, however, means simply "the Goddess," suggesting that that she may have originally been Allah's consort—or maybe the sources have confused Allah's consort for a daughter.[55] The importance of her cult seems to have declined, however.[56] By the time of Muhammad, the most powerful goddess was Al-'Uzza, goddess of love and chastity.[57] Her shrine was also to the east of Mecca, on the way to Ta'if. She inhabited three sacred trees there, and her shrine was also the site of an oracle. The Arab tribes would offer Al-'Uzza gifts and sacrifices, and ask her to intercede on their behalf with her father, Allah.[58]

Whether Hubal or Allah was the head god, one thing is sure: the name Allah definitely predates Muhammad. In fact, Muhammad's father was Abdullah, meaning "worshipper of Allah" or "servant of Allah." Perhaps what we are seeing dimly through the dust was actually in part a tribal dispute over whether Hubal or Allah was the head god. There's a powerful story that suggests social conflicts that aligned with these two gods. Muhammad's grandfather needed to fulfill a vow by sacrificing one of his own children to Hubal, and went to the Kaaba to cast Hubal's divination arrows.[59] When the arrows pointed at Abdullah, Muhammad's grandfather refused to comply, and reportedly sacrificed a hundred camels instead—a huge expense. Hubal and his cult could not have been a family favorite after that, and quite possibly already wasn't, but nonetheless associated with social factions that were hard to contest. Thus, it may have been a pointed choice that Muhammad's father had been named "worshipper of Allah."

———

Whatever the backstory—all human lives have backstories—Muhammad himself was clear that there was only one true God, and that the proper Arabic name to use to refer to him was Allah, not Hubal. He kept experiencing revelations from God for twenty-two years, reciting them to others, who memorized them and also wrote them down.[60] Within a very few years of Muhammad's death in 632, scholars assembled complete versions of the Qur'an, and agreed on a standardized version in 650.

The result is widely regarded as a literary masterpiece, aside from its theological significance. The language is often quite memorable and beautiful, and perhaps even more so in the original Arabic, which I cannot read. (Many Muslims contend that the Qur'an can truly be comprehended only in the original Arabic.) But rather than focusing on telling grand stories about notable personages and events, the Qur'an primarily rallies the believers, gives accounts of God's majesty, and sets down strictures on what one should do and should not do. Most of it reads more like Leviticus and Psalms than Genesis and Chronicles, more like the Letters of Paul than the Four Gospels, more like the *Bhagavad Gita* than the rest of the *Mahabharata*. Any stories are usually pretty short.

Muslims also gain counsel and instruction from the second great foundation of Islamic thought: the *Sunnah*—the customary practices of the Muslim community, based largely on how the Prophet lived his life. Most important are *hadith*: short sayings and descriptions of Muhammad that people remembered after his death, which have been gathered together into different collections by the various branches of Islam. The term *Sunnah* derives from the Arabic for "path" or "practice." It's a very appropriate metaphor. A helping hand on either side, the *Sunnah* and the Qur'an guide Muslims along what the Qur'an calls the "straight path" to a life of virtue—to a natural me cleansed of the micro- and macro-politics of personal ambition.[61]

More than anything else, those helping hands on that straight path lead the Muslim through the troublesome concerns of an increasingly urban and bourgeois life. Most of Islam's main "pillars," as Muslims like to call their faith's central principles, resonate with the themes of bourgeois faith—not surprisingly, perhaps, given that the Qur'an positions itself within the Abrahamic tradition.[62] Indeed, in Islam's own view, it is as old as any other Abrahamic faith. It sees itself as the unifier of the Abrahamic tradition, not a new division of it. A constant theme of the Qur'an is the connection of its revelations with those of both the Old Testament and the New Testament, from Adam and Eve to Abraham to Moses to Jesus—as well as Noah, Lot, Isaac, Jacob, Ishmael, and Mary, all of whom often appear in the Qur'an.[63] Jesus gets 25 mentions. Adam gets 26. Abraham gets 71. Moses gets 171.[64] And many Bible stories get a mention in the Qur'an, albeit often with significant differences and generally in considerably shortened form. As the Qur'an says of believers in Islam,

> We believe in God and that which has been revealed to us; in what was revealed to Abraham, Ishmael, Isaac, Jacob, and the tribes; to Moses and Jesus and the other prophets by their Lord. We make no distinction among any of them, and to Him we submit.[65]

To this ancient tradition the Qur'an adds the revelations of an additional prophet, Muhammad. One of the constant themes of his revelations are the bourgeois troubles of excess and material desire that divert people from *fitra*, the purity of our natural constitution at birth—the innocence and harmony with God we have at the moment of our creation. (*Fitra* literally means "creation," similar to the Greek and Latin for nature, *physis* and *natura*, which derive from the root words for being "born.")[66] But social life, combined with how *Iblis*— also known as *Shaytan*, the Arabic term for *Satan*—plays on our free will, easily leads us away from God and into selfish material desires, the Qur'an contends.

> By the charging steeds that pant and strike sparks with their hooves, who make dawn raids, raising a cloud of dust, and plunging into the midst of the enemy, man is ungrateful to his Lord—and He is witness to this—he is truly excessive in his love of wealth.[67]

The Qur'an sternly warns its readers about the consequences of this excess.

> Woe to every fault-finding backbiter who amasses riches, counting them over, thinking they will make him live forever. No indeed! He will be thrust into the Crusher! What will explain to you what the Crusher is? It is God's Fire, made to blaze, which rises over people's hearts. It closes in on them in towering columns.[68]

Rather, the Qur'an commands the believer to give alms.

> Believers, do not let your wealth and your children distract you from remembering God: those who do so will be the ones who lose. Give out of what We have provided for you, before death comes to one of you.[69]

In this way one can be saved from the fires of Hell.

> The most pious one will be spared this [Hellfire]—who gives his wealth away as self-purification, not to return a favour to anyone but for the sake of his Lord the Most High—and he will be well pleased.[70]

Another of the Qur'an's strongly bourgeois themes is *tawhid*, the Islamic conviction that God is one, indivisible and universal. The Qur'an sees *tawhid* as a point of difference with Christianity. "Do not speak of a 'Trinity,'" the Qur'an reads. "God is only one God, He is far above having a son, everything in the heavens and earth belongs to Him."[71] The Qur'an also does not use the image of God as a "father," and most Muslims argue that God has no gender.[72] Arabic requires a gender assignment, though; there is no neutral pronoun form. One might inquire why, if a choice has to be made, the Qur'an goes with masculine pronouns for God. But so, too, do Judaism and Christianity. And by not carrying a masculine image of God into a conceptualization of god as father, Muslims contend Islam is the more monotheistic, for a father implies children, which implies that the divine is not only one. I'll let the Muslim and Christian theologians argue out (if they desire) whether this is a difference in degree or form of monotheism. But I will note that Islam embraces the notion of angels and devils, including Shaytan. It does accept the existence of other spirits, some of which, like the angel Gabriel, are accorded at least semidivine status. But again, so do the other Abrahamic faiths.

Tawhid helps enable another of Islam's constant refrains: the unity of believers. One god, one people; one people, one god. Here again, Islam resonates with the other Abrahamic and bourgeois religions in the development of what

I earlier called quasi-kinship, a sense of kin-like ties that people feel cut across actual traceable blood relations—but a divinely sanctioned quasi-kinship, a natural we rooted in the goodness of the grace of God, yielding a community of the good. "You are all part of the same family," the Qur'an suggests, so

> [h]old fast to God's rope all together; do not split into factions. Remember God's favour to you: you were enemies and then He brought your hearts together and you became brothers by His grace.[73]

This feeling of family and brotherhood even among those who are not blood relations the Qur'an calls the *ummah*, the community of believers. At times, the Qur'an includes Judaism and Christianity—those it calls the "people of the book"—in the *ummah*, in line with Islam's vision of itself as the unifier of the Abrahamic tradition. But generally in the later sections of the Qur'an, the *ummah* is only the community of Muslims. As well, the Qur'an places considerable emphasis on the difference between "believers" and "disbelievers," and the need for believers to hold together.

The Qur'an encourages that holding together through a sharply bivalent conception of God's attitude toward the doings of people. God is merciful, the Qur'an frequently reassures, but often warns as well that "God is strong and severe in His punishment."[74] Similarly, the Qur'an cautions, "Who could be more wrong than someone who rejects God's revelations and turns away from them? We shall repay those who turn away with a painful punishment."[75] And it also puts the two points together, writing that "your Lord is swift in punishment, yet He is most forgiving and merciful."[76] Punishment and mercy are two of the most common words in the Qur'an.[77] Yet this too is familiarly bourgeois. Both the Old and New Testaments show plenty of the same ambivalence, and the concept of *karma*'s effects on *samsara* plays a similar moral role in the Brahmanic traditions.

This tough love incentive to follow a straight path affords considerable power to whoever articulates the rules. In the case of Christianity and Buddhism, it is Jesus and the Buddha. In the case of Islam, it is the Prophet Muhammad, God's messenger. "Whoever obeys the Messenger obeys God," the Qur'an counsels.[78] "Obey God and His Messenger if you are true believers," it later reminds its readers.[79] Quite obviously, Muhammad was, and is, accorded huge authority and honor by his followers. As with Jesus and the Buddha, followers retain enormous interest in even the smallest detail of how Muhammad led his life—his habits, his beliefs, his history—seeking guidance and giving obeisance.

There is more than a whiff of hierarchy here. It's the smell of the political in the natural conscience. In the case of Muhammad and his followers, those politics led to the establishment of the first Arabian state, with Muhammad as leader of both the faith and the government. He was also the military leader—apparently, quite a brilliant one—during the struggle of the Muslims with the disbelievers, who were mainly led by the Quraysh tribal authorities in Mecca, home of the Great Mosque and the Kaaba. Simultaneously head of the faith, government, and military, he was pretty much as powerful as a person can be.

This power and authority did not come easily. A few years after Muhammad's revelations began, he started to preach openly about the form of faith his recitations described. The Quraysh authorities were not amused and persecuted many of the early converts to Islam, including killing a slave woman owned by a Quraysh leader. (Not surprisingly, given its bourgeois concerns about wealth and power, many slaves were early on attracted to Islam.) Initially, Muhammad was protected by his clan ties and his wife Khadija's wealth and status. But Khadija died in 619, and so too did Muhammad's uncle, the leader of Muhammad's sub-clan of the Quraysh, the Banu Hashim. The next leader of the Banu Hashim was no friend of Muhammad and Islam, and withdrew the clan's protection. In 622, having heard about an assassination plot, Muhammad made his famous *Hijrah*, his migration north two hundred miles to the city then called Yathrib, and soon renamed Madinat an-Nabi, the "city of the Prophet," or Medina for short, as it is still called to this day. Many of his followers soon followed.

Muhammad seems to have realized at this time, if not earlier, that he could not establish a religion on its own. Islam would not survive without political protection. But there was no state he could turn to for support, for there was no Arabian state, and the neighboring Byzantine and the Sasanian empires were imploding. So he decided to establish one.

Muhammad went about state building in a remarkable way. One of his first acts was to establish the *Ṣahifat al-Madinah*, the Charter of Medina, what is often regarded as the first written constitution anywhere. The charter commits the nine Arab tribes then in Medina to act as one *ummah*—together with local Jews, who were quite numerous in Medina. The Jews had to follow the political lead of the Muslims, but were otherwise free to practice their own faith in their own way given that, as the charter put it, the Jews "have their religion and the Muslims have theirs."[80] The agreement with the Jews soon fell apart, though, and they switched to supporting the Quraysh in Mecca. The *ummah* of the Muslims persisted nonetheless, and they battled the Quraysh, the other pagan Arab tribes, and the Jews for the next eight years, with Muhammad as their general. Usually they won, including surviving a siege of Medina in which they were greatly outnumbered. Finally, in 630, Muhammad led about ten thousand Muslims into Mecca and took the city, promptly destroying all the idols in the Great Mosque and elsewhere, and rededicating the Kaaba solely to the worship of Allah. Within two years, the entire rest of the Arabian Peninsula had surrendered to Muhammad's authority, and most had professed conversion to Islam. A new religious tradition and a new state had been established, both headed by Muhammad.[81]

These were commanding politics. But the Qur'an had an answer for those who grumbled that this was all a power play on the part of Muhammad— essentially the same answer that Christianity gave for Jesus's assumption of a leadership position, and that Buddhism gave for the Buddha's. Although there were clear political implications in Muhammad's mission, it was not driven by politics, the Qur'an contends, for the origin of that mission lay outside the human. Rather, it sprang from the absolute goodness—the natural conscience—of the will of God. Muhammad was the messenger, the Prophet, not the author of Islam and the words of the Qur'an. He only recited the Qur'an, articulating what was revealed to him. He didn't write it. People used to ask Muhammad to "Bring [us] a different Qur'an, or change it," the Qur'an reports. Here's Muhammad's reply:

> It is not for me to change it of my own accord; I only follow what is revealed to me, for I fear the torment of an awesome Day, if I were to disobey my Lord. . . . If God had so willed, I would not have recited it to you, nor would He have made it known to you.[82]

Besides, there is nothing special about me, he would say. "I am only a human being, like you, to whom it has been revealed that your God is One."[83] And he would point out the parallels of his own situation with that of prophets who had come before him, from Abraham and Moses to Jesus. "Alas for human beings! Whenever a messenger comes to them they ridicule him."[84] He was just doing his duty, "so obey God and the Messenger. If you turn away, remember that Our Messenger's duty is only to make plain his message."[85]

His duty done and the natural we of the *ummah* set well into motion, on June 8, 632, he rested his head on the lap of his wife Aisha, and died.

————

However early Muslims may have conceived their motives, Islam stands out in having a close relationship with state and empire almost from the start.

Christianity, New Judaism, Gnosticism, Buddhism, and Jainism all begin as reactions against state and empire. Christianity and Buddhism—through later politics that might well have surprised and upset their founders—eventually became embraced by the very empires they contested, gaining a mighty boost. New Judaism, Gnosticism, and Jainism never gained such support, and remain far smaller traditions today. Hinduism seems to have had a more ambivalent political birth, being neither anti-empire nor immediately embraced by empire, although in time it was, leading to its own governmental boost.[86]

At the time of Muhammad's death, Islam had the support of only a state, not an empire. But that was shortly to change. Arabian power swept across an astonishingly large territory at astounding speed. The Sasanian-Byzantine War had just ended in 628, and neither side could muster up much resistance, their armies and treasuries depleted by decades of fighting. By 637, led by some of Muhammad's former comrades in arms, Arab armies had taken Syria from the Byzantines and Iraq from the Sasanians. By 642, they had conquered Palestine and Egypt and broken the back of the entire Sasanian Empire, although it took another ten years before the Arabs had complete control of it. Over the next hundred years, they worked their way north into Anatolia, west over all of North Africa and up into Spain, and east into Afghanistan and Pakistan. At fifteen million square kilometers, the Arabian Empire had become the largest empire yet—topping even the Roman Empire and the Alexandrian Empire.[87]

Although the Arabian Empire spread rapidly, its Islamic core shortly underwent a major schism, a schism that is very much with us still today: Shia versus Sunni. Despite any religious allegiances, empires are all about ambition and bring conflict along with attempts to impose unity. In the Arabian Empire, the divisiveness of unity manifested in a dispute over who was the rightful successor of Muhammad, and thus also a debate over the rightful way for the successor to be chosen. One faction supported Abu Bakr, the father of Aisha, Muhammad's favorite wife among those he married after the death of Khadija. Another faction supported Ali Ibn Abi Talib, Muhammad's cousin and son-in-law, married to Fatimah, Muhammad's only surviving child and daughter of Khadija. The idea that a woman would succeed Muhammad was not socially tenable at the time. Neither Aisha nor Fatimah was championed to take over, but rather a man closely connected to them. Yet neither of those men had a claim that commanded a clear consensus. Which was better, being Muhammad's father-in-law or being his cousin and son-in-law? Abu Bakr and Ali were both from Muhammad's tribe, the Quraysh. But they were from different clans, which didn't help with consensus building. In the turmoil that followed, the supporters of Ali came to call themselves the Shia, an abbreviation of Shiatu Ali, meaning the "followers of Ali." Those who regard Abu Bakr as the rightful successor of Muhammad came to call themselves the Sunni, the followers of the Sunnah, the "path" that leads from Muhammad's teachings.

Things got bloody fast. Abu Bakr won out initially and became widely regarded as what the Sunni call the *kalifat Allah*, the caliph, meaning "deputy of God." Abu Bakr even died a natural death. But he ruled for only two years. The next two men to control the caliphate, Umar and Uthman, were both assassinated. Ali finally was elected to serve in 656, making him the fourth caliph in the reckoning of the Sunni and the first true successor of Muhammad in the reckoning of the Shia, who use the term "imam" (which simply means "leader") instead of "caliph." But then, five years later, he too was assassinated. Much blood continues to flow from this gash in the natural we of the *ummah*.

Despite the contentiousness at the top, huge numbers of people in the conquered regions converted to Islam, many willingly. And not surprisingly: the direction of the new tide of power was clear enough, even if there was some significant oscillation at its gravitational center. Jews and Christians were not required to convert. As "People of the Book," they enjoyed a somewhat protected status, as long as they paid their taxes and did not dispute Arab political control. Still, those were big caveats. The political incentive to convert was strong. Islam gained great social advantage through its association with a vast empire, as had Christianity, Buddhism, and Hinduism.

Conversion to Islam was not only a matter of advantage, though. (Nor was it for other traditions that gained imperial support.) Islam also spread because a great many people both learned about it and found it spiritually appealing. Most of those who took up Islam, however, could hardly be described as following bourgeois rhythms of life. Few areas conquered by the Arabian Empire were highly urbanized. These were mainly rural peoples. Rather, Islam's appeal rested as well on its electrum alloy with the pagan concerns of the agrarian majority. Yes, Islam offers a powerful vision of a supernatural basis for a natural conscience. But like Hinduism, Islam is packed with bourgeois surprises.

One such surprise is Muhammad's muted concern for the problem of desire, in comparison with the problem of disloyalty. The Qur'an and many *hadith* greatly emphasize the instillation of loyalty to the God of the people and to the people of the God, especially his messenger. *Asabiya* or "group feeling" is what Ibn Khaldun called it. Sociologists still read his 1377 book, the *Muqaddimah*, and assign it to their students.[88] (Me too.) Khaldun argued that *asabiya* is especially important for a dominantly nomadic people, such as the Arab tribes of the time, as opposed to more urban peoples who can come together on other bases of interaction, such as economic ties.[89] The challenge of binding together a rapidly growing and far-flung empire gave even more impetus to a great emphasis on loyalty, as well as helping overcome the conflict Ibn Khaldun saw between the mounting wealth of the few in the cities in comparison to the continued poverty of the agrarian majority. Of course, Christianity, Judaism, Buddhism, and other bourgeois traditions also emphasize loyalty, but in closer balance with concerns about the troubles of desire, as their teachings focused more on the moral needs of urban folk. To put it another way, the social organizational problem of Islam and the Arabian Empire was more horizontal, less vertical.

Desire concerned Muhammad too, as I noted earlier. But his concerns centered on excess and selfishness rather than desire itself. The Qur'an does not denounce wealth in the manner of Jesus's saying that it is harder for a camel to pass through the eye of a needle than it is for a rich person to enter heaven.[90] Rather, the Qur'an condemns those who do not share their wealth with the broader community, supporting those in need through giving alms, as in the quotes I gave above. The Qur'an also speaks out against usury, while favoring trade and the amassing of wealth, even arguing that God will reward the alms-giver with good economic fortune. One is to give charity to the poor, not loans with interest. It's worth hearing from the Qur'an at length on the subject, as it is such a strikingly different take from common practices elsewhere:

> God has allowed trade and forbidden usury. God blights usury, but blesses charitable deeds with multiple increase: He does not love the ungrateful sinner. Those who believe, do good deeds, keep up the prayer, and pay the prescribed alms will have their reward with their Lord: no fear for them, nor will they grieve. You who believe, beware of God: give up any outstanding dues from usury, if you are true believers. If you do not, then be warned of war from God and His Messenger. You shall have your capital if you repent, and without suffering loss or causing others to suffer loss.[91]

Many Muslims still take the injunctions to give alms and forbid usury quite seriously. For example, Islamic banks often operate on the notion of joint responsibility with the debtor for the repayment of loans, encouraging economic mutualism, what is sometimes called "Islamic banking." And it seems to work. To this day, most dominantly Islamic countries have considerably lower levels of economic inequality than most dominantly Christian, Hindu, or Buddhist countries, as well as than Israel, the only dominantly Jewish country.[92]

Let's turn to sexual desire and its relations of gender and power. Islam is widely regarded to be anti-sex—as well as anti-women, given the misogynist notion among some Muslims that women are at fault for instilling lust in men, as well as all the charged debate about the hijab, burqa, and niqab. And true enough, one does not find a lot to cheer the feminist in the Qur'an—at least as feminism is usually understood in the West, including by me.[93] But, once again, nor does one in the Bible or the Buddhist canon. Christians today often pass quickly over passages that don't fit their lives (as they should) such as Paul's injunctions that women need to veil themselves while praying, that wives "be subject to your husbands as you are to the Lord" because "the husband is the head of the wife," and that "women should be silent in the churches" because they "should be subordinate."[94] Buddhists similarly move fast over lines like the Buddha's phallocentric advice that one should "[g]uard against looking on a woman. If ye see a woman, let it be as though ye saw her not, and have no conversation with her." For a woman is manipulative and "desires to captivate with the charms of her beauty, and thus to rob men of their steadfast heart." Therefore, a Buddhist man had best protect himself "by regarding her tears and her smiles as enemies."[95]

One should not confuse current laws and customs with those of an earlier day, as described in the Qur'an, the Bible, the sayings of the Buddha, or any other ancient religious document. Indeed, sometimes our religious traditions were more liberal in ancient times than many of our current laws and customs.

Take how many of the *hadith* describe the sexuality of Muhammad. Jesus, the Buddha, and Mahavira do not engage in sex, say the scriptures of their traditions, and each of these great religious figures rejects family life. But many *hadith* plainly describe Muhammad as experiencing sexual desire, and as frequently acting on it. Not only is he married, eventually to a large number of wives, many *hadith* also describe his sexual practices in some intimate detail. We learn in one *hadith* collection, the *Kitab Al-Taharah* of *Sahih Muslim*, that "[o]ne day the Prophet (peace be upon him) had intercourse with all his wives," and that "[h]e took a bath after each intercourse."[96] In another, we even learn the details of precisely how he bathed himself after intercourse.[97]

During early Islamic times, Arabian culture exhibited a frankness in sexual and bodily matters would later shock the sensibilities of the Victorians. The tales collected in *1001 Arabian Nights* were notorious for their frequently bawdy storylines. Muḥammad ibn Muḥammad al-Nafzawi's *The Perfumed Garden* is a twelfth-century work that is pretty much an Arabian sex manual, complete with extensive advice on sexual technique for the mutual pleasure of the parties involved, including both heterosexual and homosexual gratification.[98] Sir Richard Burton's English translations of both were so offensive that, initially, they could be released only to the members of a private club.

Many *hadith* are also quite frank about excreta, a topic that scarcely appears in more dominantly bourgeois traditions like Christianity and Buddhism. We learn that when Muhammad "went (outside) to relieve himself, he went to a far-off place."[99] And we learn of Muhammad's view that "[w]hen any of you goes to the privy, he should not face or turn his back towards the qiblah [the direction for prayer]. [And] he should not cleanse with his right hand."[100] These are topics bourgeois culture has often found too rude even to mention, however real they are to all our lives.[101]

Menstruation, a topic that is quite real to the lives of women, also gets considerable discussion in many *hadith*, with two entire books of *hadith* devoted to the matter.[102] The Bible does at times mention the menses, but usually with a phallocentric horror and disdain. The *hadith* collections are still quite phallocentric on this subject, as on many others. It too is a male-dominated work written in a male-dominated time. But they report Muhammad as basically believing that, rather than isolating and seeing a woman as polluted during menstruation, a man ought, well, to give her a hug. One *hadith* puts it this way, according to the authority of Muhammad's wife Aisha: "When anyone amongst us (amongst the wives of the Holy Prophet) menstruated, the Messenger of Allah (may peace be upon him) asked her to tie a waist-wrapper over her (body) and then embraced her."[103]

Early Islam was also a time of some impressively strong women, even as female deities like Allat and Al-'Uzza were being discarded. Khadija perhaps is the most notable, given that she hired and proposed to Muhammad, that she was a successful and wealthy merchant in her own right, and that she was Islam's first convert—perhaps even before Muhammad himself, as she is the one who convinces him his visions are real.

Muhammad's youngest wife, Aisha, has an equally powerful narrative. She was none too fond of Ali, her father's rival as Muhammad's successor. And when Ali finally gained the caliphate, she led an army against him, launching a civil war known as the First Fitna. She won the opening battle, capturing the city of Basra. When Ali's army fought to retake Basra, Aisha led her army again, directing them from the back of a camel. This time she lost, but was ultimately spared by Ali. She went on to become one of the principal sources for *hadith*.

A rough parallel would be if the Gnostic "Gospel of Mary" was regarded as canonical in Christianity, instead of only male-authored gospels.[104]

Aisha was not the only woman warrior of the time. Nusayba bint Ka'b al-Ansariyya fought along the men during the Muslims' battles against the Meccans, and is credited with saving Muhammad's life during the disastrous Battle of Uhud when she shielded him, sustaining numerous lance and arrow wounds herself. Khawlah bint al-Azwar was a prominent soldier during the Arabian conquests, fighting in Syria, Jordan, and Palestine. The early records of the Arabian Empire also celebrate many prominent female scholars, including the mathematician Lubna of Cordoba and the legal theorists Faṭima bint Abi al-Qasim and Zaynab bint Ahmad. Plus a number of women became heads of state during early Islamic times, albeit never caliph or imam.

Nonetheless, the social stature of women in Islam weakened as the centuries unfolded, similar to other faiths closely associated with the spread of empires and their militarism, monetarization, improved record keeping, and centralization, all of which advantaged men over women. Although women are quite capable of physical violence, and there are records of women soldiers in ancient times, in Arabia and elsewhere, men are on the whole advantaged over women in physical combat, and thus in the social power that comes with it. Coined money and improved transport technologies facilitated trade at a distance, tending to promote male economic transcendence and female economic immanence, concentrating financial power in male hands while women's labor remained relatively local and outside of coined value. Techniques of better record keeping helped ensure that taxes, loans, and bills were paid and money differentially accumulated, as I've discussed. But better record keeping also provided a ready opportunity for gender hierarchy by the simple expedient of denying most women the opportunity to become literate. Better record keeping combined with militarism and coinage to promote the centralization of the state, consolidating male power. The social conditions of electrum faiths perhaps provided more scope for women's power than more dominantly bourgeois faiths, but not enough to prevent electrum men from eventually extracting almost all the gold from the alloy.

———

In addition to Islam's significantly more accommodating takes (at least initially) on both material and sexual desire, it articulates two more areas of bourgeois surprise: a more immanent conception of the divine, and a considerable emphasis on issues of agriculture and ecology.

Despite an unusually abstract conception of God—or maybe in part because of it and a corresponding need for some balance with immanence—

the Islamic divine is also quite personal. The Qur'an repeatedly describes God as aware of every thought and action of every person. You cannot hide anything from God. Don't even try. God is a witness to everything anyone does, both bad and good, and weighs out the appropriate rewards and punishments—all of which portrays God as quite attentive and involved in people's personal lives. Plus Islam makes as big a deal about Muhammad and his life on the Earth, and each and everything he ever did, as Christianity does about Jesus and Buddhism does about the Buddha, as I noted above. The Qur'an repeatedly emphasizes that Muhammad was a person and not a god, which is a huge part of his emotional role in Islam: he was here, immanent in the concrete of the everyday, an example for everyone of how to live a virtuous life. Nonetheless, although Islamic doctrine may often say otherwise, from a sociological point of view Muhammad is at least semidivine, given the holiness that Islam ascribes to every detail of his life. This conceptual borderline gives a sacredness to his immanence.

Islam also gives its adherents a powerful experience of divine immanence through its strong focus on place. For all its universalism, Islam considers one spot on the planet, the Kaaba with its Black Stone, the center of its worship. For all its universalism, Islam expects that all Muslims, at least once in their lives, will make the pilgrimage, the *hajj*, to Mecca and circle the Kaaba seven times. For all its universalism, Islam expects its followers to face the direction of the Kaaba—from wherever on the planet they happen at that moment to be—during each of the five daily prayers of an observant Muslim (often combined into three prayers by the Shia). Such practices bring transcendent notions of quasi-kinship, of *asabiya*, from the then and there into the immanence of the here and now.

Judaism may nearly be a match for Islam in its focus on place, leading to much conflict, of course. *Lashanah haba'ah biy'rushalaim*—"next year in Jerusalem"—is the Zionist concluding line of the Passover service. Christians and Buddhists also encounter the divine in the concreteness of place. Christians are passionate about Jerusalem too, as Buddhists are about Lumbini, the site of Buddha's birth. Yet Christianity and Buddhism demand no equivalent of the *hajj*. They do not ask all their faithful to face the same direction many times a day as they kneel in prayer, wherever they are. Nor does Judaism, although Jews generally lay out synagogues so they face Jerusalem, and Christians often plan churches so they face east, toward the rising sun.

We're talking matters of degree here, though. The sociologist must note that all the bourgeois faiths, however transcendent their philosophies, find need to provide ways to experience meaning immanently as well. The political scientist might note the same of empires.

Islam stands out more in the attention it gives to agricultural and ecological concerns. Consider the striking difference in Islam's conception of Heaven. The virtuous Christian looks to be admitted in the afterlife into what St. Augustine called the "Heavenly City," a place where there is no desire, unlike the "Earthly City." Instead of a heavenly city, the virtuous Muslim looks to be admitted into a heavenly garden, where food and water abounds. Consider this promise in the Qur'an: "As for those who believe and do good deeds, We shall admit them into Gardens graced with flowing streams and there they will remain forever."[105] They will be "given sustenance from the fruits of these Gardens" and will have "pure spouses" there.[106] In the Qur'an's vision, then, Heaven is not a place where we do not need to eat and do not have sexual desire. It is where our hungers are forever and easily satisfied.

Along with its more positive take on desire, the Qur'an has a more positive take on our *fitra*, our human nature, and on nature more generally. The problem is the *shayateen*, the devils, and the chief *shaytan*, *Iblis*, who tempt humans away from their *fitra*. The problem is not *fitra* itself. There is no original sin in Islam. Although the Qur'an does tell the story of Adam and Eve being seduced by *Iblis* into eating from the forbidden tree, God later forgives them.[107] Islamic legends do sometimes offer a third nature construction of the *shayateen* as taking the form of insects, snakes, hot desert wind, and other aspects of ecology that humans often find unpleasant, indirectly rooting our politics in a vision of nature as the source of evil. But *Iblis* and the other *shayateen* are not described as having material form in the Qur'an. Rather, they are creatures of light.

The Qur'an also repeatedly emphasizes God as the source of the sustenance we gain from the Earth. Take this passage from Sura 6, "Livestock":

> It is He who sends down water from the sky. With it We produce the shoots of each plant, then bring greenery from it, and from that We bring out grains, one riding on the other in close-packed rows. From the date palm come clusters of low-hanging dates, and there are gardens of vines, olives, and pomegranates, alike yet different. Watch their fruits as they grow and ripen! In all this there are signs for those who would believe.[108]

The farmer and camel herder can find here much of relevance to their daily lives—to the questions that are forever before them concerning the unreliability of sustenance. While passages like these can be found in the earlier literature of their traditions, these are questions that Jesus, Mahavira, and the Buddha themselves barely addressed—or at least questions whose answers those who wrote down the newer scriptures felt were not particularly important to their main audiences, and did not record.

And like Hinduism, Islam retains a very ancient and powerful agrarian faith practice: sacrifice of agricultural animals. The Old Testament is full of laws that require the sacrifice of a chicken, dove, lamb, goat, or cow. But these practices are virtually unheard of for Jews and Christians today. In Islam, on the other hand, *Eid Al-Adha*—the "Festival of the Sacrifice"—remains one of the most central and sacred rites, for it concludes the annual *hajj*. Muslims all around the world celebrate *Eid Al-Adha*, giving them a chance to experience the meaning of the *hajj*, even if they are not performing the pilgrimage themselves. The festival also celebrates Abraham's willingness to sacrifice his own son to show his fealty to God—a story that appears in both the Old Testament and the Qur'an, albeit with significant differences—before God converts the test to an animal sacrifice at the last moment. If a family can afford it, they sacrifice a lamb, a goat, a cow, or even a camel, often in the yards of their own homes. People give much of the meat away to the poor as a form of *zakat*.

The Qur'an also describes God as the designer, creator, and motivating power behind ecological relations more generally, and repeatedly emphasizes this point, as in this passage:

> It is God who splits open the seed and the fruit stone: He brings out the living from the dead and the dead from the living—that is God—so how can you turn away from the truth? He makes the dawn break; He makes the night for rest; and He made the sun and the moon to a precise measure. That is the design of the Almighty, the All Knowing.[109]

Again, these themes can be found in the older literatures of Christianity, New Judaism, Buddhism, and Jainism. But they are not the themes that these great departures themselves addressed, nor are they the themes that they emphasize today. Look within and, yes, one will find that these traditions, too, are alloys. All culture is. But the parts they typically burnish and shine bring out considerably more glint of gold than of silver.

The Good

8

Nonpolitical Politics

BUT ALL THAT GLITTERS is not gold. *Non omne quod nitet aurum est.* When we go digging for the goodness of the absolute, so fierce our passions can be that we do not inspect with care what we dig up. Nor do we reflect deeply on our means of digging, however deep our mining may go. Excavating a labyrinth in the dark, we may scarcely note the rubble, the subsidence, the pollution, the lives damaged and lost. We may not see the mess such mining leaves behind for those still on the surface, because that is precisely its point: to try to leave the mess, the mess of politics, behind.

And yet not leave it. It is for reasons of the surface that we go looking for golden absolutes anyway. Our social lives, with all their conflicts and concords, are what give absolutes their hoped for value. The glitter of the absolute turns out—once we turn this ore from side to side, inspecting its reflections—to be the sheen of the political. Although sought as an escape from politics, absolutes have their greatest attraction because of how they can be used in politics: but in a special kind of politics, what I will call *nonpolitical politics*. An absolute seems to be politically innocent from human affairs, due to its separation, deep in the ground or high in the sky, in nature or the divine. Thus, an absolute's advocates feel their advocacy to be similarly innocent. They can therefore advance interests in human debate that seem to them disinterested, whatever the implications may be for the hierarchies and comities of our lives.

And yet, routinely, it is the advocates themselves who experience most of the advantages of such understandings of untarnished good.

————

Nothing brings the powers, and potential horrors, of nonpolitical politics to mind for me like my own small experience with gold mining. My wife Diane and I were visiting our friend Karl Muller in South Africa, where we had never been before. (I've since been many times, working with my colleague Mpumelelo Ncwadi, as chapter 2 describes.) This was during the height of apartheid. Karl is a White man, born in South Africa (although he is now a citizen of Swaziland), and a political radical. He was eager to show us his birth country, warts and all, so we might better understand apartheid and spread the word back in America. Gold mines were at the heart of the apartheid economy, and infamously dangerous and racist places.[1] Karl thought touring one would highlight apartheid's injustices, and somehow or other, he was able to parley my undergraduate geology degree into a visit.[2] He also secured special permission for Diane to join us, as women at the time were banned from the exclusively male world of the mines.[3]

So it was that on October 15, 1984, the three of us found ourselves standing nearly four thousand feet underground, hunched over and covering our ears, trying to save our hearing from the loudest sound we had ever heard. We had been guided there by a section manager of the gold mine, who was White like the three of us. First, he had taken us to special locker rooms for Whites where we changed into boots, overalls, and helmets with lights. When we came out, the manager waved us over to where he was standing with two assistants, both slim Black men, one with a clipboard and pen and the other with a small satchel over his shoulder. We headed to the shaft and what they called the "cage," a metal elevator car with an open latticework floor, roof, and sides.

On the ten-minute trip down, the manager decided to give us an education about why apartheid was in the best interests of all concerned, and how the mine racially organized its various jobs accordingly. "We understand our Blacks," he assured us. I glanced over at the assistants who were with us. They were impassive as the manager explained how it was important to understand what Blacks were capable of doing and what they were not capable of doing, as well as recognizing the different skills of each tribal and national group.

"Mozambicans are clean—they make good tea boys," he explained. "Angolans are smart, so they are great at cleaning toilets." It was unclear why being smart suited one for cleaning toilets. Was that supposed to be an attempt at humor? While we were trying to figure it out, he went on, explaining that "Swazis make good drill boys," as well as other attributions about the capacities and appropriate employment of various Black tribes and nationalities. Whites didn't do any of these jobs, but there was no need for him to say that, and he didn't. It was evident enough. And we never heard him refer to White mine employees as "boys."

I looked over again at the two assistants, standing together with us in the elevator car. They gave no indication of even having heard what the manager had said. I wondered if they spoke English, and indeed if they were even part of our party or just taking the same car down into the mine with us. (It was only later that I learned that Blacks and Whites typically did not ride together in the cage.)

I looked over as well at Diane and Karl, catching their eyes. We were all in shock. While the manager's focus was momentarily elsewhere, I quickly gestured with my hands about whether we should contest his outrageous statements. Karl shook his head. Something in the manager's manner made it plain that we were there to listen, not debate and discuss. Close as we were in the cage, it was not a place for dialogue.

We emerged at the twelve-hundred-meter level (about thirty-nine hundred feet down), the shallowest working area of the mine at the time. (Today, the deepest South African gold mines reach down nearly four kilometers—almost two and a half miles.) It was surprisingly well-lit and cool. Continuing his explanation of how well everyone is treated and how much "we understand our Blacks," the manager took us over to see a rest area for the miners, which also featured a board for hanging up tools, painted with two-dimensional silhouettes of the tools that were supposed to be hung on each hook. The two assistants came along with us. Evidently, they were indeed a part of our party. The manager proudly pointed to the board and said, "we paint the silhouettes because Blacks can't see in three dimensions. You see, we know their nature."

Can't see in three dimensions? By nature? Was he pulling our leg, and maybe those of his two assistants? But there was no smile, no hint of a joke, however unkind and unfunny. (I afterward learned from South African friends that this was a relatively common belief among Whites during apartheid.)

That was not the only bizarre biological claim the manager made to us. Earlier he had explained how the mine company has to carefully select which Blacks to employ, putting them through a grueling weeklong physical training session in a massive steam room called a climatic chamber or an acclimatization chamber.[4] "Blacks are hot-blooded, not just warm-blooded," the manager explained. "Some of them their blood will boil if you overheat them." Blood will boil? Likely in anger at this kind of treatment—which is probably what the training really served to detect, eliminating those who were unwilling to tolerate the abusive conditions of the mine's racial hierarchy. (White miners, we learned, didn't have to take the acclimatization training.)

The assistants remained impassive as the manager went on to explain that "Blacks aren't stupid. In fact, they are great linguists," referring to the click languages like isiXhosa that centuries of White overlords have struggled to wrap their tongues around. "But the thing is," he continued, "they just can't think logically or abstractly."

Finally, to our great relief, he finished this line of explanation and instruction, and took us over to see the cooling equipment that kept this level of the mine so comfortable. I felt a desperate need to take the two assistants aside and say that I didn't agree with what the manager was saying—that this was complete crap—but there didn't seem any way to do so. I hoped they in fact didn't speak English and didn't know what he was saying.

The manager wanted to orient us under the ground, and reached for the clipboard and pen one assistant was carrying. Apparently, that was his role during our visit: to carry the manager's clipboard and pen. The manager made a little sketch, showed us, and handed the clipboard and pen back to the man. The manager didn't use the clipboard and pen again, but the man continued with us the entire time we were underground.

The manager told us he was happy to take us wherever we wanted to go in the mine. "We don't have anything to hide," he said. So I asked to see the working face of the mine and for a demonstration of rock drilling. The manager looked momentarily taken aback, but agreed. The manager had a word in Afrikaans with another White man—evidently the supervisor of this working level—and some arrangement was hastily made.

As we walked and clambered up and down ladders, the lighting gave out, the ceilings got lower and lower, the floors became covered with loose rock, and it got intensely hot. By the time we reached the working face, the tunnel was maybe four or five feet high, depending on the exact spot, and steeply sloped. We couldn't stand upright. Neither could the miner, a small but muscled Black man. As we approached, he was resting by the rock face, stripped to his waist and covered with sweat, his drill laying on the sloping floor beside him. He had no goggles, no safety gloves, and was wearing only an ill-fitting helmet, ripped trousers rolled up to his knees, and thin, molded rubber boots, like one might wear in the rain. They were definitely not steel-toed. And no ear protection (which we didn't have either). The manager said something, the supervisor pointed, and the miner picked up the drill. (We were later told it weighed about ninety pounds.) With impressive strength, the miner slung the drill up into a horizontal position, despite the low ceiling and the sloping floor with its covering of loose rubble. He turned the drill on.

It was like standing inside an earthquake.

I looked over at the manager, grinning at our discomfort as we flattened our hands over our ears. How could he believe such incredibly thin justification for such cruelty and exploitation? Evidently, because for him it seemed plenty thick enough. For him, it seemed just, and not political. For him, it seemed a matter of nature. Indeed, he had said exactly that.

When we left the rock face, sweaty and dusty from our few minutes there, ears ringing, the manager stopped us in a wider spot with a higher ceiling. He made some indication to the other of the two men who had been accompanying us, the one with the satchel. We then found out why he too was along. It was an insulated satchel, and he reached in and pulled out a cold Coke for each of us—for each of us White people, that is. I rather doubt that the four Cokes seemed just, apolitical, or natural to those two men. I think they were just as hot and thirsty as we were.

Then we headed to the cage for the ride back to the top, and, as it turned out, for another little demonstration by the manager. We emerged, blinking, into the noonday sun. As we talked with the mine manager, the two men wandered off across the yard, thinking they were done. But when they had gotten perhaps a hundred feet away, the mine manager lifted his hand and gave a sharp snap to his fingers. It was as if the men had hit the end of a bungee cord. They came zinging back, while the manager took out a pack of cigarettes from a pocket. He brought a cigarette to his mouth and bent slightly forward as one of the men produced a lighter and lit it for him. Then he waved the men away.

That wasn't nature either. That was power.

———

Some ideas just grab you and won't let go. They toss you high, swing you low, and spin you around until you are dizzy and giddy with their promise. Such an idea is the thought that there are moral realms beyond politics upon which we can base our actions and values, allowing the grace of the innocence of the absolute. Ideas about nature are a common foundation for such a conscience, what I have been calling a natural conscience. So are ideas of the supernatural. Other forms of reasoning can be as well. Key is our sense that the idea gives our motives grounds that we ourselves did not choose. We may then in good conscience, we believe, enact politics based on these motives that we contend derive from the nonpolitical. This is what I mean by nonpolitical politics, the paradox of pursuing interests that we believe are not based in interests—indeed, that we feel we may legitimately pursue precisely because we believe these interests are not based on interests.

The moral philosopher in all of us wants to find a sound basis for the good. On the whole, this is a welcome desire. But the sociologist in all of us should also recognize that we need to tread carefully with eyes wide open, and with mouth and ears ready to give and receive critique. The good, when we treat it as an absolute, is so seductive we may hardly notice when we are using it to do quite bad things—what I called the conundrum of the absolute in the first chapter.

I trust I am on solid moral ground when I declare that the manager of that South African gold mine was enacting bad things. But I have no doubt that he regarded himself as a good person, minus the occasional lapse. (No one's perfect, after all.) At least, he went to great lengths to describe the procedures at the mine as based on the good—as treating people appropriately, according to their nature. Maybe it looked unfair from the perspective of the visitor to South Africa, unfamiliar with what the manager saw as the different capacities of Blacks and Whites. But he didn't choose to give Blacks and Whites different capacities. It wasn't his own interests that he was pursuing. There was nothing to hide. Everything was on the surface in the underground of the mine. Or so he believed he could claim to us.

I think the manager was well aware we did not agree. That was evident in his manner throughout our time with him. He showed little interest in learning about our reasoning, or about the reasoning of the two Black mine workers who were with us. Nonetheless, these were claims he needed to make to us and to the mine workers, and thereby make to himself personally and to the world politically. Few can find much comfort in the thought that others disapprove of us. Few are so confident in our comforts that we believe them unassailable. And so he sought a natural other—a first nature apart from human manipulation and therefore good, yielding a second nature—and a natural me and natural we that follows its guidance, and thus a natural conscience upon which to rest his moral soul.

We may take this as a sociological commonplace: that when people do things that others likely see as bad or even evil, or that they themselves might regard as bad or evil in another context, they generally construct it in their own minds as following a form of the good and just. One of the great questions of a moral sociology must be how people can construct the bad as the good—as well as the good as the bad.[5] The nonpolitical politics of the natural conscience are a common means of that construction, whether on the part of that mine manager or on the part of so much other social mischief in this difficult and beautiful world.

———

The night I first met Mpumelelo I told him about that mine tour. He had mentioned that he has a degree in mining engineering and used to work in a gold mine—a different mine, it turned out, but one close by. Thinking it might be a point of connection, I told him about the manager, the assistants, the scene at the rock face, the satchel with the cold Cokes, and the men being called back to light the manager's cigarette. He confirmed that what we experienced was not out of the ordinary. And he told an even worse story about how the cage at his mine had multiple levels, with the upper level for White miners, and how the White miners would open the trap door between the levels and urinate on the Black miners below on the trip down.

"That's what it was like," Mpumi said. "But the thing is this, Mike. They had to show that they were different from us. Apartheid absolutely depended on that."

Mpumi was pointing to the third dimension of the natural conscience, the sense of a natural we. And he was pointing as well at how a natural we commonly takes shape as a double construction with a *natural them*. Although I believe not unavoidably, the sense of natural we is routinely highly bounded and hierarchical, based on a point of difference whose origin one ascribes to a natural other. Contending that the boundaries and hierarchies of human communities are for political gain is not a persuasive way to maintain those boundaries and hierarchies. Whether intentionally or not, the mine manager looked to nature to support those divisions, using the splits in the ancient triangle to maintain splits in human society—to find what he felt to be a nonpolitical thee, me, we, and them.[6]

Yet the double construction of a natural we and natural them is highly political, despite its claims to the contrary. Of course. We are political beings, whether people of the *polis* or people of the countryside, people rich or poor, people advantaged or hindered along the many axes of social privilege. I will argue in the last chapter that there is no necessary cause for sorrow in our political character, although there very well may be in the character of our politics. (My argument there won't be surprising. It will, I believe, be familiar to how we commonly lead our lives and deal with the conflicts between us.) Nonetheless, we often seek a basis for fending off the social attributions others make and the political motivations they pursue, finding the good in what others may sometimes regard as the bad.

But how? Do I just say, no, I'm right and you're wrong—that my concept of nature is the correct one and yours isn't? What if you say the same thing right back at me? The solipsistic thought that the only truth is my truth is difficult to maintain for long, for the self is always in social context and social context is always in the self. Far easier it is when I conceive some others to be similarly constituted to me. The natural conscience commonly provides this ease by creating not only the sense of the goodness of a natural other and a natural me but as well the goodness of a natural we—a we that I understand in contrast to a them, or I must accept the vantages and disadvantages of that them as my own. Besides, it is far easier for me to protect any advantages I may gain via the nonpolitical politics of the natural we and them when similar others are similarly advantaged.

Which raises an important question: are nonpolitical politics always just a moral Trojan horse, where we hide our conspiracy as we gain access to the citadels of power? For it is certainly remarkably common that the nonpolitical politics we hear advanced in social life look an awful lot like the political politics of social life.

Conspiracies do happen. People do collaborate and coordinate in the framing of narratives that promote mutually advantageous outcomes, from corporate advertising to social movements to press releases to selective reporting to state censorship.[7] But even in these circumstances, the collaborators sleep easier and better maintain each other's respect when they feel that the conniving furthers purposes that are deeper or higher, derived from outside the human.

Thus, there is generally no need to sniff inside morality for the cigar smoke that rankled Thoreau's nose in order to account for the common fit of proposition and position. We need only make the following sociological assumption: *that people tend not to challenge ideas that support their interests.* I will call it *interests bias.*[8] This is perhaps the most basic observation of the sociology of knowledge.[9] No conscious plan required. No need to light up cigars with others. The effort entailed is lack of effort. Face it, we normally don't employ much intellectual rigor when we find a happy matchup between what we believe and what we want. There just isn't the electricity there to set off the alarm bells of critique—at least not our own alarm bells.

———

It is not only in racism that we encounter interests bias and the use of nature in nonpolitical politics. Alas, we can also sometimes find it in environmentalism—perhaps most tragically in the creation of parks, reserves, national forests, and wilderness areas.[10] This cuts close to the bone for me. I'm an environmentalist, and I've worked for decades on creating nature reserves and other forms of environmental protection.[11]

My friend David Nickell is all too familiar with being subjected to this form of nonpolitical politics. Back in 2006, I emailed David that I was giving a talk fairly close to his farm. He emailed back the next morning inviting me to stay a couple of nights. A few weeks later, he and I were walking together through the nearby woods and meadows of what used to be his home: the Land Between the Rivers, what the US National Forest Service has renamed the Land Between the Lakes National Recreation Area.

In far western Kentucky and extending south into Tennessee, two mighty rivers—the Tennessee and the Cumberland—run north in close parallel. The result is a kind of inland peninsula about five miles across and fifty miles long. Upward of a thousand families like David's used to live there. Used to: in the 1940s, the authorities put a dam on the Tennessee, and in the 1960s they followed with a dam on the Cumberland, using eminent domain to claim all the land in between for a reserve and recreation area.

The Land Between the Rivers people didn't go quietly. They'd lived there for generations. As we walk, David tells me the story of Miss Babe, a neighbor woman in her sixties who lived alone on her small farm.

"The government men were approaching her two-story frame house to present her with the condemnation papers. She told them to get back in their truck but they ignored her." Miss Babe raised her shotgun. "One barrel took out the windshield. The second barrel offered enough reason for the government men to scramble to their truck and head back towards wherever it is government men come from."[12]

I'm amazed at her fortitude, but David tells me the story has a bad ending. The "government men" convinced a neighbor to drive Miss Babe to a meeting in town. (She did not own a vehicle.) But there was no meeting. And while the neighbor was driving Miss Babe, they burned her house down. David describes Miss Babe's reaction when she returned later that day.

"Rounding the curve at the top of ridge they saw the smoke. According to the man doing the driving she slumped in her seat and hung her head, but said nothing."

David pauses, and I with him.

Then, in a hoarse whisper, David continues, "They had pushed her house into a pile with a bulldozer and set it afire—all her possessions still inside."[13]

We come to David's family's former homestead. It's spring and a great bank of his mother's jonquils burst white and yellow from a small clearing in the forest. David explains that jonquils mark the location of former homes throughout the area, and I think back on several other jonquil patches we had passed earlier. I take David's picture in front of his mom's jonquils.

I'm dazed by the callous tragedy of it all. How could the officials bring themselves to do this, I ask David when we get back into his truck. David explains that they thought they were doing the right thing. Local people had maintained a collectively managed commons in the Land Between the Rivers, a large section of woods they called "the Coalins." Nobody knows where the name the Coalins came from, David tells me. But it was full of wild turkey and deer, due to local people's sound management. It may be hard to believe now, but turkey and deer had virtually disappeared from the rest of Kentucky. So hunters and environmentalists wanted the Coalins for a reserve, as well as to use the local flock and herd to repopulate turkey and deer elsewhere. Others wanted the entire Land Between the Rivers area for flood control, water supply, and possibly hydropower. These are all ecological purposes, they contended in various ways—purposes that came from nature, not politics. And the tourism, the hunting development, the water regulation, and the cheap power would be great for the economy, that seemingly inescapable natural absolute. Besides, muttered outsiders, the local people were just "hicks" and "hillbillies" anyway—a natural them.

Back at his house that evening, David points out the interests bias of the "government men": that they had careers to advance and incomes to maintain. He tells the story of one of the federal attorneys who condemned the land. David explains that a local television station interviewed the attorney years after the removals were complete. The interviewer apparently asked the attorney the same question I had asked: How could the officials bring themselves to do this? The attorney replied that he was just doing his job and had thought nothing about it but now felt terribly. "If I die and go to Hell," David quoted the attorney, "it won't be for drinking whiskey and chasing women; it will be for what I helped do to the Between the Rivers people."[14]

———

The mine manager and that attorney are not alone in the list of those who have sought to use nature in this invidious way, sanctioning not only the double construction of a natural we with a natural them but a natural hierarchy of we and them. I will not attempt to review this sorry history here, or to detail its continuing legacy in the politics of today.[15] Rather, I will hope that I have provided enough in these two examples to encourage readers to be alert to this form of argument when they encounter it.

I hope we can also be more alert to the parallel use of the divine in the nonpolitical politics of legitimating hierarchy. To help with that watchfulness, I'll give an example of this use, too. Yet it is difficult to do so without giving offense to someone—especially since I do not have space to provide a comprehensive review from all the bourgeois faiths. So there is a risk that I may be perceived as picking on the particular faith tradition of the example I give. I'll have to accept that risk, while mentioning that I could have drawn examples from any of the bourgeois faith traditions that I have discussed in this book, including the more electrum ones.

The example I'll give are the writings of the Protestant reformers Martin Luther and John Calvin—but, to repeat, not because of any special venom for Protestantism. Rather, I use this example because it also gives me a chance to discuss the rise of this major development in the world's largest religion, and its relationship to the history of bourgeois life. In a more perfect book than the one I have written, I would have found a way to fit the Protestant Reformation into the chapter on Christianity. There simply wasn't room. So I'll use my discussion of the nonpolitical politics of Luther's and Calvin's natural conscience as an opportunity to also squeeze in a bit of this history—which begins with Catholicism.

––––––––

"Rue Saint-Agricol? Did you ever hear of a Saint Agricol?" I asked my wife Diane as we took a left off Place de l'Horloge, the main square of Avignon. We were exploring the city on one of our first weekends living there during the sabbatical I describe a bit in chapter 5.

"Nope, never heard of that saint," Diane replied. "There're a lot them! But I think Rue Saint-Agricol leads to a church with the same name. Saw that on the map."

Right she was. Other than Jerusalem or Rome, Avignon could justly claim to be the most Christian city in the world. In addition to the cathedral—Notre Dame des Doms, the former seat of Christendom during the fourteenth century, when the Papacy temporarily moved to Avignon—the old city inside the walls has another ten churches. (It also has a stunning nineteenth-century synagogue in the former Jewish quarter.) One of those churches is Église Saint-Agricol d'Avignon, the oldest church in the city other than Notre Dame des Doms. It dates back to the tenth century CE, although most of what we see today comes from a major reconstruction of the Église in 1321 CE, plus a few later renovations.

"Intriguing name," I mused. "It must mean something agricultural."

"There's the church. It looks really interesting. Shall we go in?"

Walking around in the ancient gloom, we soon learned that Saint Agricol did indeed have an agricultural connection. His name came from the Latin *agricola*, which means farmer (as we ought to have remembered). But he wasn't a farmer. He was the son of a Bishop of Avignon, and eventually went on to become Bishop of Avignon himself. (The Catholic injunction for priestly celibacy was rather loosely enforced at the time.) His prayers saved the city from an invasion of storks who were dropping dead snakes everywhere, causing disease, we garnered from a sign in the church. Because of his intercession, the storks reportedly grabbed up all the snakes in their beaks and flew away. Agricol was deemed a saint shortly after his death in 700 CE. Agricol became immensely popular when people found that, apparently, prayers to him could bring rain, good weather, and plentiful harvests. He is now considered the patron saint of Avignon. There's a huge painting of him in the church, successfully pleading with Jesus to save the city from the storks. His relics are in a small reliquary just below the painting.

"Cool!" I exclaimed when we came back out of Église Saint-Agricol. "Fabulous church."

"I loved it too," agreed Diane. "But you know, Mike, it didn't seem very bourgeois. But it is certainly Christian. How are you going to explain that?"

A fair question, and it's one that had me stumped for a while. The accounts of Saint Agricol do indeed have a strongly pagan flavor to them. His name and powers clearly respond to pagan concerns for agricultural sustenance. His feat of stopping the stork invasion also shows a strong command of an ecology, a nature, which is by no means necessarily good. And he has a highly immanent presence. This is where one comes to pray to Saint Agricol, not some other place. He has no other church dedicated to him. Not only are his relics in the church, he was born in Avignon, he died in Avignon, and now he is the patron saint of Avignon—and only of Avignon.[16] He is not just Saint Agricol. He is Saint Agricol d'Avignon. And he is indeed Christian, a faith that does not today typically emphasize pagan silver.

But the time of Saint Agricol and the seven hundred or so years that followed his life—from his birth in 630 CE to about 1400 CE—was not a very bourgeois period in Europe. During the European Middle Ages, after the collapse of the Roman Empire, urbanism underwent a major decline. Once a city of a million, Rome had been reduced to about fifteen thousand inhabitants by about 1300 CE, when most of Église Saint-Agricol was built. By then, there were only a few cities greater than fifty thousand inhabitants in size: Constantinople, Florence, Milan, Paris, and Venice. Most were under ten thousand.[17] And this was before the Black Death, which killed about 60 percent of Europeans between 1346 and 1353, greatly reducing even further the size of the cities that remained.[18] The Roman Empire had never been a majority urban society. Even at its peak, roughly 75 percent of people continued to live agrarian lives.[19] But the proportion of urban people in the Roman Empire's former area shrank well into the low single digits during "the calamitous 14th century," as Barbara Tuchman aptly termed it.[20]

This period of urban collapse saw a corresponding effervescence of new saints, now mostly forgotten, that adherents felt had pagan powers—like Saint Agricol. The class background of these electrum saints didn't matter. What mattered was that they spoke to pagan concerns. People looked to Saint Solange of Bourges, a virgin shepherdess who died in 880, for help with rain and to protect shepherds and shepherdesses. They also looked to Saint Heribert of Cologne, an archbishop who died in 1021, for help with rain and drought. They looked to Saint Engelmaro, a peasant who died in 1100, to protect their cattle and bring good weather and harvests. They looked to Saint Isidore, who was a farmer and died in 1130, for protection for farmers, farm workers, livestock, and rural communities. They looked to Saint Julian of Cuenca, a philosophy professor who became a hermit and died in 1208, both to bring rain and to assist the craft of basket making. Other pagan help was sought from saints Odo of Cluny, Theodore of Sykeon, Phocas the Gardener, and others whose patronage was believed to aid the agrarian concerns of rural folks.

These were not the nonpolitical politics of a natural conscience, concerned with the problems of desire. These were direct requests from the divine for assistance with ecological sustenance in an often-dire world.

———

Nonpolitical politics made a major return on October 31, 1517, however. That was the day a thirty-four-year-old theologian named Martin Luther sent a letter to the Archbishop of Mainz, along with a work that came to be known as the *Ninety-Five Theses*, but that Luther had titled the *Disputation of Martin Luther on the Power and Efficacy of Indulgences.* (Contrary to the widespread story, there is no evidence that he ever nailed the *Ninety-Five Theses* to the door of the Castle Church of Wittenberg, Germany.) An indulgence was a theological forgiveness that one could purchase from the Church to compensate for some bad action, increasing one's chances to get into Heaven, despite the transgression. The Church used indulgences as a major source of funding for its operations. Luther thought that the practice corrupted the Church, and he declared in his sixth thesis that the Church "cannot remit any guilt, except by declaring and showing that it has been remitted by God." This move to eliminate human judgment was an attempt to restore a nonpolitical divine. Although initially hugely controversial, it turned out to be hugely popular. And who remembers Saint Agricol now, aside from the residents of Avignon and a few tourists?

Protestantism (and the changes it in time encouraged in Catholicism) turned out to be hugely popular because Europe had changed a lot in the two centuries since the nadir of European urbanism in the eighth to fourteenth centuries. The Renaissance is often described as a cultural and intellectual movement, but it was equally economic and geographic. It was a time of massive economic growth and expansion of trade, due to improvements in shipping, manufacturing, and banking—which supported, and were supported by, the cultural and intellectual innovations. Cities grew once again. London, Naples, and Paris all had at least four hundred thousand inhabitants by 1650, and cities of fifty thousand or more were common. Luc-Normand Tellier calls it an "urbexplosion," writing that "the rate of urbanization of Christian Western Europe reached again the level it had under the Roman Empire, one thousand years before."[21] It was, in short, a *bourgeois echo*.[22]

Luther wasn't the only one who heard this echo. It resonated for many because along with the growing cities of the growing economy came the renewed growth of class. But what justified the renewed inequalities? As Max Weber famously argued, Protestantism contended that these inequalities were, at least potentially, justified by God—by the goodness of God's impartiality in the machinations of human affairs.[23] Calvin was particularly explicit about this interpretation. In his view, the grace to go to Heaven depended upon fulfilling one's duty to one's assigned station in life, one's "calling," an assignment that comes from God. As Calvin put it in his *Institutes of Christianity*, sounding like he had just put down a copy of the *Bhagavad Gita* before he picked up his quill:

> [T]he Lord enjoins every one of us, in all the actions of life, to have respect to our own calling. He knows the boiling restlessness of the human mind, the fickleness with which it is borne hither and thither, its eagerness to hold opposites at one time in its grasp, its ambition. Therefore, lest all things should be thrown into confusion by our folly and rashness, he has assigned distinct duties to each in the different modes of life. And that no one may presume to overstep his proper limits, he has distinguished the different modes of life by the name of callings. Every man's mode of life, therefore, is a kind of station assigned him by the Lord, that he may not be always driven about at random.[24]

There was a certain equality in this notion of divinely assigned stations, for everyone had one. But there was also a significant stinger: no one was "to overstep his proper limits." As Weber noted, the notion of duty to one's assigned station gave "the comforting assurance that the unequal distribution of the goods of this world was a special dispensation of Divine Providence" that we ought not to question.[25] Wealth, or the lack of it, was no one's fault. You couldn't be blamed for being rich, nor should you begrudge being poor. It was all for the good because it came from the good, ordained by God.

The bourgeois echo was thus a matter not just of class but of its characteristic moral argument: nonpolitical politics.

––––––

I'm standing in front of a handsome stucco and brownstone apartment building, five stories high, on a quiet, shady street in Frankfurt-am-Main, Germany: 43 Günthersburgallee. My wife's father—we all called him Opa after our kids were born—lived here before World War II. I'm thinking about how nonpolitical politics can also be based on combining absolute ideas of nature with those of the divine, not just one or the other, and in the process creating doubly absolute conceptions of community and hierarchy, of natural we and natural them.

Opa's family were German Jews. Opa's father owned a leather wholesaling business across the river in Offenbach, making a comfortable enough living to purchase 43 Günthersburgallee. The family's apartment was on what Americans call the second floor and Europeans call the first floor.

Hitler was elected chancellor in 1933. Opa was seven and attended a fine private school, and he was one of just three Jews in his class. One day shortly after Hitler's election, the teacher took Opa and the other two Jewish boys aside and quietly suggested that they should not come to school the next day. Opa was puzzled as he told his parents the story that evening. But they understood. They immediately transferred Opa to an all-Jewish school, as did his friends' parents with their children.

I'm thinking about this episode as I look at 43 Günthersburgallee. The sign on the driveway to the back of the building says "Einfarht freihalten!" which basically means "keep the access open." If only: later in 1933, on September 3, Hitler gave a speech in Nurnberg on his view of a "higher race" that had the right to dominate "lower" races in the fight for *lebensraum* or "living space"—a right granted by nature, he claimed. In Hitler's words,

The higher race—at first "higher" in the sense of possessing a greater gift for organization—subjects to itself a lower race and thus constitutes a relationship which now embraces races of unequal value. Thus there results the subjection of a number of people under the will often of only a few persons, a subjection based simply on the right of the stronger, a right which, as we see it in Nature, can be regarded as the sole conceivable right because founded on reason.[26]

Hitler brewed here a dangerous moral mix, combining notions of absolute nature with hierarchical notions of natural we and natural them. And who had the favor of being in the "higher race" or "master race"? In his view, only those with "German blood." As the Nazi party platform of 1920 put it,

> Only a member of the race [referring to the "master race"] can be a citizen. A member of the race can only be one who is of German blood, without consideration of creed. Consequently no Jew can be a member of the race.[27]

There was a certain ecumenicalism to the Nazi view of the German master race, however, accepting all those with German blood "without consideration of creed." But the moral absolutism of Nazism was also plainly religious as well. It initially welcomed German Catholics like Hitler as well as German Protestants, although later advocated only Protestantism, conveniently overlooking Hitler's own upbringing—not to mention his Jewish grandfather. Jews, however, were defined as immediately non-German by virtue of their Jewishness, no matter how long their families had been in Germany, which was well over a millennium for many of them. And German converts to Judaism were no longer considered members of the German master race. As a German court during the Nazi years ruled concerning one such convert to Judaism, "in cases when the individual involved feels bound to Jewry in spite of his Aryan blood, and shows this fact externally, his attitude is decisive."[28] Yes, Nazis defined Jews as a race, a natural them based on ideas of nature, but everyone also knew them to follow a different religion. Jews thus served twice over in the creation of the moral contrast necessary for envisioning an absolute community, derived from absolute conceptions of both sides of the base of the ancient triangle: nature and supernature.

Moreover, although Hitler himself seems to have been an atheist, he commonly spoke about God in his speeches, especially to advocate what Nazis called "positive Christianity." Under this view, all Jewish-composed texts had to be rejected from Christianity, including the entire Old Testament, and Jesus had to be defined as "Aryan" and not the Jew he was. Positive Christianity also was an attempt to merge Christianity into Nazism. As the Reichsminister for Church Affairs put it, "True Christianity is represented by the party, and the

German people are now called by the party and especially the Führer to real Christianity. . . . The Führer is the herald of a new revelation."[29]

Directly opposite 43 Günthersburgallee is a lovely little neighborhood park, with playgrounds, a basketball court, and benches scattered among the trees and grass. I cross the street to have a look at it. Opa must have played there, as well as his brother. But not after November 9, 1938—Kristallnacht, the "night of broken glass" when civilians and paramilitary forces smashed Jewish homes, shops, schools, and synagogues across Germany. Opa's father's leather business in Offenbach was among those destroyed.[30] Tens of thousands of Jews were arrested and sent to concentration camps. Jews began going out as little as possible, hoping to avoid notice.

The Gestapo came around to 43 Günthersburgallee too. They demanded to see Opa's father. They found him in bed, pretending to be sick. The soldiers weren't convinced. Still, they told him if he could get a certificate from a non-Jewish doctor documenting that he was sick, they wouldn't take him away. Opa's mother called a Christian doctor who agreed to come to the house. The doctor signed a certificate saying Opa's father had an infectious disease and gave him some pills that made him run a fever. Then the doctor quietly took his leave, refusing payment. When the soldiers came back, they accepted the certificate and left, leaving Opa's father home in bed.

The family recognized that they would all have to leave, if they could. Sensing trouble, Opa's parents had already sent his older brother to England the previous year. Opa had been too young, they felt. That didn't matter now. Opa would have to go—and to go alone, if necessary, even though he was just thirteen.

They heard of a man at the travel documents office who took bribes. But the family had almost no money. Opa's father's business had been destroyed and their bank funds impounded. Plus it would take too long and attract too much suspicion to sell 43 Günthersburgallee. Desperate, Opa's mother sold her jewels and other family valuables. Opa's father still had to pretend to be sick in bed, so Opa headed off to the travel office on his bicycle with a huge packet of cash. Opa found the man. He took the money without question and gave Opa an exit visa. In December, just a few weeks after Kristallnacht, Opa took a train alone for England, not knowing whether his parents would follow.

A couple of weeks later, out of the blue, a woman knocked on the door of 43 Günthersburgallee, a complete stranger. Her boyfriend was making arrangements for Jews, she said, so he could save up enough to marry her. It wouldn't be cheap, however. Somehow Opa's parents scraped together enough other cash. The woman came back. They gave her the funds, hoping the arrangement wasn't just a scam. A few days later she came back once again and handed them the necessary papers. Opa's parents packed a few clothes and left immediately for England. In time, Opa, his brother, and his parents made it to the United States.

Not all of Opa's relatives were so fortunate. Frankfurt has put little square metal markers into the sidewalks outside the homes of Jews who died in the concentration camps, one for each person who died, listing their name, their birthdate, the year they were arrested, and the camp they were sent to. I cross back from the park and look at the six markers outside 43 Günthersburgallee. Max, Simon, and Frieda Stein. Julius, Jenny Klara, and Kurt Flörsheim. I'm fighting back tears. Some cousins of Opa's mother had moved into 43 Günthersburgallee just before Kristallnacht. They remained after Opa's immediate family left, hiding and hoping. I don't know if their names were Stein or Flörsheim. No one in the family remembers now.

But the Steins and the Flörsheims were certainly someone's cousins. Indeed, no matter the politics, they were everyone's cousins. We all are. At least that's the only vision of the natural I can accept, I find myself thinking as I take a last look at 43 Günthersburgallee: one that glitters with the inclusion of us all—a natural we with no natural them.

9

Awesome Coolness

TO HAVE THAT GLITTER of us all, though, we'll have to have to recognize that culture is an alloy, a melding of traditions and peoples and their insights and experiences. It's not all gold or all silver. And we'll also have to recognize, quite obviously, that we do not form a cultural alloy by forever opposing our differences. Rather, we amalgamate both through the easy fusing of where we agree and the compelling sparkles of where we don't.

At least James R. Walker and the Lakota Sioux shamans of South Dakota's Pine Ridge Reservation were some who made such an the attempt. Not many recall Walker and the Pine Ridge shamans today. But they achieved a remarkable synthesis.

Walker was a physician and he came to Pine Ridge in 1896, the only Western-trained doctor for its seven thousand residents. Pine Ridge was one of the remaining shards of the Great Sioux Reservation, which at the time of its establishment in 1868 encompassed the entire western half of South Dakota. Already by 1877 the US Congress had taken a third back, and then took back another third in 1889, allotting the land in 320-acre gifts to White settlers. Needless to say, the Sioux felt deeply betrayed. It got worse. The next year a hundred fifty-three Lakota men, women, and children were slaughtered in the snow by the 7th US Cavalry Regiment, using rifles and Hotchkiss guns, an early form of machine gun. The horror took place in a small canyon on Pine Ridge named Wounded Knee, and was thereafter called the Wounded Knee Massacre. The Lakota had been dancing the Ghost Dance, a semi-Christian ritual that was supposed to lead to the coming of an Indian messiah who would sweep Whites from North America, restore the buffalo herds, and bring peace throughout the land. The White authorities got nervous and called in the cavalry to put a stop to the dancing and to disarm the Indians. There was a misunderstanding with a Lakota man who was a deaf-mute and didn't under-stand what the soldiers were saying about giving up his gun. A shot was fired (no one knows who fired it) and then many more.

The effects of the tragedy and the land loss were still everywhere to be seen when Walker arrived on the reservation six years later.[1] The Lakota were in rough shape—economically, emotionally, culturally, physically. People were poor and sick, hopeless and neglected. Many were near starvation. Nearly all were in desperation.

Tuberculosis was especially rampant. Walker couldn't handle all the neces-sary medical work alone, so he decided to try a novel approach: training tradi-tional medicine men to treat tuberculosis. The medicine men agreed to learn Walker's techniques, but on one condition. He also had to learn theirs. Walker agreed in turn, and after many years of instruction the medicine men inducted him into the Buffalo Society as a full Lakota shaman. Not many Whites of James Walker's time could have won this kind of trust and acceptance from a people who had every reason to suspect his intentions. He must have been a remarkable man, as remarkable as the Lakota medicine men must have been to connect across the horrors of their encounters with Whites.

It was not only a matter of trust and appreciation of difference, though. The medicine men were worried that their wisdom would soon be lost. The younger generations were all adopting Western dress and turning to Chris-tianity, due both to cultural pressure from missionaries and to a sense of cultural vacuum from the pervasive feeling that the Christian god must be stronger than the native ones. So in addition to training him, the medicine men asked Walker to record what they knew. Walker spent years interviewing the local shamans and published several articles and one book. Decades after his death, other scholars compiled four further books based on his careful notes and transcripts.[2] His writings are the main source we have today on much of tra-ditional Lakota belief.

Walker might have given us even more, but in 1913 another Western doctor visited Pine Ridge and was shocked by Walker's approach. Walker defended himself as best he could to his superiors back in Washington. Nonetheless the US government summarily retired him from service. He left the reservation on April 1, 1914, never to return.

Before he left Walker dedicated himself to learning what more he could. He was particularly concerned about his understanding of a central feature of Lakota belief—indeed, the very centermost feature: the meaning of *Wakan Tanka*. So he decided to visit a shaman called Finger, an "old and conservative" man, as Walker described him.[3] It didn't go well. They sat awkwardly together long into the night, not saying much. Walker eventually decided to head home to bed, stood up, and started walking back to his quarters. Suddenly, a brilliant meteor streaked across the sky.

"Wohpe!" Finger cried. "Wohpe-e-e-e!"

Walker came back and watched Finger burn sweet grass over a fire and intone some prayers which Walker, himself now a Lakota shaman, still didn't know. Walker asked the meaning of the prayers. Finger agreed to explain it all to him, but some other evening, it being quite late.

A few weeks later they got together again—just five days before Walker was due to leave the reservation.[4] This time they talked all night. Finger explained that a shooting star is an appearance of *Wohpe*, another name for the *Beautiful Woman*, and is a form of *Wakan Tanka*. The *Beautiful Woman* is set in motion by *Skan*, the force that sets all motion into motion. *Skan* is another manifestation of *Wakan Tanka*. So too is the Rock, the Earth, the Moon, the Wind, the Winged, and the Sun—all told, eight manifestations of *Wakan Tanka*.

Walker was baffled. Let me quote from Walker's transcript of his conversation with Finger.[5]

> "Then there are eight *Wakan Tanka*, are there?" asked Walker.
>
> "No, there is but one," Finger replied.
>
> "You have named eight but say there is but one. How can this be?"
>
> "That is right. I have named eight. There are four: the Sun, *Skan*, the Rock, and the Earth."
>
> This was head-spinning. Eight had become one and then immediately became four. "[But] you named four others, the Moon, the Wind, the Winged, and the Beautiful Woman, and said they were *Wakan Tanka*, did you not?"
>
> "Yes. But these four are the same as the *Wakan Tanka*. The Sun and the Moon are the same, the *Skan* and the Wind are the same, the Rock and the Winged are the same, and the Earth and the Beautiful Woman are the same. These eight are only one. The shamans know how this is, but the people do not know. It is *wakan*."

And then, suddenly, at least a little, Walker understood. The answer was both easier and harder than he imagined. For what *wakan* means in direct translation is "mystery," and what *Wakan Tanka* means in direct translation is "great mystery." This direct translation is exactly what the Lakota Sioux medicine men meant, Walker finally realized. The heart of everything—both before and after everything, in everything, and setting everything into motion—was that which, as Finger put it, "has no birth" and "has no death:" the Great Mystery.[6]

———

Religious scholars call what Finger described to Walker a form of pantheism: a sense of a divine that suffuses the universe and provides a oneness to the diversity of the all. For Finger, that suffused diversity included manifestations of nature, supernature, and the human, a pagan entanglement of difference that is nonetheless unified. Yet not only pagan. There is widespread unity in this unity of the widespread. Closely related ideas can be encountered in tradition after tradition, from pagan to bourgeois. Walker eventually got what Finger was talking about because, I imagine, he had already gotten it before.

Some aspects of Finger's formulation sound characteristically pagan. The Great Mystery of *Wakan Tanka* manifests the forces of ecology and sustenance: the light of the Sun and the Moon, the materiality of the Rock and the Wind, the fertility of the Earth and the Beautiful Woman, all enlivened and motivated by *Skan* and the Wind. But a Daoist could very easily hear in Finger's words a resonance with the idea of the *dao*, the natural Way of things that we can encounter everywhere and in everything, if we just allow ourselves freedom from intention. A Hindu would quite likely immediately feel a strong resonance with the idea of *brahman*, the unifying and unchanging spirit and source of change in and behind everything, or the idea of *shakti*, the creative energy that emanates from *brahman*. A Platonist might nod in agreement and say *Wakan Tanka* sounds like the Good that Plato argued lies behind the experience of our senses and emanates the "forms" of existence.

Crucially, all of these traditions find as well an unknown quality to this unifying divine presence. Yes, they offer an explanation for our experience—an explanation for the unexplained—by pointing to a kind of transcendent immanence, a motivating presence, in the all. But there the explanation stops and the adherent is invited into wonder, divine wonder.

And how different are any of these ideas from the Buddhist's sense of *anatman*, the fundamental lack of distinction between self and other—the inherent unity in and of the all? Or how different are any of these ideas from the Abrahamic religions and their sense of the universe as God's creation? Yes, the Abrahamic vision sees this holiness as stemming from a discrete entity, a transcendent god, a *super*nature. But the hand—if it is indeed a hand, as Michelangelo's ceiling for the Sistine Chapel suggests—of this unifying divine can be felt intimately and immanently in the workings of the world and all we experience. To the Jew, the Christian, and the Muslim, it is all God's work.

However transcendent *YHWH*, the *Father*, or *Allah* may be, the adherent also has a strong sense of the everywhereness and everythingness of the divine, and an explanation of everywhere and everything thereby. So too for a Bahá'í, a Unitarian, a Theosophist, or a Transcendentalist. Yet as well, the adherent gains a wonder for what is not known along with a reverence for what all faiths variously contend is known.

Many centuries of scholars have reflected on these parallels across traditions. Recent writers like Karen Armstrong, Robert Forman, Harry Oldmeadow, Sayyed Nasr, Huston Smith, and William Stoddart all try to point out these resonances to a world that often seems more intent on its differences. Writers like Aldous Huxley, Ananda Kentish Coomaraswamy, and Frithjof Schuon tried to do so for mid-twentieth-century generations. If we go back to 1540, we can find Agostino Steuco calling it the "perennial philosophy" in his ten-volume treatise *De Perenni Philosophia*. As Steuco put it, there is "one principle of all things, of which there has always been one and the same knowledge among all peoples."[7] Steuco's term was revived by Aldous Huxley in an influential 1945 book and is still widely used today.[8]

Some writers have sought a basis for universal religious truth in these similarities. That is not the sociologist's task. Rather, the sociologist looks for both similarities and differences in our varying beliefs and considers their social conditions and possibilities. And when we look with the sociologist's eye, we readily find that a sense of the everywhereness and everythingness of a divine that can never be fully known is indeed very common—although understood in many varying ways, from *Wakan Tanka* to *Brahman* to the *Dao* to *YHWH*, *Pateras, Allah*, and more. As I'll come to, I don't think "perennial philosophy" is the best term for this diverse commonality. But let's go with it for now.

————

A case can also be made that something like perennial philosophy also extends into a realm of thought we typically do not regard as a kind of religious tradition: scientific studies of nature. At least Gottfried Leibnitz, the Renaissance polymath and co-inventor of calculus, thought so. He even used the phrase "perennial philosophy" in some of his later writings.[9] Leibnitz was a rationalist, but he found the mind of the divine everywhere. In his view, all materiality could be reduced to infinitesimal bits he called "monads" that acted out the "pre-established harmony" established by the divine. Why do things act as they do? Because God set them up that way. Why did God set them up in this way? We don't know. That's a mystery. But it's a good mystery, thought Leibnitz. He is famous for arguing that, although we do not understand the course of things, we may rest assured that it is all actually for the good, even when it seems evil and wrong to us.

Baruch Spinoza, a contemporary of Leibnitz, had a broadly similar but significantly drier view. He and Leibnitz got together to debate the issue in 1676, near the end of Spinoza's life. Spinoza had just published his principal work, *Ethics*. Leibnitz loved its rationalism and hated its distant conception of an indifferent divine. They apparently argued for three days in Spinoza's room in a redbrick house beside a canal on the outskirts of The Hague, where Spinoza earned a meager living as a lens grinder. Spinoza contended that God thoroughly imbues the material world, and indeed that the material world *is* God. Or perhaps that the material world is part of God, God being something larger—a view technically called panentheism, meaning everything in God, rather than pantheism, meaning God in everything. But that was a fine point of their argument. The main disagreement was Spinoza's view that this divinely imbued logic determines everything almost as a kind of ineluctable mechanism. God does not make moral choices along the way about what is the best outcome, he contended. Rather, God is the deep logic that makes the outcomes, all set in motion long ago and still ticking along, but with no moral judgment. Crucially for Spinoza, articulating an assessment familiar to pagan traditions, those outcomes are not necessarily for the good. The good just isn't relevant here. Leibnitz couldn't go along with that, calling such a view "horrible," "terrifying," and "intolerably impudent."[10]

Yet despite all their rationalism, neither Leibnitz nor Spinoza professed to really understand the deepest what and why of the universe. They just disagreed on where to draw the line between what we can know and what we can't. For Spinoza, it stopped at the point where we note that the universe is extraordinarily ordered and conclude that such ordering indicates a divine actor in and behind it all. Leibnitz contended that we can know more than that: we can also know that the divine actor does everything for the good, even if we are often puzzled and distressed because of our own small understanding of the good. Yet for both, you eventually hit a point of deep and great mystery.

Science today generally doesn't bother to engage questions of the in it all, behind it all, and possible good of it all. But that doesn't mean that individual scientists don't. A 2009 Gallup Poll in the United States, for example, found that 51 percent of US scientists believe a divine actor or some kind of higher power put (and, for some, still puts) the universe into motion.[11]

Albert Einstein is a famous case in point. Commentators have long hung on every word of Einstein, as the leading icon of scientific thought in the modern era. Einstein was as much a humanist as a physicist, and in a 1940 paper presented at a symposium on "Science, Philosophy, and Religion in their Relationship to the Democratic Way of Life," he wrote, in a line that has become canonical for many, "Science without religion is lame, religion without science is blind."[12] By that he meant we should look to religion for our ends, but to science for our means. In Einstein's words, "Though religion may be that which determines the goal, it has, nevertheless, learned from science, in the broadest sense, what means will contribute to the attainment of the goals it has set up."[13]

Einstein's comfort with talking in religious terms remains controversial to this day among scientific proponents of atheism like the evolutionary biologist Richard Dawkins. His theory of the "selfish gene" brought Dawkins to scholarly prominence. More recently, his 2006 best-seller *The God Delusion* brought Dawkins to popular prominence as probably the best-known proponent of atheism today, and especially of an activist version of atheism often referred to as the "new atheism."[14] That Einstein—that this idol of science—was comfortable with religion troubles the new atheist position.

Seeking the grace of Einstein's cultural authority, Dawkins argues that Einstein in fact really was "atheistic," even though Einstein described himself as an agnostic and toyed with calling himself a pantheist. In a 1930 interview, Einstein said, "I'm not an atheist. I don't think I can call myself a pantheist. The problem involved is too vast for our limited minds."[15] In a 1950 letter, after another twenty years of reflecting on the matter, he wrote, "My position concerning God is that of an agnostic."[16]

But Einstein also was very firm in rejecting theism, the idea of a monotheistic god who directs and intervenes in our personal lives, and who is some form of person: what is often called the idea of a "personal god." As Einstein wrote in a letter in 1952, "The idea of a personal God is quite alien to me and seems even naïve."[17] But in that 1930 interview where he declared he was neither an atheist nor a pantheist, Einstein went on to say something that Lakota Sioux would very much understand:

> We are in the position of a little child entering a huge library filled with books in many languages. The child knows someone must have written those books. It does not know how. It does not understand the languages in which they are written. The child dimly suspects a mysterious order in the arrangement of the books but doesn't know what it is. That, it seems to me, is the attitude of even the most intelligent human being toward God. We see the universe marvelously arranged and obeying certain laws but only

dimly understand these laws. Our limited minds grasp the mysterious force that moves the constellations.[18]

Here Einstein sounds the theme of the mysteriousness of the universe, and how wonderful a marvel it is, closely akin to the notion of *Wakan Tanka*, the Great Mystery. In so doing, Einstein makes plain that agnosticism—which comes from the Greek for "not knowing"—is not necessarily a lack of commitment to any position, a sort of theological fence sitting. Many agnostics contend, quite committedly, that the question of god or gods is something we simply can't answer, and maybe a question we don't even know how to ask. The shaman Finger would understand. For agnostics like Einstein, though, this mystery isn't just a mystery. It's a holy mystery. That is, the mysteriousness is exactly what we should be worshipping. We might call this view "spiritual agnosticism." Here's how Einstein described it:

If something is in me which can be called religious then it is the unbounded admiration for the structure of the world so far as our science can reveal it.[19]

For Einstein, then, scientific discovery does not disenchant the world. It does not take away the mystery. Rather, it reaffirms the mystery, for it is truly incredible, the most incredible thing we can know, that such a structure has come into being. Figuring out or discovering a scientific answer always raises more questions about that structure and how it could possibly have come to be. The questioning, the recognition that there is so much that we do not know, never stops. Rather, it ever grows, eliciting continual amazement and awe that is deeply meaningful to scientists, as it is to non-scientists. Let me quote Einstein one last time:

The most beautiful and deepest experience [anyone] can have is the sense of the mysterious. It is the underlying principle of religion as well as all serious endeavor in art and science. [Anyone] who has not had this experience seems to me, if not dead, then at least blind. To sense that behind anything that can be experienced there is something that our mind cannot grasp and whose beauty and sublimity reaches us only indirectly and as a feeble reflection, this is religiousness. In this sense I am religious. To me it suffices to wonder at these secrets and to accept humbly to grasp with my mind a mere image of the lofty structure of all that is there.[20]

Dawkins quotes much of this passage in *The God Delusion*.[21] And Dawkins immediately follows it with a rather spiritual statement of his own: "In this sense I too am religious, with the reservation that 'cannot grasp' does not have to mean 'forever ungraspable.'[22] Dawkins is not an agnostic. He is absolutely certain there is no god or gods, especially a personal or theistic god. He thinks the question of the existence of god or gods can be asked and answered, and the answer is a resounding no. That is the defining belief of atheism: It is a-theistic. But even though Dawkins is an atheist—he calls himself a "staunch" atheist in his book—Dawkins as a scientist has clearly often found himself overwhelmed by how truly amazing it all is, an amazement that even his level of commitment to strong atheism does not defuse.[23]

Ronald Dworkin calls this view "religious atheism," in part to criticize Dawkins.[24] And indeed, Dawkins doesn't like such language to describe his views. Despite his grudging response to Einstein that "in this sense I too am religious," Dawkins says, "I prefer not to call myself religious because it is misleading."[25] So let's not call him religious. Let's take him at his word, unless we want to start calling science a religion—which perhaps in some senses it is, as many have suggested, or should be, as many others have suggested.[26] But scientists, even religious ones, usually don't like to see the scientific endeavor that way, as least not publicly. So maybe we could ratchet down the point a bit and call Dawkins's reverence for the "beauty and sublimity" of the all a "spiritual atheism," in parallel with spiritual agnosticism. My guess is that Dawkins wouldn't like that term either, though. It implies an unseen presence, a spirit, that Dawkins would not be able to detect in any meter or test tube.

Nor would Dawkins likely be any happier about calling his view part of the perennial philosophy, for the uses of this term have also always implied the presence of a spirit—and not just a spirit, but a guiding spirit. I would add as well that perennial philosophy is, like Axialism, a rather evolutionist and civilizationist term, hinting at a kind of unfolding sequence and a moving up from paganism to what I have been calling bourgeois faiths. It is thus potentially chauvinistic. Plus to call one of these various views of the unknown a "philosophy," let alone a common and perennial "philosophy," seems to rush to a confidence that anyone has this all worked out. Rather, it seems to me that the point is no one does.

———

May I hazard a different term, then—one that I think embraces pantheism, perennial philosophy, spiritual agnosticism, and Dawkins's passion for the dispassionate? Perhaps we could call it, with both humor and seriousness, the recognition of the **AWESOME COOLNESS** of the universe.

At least this is a term that I have been tossing around in conversations and lectures in recent years. My students love it. I confess that some people have told me they get the point, but would rather I used a more technical sounding term. I'm going to go with the students, though, in part because I like the term's lightheartedness and the unifying chuckle of recognition it generally elicits. But I don't care what anyone calls this recognition—as long as they do indeed get the point.

To help people get the point, maybe I ought to define awesome coolness. But I think it would be internally contradictory to do so. Instead, I'll describe it: However dull and dismal we may often find the cold truths of logic, it is quite mind-blowing to consider—to deeply consider—just why it is that 1 plus 1 equals 2, here, there, and everywhere. Yes, we can imagine dope smokers sitting around in bell bottoms contemplating that fact. But it really is the sort of thing that would break your brain if you tried—deeply tried—to puzzle it out. Or consider that 2 is the only prime number that is even. That makes 2 pretty odd. Or consider that π is 3.141592653589793238462643383279502884197169399375105820974944592307816164, and on and on and on ad infinitum, until you decide that your circle is as round as you'll be able to get it in this life.

Or consider that all our cells contain in them these incredible little power plants we call mitochondria that break down nutrients and make chemical energy and that seem to have begun eons ago in evolution from a bacterial invasion into some cell that craftily captured the invader and put it to work, making that cell so successful that it passed this amazing feature on to the trillions of cellular progeny that make up each one of us.

Or consider that the ruby-throated hummingbirds I may be fortunate enough to admire flitting around my garden in the summer in Wisconsin, where I live, may spend the coldest months of the year in Central America, and may get there by flying up to five hundred miles across the Gulf of Mexico at the speed of a galloping horse, through wind and rain, all in a single twenty-hour flight—even though an adult ruby-throated hummingbird weighs only about three and a half grams, lighter than a nickel coin.

Or consider that if you fill in the piano keys around an A-major chord with the notes of a G-major-seventh chord you get a clashing dissonance that makes you want to run from the room, unless you are a fan of the abstract and harsh in music, but if you stack the notes of a G-major-seventh chord in the register up from the A-major chord you get the resonant vibrancy of an A-thirteenth chord, so loved by jazz musicians, tickling the cilia of your labyrinths and echoing from the sonorous air into the inner receptivities of your imagination.

Or consider that there are reaches and reaches and reaches of space and time out there, showing that the form of our world and the homey confines of our solar system are part of a vastness of possibilities, and that something, someone, or some *somehow* must have brought this immensity into being and motion, whether you call it *Wakan Tanka* or another name or maybe no name at all.

These are awesomely cool facts, every one.

"And if you don't think so, well, tough luck, Buster," as my daughter Eleanor put it to me, looking over my shoulder as I was typing a draft of this chapter. "You go find another planet, another social system, another galaxy, another universe that's cooler and more awesome and show it to us all." Exactly.

————

Surely this is something we can agree upon—even if we don't agree on the terms for it. I say can because we apparently do, from atheist to agnostic to bourgeois to pagan. So why do we fight so much about it? Can't we just live with the thought that others have different languages for trying to describe the indescribable? After all if life, the universe, and everything are indescribable it should be no surprise that people in all their variety would try to describe them differently.

But we humans do not find it easy to hold on to a common recognition of our common recognition. Faced with questions we think we need to answer, we lose our openness to wonder and replace it with absolutes that divide the world and its peoples into disturbingly clear categories. Why? *Because ideas are never only about the ideas themselves.* They are also about the social relations in which those ideas are embedded, and the social relations that these ideas put together and hold apart.

I went back and forth in my mind for a day before I settled on the word "never" up above. At first I had it as *rarely* only about the ideas themselves. But I couldn't think of an instance in which it wasn't so, and I still can't. Then I tried *rarely, if ever.* That seemed unnecessarily tentative. If the water's clear and your nerve is up, you might as well dive. What makes that water clear is what others often regard as the basis of its murkiness: The recognition that ideas always emerge from a social context, oriented toward a social context. How could it be otherwise? Ideas must come from somewhere and some people, directed toward other wheres and other people. Or we would never have heard of them.

The main factor in this turbidity, argued Michel Foucault across his vast oeuvre, is that any social context always has power relations—power relations that yield the ideas and ideas that yield the power relations. "Power-knowledge" is what Foucault called it. It's an awkward term, and maybe appropriately so. It makes an awkward point: Knowledge isn't neutral. It comes from people, with all their foibles and ambitions. Plus the problem is recursive, said Foucault. Our foibles and ambitions come from our knowledge and how it leads us to organize our lives as much as the other way around. There's no easy exit, he contended, and maybe no exit at all.

Such a recognition can yield a sourness in our political thought. There is much cause for this caustic view. Social life and its politics give us plenty to be sour about, maybe even more than we are generally aware of. (Foucault thought, like fish and water, we aren't aware of most of it.) But the relationship between knowledge and the power relations of social context is not wholly negative. We want our ideas to relate to our contexts. That's why we think of them. And not all our interests are bad. Nor is it bad to have the power to implement the ones we regard as plausibly good—as long as we remain open to challenge about that plausibility, challenge from others and challenge from our own selves, continually invigorating and developing our reasoning.

It's also very helpful to know where and whom ideas come from, for knowing their social location helps us judge the plausible goodness of ideas precisely by identifying their social relations, and therefore their power relations too. We know others see things differently because we know that we see things differently. That too is not necessarily bad. The difference of others is why it is so often so very rewarding to talk to them and to find out what they see. They have had experiences that we have not as surely as we are not them. The trouble comes when we see things differently so that we may be seen differently. The trouble comes when we bound our ideas so we may bound our groups. The trouble comes when our ideas and ideals yield a natural we and a natural them.

As the sociologist of religion Paul Lichterman notes, "People, however, also use religion to define collective identities. Public groups, for instance, often use religious language to understand who they are, and how they relate to insiders and outsiders, apart from justifying opinions on specific issues or group goals."[27] We use our ideas about nature this way too, whether those ideas come from a scientist's lab or from the lab of everyday life. We're never just talking about nature or religion. We're also talking about community. We're talking about the ancient triangle.

What we know is who we are, and who we are is what we know. To be someone is to have knowledge, both knowledge that others have and knowledge that others don't. That commonality of knowledge connects us to others and that difference of knowledge gives us our sense of individuality—which in turn also connects us to others, for without individuality there would be nothing to connect from, or to. We would already be connected, and community would not be such an ever-present issue for humankind, and such a source of both our joys and our disappointments.

We need to seek that connection because most of what we know we gain with the assistance of others. Who has time to do all one's own experiments on what is the truth of the world? Besides, others have learned valuable things, sometimes even through tragedy. Why repeat those misfortunes just to see if you really will hit the pavement hard if you jump out of a tall building, attempting to fly by flapping your arms? Do you really need to try every mushroom species for yourself? Does no one have any worthy advice for us? Actually they do, as we have all learned, often to our chagrin. So we turn to others, others we trust because of our sense of communion with them, to gain knowledge that we don't have the time, skills, or opportunity to determine on our own. It's an ongoing process that brings us into the cultures of our communities, and that I like to call *knowledge cultivation*.[28] To put it in language like Foucault's, it's a matter of power-knowledge-identity. But that's even more awkward to say. So I like to use the metaphor of cultivation, a cultivation that runs very deep.

There's a subtle and powerful corollary to how we cultivate knowledge. Even more than turning to others for knowledge, we turn to others for guidance about what we can safely avoid learning about. We have to. Every moment of every day when we are awake, we are attending to some possible sources of information about our world and situation, and simultaneously not attending to an infinite amount of other possible sources. Some of those sources of information we evaluate on our own because they are right around us, streaming into the senses: light, sound, smell, taste, feel. But also we are making decisions about whom to talk to and listen to, and what to read and watch—and, what is a far larger category, whom and what not to. You won't have time to peruse the *Huffington Post* on your tablet if you have just devoted your fifteen minutes of reading time at breakfast to reading *Le Monde*, the *New York Times*, or the latest postings from *Fox News*. There is simply way more to read than you can get through. If you check out a book from the library today, or maybe even a half dozen, that's great, but there are tens and tens of thousands of others you will never read. You won't live that long. Plus about another two million new ones are published every year around the world.[29] If you take a few courses at your local university, wonderful, but then you can't take any of the hundreds of others that are probably on offer at the same times. How will you know if those sources and courses you did not attend to were safe to ignore? Maybe they contained some vital information that is very relevant to your life and where it could be heading. But you can't know for sure, because you haven't looked or listened. And you can't. There is way, way, way too much out there.

So how do you decide? Through the same cultivations of social trust and identity that bring knowledge to you and help constitute your social identity. But in this case, they are not cultivating knowledge. They are helping us with a necessary problem of daily life: the *cultivation of the ignorable*, our sense of what is safe to disregard.[30] To gain some knowledge we have to ignore a whole lot more. The ignorable is thus constitutive of knowledge.

The ignorable is not ignorance, though. I'm trying to tread carefully around the way we use the word ignorance as a put-down.[31] Let me try putting it this way. The ignorable is not necessarily something that others think one really ought to know, which is what I think we really mean by the word "ignorance." Rather, the ignorable is what others think we don't need to know, others that we trust to guide us rightly. The ignorable is what we trust we may screen out, largely tacitly, in order to focus on what our limited understanding of our context makes seem more relevant. And maybe it is. Maybe it's not. We don't know, and indeed we can't fully know. We can't know everything and be everywhere. Unlike some conceptions of the divine, we not omniscient and universal. And so we look to trusted others to guide our sense of what is germane to our lives and needs.

Thus the ignorable is also constitutive of community. You have to situate yourself within tissues of trust that help form you as a self that knows some things, and is known for knowing them, but also must rely on others for a whole lot more—even if our individualism sometimes makes this reliance hard to admit. These tissues are not easy to sever, once we are connected with them. I am talking here about who our friends are and who our friends are not. I am talking here about who we care about and who cares for us. These are closely held bonds that we neither make nor cut easily. Which means we often find ourselves similarly holding tight to our sense of knowledge and the ignorable that come from these bonds, and that create them, solidifying social relations by freezing knowledge and the ignorable into absolutes.

———

We hold particularly tightly when we think those bonds are under threat—or have been led to believe that they are. For as many a political leader has discovered, one of the surest ways to unify people is to divide them. The sociologist Howard Becker suggested a term that aptly describes this social process: "moral entrepreneurs."[32] Behind every sharp community boundary of the absolute good stand people who gain social position by carving that line into society. The absolute good then becomes the goodness of the group—a natural we divided from a natural them—and the goodness of the moral entrepreneur. Numerous are those who have figured out that one can make others feel good about themselves by using absolutes to encourage them to think ill of others—and who then feel good about those that showed them to this tragic satisfaction.

Some moral entrepreneurs become highly successful by choosing the right moment to play our uncertainties away from awesome coolness into a *fearful hotness* toward a natural them, hardened into absolutes about nature, religion, and each other. This phenomenon is familiar not only to the grand politics of the front page, but also to the micro-politics of our daily lives. Indeed, I suspect that all of us have at least on occasion tried our own moral hand at this regrettable kind of entrepreneurship. In quiet moments, I recognize that I've done it myself sometimes.

The scriptures of bourgeois faiths unfortunately provide some scope for a moral entrepreneur to encourage a fearful hotness from absolutes, just as they can also provide scope for appreciation of awesome coolness. These works were all written a long time ago, even comparatively recent religious texts like the New Testament or the *Talmud* or the Qur'an or the *Bhagavad Gita*. That age in itself provides a moral argument for reading scriptures as yielding absolutes beyond politics, and thus a basis for nonpolitical politics. Not only do bourgeois scriptures describe a divine that is beyond politics, the implicit logic goes. Their very age means that the reader from the present had no hand in crafting those scriptures, no intent in selecting their words. Thus the politics of the present cannot impugn them—or so we often accept in moments of fearful hotness, easily waving aside objections that a text must always be interpreted by someone to have any meaning. Otherwise every word is just a splash of ink on the page or of light emitting diodes on the screen.

That authoritativeness in hand, the next step for the moral entrepreneur is to encourage reading scriptures selectively in some particular moral light of the present, rather than the moral light of the context that gave rise to them. One does not have to deliberately omit or rewrite passages to merely emphasize some over others and to present their meaning with very different illumination from that which shone on the papyrus and pen of the original writers. In moments of present conflict, we lose patience with subtler readings that point out contradictions and how little we really know about the context of the past.

Consider the appalling violence in much of the Old Testament. As I argued in chapter 4, there is no particular pretense to the good in the Old Testament, especially in the earlier books. (It does tend to happier passages in the later books.) It's not a bourgeois work. It's pagan monotheism, and you don't have to look deep into other pagan traditions to find plenty of divinely inspired atrocity, as in the *Popol Vuh* and *Gilgamesh*. Yet there's an important difference in the character of these pagan divinities and their violent passions: They're powerful, but you can disagree with them. They can be wrong and you can try to get them to change their minds. You can confront and contest them, as Moses, the Divine Twins, and Gilgamesh all did. You can sometimes even defeat them. There is plenty of horror in pagan traditions, but that horror is not absolute. This may seem a fine point, but it's one that bourgeois moral entrepreneurs looking back at their faith's more pagan earlier writings have often conveniently ignored, as they sought to encourage an absolute reading of some violent passage.

The bourgeois moral entrepreneur can, of course, also try to decontextualize a faith's more recent scriptures. Consider the shocking language of Revelation, the final book of the New Testament. The Four Horseman of the Apocalypse ride out swinging swords, and Jesus and an angel swing sickles, dealing judgment on the sinfulness of the people of Babylon. The angel throws the fallen "into the great wine press of the wrath of God. And the wine press was trodden outside the city, and blood flowed from the wine press, as high as a horse's bridle, for a distance of about two hundred miles."[33] Satan fights back in the form of a dragon, leading the remaining forces of evil, and assisted by a scarlet beast with seven heads and ten horns—a beast that doesn't have a name, only a number: six hundred sixty-six. Riding the beast is a woman bedecked in jewels and purple and scarlet clothes. She does have a name, and it is written on her forehead: "Babylon the great, mother of whores and of earth's abominations."[34] Then Jesus, "clothed in a robe dipped in blood," rides out on a white horse. Even more fearsome, "from his mouth comes a sharp sword with which to strike down the nations."[35] An angel calls for birds to "Come, gather for the great supper of God, to eat the flesh of kings, the flesh of captains, the flesh of the mighty, the flesh of horses and their riders—flesh of all, both free and slave, both small and great."[36] The forces of God kill the dragon and the beast, and Jesus gives the birds plenty to eat: "And the rest were killed by the sword of the rider on the horse, the sword that came from his mouth; and all the birds were gorged with their flesh."[37]

Revelation certainly does not offer a peaceful image of a compassionate Jesus. The theologian Gregory Stevenson notes the danger here. "Historically," he writes, "Revelation has played a role in the perpetuation of violence, the justification of warfare and genocide, the stoking of vengeful fantasies, and the creation of a militant perversion of Christianity that trades in self-glorification."[38] The perpetuators, justifiers, stokers, and self-glorifiers don't stop to note that it was written for a very different purpose in a very different time.

What was Revelation's purpose and time? We don't need to know for sure to confess that it was assuredly different from ours, given two thousand years of distance. But here's what religious scholars think.

Elaine Pagels persuasively argues that Revelation was a coded call to the Jewish followers of Jesus to continue to resist the Roman Empire in the aftermath of the destruction of Jerusalem and the Jewish diaspora.[39] When John of Patmos—not to be confused with the author of the Gospel of John—set down these fiery lines around 90 CE, Christians were only just beginning to think of themselves as separate from Jews. Pagels suggests that Revelation gave a fantasy of hope to those who longed for the overthrow of the Babylon of Rome and still burned over the seven emperors of the Julio-Claudian dynasty that seem to be have been symbolized by the seven-headed beast. Although we cannot be certain, some scholars suspect that the beast's number, six hundred sixty-six, was a numerological reference to the emperor Nero. (The ancient Jewish practice of gematria assigns a numerical value to every Hebrew letter. Using gematria, the Hebrew phrase for "Emperor Nero" yields the number 666.) Nero was the last of the Julio-Claudians and the emperor who began the First Roman-Jewish War, resulting in the destruction of Jerusalem and the Second Temple in 70 CE, two years after Nero's death by suicide in 68 CE. There is also some evidence that Nero banned the John who authored Revelation to the island of Patmos—a tiny place, just thirteen square miles, twenty miles off the coast of what is now Turkey. John had plenty of personal reason to fume about Nero and the Roman-Jewish conflict.

Many Christians rightly argue, therefore, that Revelation cannot be taken out of context. Stevenson agrees but also suggests that, despite all its necessary contextuality, Revelation still has moral value—the moral value of "challenging our thinking, calling us to account, and questioning our allegiances."[40] He implies a crucial point here: we don't necessarily have to agree with everything in a scriptural tradition to value it and identify with it. Who agrees with everything their parents, spouse, and children say, even as they love them dearly and see them as themselves? Who agrees with everything that their favorite teachers and friends say, even as they revere, respect, and care for them? (Indeed, who even agrees completely with their own self?) The value of a text and of an interlocutor is as much the thoughtfulness of the disagreements they inspire in us as the qualities of the agreements. There is much potential wisdom in both. It's a matter of dialogue, not monologue. But dialogic readers of Revelation need to be wary lest, despite identifying with the text critically, they nonetheless add further fuel to the two millennia of Christian moral entrepreneurs who have used Revelation's scriptural authority for far less subtle and gentle ends.

Perhaps one might also argue that Revelation is really the pagan part of the New Testament, and that the peaceful Jesus is to be found elsewhere—that this is not a bourgeois problem. There would be a bit of truth to such a view. Revelation does at least pay attention to ecology, mainly using it as a form of punishment, as is common with pagan traditions. Pestilence, beasts, carrion-eating birds, earthquakes, volcanic eruptions, and more all make fearsome appearance in Revelation. But the divine is also presented as absolute good, albeit a terrifying absolute good. Plus Revelation shows great concern for both forms of evil, disloyalty and desire. It singles out 144,000 chosen ones as the true dedicated followers of God. And it phallocentrically reviles the corrupting power of women's sexuality as embodied by the image of Babylon as a whore. Revelation plainly manifests deeply bourgeois moral disquiet.

Moreover, Revelation is not the only book of the New Testament to present a warlike Jesus. Some chapters ago I mentioned Matthew's controversial report of Jesus saying "I have not come to bring peace, but a sword."[41] There is also Luke's account of Jesus telling his followers, "But as for these enemies of mine who did not want me to be king over them—bring them here and slaughter them in my presence."[42] Do these lines have to be appreciated within their context to be understood? Definitely. But it is also the case that, like the Old Testament, the New Testament provides the bourgeois moral entrepreneur with plenty of material for fearful hotness about a natural them.

Muslim moral entrepreneurs have used some of the Qur'an's bloodier passages to similar effect. Like the Bible, the Qur'an contains much that is as beautiful, noble, and inspiring for the worries of the present as it was for those of the past. But it also—again, like the Bible—contains many lines that can be decontextualized and marshaled in horrific and abusive ways. In the current political moment, much has been made of passages like "Let those of you who are willing to trade the life of this world for the life to come, fight in God's way. To anyone who fights in God's way, whether killed or victorious, We shall give a great reward."[43] Or "Those who wage war against God and His Messenger and strive to spread corruption in the land should be punished by death, crucifixion, the amputation of an alternate hand and foot, or banishment from the land: a disgrace for them in this world, and then a terrible punishment in the Hereafter."[44] That passage does not actually advocate starting a war, and it continues to say "unless they repent before you overpower them—in that case bear in mind that God is forgiving and merciful."[45] Nonetheless, this section of the Qur'an gives plenty of scope to the moral entrepreneur seeking justification for violence.

The Qur'an does indeed contain much that urges its readers to greater gentleness and mercy. Take the much-admired line that "if anyone kills a person . . . it is as if he kills all mankind, while if any saves a life it is as if he saves the lives of all mankind."[46] Even the controversial term *jihad*, which means to strive or to struggle, mainly occurs in contexts that would be difficult to take as implying "holy war" against nonbelievers.[47] Rather, the Qur'an's intended meaning usually is pretty clearly about striving and struggling to serve God in the face of one's sinful inclinations, as well as striving and struggling to defend Islam from its detractors. That doesn't stop the determined moral entrepreneur from cherry-picking—cherry-picking not the sweetest but the sourest and bitterest lines. And, as with the Bible, there are plenty to pick from. Even the famous line that killing-one-is-killing-all has an important caveat where I inserted ellipses above: "If anyone kills a person—unless in retribution for murder or spreading corruption in the land—it is as if. . . ." The absolutist hunting ammunition for some nonpolitical politics can do a lot with that qualification.

Such fruit can be found in the scriptures of other traditions too. There are sour and bitter cherries to be picked out of the *Talmud*, the Hindu canon, and even the generally pacifist Buddhist canon. At least militant Jews, Hindus, and Buddhists have often claimed to have found them.

———

Nature, too, can be cherry-picked for the sour and bitter, and then taken out of context and served to a natural we to motivate their displeasure. The moral entrepreneur seeking to create fear, anger, and disregard for a natural them can selectively find such fruit in nature because our ecological relations are complex and indeed sometimes quite unpleasant.

One example of such selectivity that has always given me pause is Ellsworth Huntington and his effort to connect the degree of civilization in an area with its climate.[48] Huntington was a professor at Yale in the early twentieth century. Like all Yale professors of the time, he was a White man. I'm a White man too, and a professor. Plus I have several degrees from Yale. And like me, Huntington seems to have considered that the association of Whiteness with elite places like Yale might manifest patterns of social injustice.

But Huntington felt that we can put aside our moral concern about these associations, for he believed that he demonstrated them to be due to nature, not politics.

Huntington was a geographer, so he liked maps. He sent a survey to "widely informed men" all around the world, asking them to rate the level of civilization they experienced in their locality so he could plot their results. The resulting map showed "very high" levels of civilization in rather unsurprising regions: Central and Northern Europe; the Northeast, Midwest, and West Coast of the United States; and along the temperate southeast coast of Australia, from Sydney over to Melbourne. Basically, his widely informed men found that civilization was highest wherever there was the highest proportion of White people like themselves.

Huntington's respondents also gave a few regions special downgrades that fit the common prejudices of White elites at the time. Ireland, Spain, southern Italy, Greece, Eastern Europe, and southern Canada all rated "high" instead of "very high," despite their overwhelmingly White populations. And the widely informed men rated most of Africa, South America, and Asia as "low" or "very low" in civilization, with a few "medium" scorings around areas where some Whites had settled, such as South Africa and central India, and a small zone of "high" around Buenos Aires in Argentina, a region with considerable White immigration. Japan and eastern China rated a "medium." They rated much of Africa as having no civilization at all—just a blank space on the map, the same as most of Greenland.

Huntington then compared the map of civilization to a map of what he termed "human energy according to climate." He reasoned that wherever the climate was unpleasant—wherever it was too hot or too cold for human comfort—people would be lethargic and unable to advance much in civilization. And he found the highest levels of beneficent climate pretty much wherever the highest proportion of White people lived. His conclusion: "The climate of many countries seems to be one of the great reasons why idleness, dishonesty, immorality, stupidity, and weakness of will prevail."[49] In short, White people are not to be blamed for dominating others. It's just their good fortune to have been so favored by the nature of climate.

This was considered real science at the time. Huntington's 1915 book on the subject, *Climate and Civilization*, won him much praise. The Geographical Society of Philadelphia awarded him its Elisha Kent Kane Gold Medal in 1916. In 1917, Huntington served as president of the Ecological Society of America, and in 1923 he served as president of the Association of American

Geographers. And maybe no wonder: at the time, almost all the members of these academic societies were White as well.

I say "maybe no wonder" because, even setting aside the shoddy and selective methods, the line of reasoning is incredibly sloppy. It can readily be turned around to say exactly the reverse. Wouldn't it make just as much sense to say that *easy* climates encourage laziness, stupidity, and weakness of will? Difficult climates must exert greater selective pressure for a strong will and high intelligence, because survival is more difficult. So civilization should be highest where the climate is the most challenging. Indeed, in my view, the accomplishments of the Inuit, the Yanomami, the Maasai, and Aboriginal Australians must count among the most innovative applications of strong will and high intelligence to the challenges of ecological context. But such a line of reasoning would not have done the moral work Huntington and his many fans needed: the justification of racial inequality as not due to politics but due to a power they felt to be outside of politics. Nature.

————

The absolute does not absolve. It does not absolve because it does not resolve, much as we might hope it would. Indeed, it commonly gets in the way of resolving by shutting down conversation, mistaking closing for closure. Alas, sometimes the closing is no mistake. It is the intent. Nature and religion treated as absolutes become creators and demarcators of borderlines. They become boundaries of cultivations of knowledge and the ignored—boundaries that we create and that we push each other into. We go looking for the world but find instead our own identities, formed in opposition to others instead of in dialogue with others, especially in troubling times.

I say Allah and you say Jesus. You say evolution and I say Adam and Eve. I say women's rights and you say honor and obey. You say LGBTQ rights and I say holy matrimony. I say climate change and you say God's plan.

You say Halloween is fun and I say paganism is wicked. I say sex is joy and you say sex is sin. You say science is authority and I say scripture is authority. I say equity is justice and you say equality is justice. You say we are one and I say God is one.

I say racism and you say 9/11. You say choice and I say murder. I say Black lives matter and you say all lives matter. You say the rule of law and I say the rule of the Ten Commandments. You say rights and I say the market. I say care for the environment and you say care for creation, if you say anything at all.

These, then, are the social uses, and the social abuses, of the absolute. Our certainties shape our identities, and our identities shape our certainties. We go blundering ahead, convinced that the solution to our conflicts lies in establishing the one right way for everyone—one right way that we believe is not based in our own interests, even though it happily does serve our interests. For it is, after all, everyone's one right way, we contend.

But at the same time that we go grasping for this elusive release into a nonpolitical politics, the oldest questions of the ancient triangle come right back to us, ever unanswered in the continued unfolding of time and surprise. In that unfolding, it seems to me, we can discover space for optimism about human cooperation and justice. While the origins of nonpolitical politics and fearful hotness lie in our thirst for certainty, for really knowing, the origins of political politics and awesome coolness lie in our appreciation for enigma, for never really knowing. Herein lies the most awesome and cool power of the Great Mystery: the way it encourages us to be forever open to further experience of the world and to further experience of each other.

10

The Jewel of Truth

THE FIRE HAS BURNT pretty well down now, and it's getting late. Shall we throw one last log on? Yes, that nice piece of oak. There's one more story I'd like to tell, and then talk over for a bit if you've a little more energy. A fairy tale, not too long. One log should do. I call it "The Three Lions of the Deep Earth." No, I don't need any more chocolate—for the moment, at least! Oh, but another splash in my glass would be very nice. Perfect. Thanks. You good too? Great.

––––––

Once upon a time, there was a King and a Queen who had three sons and one daughter. The sons were all handsome and clever, and the daughter was beautiful and smart. Why? Because this is a fairy tale, that's why.

One day, a prince from a neighboring kingdom came to visit, and he immediately fell in love with the daughter and she with him. They decided to wed. When the King and Queen heard of it they were overjoyed, for the visiting prince was handsome and clever like their own sons. The wedding date was set for a year hence.

The King and Queen wanted to send their daughter off in style into her new life. What to give her as a present but a new crown, set with the most beautiful jewel that could be found? Yes, that was it. They called their three sons before them and instructed them each to go out and find the most beautiful jewel that they could. The one that brought home the most beautiful jewel within the year would then be awarded rulership of the realm, for the King and Queen had tired of being monarchs.

So off the three sons went. Almost a year later, as the eldest brother was riding along the foothills of some faraway mountains, he encountered an old man with three moustaches, sitting beside the road, swinging a glittering jewel on a string.

"That is a beautiful jewel," said the eldest son.

"Yes," croaked the old man, "but not as beautiful as the Three Lions of the Deep Earth. Those are the most beautiful jewels in the world, although they are as yet uncut."

The eldest son, excited, exclaimed, "Oh wise old man, where can I find the Three Lions of the Deep Earth, and where can I get one of them cut?"

"See there," said the old man, nodding in the direction of the mountains. "You must cross the Waterfall of Love, climb the Mountain of Great Truth, and enter the Cave of the Bright Mysteries, where you will find the Three Lions of the Deep Earth. Take one, and bring it to the jewel cutters in the three huts over there, across the road."

There were indeed three jewel cutters' huts, conveniently located just across the road. Why? Because this is a fairy tale, that's why.

So the eldest son crossed the Waterfall of Love, climbed the Mountain of Great Truth, entered the Cave of the Bright Mysteries, and found the Three Lions of the Deep Earth in a recess at the back of the cavern. He took one— they all looked exactly the same, rounded and glassy and not very impressive, for they were as yet uncut—and brought it back down the mountain to the jewel cutters' huts.

One of the jewel cutters was sitting outside in the sunshine. The eldest son said to him, "I am looking for a jewel cutter. Who is the best one here?"

"It is I, of course," the cutter replied. "I was trained by a great guru in the *dharma*, the eternal laws, of jewel cutting. Let me cut your Lion of the Deep Earth." The eldest son agreed, and the jewel cutter truly cut the Lion into a beautiful jewel. The eldest son paid the jewel cutter well and happily headed for home, contented with the thought that he would gain the rulership of his parents' realm.

The next day, the middle son passed by the same road and had the same conversation with the old man with the three moustaches, crossed the Waterfall of Love, climbed the Mountain of Great Truth, entered the Cave of the Bright Mysteries, took another of the Lions of the Deep Earth, and brought it to the jewel cutters' huts.

This time, a different one of the three jewel cutters was out sitting in the sun. "I am looking for a jewel cutter," the middle son said to him. "Who is the best one here?"

"It is I, of course," the cutter replied. "I was trained by a wise monk in the *dao*, the essential Way, of jewel cutting. Let me cut your Lion of the Deep Earth." The middle son agreed, and the jewel cutter truly cut the Lion into another beautiful jewel. The middle son paid the jewel cutter well and happily headed for home, contented with the thought that it would be he who gained the rulership.

And the very next day after that, the youngest son passed by the very same road and had the very same conversation with the very same old man with the very same three moustaches. He too crossed the Waterfall of Love, climbed the Mountain of Great Truth, and entered the Cave of the Bright Mysteries. He took the last of the Three Lions of the Deep Earth, and brought it to the same three jewel cutters' huts. Why? Because this is a fairy tale, that's why.

This time, the third of the three jewel cutters was out sitting in the sun. "I am looking for a jewel cutter," said the youngest son to him. "Who is the best one here?"

"It is I, of course," the cutter replied. "I was trained by a brilliant scientist in the *nature*, the physical realities, of jewel cutting. Let me cut your Lion of the Deep Earth."

But the youngest son was good-hearted and wise beyond his years. He went and knocked on the doors of the other two huts as well, and learned about the *dharma* and the *dao* of jewel cutting too.

"You all seem like excellent jewel cutters," said the youngest son. "So I will have each of you take turns at cutting the Lion into a jewel."

The annals do not record which cutter cut first. But as each received the jewel after the other had worked it, he saw new and different possibilities for how best to bring out the brightest beauty of the Lion. Each had three turns at cutting the jewel. And when they were done, the Lion glittered with a fire and a luminance that rivaled the Sun itself. The youngest son tried to pay the three jewel cutters, but they all refused the money, so overjoyed were they at what they had accomplished together.

The three sons soon returned home with their three jewels. They laid them out in front of the King and Queen, and the King and Queen called in the sister to choose which was the most beautiful, her not knowing which brother had brought back which jewel and would therefore gain the rulership of the realm.

But the sister, like her youngest brother, was good-hearted and wise beyond her years. She looked over the jewels and said, "One of the jewels is plainly the most brilliant, and has a luminance that rivals the Sun itself. Yet I refuse to choose it, or either of the others."

"My princess," spoke the King, with some agitation, "how can you refuse? If one is the most brilliant—and I can guess which one you mean, for it truly does rival the Sun itself—choose it!"

"I will only choose it on one condition: That all three of my brothers rule together."

"But that would never work," replied the King. "As in jewel cutting, only one person can hold the tools at once."

"I mean for them to rule in turn, for a year each," replied the sister. "As in jewel cutting, when one person cuts after another he sees new and different possibilities that bring out the brightest beauty."

"Not just he. He or she," added the youngest son. "Let all three brothers rule together with our sister, each in turn finding those different possibilities of brightest beauty."

And so it was. The wedding of the sister and her prince took place the next day. She wore a crown set with the third Lion of the Deep Earth in the middle of the other two, radiating like the Sun and illuminating all the wedding party, far into the night. Plus the sister's new husband had three sisters who were beautiful and smart like her. The three brothers each married one of the sisters, and the four couples took turns at ruling, year by year in rotation.

Never before was a land ruled so justly and so wisely, with so much beauty and prosperity, and so much profound joy.

Why? Because this is a fairy tale, that's why.

————

Although it is a fairy tale, I think this fable has much truth to offer—even if I made it up.

Indeed, the truth is always something that we make up, and then re–make up as we go along, a settlement we build on the banks of the river of our lives, before passing on to some other new settlement further downstream.[1] How could it be any other way? What we call truth is a human construct, a community construct, the product of our continual mutual (if often conflictual) learning. Sometimes we hear people of faith say, no, truth comes from God, from the divine and therefore from beyond the human community, if the truth is truly divine. Sometimes we hear rationalists say, no, truth comes from science, from nature, which they too argue lies beyond the human community, if the truth is truly natural. But the sociological response is that we humans can know only as humans know, for we are just that: human.

Which doesn't necessarily make our truths less true. Maybe just the opposite. Because we make stuff up as we go along, because we are always refining our understanding, the truths we use to guide our actions have a better chance of being relevant to the conditions in which we find ourselves at any given moment.

The trouble, of course, is that we may be fooling ourselves, and perhaps fooling others, with the truths we make up. We want outcomes that are to our advantage, quite sensibly, and to the advantage of those we care about. So the temptations of mendacity pull strongly on our hearts and minds.

We all know this, having been fooled many a time in our past, and most likely having attempted some fooling on our own, at least on occasion. We have all encountered instances where it seemed plain that others had conspired to project truths that suited the politics of their interests, and where we recognized that we too had painted our desires and not our realities. And so we look for truths absolute and unchanging, stretching across history and circumstance, the better to be sure that we haven't been fooled, either by others or by ourselves, victims of a hidden conspiracy.

The trouble is, our desire to avoid such a conspiracy may make us susceptible to easy formulations that appear to be free of politics, as we silently agree to hidden conspiracies—*as long as those conspiracies remain hidden from us*, and perhaps even hidden from those who formulated them, even if that them is us. There are indeed circumstances where we consciously conspire to create truths that support our political interests, big and small. Sometimes conspiracy of ideas and interests does happen. But people can usually arrive at such support by an easier means, without engaging in deliberate manipulation: what I earlier called the "interests bias" that comes from our tendency not to fire up critical passion when our ideas and interests happily line up.

Mighty among our interests is support for the communities we trust to help us sort between what we need to know and what we may safely ignore, as I also discussed earlier. But our communities may be wrong about that need and that safety. Moreover, our communities may enact interests that do not altogether line up with our own, even though they are our own communities. A community is not sameness; it is a connection across our inevitable differences. Moral entrepreneurs may tug on that connection for purposes other than ours. They may even consciously lie to us.

In short, there is plenty of scope for being fooled in our attempts to avoid it. Thus it is great to hear from others—other people from other cultivations of knowledge and the ignorable. But an absolute does not welcome the voices of others. An absolute yields one-sided truth, truth that looks at the object of our contemplation and desire from just one perspective. It yields flat truth. It yields truth that reflects only what looks at it from that same viewpoint. It yields uninviting truth, uninviting to further reflection from other angles of vision and experience. It yields truth that embodies only one logic out of the manyness of our understandings and circumstances. An absolute may seem to give us hard truth but rather gives us truth that is all too easy, for it allows us to proceed with eyes and ears closed to challenge. Such truth is also dull truth for it mirrors only what is directly in front of it, and thus shines little and reveals little.

Instead of a one-sided approach to truth, let us have a truth with many sides, many angles of reflection, a truth that sparkles with the full light of activity around it and that draws our imagination into its interior where the glimmers play and dance as we move our perspective from side to side, incident to incident, explanation to explanation, person to person. Let us have a *jewel of truth*, a truth with many facets. And let us all contribute to cutting and recutting that jewel, and to polishing its surfaces with the grit of circumstance and experience so that it glitters and glints with more and more understandings and potentials. A jewel, through its beauty, invites the careful scrutiny of each facet from where we each stand, as we collectively seek to improve the jewel's luster and light through ever more cutting and polishing. Plus let us have not just one jewel of truth but lots and lots of them, each the work of a community of jewelers but arrayed so that they reflect upon the facets of the others, radiant with ever-changing sparklings of the all.

Such an array of jewels would reflect not a monologic but rather a *multilogical truth* that develops from our dialogues and considered agreements and disagreements with one another and the world, and that challenges us toward intellectual honesty—a truth that is not just the reflection of one flection, one bent on things, but a constant re-reflection of the many flections, the many logics, of all our lives.[2] This jewel would be no less comforting and useful for its manyness, criticality, and endless change. Rather, it would comfort us with connections and interconnections. And it would gain us the greater utility, for it emerges from the diversity of practice and know-how that it brings together, and because it gives context to truth, and therefore truth to context. In other words, a multilogical truth is a contextual truth, relative and relevant because it is relational.

But relative is not the same as relativist—at least as relativist is usually meant. Considering that views of truth may look different from the perspective of another is not to suggest that there is no truth other than the solipsism of one's personal account of experience. Nor is it to suggest that no idea, statement, or declaration about truth is any better than any other. Quite the opposite: rather, it is to suggest that others have views and experiences of value to us, that we may learn from, as we collectively scrutinize all our efforts at adding facets to the jewel, seeking to improve the results. Yes, truth is relative. That's why we often gain so much from each other's views and experiences. But truth is not solipsist any more than it is absolutist. Indeed, solipsism is just the absolutism of the personal.

I have been borrowing here from a Mahayana Buddhist image, the *jewel net of Indra*. Some colleagues of mine—their names are Loka Ashwood, Noelle Harden, and Bill Bland—and I recently suggested another metaphor for this vision of truth as the contextualized, ever-changing, connecting up of difference.[3] We called it *grounded knowledge*, knowledge that recognizes its grounding in local context but also recognizes that it ultimately connects to all other contexts, just as all grounds in a landscape ultimately connect to every other. To accept grounded knowledge does not mean denigrating your own views for being different, partial, and parochial. Nor does it mean denigrating the views of others. But nor does it mean necessarily agreeing. We each have grounds for what we know, grounds that come out of our specific experiences in our specific contexts. We can trace connections to all other grounds through welcoming yet critical evaluation of the accounts of others—but also, through them, encouraging scrutiny of our own accounts of experience. And when we do, when we consider others' experiences as our own, and in light of our own, we find that our knowledge has changed, even if we do not necessarily fully agree. It becomes not just local knowledge but multilocal knowledge, drenched in our similarities and our differences like so much water drawn from springs issuing out of many grounds, rushing together into an ever-changing stream.

———

The jewel of truth is not a new idea. It is one of the foundation stones of our sociality. And although we often seem to forget this basic insight of our social condition—or seem to want to forget it in the political heat of the moment—related ideas can be found in many traditions.

Take Judaism and its openness to debate as recorded in the Talmud. Here Jewish scholars did not merely write down the "Oral Torah." Rather, in assembling the Talmud, they combined what Jews call the *Mishnah* with what Jews call the *Gemara*. The Mishnah dates from about 200 CE and inscribes the results of centuries of religious debate over the meaning of the Oral Torah. The Gemara dates from about 500 CE, when the Talmud was first assembled, and inscribes the results of religious debate in those three intervening centuries. And the Gemara is not merely tacked on at the end of the Mishnah. Rather, the Talmud puts the commentaries of the Gemara side by side on the same pages as the relevant passages in the Mishnah. Plus the Gemara often comments on other Gemara, again often on the same page. The Talmud's debates continue on in a series of medieval commentaries called *Tosafot*, now included in most printings of the Talmud on the outer edges of the pages. The result is commentaries on commentaries on commentaries: Tosafot commenting on the Gemara, the Gemara commenting on the Mishnah, and the Mishnah recording commentaries on the Oral Torah—all of which have commentaries internal to themselves, the rabbis recorded in the Mishnah debating one another, the rabbis in the Gemara debating one another, and writers of the Tosafot debating one another as well.[4] It doesn't stop there. Judaism has long been open to new *minhag*, or local customs and traditions that contextualize practice in circumstance.

Christianity also has a strong tradition of openness to debate and deliberation. Consider the ceaseless conversation embodied in Christian *hermeneutics*, the practice of Christian biblical interpretation and reinterpretation, mediating like the Greek god Hermes between the heavens and the Earth. Indeed, the Christian dialogue of difference begins right with the Gospels. There is no one Gospel truth. There are at least four—Matthew, Mark, Luke, and John, who have many differences—encouraging Christians to continually think and rethink the origins and implications of their faith. Gnostic Christians would include at least a half dozen more Gospels, like the *Gospel of Thomas*, the *Gospel of Judas*, the *Gospel of Mary*, and the *Gospel of Truth*. The New Testament's Epistles continue the dialogue, as do the later writings of Augustine, Thomas Aquinas, Luther, Calvin, Milton, Wesley, Merton, Niebuhr, Armstrong, Cobb, Pagels, Pope Francis, and thousands and thousands more. Let us recall as well that there are over two hundred seminaries of various Christian denominations in the United States alone and dozens of scholarly journals devoted to Christian theology.

Islam too has a vast tradition of deliberation and debate. Despite all the current attempts East and West to box it into one supposed stability, Islam has a deep commitment to continual learning and change through *ijtihad*, the Islamic practice of diligent critical thinking. The two oldest degree-granting universities in the world—Morocco's University of al-Qarawiyyin (founded in 859) and Egypt's Al-Azhar University (founded in 970)—are Islamic, home to scholarly debate over *ijtihad* for over a millennium. As well, Islam maintains at least eight current *madhhabs* or schools of interpretation and jurisprudence.[5] *Ijtihad* is central to those schools, but is also independent of them. Even a scholar working within a school of thought is supposed to think through an issue independently from the school's traditions. As Muslims say, the "gates" of *ijtihad* are always open.

And in science, there is the commitment of all scientists to have their ideas and findings tested and contested by others, based on new evidence and new interpretations that bring ever more experience and perspective to bear not on truths that never change, but rather on truths that never stop changing. Although we often look to science to settle matters once and for all—to make discoveries that will hold up for all of time, like those we imagine of a Newton, a Darwin, or an Einstein—scientists themselves know that's not how it works. Newton was an alchemist. He wanted to convert base metal into gold, and he spent years looking for the elixir of life. Darwin was a sexist. He believed that evolution acts only on males because evolution requires competition and only males are competitive; the only reason why females evolve, he felt, is that they have fathers.[6] Einstein rejected quantum mechanics. He didn't like its probabilistic linearity.[7] These are all ideas that scientists of today no longer hold to, even as they continue to accept or recontextualize other aspects of the work of these foundational figures.

Science too is interpretation, but careful interpretation that scientists keep open to the careful interpretations of others. It's a dialogue—or, at least, it should be—not a monologue. It tries to answer every question but also to question every answer. Thus, the most dedicated scientists, I have long thought, are those who most sincerely want their work to go speedily out of date.[8] Because if it does, that means others found it so relevant and so important that they looked into the matter further, and brought new evidence and new perspectives to bear on it. So, of course, as we know more, our knowledge changes. In a way, as we know ever more we know ever less, for we come to see that there is so much more that we do not know with every new thing that we do know.[9] The awesome coolness of truth is that it always changes, not that it doesn't. All truth, however apparently firm, always retains an element of the mystery of the unknown. The most sincere scientist hopes that will always be the case.

Perhaps the most sincere adherent to a faith should hold this hope for a changing truth just as earnestly. It would be a hope that is highly likely to be fulfilled, if past history is any guide, for all our faith traditions have in fact changed quite a bit since their origins—as we should expect they would, the better to respond to changes in our contexts. Moreover, they all exhibit wide diversity of interpretation in the present, with their many branches, schools, sects, and constant discussion within and between them. One can see this diversity even in the life of one individual adherent of a faith. Think how different the faith understanding of, say, an eleven-year-old is likely to be than when that person is, say, mid-fifties. (Think of the appropriateness of even presenting an eleven-year-old with the original texts of a tradition—the error I made in reading the Bible as a bedtime story to my daughter when she was that age.)

And how exciting and valuable that diversity is! In the previous chapter, I noted that one does not need to agree with everything in a faith tradition to identify oneself with it, or to learn from it. The value we find in a tradition is as much in our disagreements as our agreements, as we engage with that tradition's thoughts, stories, and writings reaching out to us from the past and from elsewhere in the present. The question should not be whether a tradition is altogether right or not but whether we find it a helpful basis for thinking through, and re–thinking through, to our own moral understandings.

Now let's take another step with this line of reasoning. It is actually impossible to agree with everything in a faith tradition, just as it is impossible to agree with everything in science because, like science, no faith tradition agrees with everything in itself. The Protestant and the Catholic do not completely agree. The Orthodox Jew and the Reconstructionist Jew do not completely agree. The Shia Muslim and the Sunni Muslim do not completely agree. The Vaishnavite Hindu and the Shaivite Hindu do not completely agree. We can subdivide it further. The Baptist Protestant and the Congregationalist Protestant do not completely agree. Or even further. The Southern Baptist and the Northern Baptist do not completely agree. Or still further yet. A member of the Southern Baptist Convention and a member of the Southern Baptist Alliance do not completely agree. Or still further even yet. Been to a Southern Baptist Convention service recently—or a service at an assembly of any other denomination of any other faith tradition? A few moments of conversation with the attendees will quickly show a range of views, and not just about matters of faith: about any topic at all. That's how humans are, and we should love each other for the richness of that variety of insight.

The trouble comes when in the battle between religions, and in the battle between religions and science, adherents fall back on natural others and their communities of thee, me, we, and, regrettably, them. One thing that all sides frequently have in common is a weakness for presenting a unified and solidified conception of truth that admits no politics, especially in moments of conflict—precisely the time when we are most in need of admitting politics. Challenged, science often rushes to present itself as having methods that remove the potential for human interference in its findings. Challenged, the various denominations of bourgeois faiths typically do as well. Each falls back on a claim that it presents a truth beyond question and beyond error. But when you start out by saying you can't be wrong, it makes it very hard to admit it when you are. Of course, we all are at times. Even scientists. Even theologians. Even me. And when it is hard to admit you might be wrong, it makes it hard to have a productive conversation about what might be right.

———

Perhaps recognizing the historical and sociological context of monological traditions of truth can help us overcome these absolutist tendencies in our conversations with each other. At least that hope has been the main motivation for me in writing this book.

The context I have emphasized throughout is the difference between pagan and bourgeois: between rural, agrarian ways of living and urban, class-based ways of living. The spread of city life associated with the rise of state societies raised new moral concerns about material and sexual desire that little troubled the pagan forebears of city folk. These social uncertainties made absolutism attractive and convenient, even if often problematic and tragic. Meanwhile, those still in the country remained focused on the uncertainties of ecological sustenance and on loyalty to the social forms that helped one contend with them. Their lives were no less nor no more uncertain, but did not hinge on attempts to justify or criticize new social forms and their hierarchies of social and material standing.

These were not simply differences. I have also been arguing that they manifested, and manifested from, a deep social, cultural, and economic conflict that, I believe, we still need to reckon with. Commentators have long noted the vertical axis of conflict between the bourgeoisie and the proletariat. Equally decisive is the horizontal axis of bourgeois conflict: between bourgeois and pagan, the people of the city versus the people of the countryside. The power of urban state societies derives from this double conflict of bourgeois life—a conflict that manifests in tensions over vertical and horizontal differences in material accumulation, the transgressive powers of bourgeois sex, and the challenges both can pose to our loyalties.

I say the conflict of bourgeois and pagan and not the difference of bourgeois and pagan because our moral traditions don't just leave it at a difference. Bourgeois faiths have not been content simply to make a distinction between themselves and the pagan. They have rather been at considerable pains to label the pagan as immoral, backward, and parochial. They continue to react with embarrassment and hostility to suggestions that there is still some pagan in the bourgeois—that there is still some silver mixed in with the gold, and sometimes quite a lot. Doing so has long enabled urban state societies to argue for the morality of extending imperial reach over the realms of the pagan, gaining territory, capital, cheap labor, and an indirect means of ecological sustenance. (Urban people have to eat too.) For a faith of universal absolutes supposedly applies to all. Thus the backward pagan both threatens the civilized and needs to be controlled by the civilized, our moralities imply. Much of the contention over what we today label as race echoes these old tensions.

I have, however, been able to only hint at the connection of the double conflict to racial oppression.[10] A more substantiated case will have to await another book. This one is long enough.

––––––––

But I do want to synthesize one more important theme of this book before I close. Why do we find that we must now green our major religious traditions? Why did Pope Francis feel that he needed to release a special environmental encyclical for Catholics—his wonderful *Laudato Si'*, which has inspired more than Catholics to a greener sense of religion?[11] Why are there parallel movements within Judaism, Buddhism, Islam, Hinduism, Protestantism, and more? Why do these traditions have so much catching up with environmentalism to do? Any developed faith should have considered the Earth and our ecological relations holy already, one might well expect. Moreover, as the religious scholar Bron Taylor has noted, the greening of faith has as yet generally attained only rather pale shades of green and usually has not given ecological concerns the central place that Taylor calls "dark green religion."[12]

My argument has been that the major universal religions—that is, the religions that claim to universality—primarily respond to the moral concerns of bourgeois life. They have little to say about pagan matters of ecology and sustenance because they arose to speak to other worries, worries brought about by the rise of class and the decline of kin in the burgeoning cities of expanding states and empires. At least they have little new to say: they do all arise out of pagan traditions, with which they all retain some degree of alloy, however disguised, feared, or unacknowledged.

I sense an opportunity here, for in those alloys we can find considerable substance for deepening bourgeois religion's shades of green. Consider Passover, the favorite holiday of most Jews—the dryness of matzo aside. Almost all Jews celebrate it as a bourgeois holiday about freedom, a chance to retell the story of the Exodus from slavery and its resonances with the struggle with Rome, with the diaspora, and with continuing anti-Semitism. Jews often widen the celebration of Passover to being about everyone's freedom from poverty, oppression, and other ills of bourgeois life in contemporary class-based states, not only that of Jews—a general social justice theme increasingly appreciated by the increasing number of Christians who also commemorate Passover, in part as an acknowledgment that the Last Supper was a Passover meal in resistance to poverty, oppression, and the state. That is all great. But as I noted earlier, few recall that Passover began as *pesach*, a spring festival of ecological renewal at the time of the first ripening of barley in the agricultural calendar of the ancient Hebrews. That dry matzo, which bubbles up with no added leavening, historically symbolized the Earth's capacity for self-regeneration and revitalization, returning to life after the deadness and hardness of winter. Why not bring the Earth back in and make Passover a festival of both social and ecological renewal? Or consider the Passover *seder* plate, with its shank bone, roasted egg, bitter herbs, spring greens, and *haroseth* (a paste of fruit, nuts, and wine). Jews generally take the items on the plate to symbolize aspects of the Exodus story, such as the bitter herbs for the bitterness of slavery and *haroseth* for the mortar for the bricks Jewish slaves in the story had to make, with no comment made about the obvious agricultural and ecological resonances of each of these elements. But it so easily could be an electrum celebration: a pagan-bourgeois sacralizing of both ecological justice and social justice.[13]

Christianity also has many opportunities within its own traditions for re-embracing its entangled pagan roots. Most obvious, perhaps, would be explicitly treating Easter as the springtime celebration of rebirth that it so clearly is at a subliminal level. Jesus's resurrection from the dead in Northern Hemisphere spring resonates with the same ecological sensibilities of Passover—which perhaps should be no surprise, given that the New Testament describes Jesus's resurrection as taking place four days after the Last Supper, a Passover meal. It would not necessarily compromise Christian theology to hold that Jesus's resurrection was divinely intended to speak as well to our ecological connections. Anglo-Saxon and Germanic Christians also have the opportunity to go further with the heritage of celebrating the resurrection as Easter or *Ostern* in German, terms that derive from the ancient Germanic goddess of spring and fertility, *Eostre* or *Ostara*, whose name and attributes may derive from the even more ancient Sumerian goddess Ishtar.[14] (Most other European languages use names derived from *pesach* for the celebration of the resurrection: for example, *Pâques* in French, *Pasqua* in Italian, *Påske* in Norwegian.) Instead of passing fast with an embarrassed look over the complete absence of any mention of rabbits and eggs in biblical accounts of Jesus's death and resurrection, Christians could express reverence for, along with the fun of, the Easter Bunny as a symbol of the fertility of spring and renewal.

And why stop there with reforging an electrum connection to pagan sensibilities and traditions? Why should not Christians note with joy, rather than defensiveness, that Jesus's birthdate of December 25 corresponds with the ancient optimism of the return of the sun and longer days following what was originally the date of the Northern Hemisphere winter solstice?[15] Why not reembrace All Hallows Eve as Halloween, a time to celebrate the harvest and the Earth's provisioning through the harshness of northern winter?[16] Why not have Christians in the Southern Hemisphere celebrate all these holidays—Easter, Christmas, and Halloween—six months offset from Northern Hemisphere Christians, so as to fit the agricultural and ecological rhythms of the South? Why not think of the consumption of communion wafer and wine as a ritual of ecological communion with the "fruit of the Earth" and the "fruit of the vine"—as it is in the original Hebrew for Jewish Passover and Sabbath celebrations, from which Jesus's instructions to eat of his body and drink of his blood derive—as well as a ritual of social and theological communion? Indeed, why not think of ecological communion *as* social and theological communion? Given that eating the "fruit of the Earth" and drinking the "fruit of the vine" remain part of Jewish Passover and Sabbath celebrations, as well as virtually all other Jewish holiday celebrations, although rarely paid attention to for their ecological significance, Jews have as much opportunity here as Christians do.

I'll let others speak to the electrum potential of greater pagan-bourgeois synergy in Buddhism, Jainism, Islam, Hinduism, and other traditions for which I have less direct personal connection.[17] The observations about opportunities for pagan-bourgeois synergy that I mention above are only the start of what could be done, were all our universal religions to embrace that their adherents actually have every reason to be as concerned about ecological issues as they do about social issues. For ecological issues are social issues and social issues are ecological issues.

———

Does this pagan-bourgeois synergy mean, then, that we all join Thoreau on his walk west through the woods, away from Boston? I think not. For one thing, he probably wouldn't like it. Not only would we intrude on his solitude, we are sure to bring our politics with us (even if we do not smoke cigars). More importantly, I don't think Thoreau's west is the direction we should be trying to walk. "Eastward I go only by force; but westward I go free," he said.[18] But the west of which he spoke was but another name for the bourgeois. He thought he was walking away from the city, but he was actually walking right back toward it—right back toward the concerns about desire that bourgeois life has long raised. Much environmentalism, as is typical of our world religions, looks for a city of the good built of pure moral gold. But lusting for the absolute does not quell the troubles of desire. Rather, it accentuates them, encouraging us to walk away from the conversations we should be having with each other, with all their frustrations, yes, but also their many fulfillments.

Let's not have a bourgeois environmentalism. Our lives are too entangled for that—too entangled with one another and our ecologies. But let's not have a purely pagan environmentalism either. My point has not been to argue that pagan traditions are better and that bourgeois traditions—whether based on absolutes of nature or religion—should do all they can to become like them. If my argument comes across that way to some readers it is perhaps because our bourgeois traditions, due to their political upper hand in the long-standing pagan-bourgeois conflict, are so used to denigrating pagan traditions that any suggestion of their value seems unjust partiality and an attempt to upend and put the bottom on top and the last first. No, the issues of desire that bourgeois moral traditions intend to help us think through are indeed crucial issues. Absolutism is a clumsy and sometimes terrifying moral tool for dealing with them, however. Morality isn't so easy. It's a tangled affair—tangled because morality is entangled with the world, not apart from it.

Besides, there is a lovely effect when you mix silver and gold together into electrum. It doesn't just strike the eye as a paler yellow. The metal actually takes on a greenish luster, leading jewelers to sometimes call electrum "green gold." It's not the dusty green of tarnish. It's not the dull green of money. It's a gentle ecological luminance. So let's reforge the ancient triangle out of this green gold, and set and reset our many jewels of truth within it as we cut and recut them.

––––––

Or, to put it in terms of the other major metaphor of this book, what I am asking is that we not seek to live in a city of the good, absolute and final, separate and solved, but, rather, that we seek each other and the ever-changing worthiness of lives lived in the everywhere.

St. Augustine didn't understand the human situation in this way. In the *City of God*, he advised that

> [a]nyone can now easily gather that the blessedness which the intellectual being desires with unswerving resolution is the product of two causes working in conjunction, the untroubled enjoyment of the changeless Good, which is God, together with the certainty of remaining in him for

eternity, a certainty that admits no doubt or hesitation, no mistake or disappointment.[19]

The unswerving, untroubled enjoyment of a changeless Good. Eternal certainty with no doubt, hesitation, mistake, or disappointment. Find it in that which is external to the social and political: in God, the eternal external—external to what Augustine elsewhere termed the "standard of the flesh."[20] This hardly seems a call for openness to further learning, from and together with each other and the world.

Thoreau, for his part, similarly sought truth through separation from people and their desires. He had no doubt or hesitation about, and saw no mistake or disappointment in, seeking the goodness of truth. "No face which we can give to a matter will stead us so well at last as the truth," he wrote in the conclusion of *Walden*, his account of his two years of living alone in his lakeside shack. "This alone wears well."[21] What keeps us from finding the truth? Like Augustine, Thoreau accused the desires of our bourgeois sociality. As he put it, in one of his most quoted lines, "Rather than love, than money, than fame, give me truth."[22] That truth is the more likely the less social we are in discovering it, he contended. The solipsism of the shack led Thoreau to advise, in the conclusion to *Walden*:

> Let every one mind his own business, and endeavor to be what he was made. . . . If a man does not keep pace with his companions, perhaps it is because he hears a different drummer. Let him step to the music which he hears, however measured or far away.[23]

If Thoreau was right, why expect others to read and listen to this recommendation, since it comes from someone else? But many have. Dozens of editions of *Walden* are still in print.[24] Indeed, "a different drummer" is one of his most widely cited phrases. But as well we should feel no necessity to step along in agreement when we listen to, read about, and gain some lift from the drumming of someone else's experience. I have taken much from their writings, but I don't agree with Thoreau and Augustine about the evils of desire (among other matters). For my part, I think it all depends on the what, why, and how of our desires, and on our continued debate over the specificities of their justice. Plus I think there is nothing inherently wrong with disloyalty—including, potentially, disloyalty to the ideas of Augustine and Thoreau and the traditions and communities they represent. That too depends; there is much in our lives that deserves our loyalty and much that does not. But reading Augustine and

Thoreau has helped me hugely in coming to this very sentence, the current moment (as I write) in the stream of my understanding.

To be social, to be moral, to be just does not require concordance and conformity. It requires engagement with our differences. We all have a democratic right with regard to any notion, including what I have written here, a right that underlies all other democratic rights: the right to say I disagree, for what I think are sound reasons, so let's talk about them, and equally about your reasons, deeply and honestly.

———

How do we take up that conversation? Maybe the way we should take up every conversation: by remembering that we don't know everything. Because if you and I did know everything, why should we bother to converse anyway? There would no point, no surprise, no life to it. And life is surprise. As I like to say, if you have all the answers then you don't have all the questions.[25] Face it, you can't know everything, and nor can I. No need for despair here: it's awesomely cool that we can't, for it means we have reason to stay awake to the world and its creativities.

I am not arguing that we need to get rid of concepts and traditions like nature, religion, and community. I am not arguing that we should level our cities nor that we should dispense with bourgeois ideas because of their inevitable connection, like all ideas, to power, morality, and other manifestations of the political. I see no necessity for, nor possibility of, a postmodern world without categories. What turns our search for the good into the bad is not the ancient triangle that we forge in the smithies of urbanism. The problem is when we try to hammer the ancient triangle out of the lead of absolutes, claiming through some moral alchemy that it is actually now pure gold. But it is possible to have ideas of nature, religion, and community that are not absolute. We know we can have them because we long have had them, even if we have not always recognized them.[26]

For alongside the frequent assertions of absolutes that our politics have so often made so attractive to so many has always been another, better politics—a politics that is open to both transcendence and immanence, both the bourgeois and the pagan, and to the constant entangling work of bringing them and everything else about our lives into dialogue. The multilogical, multilocal truth of that better politics promotes what we might term *transimmanence*, an electrum understanding—a green gold truth—that carries across but also draws from local circumstance and experience, never completely resolving, and thus always evolving. It seeks not just transcendence from our traditions but immanence as well, in order to bring transcendence home and to bring home to transcendence.[27]

No, the great issue with multilogical truth is not its critical view of absolutes. Rather, its great issue is the problem of power, resulting in the sometimes enormous inequalities in people's ability to resist the experiences and entreaties of others. For dialogue is not just an exchange of words. It is as well an exchange of power, granting one another the right to speak and be heard, to disagree and be honestly taken into account. Those with greater power can more easily say what they know to be a lie or a partiality and get away with it—and can as well more easily say what they believe to be true and get away with it. Those with greater power can also more easily say what they do not know to be a lie or a partiality and not contend with, or learn from, the perspectives and insights of others. And those with greater power can more easily ignore or denigrate what they know to be well-substantiated in experience—either their own or that of others—when it contradicts their interests. There is, thus, a constant struggle for who controls the tools for cutting the jewel of truth, for we are not all equally committed to each other. We will not create conditions more favorable to dialogue and multilogical truth without addressing this striving.

The aspects of striving that I have focused on in this book are the double conflict of bourgeois life, of bourgeois versus both proletarian and pagan. Yes, it is political to undertake the work of addressing these contentions. But seeking a nature, supernature, or community that is absolute is just as political as seeking one that is not. Hiding our politics does not purge our politics. Rather than retreating behind the loftiness of the absolute, a non-absolute politics commits to perpetual openness—perpetual openness to this diverse universe.

Too much we who live dominantly bourgeois lives have looked to our traditions for the gold of Great Truths, for stabilities in the face of uncertainties, for definitions in the face of undefinability, for the power to deny the power of another. We have asked them to be traditions of the known, and they have often complied, even when it led to refueling fearful hotness, for that was often part of the intent. Perhaps they would serve us better as traditions of the unknown. As they often have been. For alongside worship of the definite, our traditions of nature, faith, and community—from science to environmentalism to universal religions to our various borderlands of community—have also given us moral means for appreciating the endless indefinite and the silver of its Great Mysteries. Our traditions of the ancient triangle do indeed have veins of this silver to draw upon, as I have tried to show. They do have the electrum, green gold capacity to open us to the awesome coolness of the unknown and to why there is no need to fear it—to open us to how, rather, the unknown releases us from our fears, most especially our fears of each other.

My point is not to call for everyone to abandon conviction. We have to go on from here with what we think we know, and we need enough conviction to have a direction in which to proceed. But let us not turn our convictions into jail sentences. We should not allow our convictions to turn us into convicts of the mind, locking ourselves up and closing ourselves off from the potential surprise present in every interaction.[28]

To put it another way, we all need starting places: the knowledge and traditions from which we began. Yet let us not turn our starting places into ending places, our confidences into defenses, our interpretations into fortifications. As we seek the good, we should be wary lest we find ourselves instead building city walls of the good: crenellated, gated, and guarded.

I'm ending on a sermon, I guess. Multilogical truth is, I hope, an everyday truth, not some rarified new discovery. But to accept it is to accept its call to moral action: we need to encourage ways of conceiving the good that promote the constant questioning and discovery that come from admitting difference—nay, welcoming difference—and thus politics. The trouble comes when we try to escape politics and to convince ourselves that we have succeeded in this escape.

And why make this futile effort at escape? The good is not the absence of politics, for there is nothing inherently bad about politics. Rather, politics is just people working out how best to get along with others, both human others and nonhuman others. That seems to me a very good thing for us to try to work out. No, instead of seeking to escape our politics, we should rather embrace our politics. For to do so is to embrace our humanity with all its needs and passions, ecologies and societies, natures and supernatures, individuals and communities, challenges and possibilities, conflicts and contentments, truths and mysteries.

NOTES

Chapter 1: The Conundrum of the Absolute

1. Thoreau (2007 [1862], 195).

2. I am giving an account here of the relaxing peace of the "out in nature frame" of doings we take to be (or stage as being) unguided by the social, as described in Brewster and Bell (2009).

3. Thoreau (2007 [1862], 185).

4. Thoreau (2007 [1862], 213).

5. Thoreau (2007 [1862], 191).

6. Thoreau (2007 [1862], 192).

7. Thoreau (2007 [1862], 191).

8. Thoreau (2007 [1862], 214).

9. Thoreau (2007 [1862], 215).

10. Thoreau (2007 [1862], 196).

11. Thoreau (2007 [1862], 202).

12. Even Thoreau was not always like "Thoreau." His mother did his laundry the entire time he lived in his cabin on the shores of Walden Pond, supposedly alone (Theroux 2004).

13. St. Augustine (2006, 175).

14. St. Augustine (2006, 180).

15. St. Augustine (2006, 127).

16. St. Augustine (2006, 131). In the interim, he'd taken on another concubine, but it wasn't a close relationship.

17. St. Augustine (2006, 177).

18. St. Augustine (2006, 181).

19. The passage is Romans 13:12–14. In this book, I use the New Revised Standard Version (NRSV) translation of the Bible. To avoid confusion, I quote the NRSV translation here, not the version given in St. Augustine (2006).

20. St. Augustine (2003, 5).

21. St. Augustine (1886, 628).

22. St. Augustine (2003, 648).

23. St. Augustine (2003, 593).

24. On the challenges and possibilities for greening religion, three foundational works are Gottlieb (2006), Nasr (1996), and Taylor (2010).

25. I conceive the triangle this way for ease of visualizing the explanation, not to give priority to the human. Indeed, it could well be argued that the base of anything is its most fundamental aspect. But I don't intend that priority either.

26. See Wirth's classic 1938 essay, "Urbanism as a Way of Life." Closely related observations can be found in Simmel's "Metropolis and Mental Life" (1950) and Weber's *The City* (1950 ([1921]).

27. "Entangled" and "entanglement" have become a popular metaphor these days, from physics to environmental anthropology (Kohn 2013, 227) and animal rights (Taylor 2017, xv). At the risk of confusion with these other uses, I use it extensively in this book.

28. Elsewhere I have described an interactive balancing of material and symbolic explanation as "ecological dialogue" (Bell 2012; Bell and Ashwood 2016).

29. This list is rather longer than the original list of Jaspers. See the next note for an explanation.

30. Jaspers's (1976 [1949]) own term was originally translated as the "Axial Period," but current scholars usually use the more mellifluous phrase "Axial Age." There has been much debate over the timing of the Axial Age and which traditions count as fitting within it. Jaspers himself put the timing at about 500 BCE but with a "spiritual process" that lasted from 800 BCE to 200 BCE. Such a timing would exclude not only Islam but also Christianity, although Jaspers clearly meant to show the foundations of Christian thought. Others like Armstrong (2006 and 2009) include Muhammad as an Axial thinker, and she notes that current scholarship dates Zoroaster from likely before 1000 BCE. These inclusions and date corrections extend the timing of the Axial Age from at least 1000 BCE to 650 CE—a very long span for a specific "period" of thought. And are there no Axial thinkers today, including Armstrong herself? For this and many other reasons, I find the notion of the Axial Age rather muddled, as the next few paragraphs explain, while still finding some value in it.

31. See especially Armstrong (2006) and Armstrong (2009).

32. Armstrong (2014) goes so far as to say we could resolve our modernist troubles if we would only more fully embrace Axial religious sensibilities.

33. Wright (2009).

34. Durkheim (1964 [1893]) and Tönnies (1940 [1931]).

35. Tönnies (1940 [1931], 18) and Durkheim (1964 [1893], 129).

36. Plus there is a third common source of the absolute that we often bring to bear on our questions of community: community itself. For by stating that a motive is for the good of the community at large, and not necessarily for the good of the individual advocate for that motive, we often try to construct a moral place beyond politics upon which to base politics. I deal little with this source here. That will have to wait for another book. This one is long enough.

37. For more on the multilogical, see Bell et al. (2011).

38. Bakhtin (1986, 170).

Chapter 2: Nature Before Nature

1. Mallory and Adams (2006, 408). No doubt PIE peoples got a version of the idea from an even earlier folk.

2. But the Minoans apparently still pronounced Zeus with a "d" instead of a "z." My source on this is not secure, however, so I've removed this minor point from the main text. The Wiki-

pedia entry on Zeus mentioned it when I consulted it on May 31, 2013, and referenced www
.palaeolexicon.com, which confirmed the point when I consulted it. However, www.palaeolex
icon.com does not give sources for its information.

3. The story is not only local. Hesiod mentions it in *The Theogeny*, as do many other classical
sources. See Ustinova (2009, 20) for a review.

4. A few kilometers away lies Zominthos, a fifty-room Minoan palace 3,900 feet up the
mountain, on the road to the cave. Apparently, Zominthos was a seasonally occupied settlement
used during the ancient tourist season until it was destroyed by earthquake in 1400 BCE—
basically, an ancient tourist trap. See www.minoancrete.com/zominthos.htm, consulted June 9,
2013.

5. Porphyry in his *Life of Pythagoras* (para. 17) describes the initiation Pythagoras endured:
spending twenty-seven days in the cave, while wrapped in black wool, followed by a sacrifice to
Zeus. My source on Plato and Epimenides is weak, though—just a tourist website: http://www
.cretanbeaches.com/Caves/Rethymno-Caves/ideon-andron-cave/, consulted March 19, 2014.

6. True, another telling of the myth locates it at the Dikteon Cave, a larger and more beautiful cave high up on Mount Dikti, which, at 7,047 feet, is the tallest mountain in eastern Crete.
Probably that telling was more popular among the people of eastern Crete, and the telling
locating the myth in the Ideon Cave, which lies a bit west of the center of Crete, was more popular at the other end of the island. A third version (Ustinova 2009, 180) offers a compromise: it
locates Zeus's birth at the Dikteon Cave, and his upbringing at the Ideon Cave.

7. De Landa (1978).

8. Chuchiak (2005, 614–615). De Landa later had a change of heart, after a difficult trial over
his behavior, and tried to record Mayan culture before more of it was lost. His *Relación de las
Cosas de Yucatan* was described by his translator, William Gates, as responsible for "ninety-nine
percent of what we know today of the [ancient] Mayas" (De Landa 1978, iii). But Gates also
noted that "he burned ninety-nine times as much knowledge of Maya history and sciences as
he has given us in his book (De Landa 1978, iv).

9. Coe et al. (2015) have recently verified the authenticity of this fragment of a fourth ancient Mayan book, known as the Grolier Codex, long in some doubt.

10. See www.newberry.org/popol-vuh, consulted June 9, 2013.

11. See www.newberry.org/popol-vuh, consulted June 9, 2013.

12. Goetz and Morley (1954).

13. The timeline of the *Popol Vuh* actually extends right up to the sixteenth century.

14. Confusingly, the corn god's name, Hun Hunahpú, is almost the same as that of one of
his sons.

15. Coe (2011).

16. *Popol Vuh*, pt. I, chap. 1. All quotations from the Goetz and Morley (1954) translation.

17. *Popol Vuh*, pt. I, chap. 2.

18. *Popol Vuh*, pt. II, chap. 3.

19. Coe (2011, 67).

20. English translations of the *Popol Vuh* sometimes use the word "nature," but only in the
sense of the character of someone or something, as in "By nature these two sons were very
wise, and great was their wisdom" (*Popol Vuh*, pt. II, chap. 1).

21. All quotes about the rise of the food chain from *Popol Vuh*, pt. II, chap. 7.

22. Porphyry copper deposits contain enrichments of several metals, not only copper, all of which have different mobilities. So the company's lab used to measure the content of four metals, as I recall, to better pin down the deposit: copper, molybdenum, silver, and gold.

23. See Stull, Bell, and Ncwadi (2016).

24. The relationship of the amaQwathi to the amaXhosa is not everywhere agreed upon. Some regard the amaQwathi as a clan of the amaXhosa, and some regard them as their own independent nation. In any event, the amaQwathi largely identify with the amaXhosa, share most of their customs, and speak isiXhosa, the language of the amaXhosa.

25. Here are a few development statistics for 2010 (ECSECC 2012). HIV/AIDS has infected 11.6 percent of the population. Some 57 percent live in poverty, according to the standard definition used in South African government statistics, compared to the national average of 44 percent. Unemployment is 27 percent. Some 7 percent aged fifteen or older have never attended school. Only 24 percent of households have piped water into their homes, compared with a national rate of 39 percent, and only 39 percent have flush or chemical toilets, compared with the national rate of 58 percent.

26. In Stull, Bell, and Ncwadi (2016), we suggest calling this cause and effect "environmental apartheid."

27. These benefits are often not recognized by scholars and administrators. See, for example, Cotula, Toulmin, and Hesse (2004), who advocate land registration to enable the state to collect taxes.

28. This was back in 1984, when much of what is now the Eastern Cape Province was still two apartheid era "homelands," Transkei and Ciskei. In chapter 8, I tell the story of my visit to a South African gold mine during that trip.

29. To learn more about the LAND project, visit thelandproject.org.

30. At this writing, the 2001 census is the most recent source of published survey data on religious affiliation in the Eastern Cape, as the 2011 census did not include questions about religion. I take the numbers in this paragraph from Statistics South Africa (2006).

31. According to a 2002 survey, 64.3 percent of all isiXhosa-speaking men have undergone circumcision (Connolly et al., 2008). Many amaXhosa circumcisions today are done in a hospital, but in rural areas the traditional practice is still quite common, although I have not seen a recent survey of the relative prevalence of hospital versus ritual circumcision.

32. The full story of the family's move is more complex, and indeed quite heartbreaking. But I'll leave it at that.

33. I take the following account of the discovery of the *Epic of Gilgamesh* from Damrosch (2006) and Malley (2012).

34. Hormuzd Rassam was not a usual archaeologist for the time. He came from a family of Chaldean Christians, a small group of whom had been in Mosul since the seventeenth century. As a teenager, Rassam learned English from Anglican missionaries and converted to Anglicanism. In 1845, the adventurer, diplomat, imperial spy, and occasional archaeologist Henry Austen Layard arrived in Mosul to dig the ruins of Nineveh. He was astounded to find an English-speaking Anglican among the native population. He hired Rassam, then nineteen years old, to be paymaster for his workforce. Rassam quickly impressed Layard with his skills and intelligence. Eight years later, the British Museum sent Rassam, who by that time had picked up a degree from Oxford, back to the ruins of Nineveh in charge of his own dig.

35. Hardly anyone remembers Rassam now. The discovery of the Palace of Ashurbanipal is usually credited to Layard, who wasn't even there. (Layard did discover the nearby Palace of Sennacherib, which was also a spectacular find.) Henry Rawlinson, one of the first translators of cuneiform scripts, tried to claim the discovery of Ashurbanipal's palace, and described Rassam as one of the diggers. Layard, on the other hand, credited Rassam, and in a letter from 1888 accused Rawlinson of what we would now call racism (Waterfield 1963, 478).

36. The "Old Persian" variant of cuneiform, a phonetic script, had been translated a few years earlier. But the Library of Ashurbanipal was pressed into the clay using Akkadian and Assyrian cuneiform, earlier scripts that mixed phonetic symbols with logographic ones representing whole words, and at the time of Rassam's expedition could not be read.

37. Mitchell (2004).

38. McIntosh (2005, 71).

39. Technically, the main temple was dedicated to Innana, the Sumerian name for Ishtar. *Gilgamesh* is mostly preserved in Akkadian, not Sumerian, and Ishtar is her Akkadian name (McIntosh 2005).

40. I favor the rendering by Mitchell (2004), which perhaps takes a few liberties of expression, but is extensively documented.

41. In pages to come, I will be describing these "widespread contemporary understandings of religion" as bourgeois.

42. Mitchell (2004, 126–127).

43. Damrosch (2006). Most commentators now accept that these parallels show cultural interconnections and syncretism, although there were some early denials, for example Heidel (1963 [1946], 223).

44. We could make similar lists for the traditions of ancient Greece, Native Americans, Japanese Shinto, the Celts, Hinduism, the Norse, and many, many more.

45. For example, Kohn (2013) describes how the Runa people of the Upper Amazon region of Ecuador understand jaguars and the forest to have thinking consciousnesses.

46. Mitchell (2004, 134).

47. George (1999), 50. The quote marks around "hand" are original in George, although he does not say why he used them. Perhaps he thought "hand" was an Akkadian euphemism for penis. One translator found these passages so delicate that he left the more ribald sections in Latin (Heidel 1963 [1946]).

48. See www.theoi.com/Olympios/ZeusLoves3.html, consulted June 17, 2013.

49. Pagels (1976).

50. Take this with a grain of salt. I recall reading somewhere that the head of the Minoan state was possibly often a woman, but now I find myself unable to track down the source. I'm still looking.

51. Shaw (2004, 82) argues that the excavators' reconstruction of the "Prince of the Lilies" as a priest-king is "not far off the mark."

52. Armstrong (2014) misses this point entirely, apparently seeking to portray early religions as more likely to incite violence than modern world religions.

53. *Iliad* 19.95–125. See Kearns (2010, 62–63).

54. A collection of ninety-five humorous obscene poems about Priapus called the *Priapeia* was popular in Roman times, and has survived to today.

55. For more on the spirited experience of place, see Bell (1997 and 2017).

56. Anderson (1991).

57. *Popol Vuh*, pt. I, chap. 5.

58. On the trickster as hero, see Scheub (2012).

59. *Theodosian Code* 16.10.25; translated by Pharr (1952).

60. See also Sandwell (2005, 89).

61. I take the translation of *pangere* from http://www.wordsense.eu/pango/#Latin, consulted August 6, 2013.

62. Mitchell (2004, 137).

63. Or so it appears from surviving frescoes.

64. Take, for example, the 29 percent difference in Midwest corn yield between 2012 and 2013 and the 59 percent difference between 1993 and 1994. Figures from http://www.index mundi.com, consulted August 6, 2013.

65. Armstrong (2014) rightly stresses the centrality of war in early city-states and their processes of accumulation. Class society has continued to use war for accumulation, but more generally finds other means to gain and maintain inequality.

66. Mitchell (2004, 168–169).

Chapter 3: The Natural Conscience

1. See Bell (1994).

2. Bell (1994, 147). Thoreau would have readily appreciated the sure moral value of the environment that Nigel felt: the sense of nature as something good, that we should follow, that we should protect. Billions today agree. It often seems we don't agree on much, but surveys from around the world show great unity on this point, at least. The World Values Survey asked thirty-six thousand people from twenty-eight countries whether it is better that humans try to "master nature" or "coexist with nature." (It took five years to do this study, which lasted from 1999 to 2004. Thirty-six thousand is a staggeringly large number of survey respondents.) The survey showed that 78 percent around the world felt it is best to coexist with nature. Only in Saudi Arabia did a majority feel the other way. (For the sources on these surveys, see World Values Survey data cited in Bell [2012, 171].)

3. The Roman philosopher Lucretius was perhaps the first to claim the Greeks invented the concept of nature. He framed the discovery of nature as a form of opposition to religion, meaning the forms of religion I have been calling pagan. I will later argue that the forms of religion I call bourgeois were deeply influenced by the concept of nature, even if they often opposed the idea, but that mostly took place after Lucretius (1957, 4–5) declared around 55 BCE that "[w]hilst human kind throughout the lands lay miserably crushed before all eyes beneath Religion . . . a Greek it was who first opposing dared raise mortal eyes that terror to withstand" with the concept of nature.

4. Lovejoy and Boas (1980 [1935], 104).

5. *Odyssey* 10:302, http://www.theoi.com/Text/HomerOdyssey10.html.

6. Lovejoy and Boas (1980 [1935], 103). The etymology of "phy" as coming from "to be" is from note 2 on 103.

7. *Oxford English Dictionary*, online edition.

8. Lloyd (1992, 10); Soper (1995, 37).

9. *Oxford English Dictionary*, online edition.

10. Williams (1983, 219).

11. Strictly speaking, we don't know if the five comedies commissioned for every Dionysia were performed one per day throughout the five-day festival. I have also taken the liberty of assuming that the play I recount below, Aristophanes's *Wealth*, was first performed at Dionysia, and not at the Lenaia, the other annual drama festival, which is not known for sure. We do know, however, the names of the other four comedies, as listed above. See Sommerstein (2001, 1).

12. In 388 BCE, the Corinthian War still raged, pitting Athens and its allies against Sparta since 395 BCE. Before that, the Peloponnesian War set Sparta against Athens from 431 to 404 BCE, and nearly resulted in the destruction of Athens. Finally, under pressure from the Persians, the Peace of Antalcidas was signed the following year in 387 BCE.

13. One of the terms of Athens's surrender at the end of the Peloponnesian War in 404 BCE was that it tear down its famous "Long Walls." But starting in 395 BCE, with the coming of the Corinthian War, the Long Walls were reconstructed, a task that was completed in 391 BCE. The tax burden to accomplish this must have been crushing.

14. On the "farmer's problem," see Bell (2004).

15. I have taken quotes from *Wealth* from two translations, depending on which strikes me as phrasing individual sections better: either Sommerstein (2001) or Sparklesoup Studios (2004), with a couple of small changes for clarity.

16. Finley (1982, 121) estimates between 60,000 and 80,000 residents of the Athenian city-state were slaves in the classical period. Elsewhere, Finley (1963, 55) estimates that Athens had a total population of 275,000 in 431 BCE, yielding a proportion of roughly one-quarter slaves. Webster (1973, 42) puts it higher, estimating about a third were slaves.

17. M. I. Finley (1982, 103) writes, however, that "I am not altogether satisfied with the evidence for this view."

18. Based on the 317 BCE census taken by Demetrius of Phalerum, which calculated 21,000 citizens and 10,000 metics. This census also recorded 400,000 slaves, but few scholars believe that figure, regarding it as a guess by Demetrius. The area of Attica doesn't seem large enough to have supported a population that size.

19. Finley (1982, 64).

20. Finley (1982, 65). Foxhall (1992; cited in Rose 2012, 211) gives similar figures.

21. Finley (1982, 65).

22. Osborne (1995, 28).

23. Webster (1973, 41).

24. However, this may not actually have been the first performance of *Wealth*. There is some evidence that Aristophanes wrote an earlier version of the play in 408 BCE, or another play by the same name (Sommerstein 2001, 28).

25. Some scholars say women never attended the drama festivals, and some say women attended only the tragedies and had to sit in the back. My approach here is to imply that the rules were not always strictly applied, especially in the company of a male relative, allowing me to portray more of the sexism of Athenian society.

26. Rose (2012) provides an overview of gender and wealth in ancient Athens.

27. Martin (2013) provides a comprehensive overview of the political history of ancient Athens. Rose (2012) provides a Marxist analysis of the class dynamics of the period.

28. Sommerstein (2001, 34).

29. Sommerstein (2001, 1) says we don't know who won the prize in 388, and Aristophanes (2005, loc. 3540) say we do know, and that Aristophanes won. In any event, it is quite amazing that we know anything at all about this kind of thing from so long ago.

30. Scholars of ancient Greek religion often describe it as a "polis religion," oriented toward a state and society built around this distinctive social form, despite its pagan origins. Kindt (2012) complains that this interpretation is overdrawn, as it neglects how everyday ancient Greeks sought a personal basis for belief, seeking to answer their own questions of context. My interpretation suggests as well that the "polis religion" of the traditional pantheon did not answer all the questions that adherents sought to resolve. But Kindt wants to see this more personal and magical basis of belief as nonpolitical. I can't agree with her there, as will become evident from my argument later in the book. To seek the nonpolitical is a form of politics. See especially chapter 8.

31. I offer here a loosely Weberian account of politics, albeit one that tries to leave analytic space for power to be seen, at least potentially, as a means and not an end, and as (again, at least potentially) non-zero-sum. Weber's classic (1946 [1919]: 78) definition of politics is "striving to share power or striving to influence the distribution of power, either among states or among groups within a state." In my phrase "contending with interests and their many conflicts," I mean to imply power as a means of such contention, but not necessarily as the point of politics in and of itself, as I worry that Weber's definition suggests. Power is potentially an interest in itself, and indeed sometimes the prime one of political actors. But not all motivation is power. As well, Weber's emphasis on "striving" about the "distribution of power" seems overly zero-sum, although he does provide some opening for a non-zero-sum understanding of power with his inclusion of the possibility of sharing power. Relatedly, I have also tried to offer a non-Hobbesian view of politics with my phrasing. Social life is not necessarily a war of all against all. There may be interests that align rather than conflict, or that simply do not conflict with those of others, with no alignment even necessary. Like a thirst for power, conflict seems to me very common in politics, but not inherent in it.

32. I am quoting the translation by C. S. Calverley (1901 [1869]), which does not mention Demeter. The translation by Hine (1982, 28), however, does.

33. See Edmonds (1912, xvi–xvii).

34. Its most infamous line is "You're sticking your prick in an unholy hole" (Shipley 2014 [2000]: 185).

35. I am no scholar of ancient Greek, but I conducted a word search for φύσις on the online Greek version of Theocritus's work at http://www.perseus.tufts.edu, and found nothing. C. S. Calverley does use the word "nature" three times in his translation of the *Idylls*, as does J. M. Edmonds—but not in the same places. (I did other electronic searches to get these counts.) In any event, neither translator could be described as fastidious in his allegiance to the original text.

36. All quotations from Horace's Tenth Epistle are from Horace (1983 [20 BCE], trans. Raffel).

37. Lau (1963, 9).

38. I speak no Chinese, but "integrity" is one of the common translations for the Daoist meaning of *de*. Confucianism uses the same word to mean something closer to "virtue."

39. Fung (1966 [1948], 284, 177).

40. I take my quotations of the *Dao De Jing* from two translations. I love Le Guin (2009) for her gender-neutrality, literary ear, and, in keeping with the original, economy of expression. I also love Lau (1963) in part because it was the first translation of the *Dao De Jing* that I read but also for his more political eye. This quote is from Le Guin (2009, 4).

41. Le Guin (2009, 110).

42. Lau (1963, 96). The next quotation ("Do without doing . . .") is from Le Guin (2009, 92).

43. Lau (1963, 109).

44. I base this translation on Merton (1965, 65), which I have updated with non-gender-specific language and with conversion of "Tao" to "Dao."

45. Virgil's *Aeneid*—basically, a retelling of Homer's epics, domesticated for Romans—mentions *natura* only once, and only in a first nature sense of essential characteristic (also like Homer). First nature also makes a few appearances in Virgil's *Georgics*—seven, by my count.

46. And in the classic translation by Garth (1961 [1717]), "nature" appears seventy-three times, twice as many times as the word *natura* appears in the original Latin.

47. Book IX, 714–763, Kline (2000).

48. Thoreau did read and admire the *Bhagavad Gita*, however, a classic Hindu work that seeks a means for overcoming desire and ambition, and says it plainly near the conclusion of *Walden* (Thoreau 1910 [1854]). For details, see Friedrich (2008). See chapter 7 for details about Hinduism, the *Bhagavad Gita*, and the problem of desire.

49. See Bell (1994) and chap. 7 of Bell (2012).

50. In a few pages, I add a third part to the natural conscience, the *natural we*. Two parts are enough for the moment.

51. For these quotes, see the section on Thoreau in chapter 1.

52. This is from a family original we call "The Oars Rise Up." I wrote the tune and co-wrote the words with my wife, Diane Mayerfeld. We've talked for years about putting it on a CD. Maybe one day we will.

53. This is from another family original, "Take Me Back to the River." I wrote the tune and co-wrote the words for this one too, mostly with my father, M. David Bell, with some lines from others. The image of "tree-green islands" was suggested by my brother, Jonathan Bell. We intend to put this song on that same CD, if it ever happens.

Chapter 4: Pagan Monotheism and the Two Evils

1. Genesis 6:5, 7. All quotes from the NRSV of the Old Testament, except where otherwise indicated.

2. Genesis 19:8.

3. Genesis 19:24. Note that the NRSV renders "Lord" as "LORD," which I find unnecessary and distracting, and have altered throughout this chapter.

4. Exodus 19:12–19.

5. Exodus 21:2–9.

6. Exodus 21:10.

7. Exodus 21:21.

8. Exodus 21:15, 17.

9. Exodus 31:15.

10. Exodus 32:9–10.

11. Exodus 32:11–12.

12. Exodus 32:14.

13. Exodus 32:26.

14. Exodus 32:26–29.

15. Exodus 32:34.

16. Exodus 32:35.

17. Barna Group (2014, Table 3.1).

18. Barna Group (2014, Table 3.11).

19. Armstrong (2006), Smith (2002), and many others.

20. Genesis 3:22.

21. Deuteronomy 32:8–9.

22. Psalms 82:1.

23. The Hebrew, of course, is spelled right to left.

24. The Dead Sea Scroll 4QDeut (as scholars technocratically label it) makes the polytheism even plainer, and reads "according to the number of the sons of Elohim" (Tov 2014, 51) instead of "according to the number of the gods."

25. Smith (2002) suggests that this use of *Elohim* results from the singularizing of an originally plural notion of the divine.

26. There is religious controversy over how to pronounce *YHWH*, the most common of the many names given for God in the Old Testament. I've already mentioned *El*, *El Elyon*, *Elohim*, and *YHWH*. God is also at times called *El Shaddai*, usually translated into English as "Lord God Almighty," and *Adonai*, translated as simply "Lord" or "Master." But there is a special complexity with *YHWH*. The oldest versions of Hebrew writing did not include vowels—only consonants. Along about the eighth century CE, though, scribes started adding diacritical marks to indicate vowel sounds, kind of like the German umlaut or the French acute accent. But to *YHWH*—the name scholars call the *Tetragrammaton*, which means "four letters" in Greek— the scribes added the approximate vowels for *Adonai* instead, even though the fit is clearly poor, to indicate one is supposed to read the word as *Adonai*. In Hebrew, that would be יְהֹוָה. But if the text already contained the word *Adonai* immediately before or after *YHWH*, the scribes instead used the diacritical marks for *Elohim*, leading to the common phrase *Adonai Elohim* in Jewish liturgy. Apparently, the scribes were holding to an old Jewish tradition that one is not supposed to write or speak God's actual name. And now no one knows the actual pronunciation of *YHWH*—except perhaps for the few who followers of the esoteric Jewish tradition of Kabbalah say are taught it in every generation, carrying the correct pronunciation forward but keeping it secret. Christians typically do not share a reticence to speak God's name. They usually render the Tetragrammaton as *Yahweh* or *Jehovah* in English. Anglophone scholars generally try to read the Tetragrammaton more or less phonetically as it would be in English, and pronounce it "Yah-weh," in the manner of many Christians, but without assuming that this is the actual pronunciation. Many Jews take some offense at these practices, I should note, and even extend their tradition of respect to the very word "God," preferring in English to write it "G-d" and to pronounce it "gee-dash-dee."

27. Note that the story of the burning bush is a later story from Acts, not Genesis or Exodus.

28. Exodus 13–15.

29. Exodus 13:21.

30. Exodus 33:14 and 40:16.

31. Exodus 40:34, 38.

32. This phrase occurs dozens of times in 1 Kings and 2 Kings.

33. 1 Kings 8:10–13.

34. The NRSV does occasionally use the English word "nature," as in "ill-natured fellow" (1 Samuel 25:25), but the word is not in the original Greek nor, I believe, the original Hebrew. I cannot claim enough skill in ancient Hebrew to ascertain this beyond doubt, but φύσις does not appear in the Septuagint, the second-century BCE Greek translation of the Hebrew which is the basis for most Old Testament translations today.

35. Job 36:30–37:5.

36. Exodus 16:14, 16:31.

37. Leviticus 26:14–16, 19–20.

38. Exodus 20:8, 23:12.

39. Leviticus 25:3–5.

40. Exodus 23:10–11.

41. Prosic (2004, 41 and 43–44). I take up the agricultural meaning of Passover again in chapters 9 and 10.

42. Exodus 23:17.

43. I heard somewhere that if the US state of Rhode Island (where I was born) were a dance floor, the entire world population could fit and join the party with six square feet apiece. Maybe we should try it.

44. See Dever (2012, 287) for the view that most ordinary Israelites actually did not follow the centralized practices of the Temple.

45. 1 Samuel 15:11.

46. Jeremiah 42:10.

47. This particular warning about God's jealousy comes from Deuteronomy 5:9.

48. Joshua 24:19.

49. Exodus 34:14.

50. For the passage in Genesis that discusses the "sons of God," see Genesis 6:1–4. For an account in the Apocrypha, see *1 Enoch* 1–36. Related material is in Jude 6–7 and *Jubilees*. For the New Testament's description of Jesus as God's "only son," see John 3:17 and 1 John 4:9.

51. The story of the Nephilim is also recounted in other ancient Israelite literature, especially the *Book of Enoch* and *Jubilees*, which describe them as a race of giants.

52. Genesis 6:1–4.

53. For example, see Wright (2009).

54. Contra Wright (2009), who I think overstates the case for monolatry in ancient Israel.

55. We start to see a transition toward a god of the good in the later books of the Old Testament.

56. Elsewhere the Old Testament uses "Ba'al" in a more generic way, not specifically tied to Moabite religion and to this Moabite mountain.

57. Numbers 25:1–5.

58. I base my account largely on the work of Armstrong (2006 and 2009), Dever (2001, 2005, and 2012), Friedman (1987 and 2003), Finkelstein (2013), Finkelstein and Silberman (2001 and 2006), Lemche (1988), Smith (2002), and Wright (2009), treading carefully through the often-conflicting interpretations.

59. Some of the prominent works of biblical minimalism are Burns and Rogerson (2012), Davies (1992), Finkelstein and Silberman (2001 and 2006), Finkelstein (2013), Gottwald (2001), Grabbe (2011), Lemche (1988), and Thompson (1992 and 1999). Unfortunately, the biblical studies literature is filled with ugly, vituperative, ad hominem attacks between the minimalists and maximalists. For a recent example, see Dever (2012, 11–34). See also Dever (2017), which is a touch more measured, but only a touch. Many biblical scholars—maybe most— find themselves in between these positions. (Biblical *mesolists*, perhaps we could call them.)

60. For reviews, see Dever (2012) and Fritz (1995).

61. Shanks (2014, 38) and Finkelstein and Silberman (2001, loc. 1414).

62. Smith (2002).

63. As Smith (2001, 14), puts it, "while early Israel recorded some traditions not shared by its neighbors, these distinctive features are relatively rare and hardly indicate a wholly different culture or religion."

64. Cline (2014).

65. Cited in Cline (2014, 9).

66. Cline (2014).

67. Cline (2014).

68. The absence of pig bones distinguishes Iron Age Israelite settlements in the highlands from earlier Canaanite settlements in the highlands, as well as from the Iron Age settlements of the Philistines along the coast, contend Finkelstein and Silberman (2001, loc. 2035). Note, however, Sapir-Hen (2016) claims that there are complexities here, especially the evidence of pig bones in the Jewish settlements of the northern Kingdom of Israel. It seems that the taboo against eating pigs was originally a practice of the southern Kingdom of Judah.

69. The translation and implications of the famous Merneptah Stele have been under debate ever since it was discovered in 1898; the dust on it has not settled yet.

70. Dever (2001) gives an overview of this broadly held conclusion among archaeologists.

71. Freud (1939) offers this speculation. The hot coal story is a midrash. The Old Testament merely notes in Exodus 4:10 that Moses was "slow of speech and slow of tongue."

72. See Exodus 12:37–38 and Numbers 1:46. Exodus gives the more general figure of 600,000.

73. I take the following figures from Shanks (2016), reporting on the results of the recent work of Hillel Geva, a biblical archaeologist at the Hebrew University of Jerusalem.

74. Dever (2012), summarizing the work of others, reports somewhat different figures, generally a bit higher. These estimates supersede the work of Broshi (1978), who used a considerably denser model of Israelite urbanism to arrive at 12 acres and 2,000 inhabitants at the reputed time of King David and 125 acres and 25,000 inhabitants at the end of the eighth century BCE—still not huge, however.

75. Dever (2012, figure IV.22).

76. Dever (2012), Finkelstein and Silberman (2001 and 2006), Matthews (2002), Smith (2001 and 2002).

77. Much of the debate here concerns use of the "low chronology" of Finkelstein versus the "high chronology" used by most archaeologists. The low chronology moves the early Iron Age archaeological assemblages forward about one hundred years, meaning that urban development of Judah was that much later. As a result, the Bible's portrayal of a more substantial State of Judah at the reputed time of David is likely to have been political mythmaking, according to followers of the low chronology. This view is hotly disputed by Dever and others.

78. Davies (2008) and Finkelstein (2013).

79. See Finkelstein and Silberman (2001 and 2006) and Davies (2008) for examples. Davies calls this the creation of "cultural memory," a phrase that has been influential in the minimalist technical literature.

80. On the archaeological dividing line between Israel and Judah, see Finkelstein and Silberman (2001, loc. 2564). On the textual evidence, see Finkelstein and Silberman (2006). For the argument that the Kingdom of Judah was initially the smaller and less significant of the pair, see Finkelstein and Silberman (2001, loc. 2567) and Finkelstein (2013). I can't comment on the archaeological evidence and the dispute over the "low chronology" (see note 77 above). But it does seem striking to me, and in keeping with the argument of this book, that the more transcendent *Elohim* would be from an earlier urbanized and developed state of Israel, and the more immanent and agrarian *YHWH* would be from a smaller, less developed urban society in Judah. See the discussion of the "documentary hypothesis" and theology of political unity below.

81. Samaria is also the name for a region that roughly corresponds with the ancient Kingdom of Israel, now roughly corresponding with the northern sections of modern Israel and the hotly contested West Bank region of Palestine, an "occupied territory" of modern Israel.

82. We know that the Jewish elite did indeed go to Babylon. Archaeologists have even discovered cuneiform ration lists from the time of Nebuchadnezzar II for grain to be dispersed to the king of Judah and his sons. These are on display at the State Museum of Berlin.

83. Chapter 6 gives more detail on the breakup of Alexander's empire.

84. Prosic (2004, 39–40).

85. On the archaeological evidence for Israelite poly-divine worship at home, including idols, see Dever (2005 and 2012).

86. Friedman (2003, 35n).

87. Genesis 2:4–7.

88. For the best accessible summary of the findings, see Friedman (2003).

89. Lemche and some other minimalists argue that all the "voices" date from the Babylonian exile to the Hasmonean Dynasty, seeing the Old Testament as a far more recent creation. It seems to me, however, that the Old Testament could be both older and more recent, constantly being rewritten out of older materials in the light of current knowledge and circumstances, as is the case of all scholarship.

90. There has been a long dispute on the temporal order of the other three voices. See Friedman (2003) for one prominent adjudication of the evidence.

91. I am following Friedman (2003) here.

92. Friedman (2003).

93. The combination of *YHWH* and *Elohim* into a single, double name occurs only in the early passages of the Pentateuch, the first five books of the Bible, and appears to be due to insertions by a later editor, who was likely seeking to better unify the Bible and its adherents.

Most translations of the Bible into English therefore render the name of god in these passages as "Lord God," not "Lord" alone, as is done in those far more numerous sections where *YHWH* appears alone. For details, see Friedman (2003), especially the second footnote on page 35.

94. Every major instance of such a god in human history is, if sexed at all, a he.

95. Such brilliance was not unique to the ancient Israelites, however. At the very least, their neighbors, the Moabites, also had such an understanding. The Mesha Stele from the ninth century BCE explains Moabite losses against the Israelites as due to their the Moabite god, Chemosh, "being angry with his land." Burnett (2016, 32).

96. Finkelstein and Silberman (2001) and Dever (2012).

97. Dever (2012, 280).

98. Smith (2001).

99. 2 Kings 22:4–6.

100. Smith (2001).

101. Among those other sources likely was Zoroastrianism, as I discuss in chapter 6.

102. We should note, however, that in some ancient cultures, the female divine could be seen as aggressive. Examples include the Athenians and their sense that their patron goddess, Athena, was a goddess of war, as well as the Sumerian view of the warlike attributes of Ishtar. But under monotheism, in keeping with increased masculinization of power associated with a centralized state and empire, it is male capacity for violence that gains legitimacy, not female capacity for it.

103. The abundance of figurines of Asherah makes plain her former theological significance. We know from the ruins of Ugarit that the Canaanites regarded her as El's consort, and many scholars suspect that Ba'al—also described as Asherah's husband—was regarded as another expression of the male divine for many ancient Israelites, equivalent to El and *YHWH*, although the Bible in its current form takes a dim view of Ba'al. For details, see Dever (2005).

Chapter 5: Why Jesus Never Talked about Farming

1. Dick died in 2013 at the age of eighty-one.

2. I take this quote and the ones that follow from my own reporting in Bell (2004, 157–158).

3. Thompson, Thompson, and Thompson (2001).

4. For a recent review of the evidence, see Ehrman (2012), who notes that pretty much all biblical scholars—many of whom are not Christian or Christian advocates—think that "whatever else you may think about Jesus, he certainly did exist." Other well-known studies of Jesus as a historical figure include Aslan (2013), Crossan (1992, 1995, 1998, and 2006), Dunn and McKnight (2005), Ferguson (1993), Freeman (2009), Green (2010), Horsley (1994, 2005, 2008, 2014), Levine (2006), Mason (2009), Wilken (2012), and Wright (2009).

5. See Mykytiuk (2015) for a recent review. For more detail, see Mason (2009).

6. Josephus (1999 [ca. 94 CE], 656); the quote is from his *Antiquities of the Jews* 20.9.1.

7. See recent issues of *Biblical Archaeology Review* for the latest in the controversy.

8. Whatever names for these works one uses are sure to annoy someone. For Jews, for example, the names "Old Testament" and "Hebrew Bible" are set within an inherently Christian frame; their term for those scriptures is simply "The Bible." Nonetheless, I'll continue on with Old Testament and New Testament, as is most common among scholars.

9. For a recent review of some of the more notable inconsistencies, see Aslan (2013).

10. See Matthew 1:18: "Now the birth of Jesus the Messiah took place in this way. When his mother Mary had been engaged to Joseph, but before they lived together, she was found to be with child from the Holy Spirit." Other details just seem downright superfluous, like the Romans compelling a passerby, Simon of Cyrene, to carry Jesus's cross for a while, as noted in Matthew 27:32, Mark 15:21, and Luke 23:26. In *Second Treatise of the Great Seth*, one of the Gnostic writings from the Nag Hammadi library, Simon of Cyrene is even said to have died on the cross in Jesus's stead, as Jesus could not die, being divine.

11. Based on the NRSV translation, the word "farmer" appears only twice in the entire New Testament, once in Timothy and one in James, and never in the Gospels. Both uses are metaphorical, not agricultural. In 2 Timothy 2:6, Paul explains that one should not expect that the rewards for following the word of Jesus will come easily. One must work, even suffer for it, just as "It is the farmer who does the work who ought to have the first share of the crops." In James 5:7, we hear encouragement for Christians to hold on and not grumble, for the coming of the Lord is near at hand. "Be patient, therefore, beloved, until the coming of the Lord. The farmer waits for the precious crop from the earth, being patient with it until it receives the early and the late rains."

12. John 10:11. My count of seventeen instances in total is again based on the NRSV.

13. John 15:1.

14. Matthew 13, Mark 4, and Luke 8.

15. Matthew 9:36–38.

16. Luke 9:62.

17. Matthew 19:29.

18. John 6:35.

19. Luke 12:22–23, 31.

20. For example, see Armstrong (2006 and 2009), Aslan (2013), Crossan (1992, 1995, 1998, and 2006), Dunn and McKnight (2005), Ferguson (1993), Freeman (2009), Green (2010), Horsley (1994, 2005, 2008, 2014), Levine (2006), Mason (2009), and Wilken (2012).

21. Antipater was originally from Idumea, a kingdom of Semites to the south and east of Judea, with its capital at Petra, a city carved into the living rock of Wadi Musa in what is now Jordan. Idumeans were Semites but not Jews—or at least only reluctantly Jews, many of them having been forced to convert a century earlier during the beginning of the Hasmonean Dynasty, which was having a go at the empire game by incorporating Idumea within Judea. That conversion was good enough for the Hasmonean elites, but many ordinary Jews never accepted it, seeing force as an inadequate basis for accepting someone into their community. Judaism today is unusual among the universal religions in making conversion difficult, seeking community strength through a strong boundary rather than through maximizing community size. Circumcision is required for male converts, and all converts have to demonstrate to the broader community that the conversion is not for any kind of advantage—a tough standard. Even those who go through a conversion ceremony are often shunned by more conservative Jews. And so it was two thousand years ago as well. Many Jews, and perhaps most, burned over the notion that a man whose family had been forced to convert to Judaism was now the real ruler of the country—especially because Antipater reported back to Rome.

22. Herod didn't actually take power until 37 BCE, however, as he had a few contenders to deal with first.

23. A point I am implying here is that there is no need to presume that, before the coming of coined money, societies did not have markets, as Polanyi (1957) argued. His vision of an ancient Mesopotamian society that "possessed neither market places nor a functioning market system of any description" (Polanyi 1957, 16) has not withstood the scrutiny of more recent archaeological evidence (Algaze 2008). Markets existed before coins. But coins greatly increased the speed, power, and consequences of markets and their tendencies toward unequal outcomes.

24. Some dispute the notion that an alphabet is an easier form of writing to learn, including Michael Coe (2012), whose work I greatly admire. Coe contends that there is nothing inherently difficult in logo-phonetic scripts like Chinese and ancient Mayan, and that readers of alphabets eventually come to read each word as a unit anyway. Generations of Chinese students I think would disagree about the equal ease of logo-phonetic writing. But, nonetheless, many cultures across the world around this time were greatly improving writing of all kinds, from alphabetic to syllabic to logo-phonetic.

25. Stone and Zimansky (2004) themselves conducted an unusually detailed archaeological survey of urban form for the medium-sized Mesopotamia city of Mashkan-shapir, a site about fifty hectares in size whose apex was around 2000 BCE. They report (p. 379) that "although not conclusive, the data from Mashkan-shapir support the idea that elites were not concentrated within Mesopotamian cities but were distributed broadly across all residential districts." But Stone (2008) also notes that early cities and states sometimes do show what she calls "exclusionary domination" along lines other than class. Her study of Ayanis—a city site from the Urartu empire, which flourished in the early Iron Age in the first half of the first millennium BCE—shows considerable spatial differentiation of wealth. But that differentiation "may be attributable to ethnic differences playing out within a highly structured and centralized economy" (p. 163). We should also note Ayanis is post–Bronze Age, and structure and centralization are accelerating, but do not yet seem to have led to what we would recognize today as class. Key here, perhaps, is the absence of coins from the site—at least Stone does not list coins among the objects found.

26. Fritz (1995, 161). Kessler (2008, 109), however, contends that by the eighth century BCE in ancient Israel "a class society had developed." It is hard to draw a sharp line with historical trends.

27. Horace (1983 [20 BCE]), Epistle 1.10 (trans. Raffel 1983).

28. Kessler (2008, 111) notes that "the decisive factor in moving ancient farming societies toward being class societies was the institution of credit."

29. Von Falkenhausen (2008), 222.

30. Marcus and Sabloff (2008, 22).

31. Marcus and Sabloff (2008, 22).

32. For details on the opulence of the townhouses in the center of Glanum, see McKay (1998 [1975], 159–164).

33. As far as I know, there are no rural Roman villas to visit near Glanum.

34. As of January 28, 2017, €9.50 is the admission price for adults at Glanum.

35. Some say 6 BCE, and others as early at 17 BCE, but 4 BCE seems to be where the weight of current scholarly opinion rests.

36. I am simplifying things a tad here, as I am often forced to do to keep this chapter coherent and readily appreciable by a general audience. Technically, the Province of Judea was

attached to Syria, and was ruled by a lower Roman order of governor called a prefect, who reported to the higher order of governor, a legate, who ruled Syria and had the rank of Roman senator. Prefects were not senators.

37. The circumstances around the travel of Jesus's parents to Bethlehem have been much debated by scholars. Luke 2 reports that Joseph wanted to take part in a census that the Romans were doing of Judea "because he was descended from the house and family of David"—in other words, to help establish his royal heritage. As well, Bethlehem was the traditional seat of the Davidic monarchy. But that particular census—known as the Census of Quirinius—took place in 6 BCE. Matthew 2 instead reports that Jesus was born in Bethlehem and that his parents immediately fled to Egypt for a short time, to avoid a supposed edict from Herod that all children in Bethlehem under age two be killed. Herod dies later that same year, according to Matthew, allowing Jesus's parents to return to the "land of Israel." But Herod died in 4 BCE, putting Jesus's birth two years later than the Census of Quirinius. More likely, argue scholars such as Aslan (2013, 32–33) and Crossan (1995, 18–33), the writers of the Gospels were trying to find a way to have Jesus be born in Bethlehem, even though his family was from Nazareth, because of the prophecy in Micah 5:2, as I shortly discuss.

38. As Aslan (2013) points out, Jesus wasn't the first to organize Jewish resistance to Rome from the relative safety of Galilee. Most notable was Judas the Galilean who helped found the Zealot movement around 6 CE. Even earlier was Athronges, a shepherd from Galilee who led an insurrection against Rome in 4 BCE. Several of these resistance organizers were also acclaimed at the time as the Messiah. For details, see Aslan (2013).

39. Matthew 2:2.

40. Horsley (1994) and Stegemann and Stegemann (1999) were some of the first to use this phrase.

41. Matthew 27:11; Mark 15:2; Luke 23:3.

42. For example, see Luke 1:27.

43. Micah 5:2, 4–5. Christians sometimes forget that the prediction of the Messiah is originally a Jewish idea, in line with the general forgetfulness of Christians about the Jewish origins of their religious tradition. Jews today, of course, disagree with Christians that Jesus is the Messiah, and some Jews continue to look to the eventual coming of the one they believe is the true Messiah.

44. Even John 7:41–42 raises this question, reporting that some contemporary local people questioned Jesus's status by asking, "Surely the Messiah does not come from Galilee, does he? Has not the scripture said that the Messiah is descended from David and comes from Bethlehem, the village where David lived?" We should also note that the Gospels do indeed give widely varying accounts of Jesus's birth and origin.

45. Luke 1:27. Luke 3:23–38 gives Jesus's supposed full genealogy from Joseph back to David, and then back to "Seth, son of Adam, son of God." The Sethian Gnostic sect in early Christianity made much of Jesus's connection to Seth, instead of Adam's sons Cain and Abel. Matthew 1:1–17 also gives Jesus's genealogy from Joseph back to David, but only back to Abraham from there. One can find here and there in Christian apologetics the claim that these are really genealogies of Mary, and that it was conventional at the time to use the male names throughout when giving a woman's genealogy. But this is pure supposition. There isn't a shred of evidence in these passages in Matthew and Luke that they were intended to be read as actually Mary's genealogy.

46. Aslan (2013). Aslan seems to overplay his argument, though, in implying that Jesus was a member of the Zealot party. More likely, he was a Pharisee, as the New Testament reports Paul as being.

47. Matthew 6:19–20.

48. Matthew 6:24.

49. Matthew 19:21.

50. Matthew 19:24.

51. Luke 18:25; Matthew 19:24; Mark 10:25.

52. Luke 18:22; Matthew 19:21; Mark 10:21.

53. John 12:14–15.

54. See chapter 1 for details.

55. Mark 10:17–19.

56. In Luke 18:19–20, the injunction against adultery is given top billing, with injunctions against murder, theft, and lying coming afterward, in that order, and honoring one's parents in the number-five slot. And there's no extra commandment about not defrauding. All in all, it's pretty much the same. The parallel passage in Matthew 19:16–19 has a similar order, but puts the commandment against murder back in the top slot, with the addition I mention in the main text.

57. Matthew 22:36–40.

58. For an account of this interaction as the basis for enduring social bonds, see Bell (1998) and Petrzelka and Bell (2000).

59. Matthew 28:19–20.

60. John 3:36.

61. Mark 6:30–44; Luke 9:12–17; John 6:1–14.

62. Matthew 15:34.

63. Orne (2017) makes a persuasive case that it does not have to be that way—that what he calls "sexy community" can unite without disruption, if we allow it to. Connection does not necessarily require disconnection.

64. Seen in this light, Jesus's retention of the commandment about honoring one's mother and father is equally about controlling desire as it is about loyalty.

65. For a review of this old debate in rural sociology, see Bell (1992).

66. McGinn (2004).

67. If anything, my figure is likely high, as about a quarter of Pompeii has yet to be excavated, and presumably more brothels still lie under the volcanic debris. I should also note that there are three instances in Pompeii's widespread graffiti of sexual services offered to women, but many fewer than those offered to men (McGinn 2004).

68. 1 Peter 2:9.

69. Matthew 12:46–50. Luke 8:19–21 and Mark 3:31–35 have similar passages.

70. Matthew 19:29.

71. John 6:53–57.

72. Luke 12:51–53.

73. Matthew 10:34.

74. Mark 11:17.

75. John 7:15–16.

76. John 5:30. There is also this similar passage in John 8:15–16: "You judge by human standards; I judge no one. Yet even if I do judge, my judgment is valid; for it is not I alone who judge, but I and the Father who sent me." See also John 5:19.

77. Mark 12:14; see also Matthew 22:16.

78. Romans 2:11 and 1 Peter 1:17.

79. Matthew 1 and Luke 1.

80. John 5:41.

81. John 8:54.

82. Jacobovici and Wilson (2014) offer a recent claim about Mary Magdalene as Jesus's sexual partner that gained a lot of attention.

83. Mark 12:17.

84. John 2:16.

85. John 2:15.

86. Crossan (1998, 586) seems troubled by the evidence that *YHWH* isn't a mercy and goodness kind of god, but I think such an interpretation is inescapable.

87. Mark 16:15.

88. Romans 12:9.

89. 2 Timothy 1:14.

90. 2 Timothy 2:3.

91. Ephesians 5:8–9.

92. Colossians 3:2–10.

93. Matthew 5:11.

94. Matthew 18:1–5.

95. John 15:4.

96. See chapter 3.

97. Romans 5:1.

98. Romans 12:5.

99. Colossians 3:12–15. For a similar passage, see 1 Peter 2:9.

100. Luke 11:28.

101. John 3:36.

102. Acts 5:29.

103. As all sociologists will know, I am again drawing heavily here on an old sociological theme, most famously articulated by Durkheim (1964 [1893]) and by Tönnies (1940 [1887]). But see chapter 1 and elsewhere for my critiques of this theme.

104. Based on a search I did for *physis* (φύσις) and *physikos* (φυσικός), using the online tool provided by biblehub.com.

105. Romans 1:20.

106. Romans 1:26–27.

107. Luke 8:22–25. Matthew 8:23–27 gives a similar account.

108. John 12:27–31.

109. Acts 9:3–6.

110. Acts 7:48.

111. Acts 17:24–25.

112. Matthew 4:1.

113. Matthew 4:4.

114. Matthew 4:7.

115. Matthew 4:8–10.

116. See Crossan (1992 and 1995) and Horsley (1994, 2008, and 2014).

117. Matthew 13:55 and Mark 6:3.

118. See especially Galatians 2:11–14 and many passages in Acts. For a recent take on the controversy and how to harmonize Paul with a less conservative Christianity, see Borg and Crossan (2009).

119. The spread of Christianity as an urban phenomenon after the death of Jesus is one of the central focuses of the seminal work of Meeks (1983 and 2002).

120. Romans 11:13.

121. The Rhône splits in two upstream from Avignon, creating Barthelasse Island in between, one of the largest fluvial islands in Europe at eight miles long.

122. Some date the foundations back to Roman times. It certainly dates from the fourteenth century, however.

123. Theodosian Code, xvi.1.2, translation by Pharr (1952).

124. My source on this line is admittedly weak. But it is too juicy to omit. It appeared in the Wikipedia entry for the "Avignon Papacy" as of August 16, 2015, and is widely repeated from there across the web. I have not been able to track down a more reliable source.

125. However, the Papacy didn't officially recognize France's annexation of Avignon until 1814.

Chapter 6: Great Departures

1. There has been a long debate about the time period the Buddha lived. It seems now that the bulk of scholarly opinion agrees with the "short chronology" in which the Buddha dies in the mid-fourth century BCE (Verardi 2011) around 368 or 370 BCE.

2. "Want not, lack not" is an ancient creed, as Marshall Sahlins (1972) once observed, that the people of northern India found newly relevant to their lives.

3. Ling (2013 [1973], 78–83).

4. Archaeologists call these "punch-marked" coins, meaning that they had a variety of symbols hammered into them in an irregular scatter across their face, instead of a single, invariant design.

5. *Jataka* I:60–65; translation by Strong (2008, 13).

6. I am following the *Lalitavistara* Sutra here. The *Nidanakatha* is similar overall (Rhys Davids 1925).

7. *Lalitavistara* F.18.b. and f.40.a (Dharmachakra Translation Committee 2013, 22).

8. The full passage in *Lalitavistara* F.42.a (Dharmachakra Translation Committee 2013, 22) is, "She was untroubled by attachment, anger, or delusion, Had no sexual desires, nor envy or ill will."

9. The full passage in the *Nidanakatha* (Rhys Davids 1925, 148) is, "The mother of a Buddha is not lustful, or corrupt as to drink, but has fulfilled the Perfections for a hundred thousand ages, and from her birth upwards has kept the five Precepts unbroken. Now this lady Maha Maya is such an one, she will be my mother."

10. Here I follow the *Nidanakatha* (Rhys Davids 1880).

11. Some versions of Siddhartha's story say that he won Yasodhara's hand by winning a sports contest.

12. *Samghabhedavastu* 1:94–119; translation by Strong (2008, 19).

13. I am following Strong (2008) here. Other versions of the story put Mara's question "who is your witness" as the last one he asks Siddhartha.

14. Strong (2008, 22).

15. Eckel (1997, 340).

16. I am giving the Buddhist interpretation of *dharma* and *karma* here. Hinduism takes these ideas somewhat differently, as chapter 7 describes.

17. Armstrong (2006, 341).

18. I am combining the translations in Strong (2008, 48) and Armstrong (2001, 187).

19. Pew Research Center (2015).

20. Ipsos Public Affairs (2016). The numbers are increasing rapidly, growing more than 50 percent since 2012.

21. Singh (2010).

22. For more on these parallels, see Linssen (1958).

23. Technically, maybe we have to say that he nearly finished the job. There was a bit at the southern end of the Indian subcontinent that Ashoka never conquered, but controlled nonetheless through proxies.

24. Citing Ashoka's own word, carved into Rock Edict 13 (Allen 2012, 413).

25. MacNair (2015, 69).

26. Pillar Edict 7, cited in Allen (2012, 423).

27. Tarn says 27,000 to 30,000, but Green and Borza (2012, 381) call that estimate "too conservative."

28. Commentators have speculated about this point for nearly two and a half millennia.

29. Arrian, *Anabasis* 12.4 (Arrian 2013 [ca. 140 CE], 177).

30. McKechnie (1989, 54).

31. The directionality is complex. For example, some scholars argue that the immaculate conception story in Buddhism postdates Christianity, although Buddhism is a significantly older tradition.

32. If I may exhibit a bit of syncretism with Jesus's parable of the sower in Mark 4.

33. Rose (2011, xix).

34. Rose (2011, xviii).

35. Actually the idea of virgin birth of a savior-like figure was possibly not a Zoroastrian first, depending on how one draws one's categorical boundaries. There are certain parallels in the myths of the Egyptian god Horus, the Hindu god Krishna, and some others around the world. As well, immaculate birth is part of the life stories told of many heroic figures, such as Alexander the Great. One legend is that he was born of a thunderbolt from Zeus into the womb of his mother, Olympias (Martin and Blackwell 2012, 4).

36. This is a Mahayana and Vajrayana Buddhist usage. In Theravada, Buddhism's other main branch, a *bodhisattva* is a person who is on her, his, or their way to Buddha-hood, and generally is reserved only as a title for Siddhartha before his enlightenment. See the discussion in the next chapter for more detail.

37. Matthew 2:1–2.

38. Jain (2010, 51).

39. I thank Diane Mayerfeld for this suggestion.

40. I thank Diane Mayerfeld for this suggestion too.

41. Jain (2010).

42. For the fullest telling of the story in the ancient sources, see Olympiodorus (trans. Griffin 2015 [ca. 550 CE], 74–75), a pagan philosopher from Alexandria who lived from ca. 500 to 570 CE.

43. Athens remained the Greek hub until Phillip II of Macedon—Alexander the Great's father—beat the Athenians at the Battle of Chaeronea in 338 BCE.

44. Buddhism is often described as non-dualist, but in my reading it is only relatively more non-dualist than most other world traditions. For example, the distinction between *dharma* and *karma* seems to me to have an inescapable degree of dualism. Indeed, that is the whole point of the distinction.

45. And it also bore some resemblance to the Vedic idea of *brahman*, which I'll discuss in the next chapter.

46. On St. Paul's use of Greek philosophical ideas, see Linsley (2014).

47. St. Augustine (2006) is very plain about it at several points in his *Confessions*.

48. John 1:1–14.

49. Josephus (1999 [ca. 94 CE]) was hardly an adherent to impartial historiography, and many contemporary scholars argue that the sweep of Jewish sects and politics was likely more complex. For example, see Boccaccini (1998) for evidence that the Essenes were connected with the Enochic party and forebears of the theologies of John the Baptist and Jesus. The trouble is, as scholars like Grabbe (1998 and 2000) emphasize, our evidence base is very fragmentary.

50. Aslan (2013).

51. I lean here mainly on Grabbe (1998 and 2000).

52. Philippians 3:4–6: "If anyone else has reason to be confident in the flesh, I have more: circumcised on the eighth day, a member of the people of Israel, of the tribe of Benjamin, a Hebrew born of Hebrews; as to the law, a Pharisee; as to zeal, a persecutor of the church; as to righteousness under the law, blameless."

53. By my count, based on the NRSV, Jesus is called a rabbi thirteen times in the New Testament.

54. Most notably, perhaps, Ehrman (2003).

55. I draw the Athanasius quote from the translation of his 39th Festal Letter given at www .newadvent.org/fathers/2806039.htm. Irenaeus, writing around 180 CE, had earlier termed them "illegitimate and secret" in his *On the Detection and Overthrow of the So-Called Gnosis*, also called *Against Heresies* (Pagels 2003, 96).

56. In addition to the fifty-two separate works, there were also a few fragments of others.

57. I draw most of the history of Arius and Athanasius that follows from Barnes (1993, 19–33), Pagels (2003, 172–181), and Freeman (2005 [2002], 163–171).

58. Technically, Christianity did not become the state religion of the Roman Empire until some decades later when the Edict of Thessalonica declared it thus on February 27, 380 CE.

59. Fortunately, through other accidents of history, scholars now have access to both the *Gospel of Judas* and the *Gospel of Mary*, although not in complete form.

60. For example, see the Ecclesia Gnostica and the Gnostic Society.

61. Some scholars now advocate moving past the term "Gnosticism," as being too broad-brush. (See the discussion in Meyers and Pagels 2007, 9–10.) But the phrase has become wide-spread and is not liable to be superseded soon, I wager.

62. Perhaps most notable here are the Princeton theologian Elaine Pagels and the actress Jane Fonda. Pagels (1979) is her most explicit discussion of the feminist possibilities of Gnos-ticism, but also see Pagels (2003). As Fonda said to an interviewer, referencing the Gnostic goddess Sophia, "When we talk about—depending on how you talk about it—God, the Al-mighty, Sophia, a greater power, whatever—can't you understand that this is beyond gender? This is beyond anything that we can imagine." www.beliefnet.com/Faiths/2005/04/Christi anity-Is-My-Spiritual-Home.aspx, consulted November 13, 2015.

63. I could continue with all fifteen syzygies, but the pattern should already be clear.

Chapter 7: Electrum Faiths

1. Rogers (2002, 29).

2. Rogers (2002).

3. However, in Ireland it was celebrated on April 20 for many centuries (Rogers 2002, 22), despite the strength of—and perhaps exactly because of the strength of, and a Christian fear of—the celebration of Samhain in that country.

4. See Johnson (2006, 64–66) for a review of the controversy.

5. One example is the Kohenet Hebrew Priestess Institute, and its work to develop "embod-ied, Earth-based, transformative Jewish ritual." See kohenet.com.

6. As McMahan (2008, 5–6) notes, "the Buddhism that has become visible in the West and among urban, educated populations in Asia involves fewer rituals, deemphasizes the mir-acles and supernatural events depicted in Buddhist literature, disposes of or reinterprets image worship, and stresses compatibility with scientific, humanistic, and democratic ideals." Some also call this form of Buddhism "Protestant Buddhism," which McMahan (2008, 7) notes was "connected with urbanization and the rise of the bourgeoisie in Ceylon, as well as other Asian nations, and mingled traditional Buddhist ethics with Victorian social mores." See also Gom-brich and Obeyesekere (1988).

7. By "discretely welcoming" pagan concerns, I have in mind the *bodhisattvas* of Mahayana Buddhism and the allowance for continued worship of traditional gods outside of Buddhism. By "incorporating some worship" of pagan divinities, I have in mind, for example, the Thera-vada Buddhism of Sri Lanka and its inclusion of Hindu gods as Buddhist gods, as well as some originally Hindu ritual (Gombrich and Obeyesekere 1988).

8. We get a bit in Harvey (1990), a classic work. Wynne (2015) is virtually silent on the matter. For a more extended critique of this selective rendering of Buddhism, see McMahan (2008).

9. On these three, I would judge Christianity as the most heavily weighted toward the bour-geois and Buddhism as it is actually practiced in Asia as the least.

10. It is with great reluctance, but a sense of mercy for the reader of this over-long book, that I do not include Mayan and Aztec traditions and the story of Quetzelcoatl/Kukulkan, as I had originally intended to do.

11. *Rig Veda*, Hymn 19 (Griffith 1896).

12. *Rig Veda*, Hymn 129 (Griffith 1896).

13. A quick look on the web will find many references to the idea of Hinduism as the "oldest religion."

14. Meadow and Kenoyer (2000), Kenoyer (2014), and Coningham and Young (2015).

15. Kenoyer (1998, 173) and Coningham and Young (2015).

16. Meadow and Kenoyer (2000) and Kenoyer (2014). In the 1960s, the famed Sir Robert Eric Mortimer Wheeler claimed there was indeed evidence of violence, but that interpretation has now been widely discredited (Coningham and Young 2015, 265–266).

17. Tahir (2008, 157).

18. If I sound anti-Maslow here, it is because I am. For more details on my views about Maslow, see Bell and Ashwood (2016).

19. See the previous chapter for details.

20. Sarma (2008, 1).

21. Doniger (2009).

22. Hiltebeitel (2011, 209).

23. However, the *Brihat Parashara Hora Shastra* likely was composed around the seventh century CE, a millennium after Vyasa lived, if he indeed is historical at all.

24. *Mahabharata* 1 (Adi Parva): 63.47 (Morris 2014).

25. I draw this telling of the story from the translation of the *Mahabharata* by Kisari Mohan Ganguli (Morris 2014).

26. As well, both Satyavati and her adoptive father, the local chief, operate ferries on the river, amplifying their metaphorical roles in boundary-crossing.

27. *Bhagavad Gita* 1.34 (Swami 2011). I draw different quotations from either the Swami or the Sargeant translations.

28. *Bhagavad Gita* 1.32–33, 37–39 (Swami 2011).

29. *Bhagavad Gita* 2.71 (Swami 2011).

30. *Bhagavad Gita* 3.7 (Swami 2011).

31. *Bhagavad Gita* 14.13 (Sargeant 2009, 714).

32. *Bhagavad Gita* 14.14 (Sargeant 2009, 714).

33. *Bhagavad Gita* 18.53 (Sargeant 2009, 714).

34. *Bhagavad Gita* 18.73 (Sargeant 2009, 734).

35. There is considerable variation in the stories told of Ganesha's birth. I take mine from the telling at www.amritapuri.org/3714/ganesha.aum, consulted December 7, 2015.

36. The *panchayatana puja* is more complex than I have made apparent, as it downgrades the Brahma/Saraswati pair and elevates Devi, the great mother goddess in their place.

37. Lang (2009).

38. Lorenzen (2006) argues—persuasively, in my view—that the contention that the idea of "Hindu" was a colonial invention is not historically accurate. The term is Persian, not British, and had long been used to distinguish Hindus from Muslims, well before the British arrived, despite the incredible variety of Hindu traditions. Similarly, see also Doniger (2009).

39. Jainism never did connect much with pagan concerns, and remains by far the smallest of these three traditions, appealing almost entirely to people who lead bourgeois lives, as I note in the previous chapter.

40. Harvey (1990, 140).

41. Harvey (1990, 140). Harvey also attributes the decline of Buddhism in India to the Muslim invasions.

42. Meanwhile, Buddhism was able to displace Hinduism from much of Southeast Asia, even converting the world's largest religious complex—Angkor Wat, originally built to honor the Hindu god Vishnu—from Hinduism to Buddhism through appeal to local elites.

43. Esposito (2005, 2–3).

44. Esposito (2005, 6) reports that Muhammad worked for Khadija for a time before marrying; other sources say it happened all at the same time.

45. Lings (1983, 35).

46. This statement is translated many ways, and is traditionally said to be the start of Sura 96:1, which Haleem (2005, 428) translates as "read." Others say "proclaim."

47. Esposito (2005, 7).

48. Eleven is the most common view, but Esposito (2003) says thirteen, and wikiislam.net says nineteen.

49. The Book of Idols (Faris 1952, 23). Over the years, there has been much speculation about Hubal, including that he was a moon god, a rain god, and a warrior god. But we have no sources on any of this—only the discussion in The Book of Idols and elsewhere that he was used for divination, based on the tossing of seven arrows.

50. The Book of Idols (Faris 1952, 23–24).

51. The Book of Idols (Faris 1952, 29) says 34, but Armstrong (2000, 11) says 360, evidently based on hadith Sahih al-Bukhari 3:43:658.

52. Some scholars speculate that the form "lah" has a common origin with Israelite and Caananite "El." The "al" in Hubal may also have same origin, and may also be a form of the once-popular Semitic god Ba'al, often discussed in the Old Testament. See Wright (2009).

53. The Book of Idols (Faris 1952, 12–13).

54. The Book of Idols (Faris 1952, 14–15).

55. Esposito (2003).

56. The Book of Idols (Faris 1952, 16).

57. The Nabateans also worshipped her, and traces of her shrine yet remain at Petra, where she was seen as a manifestation of the Greek goddess Aphrodite, and thus associated with love and chastity.

58. The Book of Idols (Faris 1952, 16–29).

59. The Book of Idols (Faris 1952, 23–24). The story is also told in the first biography of Muhammad, Ibn Ishaq's eighth-century Sirat Rasoul Allah or Life of the Messenger of God, of which an edited copy by a student has survived.

60. Some say twenty-three years, contending that the night of Muhammad's first revelation was in Ramadan on 609 CE, not 610 CE.

61. The phrase "straight path" occurs numerous times in the Qur'an, but the first occurrence is Sura 1.6 (Haleem 2005, 3), the obligatory daily prayer.

62. I am not following the convention of describing Islam as having five "pillars" of faith, as Sunni Islam and Shia Islam formulate the pillars somewhat differently.

63. The Qur'an gives no mention of the Talmud, however, which was only then becoming central to Jewish faith and practice, having been assembled in just the previous century.

64. I take my counts from the Haleem (2005) translation.

65. Qur'an 2.136 (Dawood 1999 [1956], 23). I use the Dawood translation here instead of Haleem (2005) because of its use of the word "submit," which seems to me more in keeping with the meaning of Islam.

66. See chapter 3 for details on the etymology of *physis* and *natura*.

67. Qur'an 100.1–8 (Haleem 2005, 432).

68. Qur'an 104.1–9 (Haleem 2005, 436). Similarly, consider Qur'an 102.1–6 (Haleem 2005, 434): "Competing for more distracts you until you go into your graves. No indeed! You will come to know. No indeed! In the end you will come to know. No indeed! If only you knew for certain! You will most definitely see Hellfire."

69. Qur'an 63.9–10 (Haleem 2005, 374–375).

70. Qur'an 92.17–21 (Haleem 2005, 424).

71. Qur'an 4.171 (Haleem 2005, 66).

72. Islam here departs decidedly from the entirely male conception of Allah during *Jahiliyah*.

73. Qur'an 4.25 and 3.103 (Haleem 2005, 53 and 42).

74. Qur'an 8.52 (Haleem 2005, 114).

75. Qur'an 6.157 (Haleem 2005, 93).

76. Qur'an 6.165 (Haleem 2005, 93).

77. I didn't do a specific count because my Kindle program, which I have been using to derive these simple analyses, maxes out at a count of a hundred or more, unless you do some annoying fussing. "Mercy" and "punish" quickly maxed it out.

78. Qur'an 4.80 (Haleem 2005, 58).

79. Qur'an 8.1 (Haleem 2005, 110).

80. Berkey (2003, 64).

81. Or, if you prefer, a new take on an older religious tradition—the Abrahamic tradition—had been born along with a new state.

82. Qur'an 10.15–16 (Haleem 2005, 129).

83. Qur'an 18.110 (Haleem 2005, 190).

84. Qur'an 36.30 (Haleem 2005, 282).

85. Qur'an 64.12 (Haleem 2005, 129).

86. The Gupta Empire, ca. 320 to 550 CE, led to what is sometimes called the "golden age" of Hinduism.

87. There is some dispute about what to call this empire. I use the phrase "Arabian Empire" as it emanated from Arabia and had Arab leadership for centuries, until 1517. At that point, the caliphate passed to the Ottomans—Turks not Arabs. So some prefer to call the political entity that lasted from 632 to the abolishment of the caliphate in 1924 by Mutafa Kemal the "Islamic Empire," seeing it as a succession of caliphates. But although Islam and state structures have always experienced an unusually high degree of unity, this empire also included people of many other faiths, often with a remarkable degree of tolerance for this diversity. Thus, I prefer to use the phrase "Arabian Empire" for the period of the three Arabian caliphates through to 1517 and "Ottoman Empire" for the caliphate from 1517 until 1924, while noting that Shia Muslims do not use the term "caliph."

88. Khaldun (1967 [1377]).

89. The famous French founding figure of sociology, Émile Durkheim, was later to make a similar point, distinguishing between the "organic solidarity" of difference and the "mechanical solidarity" of similarity. See the discussion of Durkheim in chapter 1 for details.

90. Sura 7.40 of the Qur'an (Haleem 2005, 97) gives a version of the eye of the needle metaphor, but uses it to condemn disloyalty, not desire: "The gates of Heaven will not be open to those who rejected Our revelations and arrogantly spurned them; even if a thick rope were to pass through the eye of a needle they would not enter the Garden."

91. Qur'an 2.276–279 (Haleem 2005, 31).

92. Based on the income ratios of the top 20 percent to the bottom 20 percent. For the precise comparative figures, see Bell and Ashwood (2016, 448n183). The pattern does not hold up among the dominantly Muslim African countries, however.

93. Some feminist Muslims argue, however, that the Qur'an itself is not necessarily sexist. The trouble, they contend, is patriarchal interpretation of it. Particularly influential in this line of critique has been the work of Mernissi (1991 and 2003 [1975]).

94. On veiling, see 1 Corinthians 11; on women submitting to their husbands, see Ephesians 5:22–24; on women being silent in church, see 1 Corinthians 14:34. The full quotation for the latter is: "As in all the churches of the saints, women should be silent in the churches. For they are not permitted to speak, but should be subordinate, as the law also says."

95. Carus (1915, 78).

96. *Sahih Muslim* 1.219, http://ahadith.co.uk, consulted February 21, 2016. Note that *Sahih Muslim* is canonical for Sunni Muslims, but not for Shiites or Ibadis.

97. "When Allah's Messenger (may peace be upon him) bathed because of sexual intercourse, he first washed his hands: he then poured water with his right hand on his left hand and washed his private parts. He then performed ablution as is done for prayer. He then took some water and put his fingers and moved them through the roots of his hair. And when he found that these had been properly moistened, then poured three handfuls on his head and then poured water over his body and subsequently washed his feet." *Sahih Muslim* 3.616, http://ahadith.co.uk, consulted February 21, 2016.

98. There is considerable controversy over the homosexual sections, not surprisingly, with not everyone in agreement that they even exist. Sir Richard Burton had intended to publish a translation of the homosexual section, but his wife apparently destroyed it upon his death. Some say that Burton made that whole section up anyway.

99. *Sahih Muslim* 1.1, http://ahadith.co.uk, consulted February 21, 2016.

100. *Sahih Muslim* 1.8, http://ahadith.co.uk, consulted February 21, 2016.

101. Bakhtin (1984).

102. Both *Kitab Al-Haid*, the third book of *Sahih Muslim*, and the sixth book of volume 1 of *Sahih al-Bukhari* focus on menstruation.

103. *Sahih Muslim* 3.577, http://ahadith.co.uk, consulted February 21, 2016. Many *hadith*, mainly from Muhammad's wife Aisha, also show Muhammad making a point of distinguishing Islam from traditional Judaism's sense that menstruation is pollution. It should be noted that Shia Islam tends to be skeptical of *hadith* sourced from Aisha. However, Muhammad's embracing and close interacting with women while they are menstruating is also attested by *hadith* from other sources, as in the report of Umm Salama in *Sahih al-Bukhari* 1.6.297.

104. Once again, it should be noted that Shia Islam often doubts the authenticity of Aisha's reports.

105. Qur'an 4.57 (Haleem 2005, 56).

106. Qur'an 2.25 (Haleem 2005, 6).

107. Qur'an 20.121–122 (Haleem 2005, 201).

108. Qur'an 6.99 (Haleem 2005, 87). For similar passages, see, for example, "The Bee," Qur'an 16.1–17.

109. Qur'an 6.95–96 (Haleem 2005, 87).

Chapter 8: Nonpolitical Politics

1. At the time, working in these mines was truly horrible if you were Black. Annual fatalities—almost all Black miners—numbered in the hundreds. Conditions have somewhat improved since the end of apartheid, but the mines remain dangerous and largely organized through racial hierarchy.

2. In chapter 2, I describe some other adventures that my undergraduate degree in geology has led to over the years.

3. The rule against women in the mines was rescinded with the end of apartheid. "I am certain," Karl notes in a recent email, "that Diane was one of a very, very small handful of women who ever went down one of those mines in the apartheid days."

4. Readers interested in the use of dubious science in legitimating apartheid can find an extensive published literature on the best procedures for acclimatization.

5. The criminologist Jack Katz first raised this great question for me in his 1990 book.

6. But where a natural we draws on the moral goodness we attribute to second nature, a natural them draws on the moral badness of third nature.

7. There is an extensive sociological literature on narrative framing, which I will spare the reader.

8. I thank Kerem Morgul for suggesting the phrase "interests bias," during one of our many wonderful conversations.

9. I will also spare the reader a gazillion references on this subject, but the work of Karl Mannheim (1936) is surely a great place to begin. Other good places are the philosophies of pragmatism and dialogism—or, as I prefer to say, dialogic pragmatism—which are in large measure efforts to deal with this problem. As is this book. For more on dialogic pragmatism, see Bell (2004).

10. Guha (1989), Peluso (1996), and Cronon (1995).

11. My first work in nature reserve creation is described in Bell and Mayerfeld (1982). I also worked for many years with the New Haven Land Trust, and continue to work with the Thousand Islands Area Residents Association in Ontario. The latter work is described in Bell (2007).

12. I didn't have a recorder going as David told this story, so I'm quoting from his written account at landbetweentherivers.org, a site that was still online as of May 27, 2016.

13. Again, I'm quoting David's account at landbetweentherivers.org.

14. Now I'm quoting Nickell (2007, 178), but David also told me this story orally.

15. I would encourage the interested reader, though, to read some of the vast critical literature on the social uses of nature, maybe beginning with the text that most influenced my own

thinking: Stephen Jay Gould's 1981 book, *The Mismeasure of Man*. Much of this literature is also reviewed in Bell (2004) and Bell and Ashwood (2016).

16. Bologna has a church dedicated to San Vitale e Agricola, but that is a different Agricola who lived in the fourth century, very early in church history, and has no special agricultural powers attributed to him.

17. Pounds (1973).

18. Benedictow (2004, 383, table 38).

19. See Scheidel (2008), who argues that the "high estimate" of Roman urbanism of around 25 to 28 percent seems the most likely. Those who favor the "low estimate" argue for an urban percentage nearer 10 percent.

20. Tuchman (1978).

21. Tellier (2009, 267).

22. A former student suggested this term during a course I was teaching on the subject of this book. If memory serves me right, it was the inestimable Alex McCullough, who served as teaching assistant for that course in 2010.

23. Weber (2009 [1904]). Weber sometimes has been critiqued for appearing to suggest that capitalism arose out of Protestantism, when it is plain that capitalism was already in strong renewal at the time of Protestantism's rise. In my reading, Weber was actually making an appropriately dialogic argument, suggesting that each propelled the other.

24. Calvin (2008 [1536], 581).

25. Weber (2009 [1904], 93).

26. Office of US Chief of Counsel for Prosecution of Axis Criminality (1946, 190).

27. Office of US Chief of Counsel for Prosecution of Axis Criminality (1946, 189).

28. Hilberg (1973 [1961], 52). However, I have seen reports that the Nazi courts were confused on this point and did not all come to same conclusion.

29. Lutzer (2016).

30. The family's memory isn't 100 percent sure on this point, however. It may have been taken over by non-Jews instead of being destroyed.

Chapter 9: Awesome Coolness

1. Walker (1983, 1).

2. Dooling and Walker (2000), Walker (1983), Walker (1991), and Walker (1992 [1982]).

3. Walker (1983, 9).

4. Walker (1991, 34).

5. Walker (1917, 154–156). Note the similarity to the section in the *Upanishads* (Part II, 9th Brahmana), where two sages discuss the number of gods as, variously, 330 million, 33, 6, 3, 1 and a half, and 1.

6. Walker (1991, 34–36).

7. Schmitt (1966, 517). Unfortunately, *De Perenni Philosophia* has not been translated into English, and I am forced to rely on Schmitt's translation of this single sentence, without its context.

8. Huxley (1946 [1945]). For some examples of recent uses, see Armstrong (2006 and 2014), Holman (2008), and Nasr (1996 and 2010).

9. Schmitt (1966, 506).

10. Stewart (2007, 11).

11. Masci (2009).

12. Einstein (1954, 46).

13. Einstein (1954, 45–46).

14. See Dawkins (2006, 11–19). Together with Sam Harris, Christopher Hitchens, and Daniel Dennett, Dawkins is part of a group sometimes called the "four horsemen of the non-apocalypse."

15. Frankenberry (2008, 153).

16. Calaprice (2011, 340).

17. Calaprice (2000, 217).

18. Frankenberry (2008, 153).

19. Dawkins (2006, 15).

20. From a much cited creed of Einstein's, "What I Believe," that exists in varying translations. I cite the version in Brian (1996, 234) because that is the version Dawkins (2006) uses, as I will discuss shortly.

21. Dawkins (2006, 19) doesn't say where he got it, but it appears to be the Brian (1996, 234) version, and not the Einstein (1954, 8–11) version, nor the version in Rowe and Schulmann (2007, 226–234).

22. Dawkins (2006, 19).

23. Dawkins (2006, 13).

24. Dworkin (2013).

25. Dawkins (2006, 19).

26. Even Dawkins (1997) comes very close to advocating such a position.

27. Lichterman (2008, 83).

28. Bell (2004) and Bell and Ashwood (2016).

29. Or so Wikipedia estimates (https://en.wikipedia.org/wiki/Books_published_per _country_per_year, consulted February 28, 2017).

30. Again, see Bell (2004) and Bell and Ashwood (2016) for more on this. Although I do not spell it out here, I am also trying to provide a counterpoint to evolutionary psychological accounts of ignorance and the rejection of "facts." The evolutionary psychologists seemingly always want to rush to genetic explanations stemming from the lingering effects of living in small bands on African savannas millions of years ago, in this case ascribing people's disputation of facts to competitive advantage. The argument, basically, is that it is evolutionarily better to crush your opponent and thereby preserve your group than accept the facts that other groups present. It would seem to me that the evolutionary advantage would depend upon the fact—like the points one group might learn from another, perhaps that lions have sharp teeth and that rhinos may charge, and that you therefore might be advised to give them wide berth. See Kolbert (2017) for a recent popular presentation of this flawed evolutionary psychology view.

31. This also concerns me about the way the word "ignorance" is used in some work in science studies on the sociology of ignorance.

32. Becker (1963) uses the term somewhat differently, being more concerned with the creation and enforcement of rules that label some as deviant outsiders and others as accepted insiders, a perspective in sociology known as "functionalism," now often critiqued for its in-

attention to issues of power. I use the term "moral entrepreneur" specifically as a power move by someone who stands to gain social standing from building a group based in part on making some others look bad, and that in turn grants that higher standing to the moral entrepreneur.

33. Revelation 14:19–20.

34. Revelation 17:5.

35. Revelation 19:13–15.

36. Revelation 19:17–18.

37. Revelation 19:21.

38. Stevenson (2013, 15).

39. Pagels (2012).

40. Stevenson (2013, 16).

41. Matthew 10:34. See chapter 5.

42. Luke 19:27.

43. Qur'an 4.74 (Haleem 2005, 57–58).

44. Qur'an 5.33 (Haleem 2005, 71).

45. Qur'an 5.33 (Haleem 2005, 71).

46. Qur'an 5.32 (Haleem 2005, 70).

47. Al-Dawoody (2011, 56) lists forty-one instances of *jihad* in the Qur'an with five main meanings. He identifies twelve instances as having to do with war, but never in the sense of a "holy war" to kill unbelievers or force conversions; rather, they mainly deal with self-defense.

48. See Bell and Ashwood (2016) for a more detailed account of Huntington's argument, including reproductions of his maps, as well as several other examples of social selection in accounts of nature.

49. Huntington (1915, 294).

Chapter 10: The Jewel of Truth

1. On the metaphor of settlement, see Latour (2014).

2. For more on multilogics, see Bell et al. (2011).

3. See Ashwood et al. (2014).

4. I could also mention the special place given in most Talmud printings to the commentaries of Rabbi Shlomo Itzhaki, an eleventh-century scholar often referred to as Rashi. Plus most editions of the Talmud include short commentaries from well after the Tosafot period, included on the outer margins of the pages. But I think my point is clear enough without highlighting yet more levels of commentary on commentary on commentary.

5. This is the standard accounting, which is a bit heavy on Sunna schools, listing five of them among the eight total. Some Shi'a object that there are more.

6. Hubburd (1983 [1982]).

7. Natarajan (2008). There are those who wonder if Einstein may one day prove right on this, however.

8. I've used a version of this line before but I can't remember where.

9. The *Dao De Jing* makes a similar point in several places, especially chapter 81.

10. For more on my views on the economics of pagan oppression, and its connections to racial oppression, see my co-authored article Stull, Bell, and Ncwadi (2016).

11. Francis (2015) and DeWitt (2015).

12. Taylor (2010).

13. For, as well, ecological justice and social justice are both forms of the other.

14. Tarico (2009) reports the possible connection of Ishtar and Eostre/Ostara as a suggestion of Tony Nugent, who does not appear to have published the idea. On the evidence that the name Eostre/Ostara indicates a Germanic goddess and not a place name based on the direction east, see Shaw (2011). Shaw argues, however, that Eostre/Ostara was quite possibly part of a local cult of matron deities, and not a pan-Germanic goddess of spring or the dawn.

15. See chapter 5 for more details.

16. For more on Halloween, see chapter 7.

17. A great place for the interested reader to start is the remarkable book series on Religions of the World and Ecology, edited by Mary Evelyn Tucker and John Grim and published by Yale University Press. In that series, see Tucker and Williams (1997) on Buddhism; Foltz, Denny, and Baharuddin (2003) on Islam; Chapple (2002) on Jainism; Chapple and Tucker (2000) on Hinduism; as well as the other books in the series on Christianity, Confucianism, Daoism, Judaism, Shinto, and indigenous traditions.

18. Thoreau (2007 [1862]), 196. See chapter 1 as well.

19. St. Augustine (2003, 444).

20. St. Augustine (2003, 553).

21. Thoreau (1910 [1854], 360).

22. Thoreau (1910 [1854], 364).

23. Thoreau (1910 [1854], 358–359).

24. I counted thirty-two on Amazon published just since 2000, before I got tired of paging through screen after screen—and not counting editions of his complete works.

25. Bell (2011).

26. I have learned much in this regard from the work of Karen Armstrong. But she tends to put the matter a bit idealistically, as in her declaration (Armstrong 2009, xiii) that "religion is a practical discipline that teaches us to discover new capacities of mind and heart." I would agree that religion should be such a discipline, but I fear we must also recognize that it very often is not.

27. Here again, I feel I must disagree with Armstrong and her view of God as "utterly transcendent" (2009, ix). Similarly, Armstrong writes about the importance of *ekstasis*, or "stepping out," in religious experience. I would argue for the equal importance of "stepping in," and that one cannot truly do one without the other.

28. The sociologists of religion Peter Berger and Anton Zijderveld (2009) argue that we should adopt a stance they call "doubt," in order that we may have convictions without being fanatics. I largely agree but don't think that doubt gets it exactly. What I advocate here is celebrating the wonder of the unknown and how it opens us up to each other and the world, a more positive orientation than "doubt."

REFERENCES

Al-Dawoody, Ahmed. 2011. *The Islamic Law of War: Justifications and Regulations.* New York: Palgrave Macmillan.

Algaze, Guillermo. 2008. *Ancient Mesopotamia at the Dawn of Civilization: The Evolution of an Urban Landscape.* Chicago: University of Chicago Press.

Allen, Charles. 2012. *Ashoka: The Search for India's Lost Emperor.* New York: Overlook Press.

Anderson, Benedict R. 1991. *Imagined Communities: Reflections on the Origin and Spread of Nationalism.* Rev. ed. London: Verso.

Aristophanes. 2005. *The Eleven Comedies.* Vol 2. Project Gutenberg Ebook 8689.

Armstrong, Karen. 2000. *Islam: A Short History.* New York: Modern Library.

———. 2001. *Buddha.* London: Penguin.

———. 2006. *The Great Transformation: The Beginning of Our Religious Traditions.* New York: Anchor Books.

———. 2009. *The Case for God.* New York: Anchor Books.

———. 2014. *Fields of Blood: Religion and the History of Violence.* New York: Knopf.

Arrian. 2013 (ca. 140 CE). *Alexander the Great: The Anabasis and the Indica.* Martin Hammond, trans. Oxford: Oxford University Press.

Ashwood, Loka, Noelle Harden, Michael M. Bell, and William Bland. 2014. "Linked and Situated: Grounded Knowledge." *Rural Sociology* 79(4):427–452.

Aslan, Reza. 2013. *Zealot: The Life and Times of Jesus of Nazareth.* New York: Random House.

Bakhtin, Mikhail Mikhaïlovich. 1984. *Rabelais and His World.* Bloomington: Indiana University Press.

———. 1986. "Toward a Methodology for the Human Sciences." Pp. 156–172 in *Speech Genres and Other Late Essays,* Vern W. McGee, trans. Austin, TX: University of Texas Press.

Barna Group. 2014. *The State of the Bible: 2014.* New York: American Bible Society.

Barnes, Timothy David. 1993. *Athanasius and Constantius: Theology and Politics in the Constantinian Empire.* Cambridge, MA: Harvard University Press.

Becker, Howard S. 1963. "Moral Entrepreneurs." Pp. 147–163 in *Outsiders: Studies in the Sociology of Deviance.* New York: Free Press.

Bell, Michael M. 1992. "The Fruit of Difference: The Rural-Urban Continuum as a System of Identity." *Rural Sociology* 57(1):65–82.

———. 1994. *Childerley: Nature and Morality in a Country Village.* Chicago: University of Chicago Press.

———. 1997. "The Ghosts of Place." *Theory and Society* 26:813–836.

———. 1998. "The Dialogue of Solidarities, or Why the Lion Spared Androcles," *Sociological Focus* 31(2):181–199.

———. 2007. "In the River: A Sociohistorical Account of Dialogue and Diaspora." *Humanity and Society* 31(2–3):210–234.

———. 2011. "If You Have All the Answers, You Don't Have All the Questions." Pp. 193–232 in *The Strange Music of Social Life: A Dialogue on Dialogic Sociology*, by Michael M. Bell, with Andrew Abbott, Judith Blau, Diana Crane, Stacy Holman Jones, Shamus Kahn, Vanina Leschziner, John Levi Martin, Chris McRae, Marc Steinberg, and John Chappell Stowe, Ann Goetting, ed. Philadelphia: Temple University Press.

———. 2012. *An Invitation to Environmental Sociology*. 4th ed. Thousand Oaks, CA: Pine Forge Press. Previous English editions in 1998, 2004, and 2009. Chinese edition published in 2010 by Peking University Press.

———. 2017. "Present Tense: Everyday Animism and the Politics of Possession." Pp. 117–127 in *Microsociological Perspectives for Environmental Sociology*, Bradley H. Brewster and Anthony J. Puddephatt, eds. London and New York: Routledge.

Bell, Michael M., with Andrew Abbott, Judith Blau, Diana Crane, Stacy Holman Jones, Shamus Kahn, Vanina Leschziner, John Levi Martin, Christopher McRae, Marc Steinberg, and John Chappell Stowe. 2011. *The Strange Music of Social Life: A Dialogue on Dialogic Sociology*. Ann Goetting, ed. Philadelphia: Temple University Press.

Bell, Michael M., and Loka Ashwood. 2016. *An Invitation to Environmental Sociology*. 5th ed. Los Angeles and London: Sage.

Bell, Michael M., with Donna Bauer, Sue Jarnagin, and Greg Peter. 2004. *Farming for Us All: Practical Agriculture and the Cultivation of Sustainability*. Rural Studies Series of the Rural Sociological Society. College Station: Pennsylvania State University Press.

Bell, Michael, and Diane B. Mayerfeld. 1982. *Time and the Land: The Story of Mine Hill*. Roxbury, CT: Roxbury Land Trust.

Benedictow, Ole J. 2004. *The Black Death, 1346–1353: The Complete History*. Woodbridge, UK: Boydell Press.

Berger, Peter, and Anton Zijderveld. 2009. *In Praise of Doubt: How to Have Convictions Without Becoming a Fanatic*. New York: HarperCollins.

Berkey, Jonathan Porter. 2003. *The Formation of Islam: Religion and Society in the Near East, 600–1800*. Cambridge: Cambridge University Press.

Boccaccini, Gabriele. 1998. *Beyond the Essene Hypothesis: The Parting of the Ways between Qumran and Enochic Judaism*. Grand Rapids, MI: Eerdmans.

Borg, Marcus J., and John Dominic Crossan. 2009. *The First Paul: Reclaiming the Radical Visionary Behind the Church's Conservative Icon*. New York: Harper.

Brewster, Bradley H., and Michael M. Bell. 2009. "The Environmental Goffman: Toward an Environmental Sociology of Everyday Life." *Society and Natural Resources* 23(1):45–57.

Brian, Denis. 1996. *Einstein: A Life*. New York: John Wiley.

Broshi, Magen. 1978. "Estimating the Population of Ancient Jerusalem." *Biblical Archaeology Review* 4(2):10–15.

Burnett, Joel S. 2016. "Ammon, Moab, and Edom: Gods and Kingdoms East of the Jordan." *Biblical Archaeology Review* 42(6):26–40, 66–67.

Burns, Duncan, and J. W. Rogerson, eds. 2012. *Far from Minimal: Celebrating the Work and Influence of Philip R. Davies*. London: T&T Clark.

Calaprice, Alice, ed. 2000. *The Expanded Quotable Einstein*. Princeton, NJ: Princeton University Press.

———, ed. 2011. *The Ultimate Quotable Einstein*. Princeton, NJ: Princeton University Press.

Calverley, Charles Stuart. 1901 (1869). *The Complete Works of C. S. Calverley*. London: George Bell.

Calvin, John. 2008 (1536). *Institutes of the Christian Religion*. Henry Beveridge, trans. Peabody, MA: Hendrickson.

Carus, Paul. 1915. *The Gospel of Buddha, According to Old Records*. Chicago: Open Court.

Chapple, Christopher Key, ed. 2002. *Jainism and Ecology: Nonviolence in the Web of Life*. Religions of the World and Ecology Series. Cambridge, MA: Harvard University Press.

Chapple, Christopher Key, and Mary Evelyn Tucker, eds. 2000. *Hinduism and Ecology: The Intersection of Earth, Sky, and Water*. Religions of the World and Ecology Series. Cambridge, MA: Harvard University Press.

Chuchiak, John F. 2005. "In Servitio Dei: Fray Diego de Landa, the Franciscan Order, and the Return of the Extirpation of Idolatry in the Colonial Diocese of Yucatán, 1573–1579." *Americas* 61(4):611–646.

Cline, Eric H. 2014. *1177 BC: The Year Civilization Collapsed*. Princeton, NJ: Princeton University Press.

Coe, Michael. 2011. *The Maya*. 8th ed. New York: Thames & Hudson.

———. 2012. *Breaking the Maya Code*. 3rd ed. London: Thames & Hudson.

Coe, Michael, Stephen Houston, Mary Miller, and Karl Taube. 2015. "The Fourth Maya Codex." Pp. 116–164 in *Maya Archaeology 3*, Charles Golden, Stephen Houston, and Joel Skidmore, eds. San Francisco: Precolumbian Mesoweb Press.

Coningham, Robin, and Ruth Young. 2015. *The Archaeology of South Asia: From the Indus to Asoka, c. 6500 BCE–200 CE*. Cambridge: Cambridge University Press.

Connolly, Catherine, Leickness C. Simbayi, Rebecca Shanmugam, and Ayanda Nqeketo. 2008. "Male Circumcision and Its Relationship to HIV Infection in South Africa: Results of a National Survey in 2002." *South African Medical Journal* 98(10):789–794.

Connolly, Joy. 2004. "'Gilgamesh': The Iraq War, 2500 B.C." *New York Times Sunday Book Review*. Retrieved June 14, 2013, from www.nytimes.com.

Cotula, Lorenzo, Camilla Toulmin, and Ced Hesse. 2004. *Land Tenure and Administration in Africa: Lessons of Experience and Emerging Issues*. London: International Institute for Environment and Development.

Cronon, William. 1995. "The Trouble with Wilderness; or, Getting Back to the Wrong Nature." Pp. 69–90 in *Uncommon Ground: Toward Reinventing Nature*. New York: Norton.

Crossan, John Dominic. 1992. *The Historical Jesus: The Life of a Mediterranean Jewish Peasant*. New York: HarperCollins.

———. 1995. *Jesus: A Revolutionary Biography*. New York: Harper.

———. 1998. *The Birth of Christianity: Discovering What Happened in the Years Immediately after the Execution of Jesus*. San Francisco: HarperCollins.

———. 2006. *God and Empire: Jesus Against Rome, Then and Now*. San Francisco: Harper.

Damrosch, David. 2006. *The Buried Book: The Loss and Rediscovery of the Great Epic of Gilgamesh*. New York: Henry Holt.

Davies, Philip R. 1992. *In Search of "Ancient Israel."* Sheffield: Sheffield Academic Press.

———. 2008. *Memories of Ancient Israel: An Introduction to Biblical History—Ancient and Modern*. Louisville: Westminster John Knox.

Dawkins, Richard. 1997. "Is Science a Religion?" *Humanist* 57(1):26–29.

———. 2006. *The God Delusion*. Boston: Houghton Mifflin.

Dawood, N. J., trans. 1999 (1956). *The Koran*. London: Penguin.

De Landa, Diego. 1978. *Yucatan Before and After the Conquest*. William Gates, trans. Mineola, NY: Dover.

Department of Mineral Resources. 2015. *Annual Report: 2013–2014*. Arcadia, South Africa: Department of Mineral Resources.

Dever, William G. 2001. *What Did the Biblical Writers Know and When Did They Know It? What Archaeology Can Tell Us about the Reality of Ancient Israel*. Grand Rapids, MI: Eerdmans.

———. 2005. *Did God Have a Wife? Archaeology and Folk Religion in Ancient Israel*. Grand Rapids, MI: Eerdmans.

———. 2012. *The Lives of Ordinary People in Ancient Israel: Where Archaeology and the Bible Intersect*. Grand Rapids, MI: Eerdmans.

———. 2017. "Whom Do You Believe—The Bible or Archaeology?" *Biblical Archaeology Review* 43(3):43–47, 58.

DeWitt, Calvin B. 2015. "Carbon, Climate, and Self Control." Paper presented at the Human and Natural Ecology: Economic, Political and Cultural Implications seminar, St. Paul, MN, June 3–5.

Dharmachakra Translation Committee. 2013. *The Play in Full: Lalitavistara*. New York: 84000.

Doniger, Wendy. 2009. *The Hindus: An Alternative History*. London: Penguin.

Dooling, D. M., and James R. Walker, eds. 2000. *The Sons of the Wind: The Sacred Stories of the Lakota*. Norman: University of Oklahoma Press.

Dunn, James D. G., and Scot McKnight, eds. 2005. *The Historical Jesus in Recent Research*. Winona Lake, IN: Eisenbrauns.

Durkheim, Emile. 1964 (1893). *The Division of Labor in Society*. George Simpson, trans. New York: Free Press.

Dworkin, Ronald. 2013. *Religion without God*. Cambridge, MA: Harvard University Press.

Eckel, Malcolm David. 1997. "Is There a Buddhist Philosophy of Nature?" Pp. 327–349 in *Buddhism and Ecology: The Interconnection of Dharma and Deeds*, Mary Evelyn Tucker and Duncan Ryuken Williams, eds. Cambridge, MA: Harvard University Press.

ECSECC (Eastern Cape Socio Economic Consultative Council). 2012. *Eastern Cape Development Indicators—2012*. Eastern Cape Development Report. Retrieved July 13, 2017, from http://www.ecsecc.org.

Edmonds, J. M. 1912. *The Greek Bucolic Poets: Theocritus*. London: William Heinemann.

Ehrman, Bart. 2003. *Lost Christianities: The Battles for Scripture and the Faiths We Never Knew*. Oxford: Oxford University Press.

———. 2012. *Did Jesus Exist? The Historical Argument for Jesus of Nazareth*. San Francisco: Harper.

Einstein, Albert. 1954. *Ideas and Opinions*. New York: Crown.

Esposito, John L., ed. 2003. *Oxford Dictionary of Islam*. Oxford: Oxford University Press.

———. 2005. *Islam: The Straight Path*. Rev. 3rd ed. New York: Oxford University Press.

Faris, Nabih Amin, trans. 1952. *The Book of Idols: Being a Translation from the Arabic of the Kitāb Al-Asnām by Hisham Ibn Al-Kalbī*. Princeton, NJ: Princeton University Press.

Ferguson, Everett. 1993. *Backgrounds of Early Christianity*. 2nd ed. Grand Rapids, MI: Eerdmans.

Finkelstein, Israel. 2013. *The Forgotten Kingdom: The Archaeology and History of Northern Israel*. Atlanta, GA: Society of Biblical Literature.

Finkelstein, Israel, and Neil Asher Silberman. 2001. *The Bible Unearthed: Archaeology's New Vision of Ancient Israel and the Origin of Its Sacred Texts*. New York: Simon & Schuster.

———. 2006. *David and Solomon: In Search of the Bible's Sacred Kings and the Roots of the Western Tradition*. New York: Simon & Schuster.

Finley, Moses I. 1963. *The Ancient Greeks*. London: Penguin.

———. 1982. *Economy and Society in Ancient Greece*. New York: Viking.

Foltz, Richard C., Frederick M. Denny, and Azizan Baharuddin, eds. 2003. *Islam and Ecology: A Bestowed Trust*. Religions of the World and Ecology Series. Cambridge, MA: Harvard University Press.

Foxhall, Lin. 1992. "The Control of the Attic Landscape." Pp. 155–159 in *Agriculture in Ancient Greece: Proceedings of the Seventh International Symposium at the Swedish Institute of Athens*, Berit Wells, ed. Stockholm: P. Åströms Förlag.

Francis, Pope. 2015. *Encyclical Letter Laudato Si' of the Holy Father Francis on Care for Our Common Home*. Vatican: Vatican Press.

Frankenberry, Nancy K., ed. 2008. *The Faith of Scientists: In Their Own Words*. Princeton, NJ: Princeton University Press.

Freeman, Charles. 2005 (2002). *The Closing of the Western Mind: The Rise of Faith and the Fall of Reason*. New York: Vintage.

———. 2009. *A New History of Early Christianity*. New Haven, CT: Yale University Press.

Freud, Sigmund. 1939. *Moses and Monotheism*. New York: Knopf.

Friedman, Richard Elliott. 1987. *Who Wrote the Bible?* New York: Harper & Row.

———. 2003. *The Bible with Sources Revealed*. San Francisco: Harper.

Friedrich, Paul. 2008. *The Gita Within Walden*. Albany: State University of New York Press.

Fritz, Volkmar. 1995. *The City in Ancient Israel*. Sheffield, UK: Sheffield Academic Press.

Fung, Yu-Lan. 1966 (1948). *A Short History of Chinese Philosophy*. Derk Bodde, ed. New York: Free Press.

Gallup, Alec, and Wendy W. Simmons. 2000. "Six in Ten Americans Read Bible at Least Occasionally." *Gallup*. Retrieved June 19, 2014, from www.gallup.com.

Garth, Sir Samuel, ed. 1961 (1717). *Metamorphoses: In Fifteen Books*. New York: Heritage Press.

George, Andrew. 1999. *The Epic of Gilgamesh*. London: Penguin.

Goetz, Delia, and Sylvanus Griswold Morley. 1954. *The Book of the People: Popol Vuh, the National Book of the Ancient Quiche Maya*. Los Angeles: Plantin Press.

Gombrich, Anthony, and Gananath Obeyesekere. 1988. *Buddhism Transformed: Religious Change in Sri Lanka*. Princeton, NJ: Princeton University Press.

Gottlieb, Roger S., ed. 2006. *The Oxford Handbook of Religion and Ecology*. Oxford: Oxford University Press.

Gottwald, Norman K. 2001. *The Politics of Ancient Israel*. Louisville: Westminster John Knox.

Grabbe, Lester. 1998. "Sadducees and Pharisees." Pp. 35–62 in *Judaism in Late Antiquity: Part Three: Where We Stand: Issues and Debates in Ancient Judaism*, vol. 1, Jacob Neusner and Alan J. Avery-Peck, eds. Leiden: Brill.

———. 2000. *Judaic Religion in the Second Temple Period: Belief and Practice from the Exile to Yavneh*. London: Routledge.

———, ed. 2011. *Enquire of the Former Age: Ancient Historiography and the Writing the History of Israel*. London: T&T Clark.

Green, Bernard. 2010. *Christianity in Ancient Rome: The First Three Centuries*. London: T&T Clark.

Green, Peter, and Eugene N. Borza. 2012. *Alexander of Macedon, 356–323 B.C.: A Historical Biography*. Berkeley: University of California Press.

Griffin, Michael, trans. 2015 (ca. 550 CE). *Olympiodorus: Life of Plato and On Plato First Alcibiades 1–9*. London: Bloomsbury Academic.

Griffith, Ralph T. H., trans. 1896. *The Rig Veda*. Retrieved February 21, 2016, from www.sacred texts.com.

Guha, Ramachandra. 1989. "Radical American Environmentalism and Wilderness Preservation: A Third World Critique." *Environmental Ethics* 11:71–83.

Haleem, M. A. S. Abdel, trans. 2005. *The Qur'an*. Oxford: Oxford University Press.

Harvey, Peter. 1990. *An Introduction to Buddhism: Teachings, History, and Practices*. Cambridge: Cambridge University Press.

Heidel, Alexander. 1963 (1946). *The Gilgamesh Epic and Old Testament Parallels*. Chicago: University of Chicago Press.

Hilberg, Raul. 1973 (1961). *The Destruction of the European Jews*. New York: New Viewpoints.

Hiltebeitel, Alf. 2011. *Dharma: Its Early History in Law, Religion, and Narrative*. Oxford: Oxford University Press.

Hine, Daryl. 1982. *Theocritus: Idylls and Epigrams*. New York: Atheneum.

Holman, John. 2008. *The Return of the Perennial Philosophy: The Supreme Vision of Western Esotericism*. London: Watkins.

Horsley, Richard A. 1994. *Sociology and the Jesus Movement*. 2nd ed. New York: Continuum.

———, ed. 2005. *Christian Origins: A People's History of Christianity*. Vol. 1. Minneapolis: Fortress Press.

———. 2008. *Jesus in Context: Power, People, and Performance*. Minneapolis: Fortress Press.

———. 2014. *Jesus and the Politics of Roman Palestine*. Columbia: University of South Carolina Press.

Hubburd, Ruth. 1983 (1982). "Have Only Men Evolved?" Pp. 45–69 in *Discovering Reality: Feminist Perspectives on Epistemology, Metaphysics, Methodology, and Philosophy of Science*, Sandra Harding and Merrill B. Hintikka, eds. Dordrecht: D. Reidel.

Huntington, Ellsworth. 1915. *Climate and Civilization*. New Haven, CT: Yale University Press.

Huxley, Aldous. 1946 (1945). *The Perennial Philosophy*. London: Chatto & Windus.

Ibn-al-Kalbi. 1952 (ca. 800 CE). *The Book of Idols*. Nabih Amin Faris, trans. Princeton, NJ: Princeton University Press.

IPSOS Public Affairs. 2016. *2016 Yoga in America Study*. Retrieved July 13, 2017, from https://www.yogajournal.com.

Jacobovici, Simcha, and Barrie Wilson. 2014. *The Lost Gospel: Decoding the Ancient Text That Reveals Jesus' Marriage to Mary the Magdalene*. New York: Pegasus.

Jain, Kailash Chand. 2010. *History of Jainism*. New Delhi: D.K. Printworld.

Jaspers, Karl. 1976 (1949). *The Origin and Goal of History*. Westport, CT: Greenwood.

Johnson, Maxwell E. 2006. "The Apostolic Tradition." Pp. 32–76 in *The Oxford History of Christian Worship*, Geoffrey Wainwright and Karen B. Westerfield Tucker, eds. Oxford: Oxford University Press.

Josephus, Flavius. 1999 (ca. 94 CE). *The New Complete Works of Josephus*. Rev. ed. William Whiston, trans. Grand Rapids, MI: Kregel.

Katz, Jack. 1990. *Seductions of Crime: Moral and Sensual Attractions in Doing Evil*. New York: Basic Books.

Kearns, Emily. 2010. *Ancient Greek Religion: A Sourcebook*. Chichester, UK: Wiley-Blackwell.

Kenoyer, Jonathan Mark. 1998. *Ancient Cities of the Indus Valley Civilization*. Karachi: Oxford University Press.

———. 2014. "The Indus Civilization." Pp. 407–432 in *The Cambridge Prehistory*, Colin Renfrew and Paul Bahn, eds. Cambridge: Cambridge University Press.

Kessler, Rainer. 2008. *The Social History of Ancient Israel: An Introduction*. Minneapolis: Fortress Press.

Khaldun, Ibn. 1967 (1377). *The Muqaddimah*. Franz Rosenthal, trans. London: Routledge and Kegan Paul.

Kindt, Julia. 2012. *Rethinking Greek Religion*. Cambridge: Cambridge University Press.

Kline, A. S., trans. 2000. *Ovid's Metamorphoses*. University of Virginia Library. Retrieved July 9, 2014, from ovid.lib.virginia.edu/trans/Ovhome.htm.

Kohn, Eduardo. 2013. *How Forests Think: Toward an Anthropology Beyond the Human*. Berkeley: University of California Press.

Kolbert, Elizabeth. 2017. "Why Facts Don't Change Our Minds: New Discoveries about the Human Mind Show the Limitations of Reason." *New Yorker*, February 27. Retrieved March 3, 2017, from http://www.newyorker.com/magazine/2017/02/27/why-facts-dont-change-our-minds.

Lang, Olivia. 2009. "Hindu Sacrifice of 250,000 Animals Begins." *Guardian*, November 24. Retrieved December 8, 2015, from www.theguardian.com.

Latour, Bruno. 2014. "Another Way to Compose the Common World." *HAU: Journal of Ethnographic Theory* 4(1):301–307.

Lau, D. C., trans. 1963. *Lao Tzu: Tao Te Ching*. Harmondsworth, UK: Penguin.

Le Guin, Ursula, trans. 2009. *Lao Tzu: Tao Te Ching*. Boston: Shambhala.

Lemche, Niels P. 1988. *Ancient Israel: A New History of Israelite Society*. Sheffield, UK: JSOT Press.

Levine, Amy-Jill. 2006. *The Misunderstood Jew: The Church and the Scandal of the Jewish Jesus*. San Francisco: Harper.

Lichterman, Paul. 2008. "Religion and the Construction of Civic Identity." *American Sociological Review* 73(1):83–104.

Ling, Trevor. 2013 (1973). *The Buddha: The Social-Revolutionary Potential of Buddhism*. 2nd ed. Onalaska, WA: Pariyatti Press.

Lings, Martin. (1983). *Muhammad: His Life Based on the Earliest Sources*. New York: Inner Traditions Internationalist.

Linsley, Alice C. 2014. "Saint Paul's Application of Greek Philosophy." *Biblical Anthropology*. Retrieved October 28, 2015, from http://biblicalanthropology.blogspot.com/2014/12/saint-pauls-application-of-greek.html.

Linssen, Robert. 1958. *Living Zen*. New York: Grove Press.

Lloyd, Geoffrey E. R. 1992. "Greek Antiquity: The Invention of Nature." Pp. 1–24 in *The Concept of Nature*, John Torrance, ed. Oxford: Oxford University Press.

Lorenzen, David N. 2006. *Who Invented Hinduism? Essays on Religion in History*. New Delhi: Yoda Press.

Lovejoy, Arthur O., and George Boas. 1980 (1935). *Primitivism and Related Ideas in Antiquity*. New York: Octagon Books.

Lucretius. 1957 (ca. 55 BCE). *On the Nature of Things (De Rerum Natura)*. W. E. Leonard, trans. New York: E. P. Dutton.

Lutzer, Erwin W. 2016. *Hitler's Cross: How the Cross Was Used to Promote the Nazi Agenda*. 2nd ed. Chicago: Moody.

MacNair, Rachel M. 2015. *Religions and Nonviolence: The Rise of Effective Advocacy for Peace*. Santa Barbara, CA: ABC-CLIO.

Malley, Shawn. 2012. *From Archaeology to Spectacle in Victorian Britain: The Case of Assyria, 1845–1854*. Farnham, UK: Ashgate.

Mallory, James P., and Douglas Q. Adams. 2006. *Oxford Introduction to Proto-Indo-European and the Proto-Indo-European World*. London: Oxford University Press.

Mannheim, Karl. 1936. *Ideology and Utopia: An Introduction to the Sociology of Knowledge*. London: K. Paul, Trench, Trubner.

Marcus, Joyce, and Jeremy A. Sabloff. 2008. "Introduction." Pp. 3–26 in *The Ancient City: New Perspectives on Urbanism in the Old and New World*, Joyce Marcus and Jeremy A. Sabloff, eds. Santa Fe, NM: School for Advanced Research Press.

Martin, Thomas R. 2013. *Ancient Greece: From Prehistoric to Hellenistic Times*. 2nd ed. New Haven, CT: Yale University Press.

Martin, Thomas R., and Christopher Blackwell. 2012. *Alexander the Great: The Story of an Ancient Life*. Cambridge: Cambridge University Press.

Masci, David. 2009. "Scientists and Belief." Pew Research Center: Religion and Public Life. Retrieved May 30, 2016, from www.pewforum.org.

Mason, Steve. 2009. *Josephus, Judea, and Christian Origins: Methods and Categories*. Peabody, MA: Hendrickson.

Matthews, Victor H. 2002. *A Brief History of Ancient Israel*. Louisville: Westminster John Knox.

McGinn, Thomas A. J. 2004. "Appendices I and III: A Catalog of Possible Brothels at Pompeii and A Catalog of Possible Prostitutes at Pompeii." Pp. 267–290 and pp. 295–302 in *The Economy of Prostitution in the Roman World: A Study of Social History and the Brothel*. Ann Arbor: University of Michigan Press.

McIntosh, Jane R. 2005. *Ancient Mesopotamia: New Perspectives*. Santa Barbara, CA: ABC-CLIO.

McKay, Alexander G. 1998 (1975). *Houses, Villas, and Palaces in the Roman World*. Baltimore: Johns Hopkins University Press.

McKechnie, Paul. 1989. *Outsiders in the Greek Cities in the Fourth Century B.C.* London: Routledge.

McLaughlin, Raoul. 2010. *Rome and the Distant East: Trade Routes to the Ancient Lands of Arabia, India and China*. London: Continuum.

McMahan, David L. 2008. *The Making of Buddhist Modernism*. Oxford: Oxford University Press.

Meadow, Richard H., and Jonathan Mark Kenoyer. 2000. "The Indus Valley Mystery: One of the World's First Great Civilizations Is Still a Mystery." *Discovering Archaeology*, March/April: 38–43.

Meeks, Wayne. 1983. *The First Urban Christians: The Social World of the Apostle Paul.* New Haven, CT: Yale University Press.

———. 2002. *In Search of the Early Christians: Selected Essays.* Allen R. Hilton and H. Gregory Snyder, eds. New Haven, CT: Yale University Press.

Mernissi, Fatima. 1991. *The Veil and the Male Elite: A Feminist Interpretation of Women's Rights in Islam.* Mary Jo Lakeland, trans. Reading, MA: Perseus.

———. 2003 (1975). *Beyond the Veil: Male-Female Dynamics in Muslim Society.* Rev. ed. London: Saqi Books.

Merton, Thomas. 1965. *The Way of Chuang Tzu.* New York: New Directions.

Meyers, Marvin, and Elaine H. Pagels. 2007. "Introduction." Pp. 1–13 in *The Nag Hammadi Scriptures: The International Edition,* Marvin Meyers, ed. New York: HarperCollins.

Mitchell, Stephen. 2004. *Gilgamesh: A New English Version.* New York: Free Press.

Morris, Darryl, ed. 2014. *The Mahabharata of Krishna-Dwaipayana Vyasa: Complete 18 Parvas.* Kisari Mohan Ganguli, trans. Seattle: Pacific.

Mykytiuk, Lawrence. 2015. "Did Jesus Exist? Searching for Evidence beyond the Bible." *Biblical Archaeology Review* 41(1):44–51, 76.

Nasr, Seyyed Hossein. 1996. *Religion and the Order of Nature.* Oxford: Oxford University Press.

———. 2010. *In Search of the Sacred: A Conversation with Seyyed Hossein Nasr on His Life and Thought.* Santa Barbara, CA: Praeger.

Natarajan, Vasant. 2008. "What Einstein Meant When He Said 'God Does Not Play Dice. . . .'" *Resonance* 13(7):655–661.

Nickell, David. 2007. "Between the Rivers: A Socio-historical Account of Hegemony and Heritage." *Humanity & Society* 31(2–3):164–209.

Office of US Chief of Counsel for Prosecution of Axis Criminality. 1946. *Nazi Conspiracy and Aggression.* Vol. 1. Washington, DC: Government Printing Office.

Olympiadorus (the Younger). 2015. *Life of Plato and On Plato First Alcibiades 1–9.* Michael Griffin, trans. London: Bloomsbury.

Orne, Jason. 2017. *Boystown.* Chicago: University of Chicago Press.

Osborne, Robin. 1995. "The Economics and Politics of Slavery at Athens." Pp. 27–43 in *The Greek World,* Anton Powell, ed. London: Routledge.

Pagels, Elaine H. 1976. "What Became of God the Mother? Conflicting Images of God in Early Christianity." *Signs* 2(2):293–303.

———. 1979. "The Suppressed Gnostic Feminism." *New York Review of Books,* November 22.

———. 2003. *Beyond Belief: The Secret Gospel of Thomas.* New York: Random House.

———. 2012. *Revelations: Visions, Prophecy, and Politics in the Book of Revelation.* New York: Viking.

Peluso, Nancy Lee. 1996. " 'Reserving' Value: Conservation Ideology and State Protection of Resources." Pp. 135–165 in *Creating the Countryside: The Politics of Rural and Environmental Discourse,* Melanie DuPuis and Peter Vandergeest, eds. Philadelphia: Temple University Press.

Petrzelka, Peggy, and Michael M. Bell. 2000. "Rationality and Solidarity: The Social Organization of Common Property Resources in the Imdrhas Valley of Morocco." *Human Organization* 59(3):343–352.

Pew Research Center. 2015. "The Future of World Religions: Population Growth Projections, 2010–2050." Washington, DC: Pew Research Center.

Polanyi, Karl. 1957. "Marketless Trading in Hammurabi's Time." Pp. 12–26 in *Trade and Market in the Early Empires: Economies in History and Theory*, Karl Polanyi, Conrad M. Arensberg, and Harry W. Pearson, eds. Glencoe, IL: Free Press.

Pounds, Norman J. G. 1973. *An Historical Geography of Europe: 450 BC to AD 1330*. Cambridge: Cambridge University Press.

Prosic, Tamara. 2004. *The Development and Symbolism of Passover until 70 CE*. London: T&T Clark.

Raffel, Burton, trans. 1983. *The Essential Horace*. San Francisco: North Point Press.

Rhys Davids, T. W. 1925. *Buddhist Birth-Stories (Jataka Tales)*. New York: Dutton and Routledge.

Rogers, Nicholas. 2002. *Halloween: From Pagan Ritual to Party Night*. Oxford: Oxford University Press.

Rose, Jenny. 2011. *Zoroastrianism: An Introduction*. London: I. B. Taurus.

Rose, Peter W. 2012. *Class in Archaic Greece*. Cambridge: Cambridge University Press.

Rowe, David E., and Robert Schulmann, eds. 2007. *Einstein on Politics: His Private Thoughts and Public Stands on Nationalism, Zionism, War, Peace, and the Bomb*. Princeton, NJ: Princeton University Press.

Sahlins, Marshall. 1972. "The Original Affluent Society." Pp. 1–39 in *Stone Age Economics*. New York: Aldine.

Sandwell, Isabella. 2005. "Outlawing 'Magic' or Outlawing 'Religion'? Libanius and the Theodosian Code as Evidence for Legislation against 'Pagan' Practices." Pp. 87–124 in *The Spread of Christianity in the First Four Centuries: Essays in Explanation*, W. V. Harris, ed. Leiden: Brill.

Sapir-Hen, Lidar. 2016. "Pigs as an Ethnic Marker? You Are What You Eat." *Biblical Archaeology Review* 42(6):41–43, 70.

Sargeant, Winthrop. 2009. *The Bhagavad Gita: Twenty-Fifth-Anniversary Edition*. Albany: State University of New York Press.

Sarma, Bharadvaja. 2008. *Vyasa's Mahabharatam in Eighteen Parvas: The Great Epic of India in Summary Translation*. Kolkata: Academic Publishers.

Scheidel, Walter. 2008. "Roman Population Size: The Logic of the Debate." Pp. 17–70 in *People, Land, and Politics: Demographic Developments and the Transformation of Roman Italy, 300 BC–AD 14*, L. de Ligt and S. J. Northwood, eds. Leiden: Brill.

Scheub, Harold. 2012. *Trickster and Hero: Two Characters in the Oral and Written Traditions of the World*. Madison: University of Wisconsin Press.

Schmitt, Charles B. 1966. "Perennial Philosophy: From Agostino Steuco to Leibniz." *Journal of the History of Ideas* 27(4):505–532.

Shanks, Hershel. 2014. "Where *Is* Mount Sinai? The Case for Har Karkom and the Case for Saudi Arabia." *Biblical Archaeology Review* 40(2):30–41, 66–68.

———. 2016. "Ancient Jerusalem: The Village, the Town, the City." *Biblical Archeology Review* 42(3):51–53.

Shaw, Maria C. 2004. "The 'Priest-King' Fresco from Knossos: Man, Woman, Priest, King, or Someone Else?" *Hesperia Supplements* 33:65–84.

Shaw, Philip A. 2011. *Pagan Goddesses in the Early Germanic World: Eostre, Hreda and the Cult of Matrons*. London: Bristol Classical.

Shipley, Graham. 2014 (2000). *The Greek World after Alexander, 323–30 B.C.* Abington, UK: Routledge.

Simmel, Georg. 1950. "Metropolis and Mental Life." Pp. 409–424 in *The Sociology of Georg Simmel*, Kurt Wolff, trans. Glencoe, IL: Free Press.

Singh, S. P., ed. 2010. *History of Yoga.* Vol. 16, pt. 2 of *History of Science, Philosophy and Culture in Indian Civilization*, D. P. Chattopadhyaya, ed. New Delhi: Centre for Studies in Civilizations.

Smith, Mark S. 2001. *The Origins of Biblical Monotheism: Israel's Polytheistic Background and the Ugaritic Texts.* Oxford: Oxford University Press.

———. 2002. *The Early History of God: Yahweh and the Other Deities in Ancient Israel.* 2nd ed. Grand Rapids, MI: Eerdmans.

Sommerstein, Alan H., trans. 2001. *Wealth: The Comedies of Aristophanes.* Vol. 2. Warminster, UK: Aris & Phillips.

Soper, Kate. 1995. *What Is Nature? Culture, Politics and the Non-human.* Oxford: Blackwell.

Sparklesoup Studios, eds. 2004. *Plutus.* Irving, TX: Sparklesoup Studios.

Statistics South Africa. 2006. *Provincial Profile 2004: Eastern Cape.* Report No. 00-91-02 (2004). Pretoria: Statistics South Africa.

St. Augustine. 1886. *The City of God.* Marcus Dodds, trans. Grand Rapids, MI: Eerdmans.

———. 2003. *City of God (Concerning the City of God Against the Pagans).* Henry Bettinson, trans. London: Penguin.

———. 2006. *Confessions.* Garry Wills, trans. London: Penguin.

Stegemann, Ekkehard W., and Wolfgang Stegemann. 1999. *The Jesus Movement: A Social History of Its First Century.* Minneapolis: Fortress Press.

Stevenson, Gregory. 2013. *A Slaughtered Lamb: Revelation and the Apocalyptic Response to Evil and Suffering.* Abilene, TX: Abilene Christian University Press.

Stewart, Matthew. 2007. *The Courtier and the Heretic: Leibniz, Spinoza, and the Fate of God in the Modern World.* New York: Norton.

Stone, Elizabeth C. 2008. "A Tale of Two Cities: Lowland Mesopotamia and Highland Anatolia." Pp. 141–164 in *The Ancient City: New Perspectives on Urbanism in the Old and New World*, Joyce Marcus and Jeremy A. Sabloff, eds. Santa Fe, NM: School for Advanced Research Press.

Stone, Elizabeth C., and Paul E. Zimansky. 2004. *The Anatomy of a Mesopotamian City: Survey and Soundings at Mashkan-shapir.* Warsaw, IN: Eisenbrauns.

Strong, John S. 2008. *The Experience of Buddhism: Sources and Interpretations.* 3rd ed. Belmont, CA: Wadsworth/Thomson Learning.

Stull, Valerie, Michael M. Bell, and Mpumelelo Ncwadi. 2016. "Environmental Apartheid: Eco-Health and Rural Marginalization in South Africa." *Journal of Rural Studies* 47(A):369–380.

Swami, Shri Purohit, trans. 2001. *Bhagavad Gita: Annotated and Explained.* Woodstock, VT: SkyLight Paths.

Tahir, Naeem. 2008. *Melluhas of the Indus Valley: 8000BC—500 BC.* Islamabad: Pakistan National Council of the Arts.

Tarico, Valerie. 2009. "Ancient Sumerian Origins of the Easter Story." *Huffington Post*, May 11. Retrieved June 8, 2016, from huffingtonpost.com.

Taylor, Bron. 2010. *Dark Green Religion: Nature Spirituality and the Planetary Future.* Berkeley: University of California Press.

Taylor, Sunaura. 2017. *Beasts of Burden: Animal and Disability Liberation.* New York: New Press.

Tellier, Luc-Normand. 2009. *Urban World History: An Economic and Geographical Perspective.* Quebec, Canada: Presses de l'Université du Québec.

Theroux, Paul. 2004. "Introduction." Pp. ix–xxv in *The Maine Woods*, by Henry David Thoreau, Joseph J. Moldenhauer, ed. Princeton, NJ: Princeton University Press.

Thompson, Dick, Sharon Thompson, and Rex Thompson. 2001. *Alternatives in Agriculture: 2001 Report.* Boone, IA: Thompson On-Farm Research.

Thompson, Thomas L. 1992. *Early History of the Israelite People: From the Written and Archaeological Sources.* Leiden: Brill.

———. 1999. *The Bible in History: How Writers Create a Past.* London: Jonathan Cape.

Thoreau, Henry David. 1910 (1854). *Walden; or, Life in the Woods.* Boston: Houghton Mifflin.

———. 2007 (1862). "Walking." Pp. 185–222 in *Excursions.* Princeton, NJ: Princeton University Press.

Tönnies, Ferdinand. 1940 (1887). *Fundamental Concepts of Sociology (Gemeinschaft und Gesellschaft).* Charles P. Loomis, trans. New York: American Book Company.

———. 1940 (1931). "Gemeinschaft und Gesellschaft." Pp. 3–29 in *Fundamental Concepts of Sociology (Gemeinschaft und Gesellschaft)*, Charles P. Loomis, trans. New York: American Book Company.

Tov, Emanuel. 2014. "Searching for the 'Original' Bible: Do the Dead Sea Scrolls Help?" *Biblical Archaeology Review* 40(4):48–53, 68.

Tuchman, Barbara. 1978. *A Distant Mirror: The Calamitous 14th Century.* New York: Knopf.

Tucker, Mary Evelyn, and Duncan Ryuken Williams, eds. 1997. *Buddhism and Ecology: The Interconnection of Dharma and Deeds.* Religions of the World and Ecology Series. Cambridge, MA: Harvard University Press.

Ustinova, Yulia. 2009. *Caves and the Ancient Greek Mind: Descending Underground in the Search for Ultimate Truth.* Oxford: Oxford University Press.

Verardi, Giovanni. 2011. *Hardships and Downfall of Buddhism in India.* New Delhi: Manohar.

von Falkenhausen, Lothar. 2008. "Stages in the Development of 'Cities' in Pre-imperial China." Pp. 209–228 in *The Ancient City: New Perspectives on Urbanism in the Old and New World*, Joyce Marcus and Jeremy A. Sabloff, eds. Santa Fe, NM: School for Advanced Research Press.

Walker, James R. 1917. *The Sun Dance and Other Ceremonies of the Oglala Division of the Teton Dakota.* Anthropological Papers of the American Museum of Natural History, vol. 16, pt. 2. New York: American Museum of Natural History.

———. 1983. *Lakota Myth.* Elaine A. Jahner, ed. Omaha: University of Nebraska Press.

———. 1991. *Lakota Belief and Ritual.* Raymond J. DeMallie, ed. Lincoln: University of Nebraska Press.

———. 1992 (1982). *Lakota Society.* Raymond J. DeMallie and Elaine Jahner, eds. Lincoln: University of Nebraska Press.

Waterfield, Gordon. 1963. *Layard of Nineveh.* New York: Praeger.

Weber, Max. 1946 (1919). "Politics as a Vocation." Pp. 77–128 in *From Max Weber*, H. H. Gerth and C. Wright Mills, eds. New York: Oxford University Press.

———. 1958 (1921). *The City.* Don Martindale and Gertrud Neuwirth, trans. Glencoe, IL: Free Press.

———. 2009 (1904). *The Protestant Ethic and the Spirit of Capitalism.* Talcott Parsons, trans. Norton Critical ed. New York: Norton.

Webster, Thomas B. L. 1973. *Athenian Culture and Society.* Berkeley: University of California Press.

White, Lynn. 1967. "The Historical Roots of Our Ecological Crises." *Science* 155:1203–1207.

Wilken, Robert Louis. 2012. *The First Thousand Years: A Global History of Christianity.* New Haven, CT: Yale University Press.

Williams, Raymond. 1983. *Keywords: A Vocabulary of Culture and Society.* London: Fontana.

Wirth, Louis. 1938. "Urbanism as a Way of Life." *American Journal of Sociology* 44:1–24.

Wright, Robert. 2009. *The Evolution of God.* New York: Little, Brown.

Wynne, Alexander. 2015. *Buddhism: An Introduction.* London: I.B. Tauris.

INDEX

in the Tabernacle, 83; in the Qur'an, 204; *tawhid* and the Christian trinity, distinction between, 203. *See also* divine, the

golden rule: the Buddha's version of, 157; Jesus's version of, 127; parallels between the Buddha's and Jesus's, 159

gold mining, 219–25

good, the: as an absolute (*see* absolute(s), the); ancient triangle and, 12; Ashoka and, 178; the bourgeois and, 12–13, 167, 190, 233; Buddhism and, 154–55; constructing the bad as, 224; disagreement about, 7–8; the divine as a universal unity of in the Axial Age, 11; Gnosticism and, 176; Hinduism and, 192, 194; Islam and, 204, 206; Jainism and, 167; Jesus and, 111, 137–38; Judaism and, 172; nature and, 3, 6, 8–9, 12, 48–50, 65–76; nature before nature and, 21, 27, 35, 40–43; nature of discussed in *Bhagavad Gita*, 190–91; as non-human, 7; Old Testament and, 80, 83, 102, 176; Plato on, 169–70; as political absolute (*see* nonpolitical politics); social change from rural to urban and, 11–12; Zoroastrianism and, 163–64

Gore, Al, 7

Grabbe, Lester, 300n49

Gratian (emperor of Roman Empire), 145

Greeks, ancient: Athens (*see* Athens); life in 388 BCE: the drama competition in honor of Dionysus, 50–57; *physis*, etymological origins of, 48–50; "polis religion" of, 286n30; Theocritus and the bucolic writers, 62–66; *Wealth* by Aristophanes, 53–59

Green, Peter, 299n27

greening religion, 7, 270–73, 279n24

grounded knowledge. *See* truth

Gupta Empire, 304n86

hadith: on bodily excretions, 211; collected in the *Sunnah*, 201–2; on menstruation, 211, 305n103; on sexual practices of Muhammad, 210

Haleem, M. A. S. Abdel, 303n46, 304n65

Harden, Noelle, 265

Harris, Sam, 308n14

harvest festivals/holidays: greening of religion and, 270–72; Halloween and the Day of the Dead, 180–81; of the Old Testament, 86, 102, 117; taxation associated with, 117

Harvey, Peter, 195, 303n41

Herod (king of Judea), 116–17, 171, 293n22, 295n37

Herodotus, 166

Hesiod, 281n3

Hijrah (Muhammad's migration to Medina), 205

Hinduism: animal sacrifice in, 194; *Bhagavad Gita*, 188–91; Buddhism and, comparison of, 191–92, 195; as electrum faith, 182, 195, 197; empire and, 207; gods in, 192–94; the *Mahabharata*, reframing Vedic ideas in, 185–91; popularity of, 157; social and historical context of, the caste system and, 183–85, 190–91; in South Asia countries, 196; as unified identity across many manners of living, 194–95

Hitchens, Christopher, 308n14

Hitler, Adolf, 233–34

Homer, 49

Horace, 66–68, 71–74, 119

Horus (Egyptian god), 299n35

Hubal (pre-Islamic Arabic god), 200–201, 303n49, 303n52

humans: entangled with nature and supernature, 21 (*see also* entangled visions of nature before nature); interaction with the divine in Hindu traditions, 186–87; in nature before nature traditions, 36–38, 41

Huntington, Ellsworth, 255–57

Huxley, Aldous, 241

Hyrcanus II (king of Judea), 115–16

ideas: context and, 12–13; social relations and, 247–48. *See also* knowledge; truth

Ideon Cave, 19–21, 41, 281n6

ignorable, cultivation of, 249–50

Roman Empire (*contunued*)
    context for Jesus and Christianity, 115–17,
    123–24; the Jews and, 98; paganism, de-
    cree against, 43; social class and urban-
    rural inequality in, 120–23; urbanism
    following the collapse of, 230–31
Romans, ancient: Dyeus to *deus* (deity) for,
    19–20; the natural conscience of Horace,
    66–68; nature, etymology of, 49; nature
    for, range of positions on, 71–72
rural life. *See* agriculture and rural life

Sadducees, the, 171–72
Sahlins, Marshall, 298n2
Salome Alexandra (queen of Judea), 171
samsara, 167–68, 190–92
sannyasa, 300n38
Sapir-Hen, Lidar, 290n68
Sargon II (king of Assyria), 97
Scheidel, Walter, 307n19
Schuon, Frithjof, 241
science: contestation and interpretation,
    openness to, 267; religion and, 241–45
second nature (as a moral good), 49–
    50, 74–76, 142, 167. *See also* natural
    conscience
Seleucids, the, 98
self, the: natural connected to a nonpolitical
    community, 137–38; natural me as au-
    thentic, 74 (*see also* natural conscience);
    nonpolitical as the natural me, 73
Semites, 94–95
"Sermon at Benares" (the Buddha), 155–57
sex: in Arabian culture, 210–11; bourgeois,
    130–31, 153, 269; disruptive power of class
    and, 129–31; in Hinduism, 186–88, 192; in-
    teractiveness of the Old Testament divine
    including, 88; for Jains, 167; Jesus and,
    136; in nature before nature traditions,
    37–38; Siddhartha Gautama and, 153–54
sexism: overlooking of in Christianity and
    Buddhism, 210; social stature of women
    in Islam, 212; in the Trinity, 132. *See also*
    gender

Shalmaneser V (king of Assyria), 97
Shamash (Sumerian god), 33–34, 42
Shamhat (priestess in *Epic of Gilgamesh*),
    33, 38–39
Shaw, Maria C., 283n51
Shaw, Philip A., 310n14
Shiduri (goddess of fermentation in *Epic of
    Gilgamesh*), 39, 46
Shinto, 182, 195
Shramanas, 166
Siddhartha Gautama, 150–51, 153–57,
    299n36. *See also* Buddha, the
Silberman, Neil Asher, 290n68
Simon of Cyrene, 293n10
Siricius, 5
slavery and slaves: in Athens, 51, 54, 57–59;
    in the Bible, 78; Islam and, 205; sex
    imposed on, 131
Smith, George, 32, 34
Smith, Huston, 241
Smith, Mark S., 288n25, 290n63
solidarity: organic distinguished from
    mechanical, 11–12, 305n89
solipsism, 265
Solomon, 83
solstice, the, 181
Sommerstein, Alan H., 286n29
Sotades, 64–65
sound: "chuckling" of a lapstrake skiff,
    74–75; memory of, 47
South Africa: Eastern Cape Province, 27–31;
    gold mining and apartheid in, 220–25
Spinoza, Baruch, 242
spiritual agnosticism, 244
state, the: centralized religion and, 117,
    145, 171, 173, 177; empire and, 5, 8–9, 11,
    92–93, 115, 142, 145–47, 163, 169, 182, 190,
    206, 288; expansion of power, Iron Age
    innovations and, 118–19; growth, associa-
    tion with concern about desire, 8–9, 177,
    182, 269; growth of in India, bourgeois
    society and, 151–53, 187, 190; Jesus and
    resistance to, 124, 134, 136–37, 143–46;
    Muhammad's state building, 205–6;

A NOTE ON THE TYPE

This book has been composed in Arno, an Old-style serif typeface in the
classic Venetian tradition, designed by Robert Slimbach at Adobe.

GPSR Authorized Representative: Easy Access System Europe - Mustamäe tee 50, 10621 Tallinn, Estonia, gpsr.requests@easproject.com

www.ingramcontent.com/pod-product-compliance
Lightning Source LLC
Chambersburg PA
CBHW020454270326
41926CB00008B/598